Educating the Deaf

Educating the Deaf
Psychology, Principles, and Practices

Donald F. Moores
UNIVERSITY OF MINNESOTA

HOUGHTON MIFFLIN COMPANY · BOSTON

DALLAS   GENEVA, ILL.   HOPEWELL, N. J.   PALO ALTO   LONDON

Printed in the U.S.A.

Library of Congress Catalog Card Number: 77-72896

ISBN: 0-395-24486-2

To my parents
Deane W. Moores and Helen Sullivan Moores
from their erstwhile dropout

and
para mis suegros
Elipio A. Maestas y Eloisa Velasquez Maestas

Contents

Foreword

The education of the deaf is the most special of all areas of special education. Special education has been defined as that education which is unique, uncommon, or of unusual quality and is in addition to the procedures used with the majority of children. The special techniques that have been developed over the years to assist deaf children in processing information without the sense of hearing are certainly unique, ingenious, and highly specialized.

It is interesting to note that special education in the United States originated with the permanent organization of a school for the deaf in 1817 in Hartford, Connecticut. At that time the school was named the American Asylum for the Education of the Deaf and Dumb. In the United States this school became the center for the education of children with little or no hearing. It was a model for the development of residential schools in other states.

The specialized techniques that have been developed for teaching the deaf are many and varied, including lipreading, oralism through the use of other senses than hearing, manual communication including both sign language and fingerspelling, the use of hearing aids to utilize residual hearing, and many variations of these. As Professor Moores has brought out in this book, the development of these training techniques was not without major controversy. He presents in detail the origin of these controversies and the dialogues expressing the opposing points of view of Edward Miner Gallaudet (the advocate of the manual method) and Alexander Graham Bell (the advocate of the oral and aural methods).

These controversies have not been entirely without their benefits. Although the arguments for each side often have been on an emotional rather than on a scientific plane, the dialogue has spurred both sides to do a better job of educating deaf children. Dedicated educators have struggled for years to improve the educational programs, and a variety of models have been developed: day schools and some residential schools that emphasized a purely oral method, and residential schools that emphasized the manual method. In most cases, no single method has been used exclusively.

As a psychologist I had had little firsthand experience with deaf children until I became head of a teacher-training program that included a program for the education of teachers of the deaf. I was fascinated by the effective techniques that had been developed by teachers who were not technically versed in principles of learning, but who seemed to have developed the commonsense procedures that follow those principles: techniques for attracting the attention of a child, reinforcement techniques, frequent repetition and rehearsal, accepting approximations in speech, and the step-by-step procedures developed and used by effective and charismatic teachers.

The major problem in educating deaf children is teaching them to process language. If a child cannot hear, how can he or she learn language? And if a child cannot learn language, how does he or she learn to read or to spell or to do arithmetic? What substitute information processing techniques can be used to aid a deaf child in learning language? What are the contributions of manualism and oralism to the development of language and speech in deaf children? What research has been conducted during the past century in Europe and in America to answer some of these basic questions? Such questions are thoroughly explored and documented by Professor Moores in this very comprehensive book.

Educating the deaf: Psychology, principles and practices contains exactly what the title states. It covers not only historical development, but also the current state of the art and the current specialized techniques of education, as well as the social and psychological characteristics of the deaf and their families. The book is a sorely needed compendium of information for workers in the area: educators of the deaf, speech pathologists, rehabilitation counselors, and workers in related fields of special education. Written at a basic introductory level, it is highly suitable for use by college students majoring in the education of the deaf, in speech and hearing sciences, and in rehabilitation counseling. Its use should help advance the education of deaf children and thereby minimize their handicap.

Samuel A. Kirk

Preface

The impetus for writing this book came from a sense of frustration over the lack of a definitive work on the educational and psychological implications of deafness. The lack was first forcefully driven home when the author undertook to teach a survey course on deafness at the University of Minnesota in 1967. Although books dealing with audiological, medical, or psychological aspects of deafness were available, none of them could be considered a complete, comprehensive reference or sourcebook that met the needs of professionals dealing with deafness and deaf individuals.

The organization of the book is modeled roughly on the content of the survey course mentioned above as modified over a period of ten years. Its major sources include extensive reading and classroom experiences as a teacher of the deaf. Many of the chapters developed out of research conducted at the University of Minnesota Research, Development and Demonstration Center in Education of Handicapped Children. This includes not only the presentation of data but also the reviews of literature in Chapter 1, "Overview: Education of the Deaf"; Chapter 5, "Families and Deaf Children"; Chapter 6, "The Acquisition and Use of English"; Chapter 8, "Deafness and Mental Health"; Chapter 9, "American Sign Language and Manual Communication"; Chapter 10, "Early Intervention Programs"; and Chapter 13, "Postsecondary Education and the Economic Status of Deaf Americans."

The first draft of the book was written while the author was on sabbatical from the University of Minnesota during the 1974–1975 academic year. A revised version was used as the basic text of a course entitled "Educational, Psychological and Social Implications of Hearing Impairment" at the University of Minnesota during the summer of 1975. The present manuscript followed other revisions made on the basis of subsequent feedback.

Educating the Deaf is intended for the use of individuals representing a wide range of interests. For those whose major commitments are to the areas of deafness — for example, teachers of the deaf, speech therapists, counselors for the deaf, educational audiologists — it can serve as a basic text and sourcebook on both a graduate and undergraduate level. Such individuals would take related work in areas such as anatomy and physiology of speech and hearing mechanisms, aural rehabilitation, and methods courses in the teaching of speech, school subjects, and language to the deaf.

For a larger, more diverse, group the book would represent the primary source of information on deafness. People in this category would include parents of deaf individuals, regular classroom teachers, teachers of other types of handicapped children, tutors for specific learning disabilities, psychologists, specialists in early child development, social workers, general rehabilitation counselors, and administrators of special education programs at local, state, regional, and national levels.

Although the text does treat areas such as teaching speech, language, speechreading, and auditory training, the treatment is not designed as an exposition of methods for working with deaf individuals. For the specialist, intensive training is necessary in each of these fields as well as in anatomy and physiology of the speech and hearing mechanism, assessment of hearing, acoustics, media utilization, and curriculum adaptation. Complete texts exist in each area and the reader is referred to them.

It was decided to develop a separate methods chapter rather than dispersing the material throughout the book. For example, the section on teaching language to the deaf could have been included in Chapter 6, "The Acquisition and Use of English." Sections on the teaching of speech, use of residual hearing, and speechreading might have been placed in Chapter 10, "Early Intervention Programs" and/or in Chapter 12, "Elementary and Secondary Education."

This book contains a significant amount of historical material. This is due to my respect for the work done by those who preceded us and to my belief that understanding their efforts will help us to build on their successes while avoiding their mistakes. It should be noted that Chapter 2 deals with education in Europe only through the nineteenth century and not up to the present. Twentieth-century developments in European countries such as Sweden, the Netherlands, the Soviet Union, and Great Britain, are discussed within the context of topics covered in various other chapters.

Although portions of some chapters may be somewhat technical, the book is written in order to be of benefit to a well-informed lay person as well as to a professional whose work touches on the lives of deaf individuals. If the book manages to convey a feeling of empathy with deaf people — an acceptance of each deaf person as an individual, and an understanding of at least some of the problems faced by deaf children and adults — then the author will be satisfied that the effort of writing the book was not in vain.

D. F. M.

Acknowledgments

Because I am indebted to so many people in such a variety of ways for the writing of this book, I hesitate to undertake an enumeration for fear of inadvertently omitting the names of important contributors. The list could run literally into the hundreds. However, I would be remiss if I did not publicly acknowledge the special impact of individuals with whom I have been involved professionally under varying circumstances during my professional career and from whom I have learned so much.

My primary sources of knowledge have been deaf individuals of all ages and circumstances with whom I have interacted as dormitory counselor, graduate student, teacher, football coach, summer camp director, educational researcher, colleague, and friend. I hope my admiration for their adjustment and success in the face of an indifferent world is evident in my writing.

Four individuals have had a significant impact on me and the development of my philosophy of education. Each has shown great understanding and restraint in dealing with a restless, often contentious, personality. Dr. Edmund B. Boatner, Superintendent of the American School for the Deaf from 1935 to 1970, convinced me that I would lead a more fulfilling life as an educator of the deaf than as an experimental psychologist. He was correct and I gratefully express my appreciation. Miss Barbara Griffin was my first supervising teacher, at the Rochester, New York School for the Deaf, and it is to her that I owe my style of teaching. Her example, more than anyone else's, demonstrated the high standards that deaf students could be helped to attain. I first came in contact with Dr. Stephen Quigley when I was a graduate student at Gallaudet College and took his course, "The Psychology of Deafness." Later, at the University of Illinois, his presence motivated me to apply to the doctoral program there. Professor Quigley was my advisor during my studies in Illinois, during which time I had the opportunity to be involved in a number of research studies. Professor Quigley has made substantial contributions to educational research in the area of deafness ranging from the preschool to postsecondary level. His advice and support, both during the course of my studies and in the intervening years, are greatly appreciated. Dr. Samuel A. Kirk was director of the Institute for Research on Exceptional Children (IREC) at the University of Illinois during the same period. Dr. Kirk was a member of my doctoral committee and for a period of time I worked with him on the standardization of the Illinois Test of Psycholinguistic Abilities (ITPA). He has provided me with invaluable professional advice over the years. To a large extent the IREC with which I was affiliated as a student has provided the model for the University of Minnesota Research, Development and Demonstration Center in Education of Handicapped Children.

Several colleagues have read the manuscript at different stages of its development and have provided valuable feedback. Those especially deserving of mention are: Dr. Ursula Bellugi, Salk Institute; Dr. Edmund B. Boatner, past Superintendent, American School for the Deaf; Dr. Maxine Tull Boatner, Biographer of Edward M. Gallaudet; Mrs. Beatrice M. Burke, El Paso Public Schools; Mr. Douglas Burke, West Texas Regional Program for the Deaf; Dr. Ann Kennedy, Moncton University, Dr. Samuel Kirk, University of Arizona; Mr. Terrence O'Rourke, National Association of the Deaf; Dr. Stephen Quigley, University of Illinois; Dr. Philip Schmitt, Gallaudet College; Dr. J. Dean Twining, Ball State University; Dr. McCay Vernon, Editor, *American Annals of the Deaf*; and Dr. Boyce Williams, United States Office of Education, Social and Rehabilitation Service.

I am also indebted to several colleagues at the University of Minnesota Research, Development and Demonstration Center in Education of Handicapped Children with whom I have been affiliated in several studies in education of the deaf. Work conducted in the course of these projects has been the basis of some of the chapters of this book. Major contributors are as follows: *Evaluation of Preschool Programs* — Mrs. Karin Eyles, Mrs. Marilyn Goodwin, Mrs. Cynthia McIntyre, and Mrs. Karen Weiss; *Minnesota Early Language Development Sequence* (MELDS) — Miss Charlotte Clark and Dr. Richard Woodcock; *Deaf Children of Deaf Parents* — Mrs. Ruth Ellenberger, Mr. Robert Hoffmeister, and Mr. Patrick O'Malley; *Post-Secondary Programs* — Mr. Stephen Fisher and Mrs. Mary Jane Harlow.

Mrs. Audrey Thurlow, Principal Secretary of the University of Minnesota Research, Development and Demonstration Center in Education of Handicapped Children, typed the manuscript. Her industriousness, patience, and ability to decipher seemingly unintelligible writing are unsurpassed.

And finally to my wife and colleague, Julia Maestas y Moores, to whom I simply owe everything. Her love, encouragement, support, and insight led me through each chapter, from first outline to rough draft to final form. Without her, the book would not have been written.

Educating the Deaf

1
Overview:
Education of the Deaf

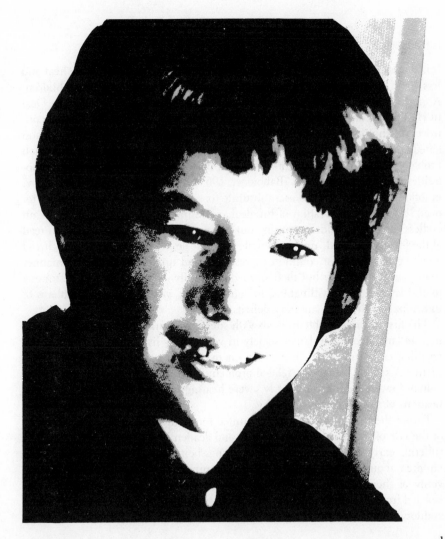

Introduction

It is doubtful that any area of its size in education has generated more heat and less light than the problem of educating severely hearing-impaired children. Almost from the time of the establishment of the American School for the Deaf in Hartford, Connecticut, in 1817, the field has been riven by debilitating controversies that have absorbed the attention and drained the energies of its most gifted educators, individuals who consequently have been reduced to approach problems within the framework of overly simplistic either-or, black-white polarities. It has been noted (Babbidge, 1965) that, in the opinion of many, emotion has been accepted as a substitute for research in determining policy for over 100 years in education of the deaf. The incontrovertible evidence — an endless stream of children pouring out of programs for the deaf unable to read at the fifth-grade level, unable to write a simple sentence, unable to speechread anything but the most common expressions, and unable to speak in a manner understandable to any but their immediate family — stands as stark testimony to an inability, or unwillingness, to come to grips with the generic problems of individuals with severe auditory deficits.

The first of these problems deals with such individuals' difficulties in mastering the language of the larger society in which they live and the effects of the resulting communication limitations on many other aspects of their development. A second, obviously related problem is the insensitivity of hearing individuals toward the impact of early severe hearing loss and the debilitating ramifications of such a lack of empathy.

Part of the frustration may be accounted for by the extremely difficult nature of the task of oral language acquisition and academic achievement for children suffering early severe deafness. Other things being equal, the ease with which children acquire the language of their community varies inversely with the severity of their hearing loss. To be isolated from the human voice is to be isolated from spoken language. While other children are able to use an intact auditory modality to build up an early mastery of the sound, shape, and sense

2

of their language, deaf children are unique in that their language acquisition may depend primarily on vision.

Children with normal hearing can be considered linguistically proficient in every sense of the word. They have a knowledge of the basic rules of their language. They can produce a potentially infinite number of novel yet appropriate utterances. Because of their unconscious mastery over the grammatical structure of their language, they can combine and recombine its elements indefinitely. They can produce and understand sentences to which they have never been exposed. They enter the formal educational situation in elementary school around age 6 with a fully developed instrument for learning: language and communication ability — an ability that they have acquired with no conscious effort on the part of their parents or themselves.

By contrast, profoundly deaf children — those with no functional response to speech — usually present an entirely different picture. Unless they have deaf parents, they probably have not acquired a language naturally and automatically. Without intensive compensatory training they may be totally nonverbal as well as nonvocal; they even may be unaware that such things as words exist. For such children language is not a facilitating device for the acquisition of knowledge. Rather it is a barrier standing between them and the full realization of their academic, intellectual, and social potentials. Typical deaf children, although of normal intelligence, find their range of experience constrained by communication limitations. They suffer, relative to other children, from a lack of opportunity to interact fully with and manipulate their environment in meaningful ways. Although deafness itself may have no effect on intellectual potential, the deafness will lead to impoverished communication skills that themselves may limit development severely, unless the children are provided compensatory tools.

Much of the curriculum in programs for deaf children has been designed to teach or develop the English proficiency that hearing children bring to the educational process. The means by which most deaf children presently learn English is a different, more laborious, and inefficient procedure. The result in terms of standard English is far below that of hearing children both qualitatively and quantitatively.

Hearing children employ their early knowledge of the sound system of their language as a vehicle to choose from a wealth of language forms pervading their environment. This involves an active process that leads to mastery of grammatical patterns. By contrast, profoundly deaf children must for the most part bypass the sound system in their quest for English grammatical competence. They perceive language primarily through visual means, that is, through speechreading (lipreading), signs, informal gestures, dactylic (fingerspelling) and/or graphemic presentation, as well as through the auditory channel. Proficiency in speechreading may be defined as interpreting the words or meaning conveyed by a speaker by watching lip and facial movements. It is a form of closure by which an individual decodes a message based on fragmentary bits of information transmitted through a distorted channel in which much of the information is lost. Speechreading is dependent on past experience with the redundancies and predictability of language based on previous linguistic experience; therefore, it is of limited utility by itself in the learning of language.

Definition of Terms

It should be emphasized that the term *hearing impaired* is not limited to individuals with a profound hearing loss. It covers the entire range of auditory impairment, encompassing not only the deaf child but also the one with a very mild loss who may understand speech without difficulty. The number of hearing-impaired children decreases as a function of the extent of loss, from mild to moderate to severe to profound levels.

Much of the confusion found among professionals dealing with children with hearing losses may be traced to an unfortunate inability to reach consensus on terminology. For some the term *hearing impaired* occurs in free variation with *hard of hearing*. For others it also includes deaf children. In addition, one person's conception of hard of hearing may overlap with another's concept of deafness.

In the final analysis any definition must be a functional one and can be accepted only within broad limits. It would be no more defensible to classify a child as deaf or hard of hearing solely on the basis of an audiometric exam than it would be to judge a child as trainable or educable mentally retarded purely on the basis of an IQ score. Other factors such as age of onset of the hearing loss, configuration of the loss, etiology, age of instigation of training, age of fitting and appropriateness of fit of the hearing aid, and family climate are all factors of prime importance.

Within this framework, terms such as *limited hearing, auditorially impaired, acoustically handicapped,* and *hearing impaired* include both of the more frequently used terms *hard of hearing* and *deaf*. The distinction between the two is usually drawn to differentiate between those for whom the auditory channel is affected but functional and those for whom the sense of hearing is nonfunctional as the primary modality for the development of language. The line between the deaf and hard of hearing for convenience has usually been drawn around a 70 to 75 dB loss through the speech range. However, no satisfactory definition other than a behavioral one has been developed. The difficulties lie (1) in trying to categorize hearing loss into discrete levels when, in actuality, they exist on continua and (2) in attempting to generalize from an audiogram alone when so many other factors also may influence the behavior of an acoustically handicapped child.

A misleading and inaccurate practice that has added to the confusion is the tendency to report an individual's loss on the basis of an unaided audiogram. This practice has been criticized (Pollack, 1964) on the grounds that substantial differences may exist between aided and unaided hearing. With appropriate fitting, training, and education some children may move across the line separating the deaf from the hard of hearing. The movement toward early diagnosis of hearing loss and fitting of hearing aids is growing. Today, for example, in some preschool programs for the hearing impaired every child is equipped with an individual hearing aid. It is much more reasonable, therefore, to refer to an individual's hearing loss under his or her normal listening condition. For an increasing proportion of young hearing-impaired children in the United States, the normal condition includes a hearing aid.

In October 1973 the Conference of Executives of American Schools for the Deaf created the ad hoc Committee to Redefine Deaf and Hard of Hearing for Educational Purposes. In the committee report (Frisina, 1974), it was noted that the term *deaf* has been used variously to mean impairment, disability, and handicap. As the committee defines it, the physical and presently irreversible *impairment* of the auditory mechanism is the cause of deafness. The terms *deaf* and *deafness* are restricted to describing the disability caused by the impairment. The *disability* is expressed in terms of speech reception as measured by speech or other sounds calibrated for frequency and intensity. The *handicap* of deafness is the extent to which a person's overall functioning is limited by the disability of deafness. Although recognizing some negative connotations of the term *deaf*, the committee recommended its retention as a generic term because of legislative and legal precedents for its use.

The committee also recommended that the term *deaf* be restricted in use only as an adjective, with *deafness* being the preferred term in reference to a state of hearing disability. Again, neither word describes or connotes the degree of handicap involved.

The following definitions (Frisina, 1974, p. 3) have been adopted by the Conference of Executives of American Schools for the Deaf.

Simple General Definitions

A *deaf person* is one whose hearing is disabled to an extent (usually 70 dB ISO or greater) that precludes the understanding of speech through the ear alone, without or with the use of a hearing aid.

A *hard-of-hearing person* is one whose hearing is disabled to an extent (usually 35 to 69 dB ISO) that makes difficult, but does not preclude, the understanding of speech through the ear alone, without or with a hearing aid.

A Definition for Educational Placement and Research

Deafness refers to the condition of individuals whose hearing is disabled and is expressed in terms of speech or other sounds calibrated for frequency and intensity. Those individuals are classified according to the following categories of deafness. The stated requirements in communication and education associated with these levels are to be assumed necessary in each infant/child/adult until proved otherwise.

Table 1.1 Summary of schools and classes for the deaf in the United States, October 1974

Schools and classes	Program data					Student data				
	Number	Preschools	Accredited high schools	Multi-handicapped programs	Total enrollment	Male	Female	Residential	Day	Multi-handicapped
Public residential schools	63	44	36	34	19,063	10,623	8,440	14,406	4,657	4,195
Private residential schools	16	11	2	6	1,501	793	708	871	630	157
Public day schools	68	59	17	29	7,269	3,828	3,441	0	7,269	1,705
Private day schools	21	19	0	4	806	427	379	0	806	82
Public day classes	489	315	114	72	21,446	11,151	10,295	47	21,399	2,730
Private day classes	45	44	2	3	810	435	375	0	810	115
Multihandicapped only	53	29	1	0	965	575	390	163	802	843
Specific handicapped facilities	31	13	2	0	1,149	640	509	891	258	1,149
Total	786	534	174	148	53,009	28,472	24,537	16,378	36,631	10,976

Source: Adapted from W. Craig and H. Craig (Eds.), "Directory of Services for the Deaf," American Annals of the Deaf, 1975, 120, 175.

1. Level I, 35 to 54 dB. Individuals in this category routinely do not require special class/school placement; they routinely do require special speech and hearing assistance.

2. Level II, 55 to 69 dB. These individuals occasionally require special class/school placement; they routinely require special speech, hearing, and language assistance.

3. Level III, 70 to 89 dB. Those in this category of deafness routinely require special class/school placement; they routinely require special speech, hearing, language, and educational assistance.

4. Level IV, 90 dB and beyond. These individuals routinely require special class/school placement; they routinely require special speech, hearing, language, and educational assistance.

Definitions Related to Age at Onset of Deafness

Prelingual deafness refers to the condition of persons whose deafness was present at birth or occurred at an age prior to the development of speech and language.

Postlingual deafness refers to the condition of persons whose deafness occurred at an age following the spontaneous acquisition of speech and language.

Educational Programs for the Deaf in the United States

At present more than 50,000 children in the United States receive some kind of special education services. Although incidence of severe hearing impairment may vary as a result of cyclical epidemics such as rubella, school enrollment figures are consistent with the estimate of Carhart (1969), which placed the incidence of deafness in the school-aged population at approximately one per thousand.

Undoubtedly there is a far larger group of children with mild and moderate hearing losses who are educated in regular classrooms without the benefit of extra help. Unfortunately it is impossible to estimate how many of these children are encountering trouble socially and academically because of reduced hearing. Most public school programs have only recently become aware of the special needs of such children, and research is quite limited. Consistent with the trend toward individualization of instruction in educational settings is the development of programs in learning disabilities, reading and speech pathology in public schools, which should benefit large numbers of children achieving below their potential largely because of moderate hearing losses.

Craig and Craig (1975, p. 175) report a total of 53,009 children in schools and classes for the deaf as of October 1974 (Table 1.1). Following a pattern that has remained consistent since the nineteenth century, males account for somewhat more than one-half the total, in this case outnumbering females 28,472 to 24,537, a ratio of 54 to 46%.

During the baby boom in the United States from 1947 to 1959 the numbers of children in the population and in the schools increased at a faster rate than at any time in our history. The number of deaf children in programs for the deaf has increased at an even faster rate, more so than would be expected solely on the basis of population growth. In fact the expansion has continued even as the number of school-aged children has leveled off and declined. As an example, in 1961 a total of 28,529 children were enrolled in all programs for the deaf, including preschool (Doctor, 1962), only slightly more than one-half the number enrolled in 1974.

One explanation for the rising figures must be the rubella epidemic of the early 1960s. A disproportionate number of deaf children were born during that period and are still present in large numbers in school programs. Of greater impact has been a movement to provide services to a wider range of children. Home training and parent counseling programs, either separately or in coordination with preschool programs, are now common. More public day schools and residential schools are accepting responsibility to serve multihandicapped deaf children, many of whom would have received no services or would have been institutionalized in the past. There are indications of at least the beginnings of a commitment to provide adequate services to deaf children from minority groups. Finally, under the special impact of federal legislation, more children with less severe hearing losses are receiving support services in integrated settings.

Programmatic Provisions

Traditionally, the majority of deaf children have been educated in residential schools for the deaf. Since World War II there has been a trend toward substantial growth of public school programs, especially in large metropolitan areas. This has been accompanied by a growing tendency in many residential schools, especially those near large metropolitan areas, to educate large numbers of their students as day pupils.

By 1974 public school enrollment represented the largest single category, with 21,446 children followed by 20,564 children enrolled in 63 public residential schools (19,063 students) and 16 private residential schools (1,501 students). Of the students in residential schools, 5,287, or 25%, were day students. Overall, 36,631 children were day students, almost 70% of the total.

Changing Populations

There seems to be agreement among educators of the deaf that programs are now serving children with different characteristics. First, there may be more children with multiple handicaps enrolled in programs. More programs are now committed to serving such children. It is possible that the number of such children is increasing. Vernon (1969) has discussed how advances in medicine may save the lives of children who in previous generations might have died. These children may survive, but many may suffer from severe multiple handicaps.

The data in Table 1.1 reveal that 10,976 children enrolled in programs in October 1974 were categorized as multihandicapped, representing more than 20% of the total. The figures represent merely the number of children already in programs identified as multihandicapped. Undeniably there are many more children in institutions for the retarded, in public school programs for trainable mentally retarded and autistic children, and at home. It is impossible to make even an educated guess concerning the number of unidentified children.

Postsecondary Programs

Since 1864 Gallaudet College in Washington, D.C., has existed as the only liberal arts college for the deaf in the world. The enrollment is in excess of 1,000, including students from all over the world, and is federally funded. In addition to the undergraduate college, Gallaudet has provided leadership in career education and hosts model elementary and secondary schools for the deaf. The graduate department, which accepts both deaf and hearing students, offers degrees in education of the deaf, audiology, and counseling and guidance.

In 1968 the federal government established the National-Technical Institute for the Deaf (NTID) as an affiliate of the Rochester (New York) Institute of Technology. NTID offers advanced vocational and technical training to deaf students who are at approximately the same academic level as Gallaudet College students.

Three regional vocational programs were established by the federal government within existing vocational facilities for students with normal hearing. These programs are in Seattle, Washington; New Orleans, Louisiana; and St. Paul, Minnesota. In addition, following federal legislation mandating vocational training for handicapped students, and specification of "set-aside" monies to fund such training, a large number of vocational programs based on the Seattle, New Orleans, and St. Paul models have been established since 1969. Rawlings, Trybus, Delgado, and Stuckless (1975) identified a total of 43 postsecondary programs for the deaf in 1975.

Educational Placement: The Question of Mainstreaming

Beginning with an article by Dunn (1968) entitled "Special education for the mildly retarded: Is much of it justified?" educators of the retarded have questioned the practice of assigning educable mentally retarded children to segregated classes. In the six-year period from 1968 to 1974 over 30 articles related to integration of handicapped children into regular classes appeared in the journal *Exceptional Children* alone (Warfield, 1974). The term *mainstreaming* received wide acceptance and in some programs was perceived as successful.

During the same period of time a series of court cases dealing with educational provisions for handicapped individuals were decided. Treatment of these cases and implications for education may be found in Abeson (1972, 1974); Kuriloff, True, Kirp, and Buss (1974); and Turnbull (1975). The two most important cases were *Pennsylvania Association for Retarded Citizens (PARC)* v. *Commonwealth of Pennsylvania* and *Mills* v. *Board of Education of the District of Columbia*. Rulings on these cases have declared illegal practices that exclude handicapped individuals from educational opportunities. The PARC decision established that all retarded children had the right to a free public education and required the state to identify all retarded children excluded from such education as well as to evaluate those already in special classes.

In both the PARC and Mills cases it was declared that regular class placement was preferable to placement in special classes, which in turn was preferable to institutionalization. From this, it may follow that a retarded child — and by extension any handicapped child — should not be placed in an institutional setting that is not demonstrably *superior* to education in regular or special classes. If children are removed from the home for educational purposes, the burden of proof is on the educators.

The decisions concerning the rights of all children to an education should have little impact on deaf children who have no additional severe handicaps. It is unlikely that many such children are excluded from an education at present. The decision that states should *identify* and serve children currently excluded from education, if implemented, should have a tremendous impact on those deaf individuals suffering from additional handicaps who have not been identified and who are now receiving no education. It should be noted that identification and education of such a population is extremely difficult. In an analysis of the outcomes of the PARC case, Kuriloff and associates (1974) noted that implementation of the consent agreement was uneven and only partially effective. They concluded:

But PARC too readily embraced the view that judicial mandate insures change. Courts are not, indeed should not be, superschool administrators. . . . In short, a decree such as PARC appears, in retrospect, a necessary but not sufficient condition for educational change. Only those charged with the responsibility to educate children can give meaning to such ambiguous concepts as "appropriate" education. (p. 41)

It is not surprising that educators of the deaf have expressed mixed reactions to the rulings that handicapped children are best served in "normal" settings and that placement in special schools is least desirable educationally. Although residential schools may in no way be equated with institutions for the

retarded, the implications of the above decisions raise some basic issues concerning the role of residential schools for the deaf. Biklen (1975) reported on a suit initiated to establish a program for the deaf in Syracuse, New York. At the time of the suit, there were over 100 deaf children in the community, all of whom were attending residential schools beyond commuting distance. Biklen claimed (p. 383) that the school district saved money by excluding deaf children from local schools and enrolling them in state-funded residential schools. Biklen reported that within a few months of the filing of the legal complaint, local school districts promised immediate implementation of programs and invited parents to participate in the planning and implementation. The suit was dropped.

Approaching the question from the perspective of a superintendent of a residential school for the deaf, Brill (1975) stated:

We seem to be in an era of simplistic solutions to complex problems. The less one knows about the details of the situation the easier it is to generalize and pronounce panaceas. Unfortunately, jurists, lawyers, legislators, general educators, and strangely enough, parents of many deaf children, know very little about the actual educational problems facing deaf children. (p. 377)

Brill argued that the prelingually deaf child requires a very special educational program and should be in a small class of six to eight pupils who are of approximately the same age and educational level. Brill recommends no program be developed unless it can ensure at least some homogeneity of grouping. He recommended a minimum of 40 children at the elementary level and 150 for a secondary program. Brill notes that the real issue is not whether a state has a responsibility for providing appropriately for a child but rather *who* shall determine what is appropriate. In *Case* v. *State of California* it was found that the professional staff of a school for the deaf was most competent in determining the appropriate placement for a particular deaf child with additional handicapping conditions.

Although they provide different orientations the positions of Biklen and Brill are not diametrically opposed. Brill has criticized the trend of establishing programs in small school districts with inadequate population bases. Biklen reported on efforts by a group of parents in a relatively large metropolitan area to provide services to over 100 deaf children who were attending residential schools and for whom there were no options. Both these positions seem reasonable to the author. The extent to which decisions such as these in the Mills and PARC cases cause a proliferation of one-teacher programs remains to be seen.

Educators of the Retarded and Mainstreaming

It is not accidental that the strongest advocates for the recent trends toward mainstreaming are drawn predominantly from the ranks of educators of the educable mentally retarded or that educators of the educable mentally retarded are leading the way in mainstreaming of other categories of handicapping conditions. For example, the major work on integration of deaf children has been written by an educator of the retarded (Birch, 1975) along the lines of a previous work on mainstreaming of educable mentally retarded children (Birch, 1974). An examination of trends in education of the retarded is necessary to gain an appreciation of the situation.

According to Kirk (1975) a major reason for the current support and popularity of mainstreaming for the mentally retarded is that many children in the past have been mislabeled as mentally retarded and inappropriately placed in special schools. Beginning in the 1920s and 1930s the upper-range IQs of children eligible for special classes increased from 70 to 75 to 80 and in some places to 85. By 1962 the American Association on Mental Deficiency (AAMD) defined retardation as −1 standard deviation below the mean, an IQ of about 85 (Kirk, 1975). As a result, the number of children in special classes for the retarded in the United States increased from 113,565 in 1952 to 703,800 in 1969, an increase of over 600% in 17 years (Kirk, 1975).

In short, the situation became intolerable in a number of ways. First, it was clear that testing and placement procedures were biased racially and ethnically. Black and Spanish-surnamed children were assigned to such classes in disproportionate numbers (Mercer, 1973). Second, there was no justification for segregating children purely on the basis of an IQ score of 85, especially those children using a different language or dialect from that of the tester. Garrison and Hamil (1971) estimated that 25% of the children in classes for the educable mentally retarded were misplaced.

The reaction by educators of the retarded has been dramatic. The American Association on Mental Deficiency has changed the psychometric definition of retardation to −2 standard deviations below the mean, or an IQ of about 70 (Grossman, 1973). In other words educators of the retarded are proclaiming major advances on the basis of the fact that (1) they are beginning to abandon racist practices which they themselves initiated; (2) they are mainstreaming children who never should have been in special classes in the first place; and (3) they have revised their psychometric definition of mental retardation to that employed 50 years ago. One must wonder how such educators can perceive their efforts as anything more than a belated attempt to right past wrongs. Educators of the deaf, with a longer and more consistent history in the education of handicapped children, should proceed with making decisions concerning placement without being subjected to undue influence from other fields.

The Placement of Deaf Children

Because the first schools for the deaf in Europe and the United States were residential facilities, most educators mistakenly assume that interest in educating deaf children contiguous to hearing peers is a relatively recent phenomenon. In reality educators of the deaf have long been sensitive to the desirability of having deaf children live at home and interact with hearing peers. It is not well known that many of the first residential schools were established originally as day programs. Two of the first three schools for the deaf in the United States, the New York school and the Pennsylvania school, started out in this way (Best, 1943).

There also has been at least some interest expressed for over 150 years in the concept of having deaf and hearing children learn together. Gordon (1885a) reviewed attempts to educate the deaf in public schools as early as 1815, when Stephani in Bavaria declared that institutions for the deaf were useless luxuries. In 1821 Graser established an experimental school in Bavaria in which deaf children were integrated with special tutoring and associated with hearing children as much as possible. By 1823 six-day programs had been established. According to Gordon instruction of the deaf was endorsed enthusiastically as a part of the public school system, with one of the major motivations being economy of cost.

Gordon quoted a report from the German Ministry of Education in 1828 as follows: "In the course of ten years it will easily be brought about that in all the provinces of the Kingdom provision will be made for the education of all the unfortunate deaf and dumb" (p. 125). Gordon reported, however, that the experiment failed, and the prophesy was not fulfilled. By 1854 the Inspector of Deaf-Mute Instruction wrote, "Of a common instruction of the deaf and hearing in the same classes no one any longer speaks" (Gordon, 1885a, p. 126). In 1858 Moritz Hill concluded:

I have followed with care the results throughout Germany, and I have been compelled finally to recognize the illusory character of the system. School authorities and families are positively opposed to having deaf mute children in the schools, because they are always a detriment to the hearing children. The hope that each deaf mute could receive necessary instruction at home in common with hearing children and without injury to the latter has been abandoned. The results of the entire system have been slight. (Gordon, 1885a, p. 126)

Gordon stated (p. 126) that in 1871 approximately 40% of the deaf children in Prussia were educated in common schools and 60% in institutions. By 1881 not one deaf child was left in the common schools. Gordon reported that the German experiment was tried throughout central and northern Europe with similar results. Concerning the work of Blanchet in France, Gordon presented the following chronology:

1836. Blanchet proposed coeducation of the deaf and hearing. He suggested closing institutions except for orphans and the poor.
1848. Blanchet opened two integrated schools in Paris.
1850. Ten schools were in operation.
1855. The Council of Public Education reported: . . . this system which receives deaf mutes in their early childhood has the immense advantage of retaining them in the bosoms of their families, and of placing them in schools in the midst of hearing pupils who become their companions in study and in play, and thus form ties

of comradeship and affection which can have upon their future only the happiest influence.

1857. Blanchet published "Upon the means of generalizing the education of deaf mutes without separating them from the family and from those who speak."

1858. The French Ministry of Education officially endorsed the Blanchet System.

1859. The Ministry withdrew its endorsement.

1882. An estimated 30 pupils remained in the system. (pp. 131–134)

Mainstreaming was attempted in the Soviet Union following the revolution. However, the results were negligible. The system was abandoned and replaced by segregated educational facilities that placed greater emphasis on the development of a curriculum specifically designed for use with deaf children (Gallagher & Martin, 1974).

In the United States as early as 1852, Bartlett (1852) had established an integrated "family" school serving both hearing and deaf children. The numbers of deaf children integrated at least to some extent in programs with the hearing have increased steadily since World War II. The trend has been most marked at the postsecondary level. Excluding Gallaudet College, all 26 programs listed in the 1973 Guide to College/Career Programs for Deaf Students (Stuckless & Delgado, 1973) and all 43 programs listed in the 1975 Guide (Rawlings et al., 1975) were located within facilities for students with normal hearing and provided for at least some shared course work. It is surprising that such a trend has been accompanied by so little reaction or even comment.

Many educators of the deaf have expressed reservations concerning the desirability of the mainstreaming trend because of past practices that "integrated" deaf children but failed to provide them with necessary support services (Brill, 1975; Vernon & Prickett, 1976). Such "integration" typically involved placement of a deaf child in spatial contiguity to hearing children with occasional help from a speech therapist or resource teacher but with little or no systematic attention to curriculum modifications, social-emotional development, or sensitivization of teachers and hearing students to the needs of the deaf child. Vernon and Prickett (1976) state that this is easily the most widely used form of mainstreaming now being practiced in the United States and conclude that it has failed miserably the overwhelming majority of children who have been exposed to it. Vernon and Prickett are careful to state that they are not necessarily opposed to the concept of mainstreaming but rather to the abuse of the concept and to the inappropriate manner in which it has developed in a majority of cases.

Research related to integration is quite limited and of questionable generalizability. This is especially true of those employing such "new" ideas as using sign language in integrated classes (Holcomb, 1970; Mangan, 1975). Overall, however, it appears that the process is continuing on a rational basis, and there does not appear to be any strong movement to abandon deaf children to the tender mercies of mainstream classes without strong support services.

Methodology*

The Methods Controversy

The methods controversy, which has been raging for over 200 years, perhaps has accounted for more confusion than any other question concerned with the hearing impaired. The issues have been distorted beyond recognition, and it is not surprising that these are misunderstood by professionals on the periphery. It is inaccurate to speak of an oral-manual controversy because no present-day educators of the hearing impaired advocate a "pure" or "rigid" manual position. Educators of the hearing impaired in the United States are oralists, and all are concerned with developing a child's ability to speak and understand the spoken word to the highest degree possible. The difference is between oral-alone educators, who argue that all children must be educated by purely oral methods, and the oral-plus educators, who argue that at least some children would progress more satisfactorily with simultaneous or combined oral-manual presentation. At present, although variations exist, four basic methods of instruction may be identified in the United States: the oral method, the auditory method, the Rochester method, and the simultaneous method.

1. Oral method. In this method, also called the oral-aural method, children receive input through speechreading (lipreading) and amplification of sound, and they express themselves through speech. Gestures and signs are prohibited. In its purest form reading and writing are discouraged in the early years as a potential inhibitor to the development of oral skills.

2. Auditory method. This method, as opposed to the oral, is basically unisensory. It concentrates on developing listening skills in children, who are expected to rely primarily on hearing. Reading and writing usually are discouraged, as is a dependence on speechreading. Although developed for children with moderate losses, some attempts have been made to use this method with profoundly impaired children.

3. Rochester method. This is a combination of the oral method plus fingerspelling. The children receive information through speechreading, amplification, and fingerspelling, and they express themselves through speech and fingerspelling. Reading and writing usually are given great emphasis. When practiced correctly, the teacher spells in the manual alphabet every letter of every word in coordination with speech. A proficient teacher can present at the rate of approximately 100 words per minute. This approach is quite similar to the system of neo-oralism developed in the Soviet Union.

4. Simultaneous method. This is a combination of the oral method plus signs and fingerspelling. The children receive input through speechreading, ampli-

* This section is based on a section, "Methods of Instruction," which appeared in Moores, D., A review of education of the deaf. In L. Mann & D. Sabatino (Eds.), *The Third Review of Special Education.* New York: Grune & Stratton, 1976, pp. 19–52.

fication, signs, and fingerspelling. They express themselves in speech, signs, and fingerspelling. Signs are differentiated from fingerspelling in that they represent complete words or ideas. A proficient teacher will sign in coordination with the spoken word.

The term *total communication* has received wide attention in recent years. Some educators refer to it as an extension of the simultaneous method, while others see it as a system that provides children on the basis of individual needs. Complete treatment of these issues and research findings are presented in later chapters.

Recent Trends

Until quite recently, the oral method has been predominant. Its ascendancy may be traced as far back as the International Congress on Deafness in Milan, Italy, in 1880, during which a resolution was passed stating that the use of manual communication of any kind would restrict or prevent the growth of speech and language skills in deaf children.

Almost without exception, programs for the deaf have followed a completely oral approach, at least through elementary grades. This includes even the "manual" schools, in which simultaneous methods of instruction typically have not been introduced into the classroom for students below age 12. In view of this it might be argued that the history of failure of education of the deaf for the past 100 years is a history of failure of the completely oral method, that it is more appropriate for children with moderate to severe losses than for those with severe to profound losses. A spate of articles (W. Bruce, 1970; Karlin, 1969; Miller, 1970) appearing in the *Volta Review*, an American journal dedicated to the advancement of oral methods, has reacted strongly against such an interpretation.

Although one of the goals of education of the hearing impaired is to produce children proficient in speech and speechreading, the reality must be faced that rigid adherence to learning language by means of speech and speechreading, even with the best of auditory training, is self-defeating for many deaf children. Lowell (1959) and Wright (1917) report that a primary requisite for speechreading is grammatical ability. Deaf people, after years of training in speechreading, cannot speechread as well as hard-of-hearing people (Costello, 1957) because they lack the ability to utilize context and anticipate, integrate, and interpret in consistent grammatical patterns those sounds, words, and phrases which are difficult to distinguish from the lips. Many distinct sounds in English either look like other sounds (e.g., /p/, /b/, /m/), or present very limited clues (e.g., /k/, /g/, /h/). The less residual learning an individual possesses, the more difficult decoding becomes. The task of speechreaders, then, is complex; to understand utterances they must differentiate among sounds that look similar on a speaker's lips and at the same time perform closure — that is, fill in — on parts of the message that are not readily available to the eyes. A. G. Bell, a leading exponent of the development of oral skills in hearing-impaired children, was aware of these difficulties and was quoted (Deland, 1923) as stating:

Spoken language I would have used by the pupil from the commencement of his education to the end of it; but spoken language I would not have as a means of communication with the pupil in the earliest stages of education, because it is not clear to the eye and requires a knowledge of language to unravel the ambiguities. In that case I would have the teacher use written language and I do not think that the manual language (fingerspelling) differs from written language except in this, that it is better and more expeditious. (p. 37)

The auditory method (also known as *acoupedics*) in its unisensory form can be traced to the success of people such as Wedenberg (1954) in Sweden and Whetnall and Fry (1964) in Great Britain with severely hard-of-hearing children. The auditory method in the United States and Canada, patterned after the work in western and northern Europe, has been used mostly with preschool-aged children (Griffiths, 1967a; Ling, 1964; McCroskey, 1968; Stewart, Pollack, & Downs, 1964), and some attempts have been made to extend it to even the most severely hearing-impaired child (Griffiths, 1967a; McCroskey, 1968; Stewart et al., 1964).

Whetnall and Fry were especially effective in promoting the educational separation of deaf and hard-of-hearing children and in providing services for more hard-of-hearing children within the regular public school situation in Great Britain. The benefits for hard-of-hearing children were immediate. Separate treatment of deaf children has served so far only to point up the extent of their failure. In the report *Survey of children born in 1947 who were in schools for the deaf in 1962–1963* (1964) it was reported that only 11.6% of the students could carry on a reasonably clear conversation in speech and speechreading.

The question of methodology was deemed serious enough to appoint a committee to investigate the possible use of signs and fingerspelling in Great Britain. The report (*Education of deaf children*, 1968) concluded that more study was needed. An interesting sidelight to the report was the enthusiastic reaction of educators sent to observe programs in the Soviet Union, which had rejected as unsatisfactory traditional oral methods in favor of neo-oralism, a combination of speech and fingerspelling similar to the Rochester method in the United States. The observers reported:

The children of four, five, and six years old whom we saw in class certainly understood their teacher well, and mostly spoke freely and often with good voice, although they were regarded as being profoundly deaf and were unselected groups. We could not judge the intelligibility of the speech, but our interpreter (who had never previously seen a deaf child) said that she could understand some of them. The children were also very lively and spontaneous, and did not appear to be oppressed by the methods used, which might strike someone accustomed to English methods as unsuitable for young children.

It appeared to us, from what we were shown, that the Russians are more successful than we are in the development of language, vocabulary and speech in deaf children once they enter the educational system. This seemed to us a strong point in favor of their method (use of fingerspelling from the very start as an instrument for the development of language, communication and speech), the investigation of which was the main object of our visit. (pp. 44-45)

This enthusiasm matched that of Morkovin's (1960a) observations after visiting the Soviet Union. The Russians claim by starting fingerspelling in the home and nursery at age 2 the child is able to develop a vocabulary of several thousand words by 6 years of age. They also report that, rather than inhibiting oral development, the use of fingerspelling enhances speech and speechreading skills (Moores, 1972a). The claims have created a renewed interest in the Rochester method, which first was used in the United States in 1878 at the Rochester, New York, School for the Deaf (Scouten, 1942). Anecdotal substantiation is provided by the case of Howard Hofsteator (1959), a deaf individual whose parents provided an early language environment through fingerspelling all conversations. They would read to him from books by placing their hands close to the printed page, spelling the stories, enabling him to read at a very early age. Several preschool programs using the Rochester method have been developed in the United States.

A reservation concerning the use of the method with young children should be noted. Possibly the presentation of connected English by means of rapidly changing hand configurations places too great a burden on the perceptual and cognitive abilities of children. Their ability to form letters manually also may be limited. No such difficulty was encountered by Hofsteator, but perhaps he was an exceptional case. It might be more beneficial to develop basic grammars by means of selected signs, later placing an emphasis on spelling congruent with the introduction of the printed word after age 3.

The possible use of total communication (or the simultaneous method) with very young children is also gaining support throughout the country, a support that may be traced to a number of factors, including: (1) the evidence that deaf children with deaf parents achieve more academically than do those with hearing parents; (2) the growing tendency to accept the language of signs as a legitimate mode of communication; (3) dissatisfaction with results of traditional methods with the profoundly deaf; (4) the increasing militancy of deaf adults who are only beginning to make an impact on the field, the majority of whom, despite their own rigid oral training, strongly support the use of the simultaneous method. *The Deaf American*, a journal produced by deaf professionals, has been particularly active on this question. It is significant that the first public school program to use the simultaneous method with young deaf children — in Santa Ana, California in 1968 — at the time was also the only program for the hearing impaired in the United States to be directed by a hearing-impaired person.

Deaf Individuals and Minority Group Membership

As might be expected, educational services to deaf individuals from "minority" groups — or, more appropriately, politically and economically disadvantaged groups — have been inferior to those provided to most deaf individuals. Although most data are restricted to the black population, the evidence suggests that deaf Spanish-surnamed and Native American individuals also suffer from the double handicap of minority group discrimination and deafness (Alcocer, 1974; McCahill, 1971).

Deaf Black Individuals

The enormous difficulties of a deaf individual with minority group membership may be illustrated by the lack of even adequate representation in the census dating back to 1830. In each census from 1830 to 1930 blacks were represented as being a much smaller percentage of the deaf population than would be expected on the basis of general population distributions. Before the Civil War blacks composed 20% or more of the population of the United States but only about 10% of the counted deaf population (Best, 1943).

In 1852 H. Peet reported approximate incidence rates of 1 deaf person per 2,000 population among white Americans; 1 per 3,000 among free black Americans; and an incredible 1 per 6,500 among black slaves. Peet acknowledged there was "probably greater inaccuracy" (p. 20) in the figures for the black population than for the white. By the time of the 1930 census, the last census that gathered data on hearing impairment, the incidence rate for whites was given as approximately 1 per 1,400 and for blacks as 1 per 2,100. Expressed another way, according to census figures blacks accounted for approximately 10% of the general American population in 1930 but only 7.4% of the deaf population (Best, 1943, p. 42).

Studies since World War II also have consistently reported a lower incidence of deafness among blacks than among whites (Furfey & Harte, 1964, 1968; Lunde & Bigman, 1959; Schein & Delk, 1974). Like Best and Peet, all these studies acknowledge that the identification procedures may miss a somewhat larger proportion of the deaf black population than of the deaf white population. However, all have concluded that, even allowing for underenumeration, the differences in incidence figures were so great that there were real differences in the incidence of deafness between the black and white populations of the United States, which to some extent could result from genetic differences.

Such a conclusion has become almost an unquestioned assumption among many educators of the deaf, an assumption that probably has been detrimental to deaf black individuals. Grievous underestimation of the size of a population inevitably leads to underestimation of the needs of such a population. Bowe (1971a) and Anderson and Bowe (1972) have pointed out that deaf black people frequently are isolated from deaf white people and seldom join clubs for the deaf, which usually are in different parts of town and which have discouraged black membership, except for the case of athletes. In many cases deaf blacks either are not aware of educational and vocational services available or do not have the necessary transportation to take advantage of them. Because recent census attempts have worked closely through deaf groups, the numbers of deaf black adults identified inevitably are low and nonrepresentative. Lunde and Bigman (1959), for example, identified only 344 deaf black adults out of a sample of 10,100 persons.

Wide fluctuations in previous census figures also should provide a cautionary note. For example, according to census figures blacks made up 4.2% of the deaf population in 1920 and 7.4% in 1930 (Best, 1943, p. 134), although they accounted for roughly 10% of the general population in both cases. The differences simply are not credible. One can conclude only that the census procedures have been of little or no benefit in providing even rough estimates of the extent of deafness in the black population.

The results of previous studies, which have concentrated on adults, are contradicted by school enrollment data. Gentile and McCarthy (1973) investigated the ethnic origin of 33,711 students enrolled in programs for the hearing impaired in 1971–1972. They reported that 4,057, or 12% of the total, were identified as black. If the 3,919 children for whom data were not available are excluded, then 13.8% of 29,268 deaf students were black. These figures seem consistent with general population figures and are much more reasonable than past estimates.

In addition to underenumeration, deaf black people have experienced much the same kind of discrimination faced by hearing blacks. In 1949 there were separate schools for deaf black students in thirteen states; as late as 1963 eight states maintained separate facilities (Babbidge, 1965). The physical plants and training levels of the teachers in these schools were markedly inferior. Gallaudet College practiced racial discrimination and did not accept black students until 1945 (Bowe, 1971a). Deaf black people tend to have less adequate education and to be depressed economically (Best, 1943; Furfey & Harte, 1964, 1968; Lunde & Bigman, 1959; Schein & Delk, 1974), even among samples that are not representative. Finally, just as in educational programs for children with normal hearing, deaf black people tend to be classified as retarded in disproportionate numbers. Gentile and McCarthy (1973, p. 28) reported that blacks make up 12% of the deaf student population but 22% of the deaf population that is classified as mentally retarded.

Deaf Spanish-Surnamed Individuals

It first should be noted that the term *Spanish-surnamed* is only one of several labels that might be used, none of which is completely accurate. Basically, the three largest groups in the population under consideration have originated in Puerto Rico, Cuba, and Mexico, including those parts of the southwestern United States conquered in the Mexican-American War. Each of the groups varies according to ethnic composition and to some extent culture. What they do share is a common language, Spanish, and the Spanish colonial heritage.

The situation of deaf Spanish-surnamed individuals, or of the Puerto Rican, Cuban, and Chicano* components, is less well known than that of other groups. Most investigations of deaf "minority" group people are restricted to the black population or incorrectly assume that the deaf Spanish-surnamed population is negligible. It is unclear the extent to which Spanish-surnamed individuals have been included in *nonwhite* and *white* categories. Some investigators have tended to use the terms *nonwhite* and *black* interchangeably. For example, Schein and Dalk refer to "non-white" census figures (1974, p. 30), which really refers to the *black* category (Best, 1943, p. 134).

Best (1943, p. 134) shows that the 1930 census carried the category *Mexican* and that people in this category made up 1.2% of the general population and only 0.7% of the deaf population. The estimate of the Mexican population at that time was completely inadequate. In addition to language barriers many of the people in this category were understandably reserved about divulging information to any census taker. McWilliams (1968), for example, reports that the Mexican population in the United States was estimated at 1.5 million in 1930. At that time the United States undertook the most massive deportation effort in its history in an attempt to return Mexican workers to Mexico and free up jobs for Anglo workers. In a four-year period an estimated 3.8 million people were deported (Alford, 1972; McWilliams, 1968). Among this group were American citizens by birth. Although the majority of deportations were made from border states, some were made from as far away as Minnesota (McWilliams, 1968). Even if some of the cases returned from Mexico to be deported again, it is obvious that original population estimates were low. The situation is similar today for many Spanish-surnamed individuals of Mexican citizenry (obviously not for the Puerto Rican and Cuban groups) who may not be legal residents of the United States. Thus population counts must be low. Census data from 1970 provide an estimate of approximately 10 million Spanish-surnamed individuals, of whom about 6 million would be Mexican-American. Unofficial estimates ran as high as 12 million, with one prediction that the population would reach 20 million in a short time (McWilliams, 1968).

Obviously, then, such a population base would provide more than a small number of deaf children to the school population. As such it is surprising that the deaf Spanish-surnamed population has received little attention. The major effort has been in the development of training procedures for teachers of deaf children from bilingual homes (Grant, 1973). Schein and Delk, in *The deaf population of the United States* (1974), do not even address the issue.

Gentile and McCarthy (1973) reported that 2,060 of 33,711 deaf students,

---

* The term *Chicano* is used to connote the Mexican-Indian and Spanish influence on individuals living in the United States, individuals distinct from the Mexican and the Anglo. For a treatment of the term see Renden (1971).

6.1% of the total, in programs for the hearing impaired in 1971–1972 were classified as *Spanish-American*.   If we subtract the 3,919 students for whom ethnic origin information was not available, Spanish-American students made up 7% of the total sample of 29,268 for whom information was available. Those figures seem consistent with general population estimates, but given limited educational opportunities available to Spanish-surnamed individuals with normal hearing, it may be assumed that deaf children in this category are not receiving adequate services.

Other Minority Groups

If information about deaf black individuals is limited, and information about deaf Spanish-surnamed individuals is negligible, then information on other groups is nonexistent.   Again, one may assume that such individuals face additional obstacles, but research is necessary to establish the nature and extent of the obstacles.

Teachers of the Deaf

Given a total enrollment of 53,009 deaf students in classes in 1974 (Craig & Craig, 1975, p. 175), it may come as somewhat of a surprise to those accustomed to pupil-teacher ratios of 25:1 or greater in regular classes to find a total educational staff of 15,745, of whom 9,004 were instructors and 2,294 were teacher's aides (Craig & Craig, 1975, p. 175).   Although variations exist as a function of the type of education program offered (e.g., self-contained, resource room, itinerant model), a pupil-teacher ratio of roughly 6:1 appears to be the norm.

Given the specialized nature of educating deaf children, class size tends to be much smaller, and a class of four children is not unusual, especially at younger ages.   Several states have limits on class size, and it is rare — even with secondary-aged students — to encounter classes in excess of 12 to 14 students.

Traditionally, the major sources of teachers were residential schools for the deaf, which developed their own teacher training programs.   Through the impetus of support provided by the U.S. Office of Education's Bureau of Education for the Handicapped, beginning in the 1960s a growing number of colleges and universities have offered programs for training teachers of the deaf.   In 1974, 71 colleges and universities in 32 states and the District of Columbia offered programs at the undergraduate and graduate levels to train teachers of the deaf (Craig & Craig, 1975, pp. 195–203).   A total of 1,196 individuals completed training programs in 1974.   The five largest programs, in terms of numbers of trainees finishing, are listed in Table 1.2.   The University of Tennessee had 70 trainees complete a program in 1974 and is the only one of the

Table 1.2   Five largest programs for training teachers of the deaf in the United States, 1974

Program	Location	Number of trainees finishing in 1974
University of Tennessee	Knoxville, Tennessee	70
Kent State University	Kent, Ohio	52
Eastern Michigan University	Ypsilanti, Michigan	38
Illinois State University	Normal, Illinois	37
Ball State University	Muncie, Indiana	37

SOURCE: Adapted from W. Craig and H. Craig (Eds.), "Directory of Services for the Deaf," *American Annals of the Deaf,* 1975, 120, 195–203.

Table 1.3   States with largest numbers of trainees finishing programs for training teachers of the deaf, 1974

State	Number of training programs	Number of trainees finishing in 1974
Texas	8	134
New York	5	113
California	7	86
Illinois	4	86
Ohio	3	83
Total	27	502

SOURCE: Adapted from W. Craig and H. Craig (Eds.), "Directory of Services for the Deaf," *American Annals of the Deaf,* 1975, 120, 195–203.

five largest programs outside of the Midwest. It should be noted that the programs are located within universities with a strong teacher training tradition and with relatively less emphasis on educational research.

Table 1.3 indicates that approximately 40% of trainees finishing in 1974 (502 of 1,196) are from programs in five states, with Texas accounting for 134 trainees. All five states are among the most populous in the United States. Although California and New York, the two most populous states, might be expected to train more individuals, the figures in general appear consistent with population figures.

Deaf Teachers

The impact of deaf individuals upon the field of education of the deaf has been quite variable. At the beginning, deaf individuals were quite prominent. The first teacher at the first school for the deaf in America was Laurent Clerc, a deaf man. Schools were founded by deaf individuals in several states, including Arkansas, Florida, Indiana, Kansas, New Mexico, and Oregon (J. Jones, 1918, p. 7). There was a gradual increase in the percentage of deaf teachers over a period of years until shortly after the Civil War and a decrease after that. Jones (1918) reported that 36% of the teaching staff was deaf in 1851 and 42.5% in 1870. By 1895 the figure was 22% and had dropped to 14.5% by 1917. In commenting on the situation Jones stated, "This is no reflection on the deaf as teachers but is the result of the rapid growth of speech teaching which calls for hearing people" (p. 12).

Another reason for the trend against the employment of deaf teachers was the opposition of the influential Alexander Graham Bell (1883a, 1884), who went so far as to present Senate testimony against establishment of a teacher training program for students with normal hearing at Gallaudet College on the grounds that the college would also accept deaf students into the program (M. Boatner, 1959b; R. Bruce, 1973).

The situation for deaf teachers remained relatively constant for the years between World War I and World War II. Day, Fusfeld, and Pintner (1928) reported that deaf individuals made up 16% of the academic teaching staffs in residential schools (p. 31) and that they were not represented on the staffs of day schools in America, in which at that time only 1 of 13 programs allowed any type of manual communication.

In 1961 there were 503 deaf teachers of the deaf in the United States (Doctor, 1962, p. 158) or 11.7% of the total of 4,309 teachers. Deaf teachers were restricted almost completely to public residential schools, which employed 488 of the 503 deaf teachers. Of the remaining 15 deaf teachers, 8 were teaching in public day classes, 6 in private residential schools, and 1 in a public day school. Table 1.4 provides comparable information on the distribution of deaf teachers in 1974.

Examination of Table 1.4 reveals a number of interesting facts. First, there was a significant increase in the number of deaf teachers from 1961 (503) to 1973 (1,077). More significant, however, is the evidence that deaf teachers were no longer confined to residential schools. The most dramatic increases in the numbers of deaf teachers from 1961 to 1973 occurred in the public day schools (from 1 to 100) and the public day classes (8 to 219), to the extent that by 1974 30% of the deaf teachers of the deaf (319 of 1,077) were teaching in public school day programs as compared with less than 2% (9 of 503) in 1961.

A number of factors are influencing the growing trend to hire deaf teachers in day programs. The two major ones appear to be the movement in day programs toward combined oral-manual instruction and the growing consensus

Table 1.4 Distribution of deaf teachers of the deaf, October 1974

Type of educational facility	Number of deaf teachers
Public residential school	694
Private residential school	18
Public day school	100
Private day school	8
Public day class	219
Private day class	8
Multihandicapped facility	20
Specific handicapped facility	10
Total	1,077

SOURCE: Adapted from W. Craig and H. Craig (Eds.), "Directory of Services for the Deaf," *American Annals of the Deaf*, 1975, *120*, 175.

that the presence of deaf teachers does not detract from the development of oral skills in deaf children.

However, in some ways, the relative position of deaf teachers deteriorated during the above period. The percentage of teachers of the deaf who were deaf themselves increased only from 11.7% in 1961 (503 of 4,309) to 12% in 1974 (1,077 of 9,004). The increase in the number of deaf teachers barely kept pace with the increase in the total instructional staff, which more than doubled. As previously mentioned, the number of children in programs increased from 28,529 in 1961 to 53,009 in 1974.

Interpretation of the data is difficult, but the author believes that a number of forces have been operating which have served to keep the impact of deaf teachers at a minimum. First would be systematic discrimination against the deaf by teacher training programs. Before 1970 the majority of programs had never accepted deaf students, and, even in the face of procedures obviously designed to eliminate deaf applicants, the Bureau of Education of the Handicapped did not move to withdraw support from such programs. Most deaf teachers, then, were graduates of Gallaudet College with undergraduate degrees, not necessarily in education. Gallaudet itself was slow to accept deaf students into its graduate program. Also, before 1970, those programs accepting deaf students tended to "track" them toward teaching at junior and senior high school levels on the grounds that most educational programs for the deaf placed an almost exclusive emphasis on speech in preschool and elementary grades and would not hire deaf teachers to work with young children.

In the decade of the 1960s the greatest increase in the demand for teachers was in public school programs to work with preschool children. As the public schools searched for personnel, preferably with advanced degrees, the supply of deaf individuals able to meet state certification requirements (which also frequently were discriminatory) did not meet the demand. The situation is improving as more and more training programs have moved to accept deaf applicants and as deaf individuals are attending graduate programs in increasing numbers, but the time is not yet in sight when the influence of deaf individuals on the education of the deaf will be what by right it should be.

Summary

The education of deaf children in the United States has been an area of controversy since the opening of the first school in 1817, with the controversies militating against the development of effective intervention strategies of benefit to the deaf. The greatest problems faced by deaf individuals are related to problems of communication with the dominant society and to the insensitivity of most hearing individuals to the problems of deafness and the resultant lack of empathy for deaf individuals.

Difficulties in definition and categorization of hearing loss complicate the issues because there is no necessary one-to-one relationship between a disability expressed in quantitative terms (for example, a certain decibel-level hearing loss across the speech range) and the way in which an individual functions qualitatively. Other factors such as etiology, age of onset of the loss, age of initiation of training, and neurological integrity also will influence the extent to which the disability of deafness handicaps an individual in day-to-day functioning.

Several types of educational programs for the deaf exist in the United States, with the majority of children being educated in public school day classes and state-supported residential schools. Recent trends have expanded provisions for preschool children, for multihandicapped children, for children from minority groups, and for children with less severe hearing losses functioning in integrated settings.

Beginning in 1968 postsecondary opportunities for the deaf have expanded considerably, especially in the vocational-technical area. Deaf teachers have been accepted into public school programs in increasing numbers.

2
Historical Perspectives: Europe to the Nineteenth Century

Prehistoric Times

Although deafness probably always has been part of the human condition, the incidence of deafness and conditions under which deaf individuals lived in prehistoric, and even classical, times can only be a matter of conjecture. It may be assumed that the status and roles of the deaf varied as a function of the types of society in which they found themselves — such as hunter, hunter–gatherer, agrarian, and so on — and the demands imposed upon them by society.

In terms of incidence rates, it is quite possible that deafness was relatively more common than at present. For example, in recent times antibiotics have greatly reduced deafness that results from meningitis, scarlet fever, and bilateral suppurative otitis media. It is logical to assume that these and other diseases took their toll of past civilizations to at least the same extent as they did in industrialized societies until the recent past. It is also doubtful that, in the areas where it was practiced, infanticide could have had much effect in the incidence of deafness on a population. First, even today, under favorable conditions a diagnosis of deafness frequently is not made until after infancy. Second, it is probable that large proportions of the deaf populations of the societies under consideration were of the acquired or adventitious variety.

Even though individual tribes and cultures might have imposed limitations and even acted punitively toward the deaf, it is difficult to imagine any culture so dependent on hearing that deaf individuals could not participate and contribute. It might be argued that the deaf have faced the greatest disadvantage relative to normally hearing persons in those societies which have been influenced most heavily by the Judeo-Hellenic tradition, that is, European and American societies. This of course could be explained by the greater emphasis placed on the spoken word and its preeminent role in religious as well as intellectual functions. Although all cultures apparently have attached magical and mystical qualities to at least some spoken words, nowhere has it been more strongly illustrated than in Genesis I: "In the beginning was the Word." Thus there were biblical sanctions against the marriage of "deaf-mutes," and during medieval times the deaf were not allowed to receive communion because they were unable to confess their sins.   It is not known whether the deaf in other great societies — such as those in ancient Egypt, Central and South America, Indonesia, China, Japan, Africa, India, and Southeast Asia — labored under similar restrictions.   For example, Degerando (1827) suggested that in societies such as ancient Egypt and China, where writing was based on meanings and did not rely on an alphabet, the deaf may have been instructed to read.   Peet (1851) strongly disagreed with this supposition.   Unfortunately, the only historical information presently available is restricted to a basically European framework.   There is always a possibility that with the decreasing Eurocentricism of the world pertinent information may be uncovered from unanticipated sources.

Classical Greece and Rome

In spite of the orientation toward the primacy of the spoken word, conditions probably were not as harsh as they have been painted by many educators of the deaf writing on the subject.   Aristotle has been portrayed as a villain because in 355 B.C. he wrote, "Men that are deaf are also speechless; that is they can make vocal sounds but they cannot speak."

Greek philosophers generally believed that thought could be conceived only through the medium of articulate words.   Because Aristotle had styled the ear the organ of instruction and believed that hearing contributed the most to intelligence, he has been accused by many of keeping the deaf in ignorance for 2,000 years (Deland, 1931).   This, coupled with the belief that his statement "Let it be a law that nothing imperfect should be brought up" led to the destruction of deaf children by the Spartans, Athenians, and Romans served to make the name of Aristotle anathema among some educators of the deaf.

Aristotle's bad standing is in large part undeserved.   His statement was taken out of context and was distorted and misinterpreted.   His quote is merely a statement of fact that holds true today; that is, a child who is born deaf will not learn to speak, without special training.   In Aristotle's time, there was no speech training.   Therefore the conditions of deafness and muteness were considered to be interrelated.   In 1851 H. Peet reported that in some biblical passages the same word (kophoi) is used to connote both deaf and dumb (or mute). This is not clear in English translations.   For example, Matthew IX, 13 reads "The dumb spoke" and Matthew XI, 5 reads "The deaf hear."   In both cases, the same term, kophoi, is used.   The term also had negative implications and denoted dull of mind.   Peet noted that Aristotle used separate terms to distinguish between deaf and mute (or speechless).   In the context of his writing the negative connotations attributed to his statement are not justifiable.

Also it is doubtful that Aristotle's dictum on imperfection, no matter how abhorrent to present-day readers, actually led to the destruction of many deaf babies. As previously noted, diagnosis of deafness at birth, when Greek babies were inspected, is difficult even today, and physically normal deaf babies manifest no differences from physically normal hearing babies.

The fact that deaf individuals existed and were accepted by Greek society is attested to by the following exchange between Socrates and Hermogenes in Plato's *Cratylus* (Levinson, 1967):

SOCRATES: And here I will ask you a question: Suppose that we had no voice or tongue, and wanted to indicate objects to one another, should we not, like the deaf and dumb, make signs with the hands, head and the rest of the body?

HERMOGENES: How could it be otherwise, Socrates?

SOCRATES: We should imitate the nature of the thing; the elevation of our hands to heaven would mean lightness and upwardness; heaviness and downwardness would be expressed by letting them drop to the ground; . . . (p. 359)

Another ancient writer whose references to deafness have been misinterpreted was St. Augustine, who in the course of a discussion on original man, remarked (Fay, 1912): "For what fault is so great innocence sometimes born blind and sometimes deaf? A defect moreover which is a hindrance to faith itself, according to the Apostle who says, 'So then faith cometh by hearing' " (p. 213). From this Augustine was interpreted as depriving the deaf of immortality (Arnold, 1879; Farrar, 1923), an interpretation that was refuted by Fay (1912) by reference to several other statements of Augustine, among which the most famous is as follows:

If a man and woman of this kind (deaf) were united in marriage and for any reason they were transferred to some solitary place where, however, they might be able to live, if they should have a son, who was not deaf, how would the latter speak with his parents? How can you think he would do otherwise than reply by gestures to the signs which his parents make to him? However a small boy could not do even this; therefore my reasoning remains sound, for what does it matter, as he grows up whether he speaks or makes gestures, since both these pertain to the soul. (p. 213)

The Justinian Code (530 A.D.)

The Romans appear to have devoted a great deal of time and thought to the legal status of deaf individuals, at least toward the end of the Roman Empire. The Justinian Code (530 A.D.), which has been criticized for depriving the deaf of their rights, actually reflects a great amount of care in classification of individuals and was far more humane than restrictions placed on them during the Middle Ages. In attempting to be comprehensive and fair, the developers of the Justinian Code identified five classifications or combinations of deafness and muteness, as presented below (H. Peet, 1851):

Maintaining the distinction between the deaf and the dumb since the two defects are not always combined, we ordain

1. That if one is afflicted with both diseases at once, that is to say, if from natural causes he can neither hear nor speak, he shall neither make a will nor any form of bequest, nor shall he be allowed to grant freedom by manumission nor in any other way. And this decree is to be binding on both males and females.
2. But where in either male or female, the same condition has been brought about by calamity, not from birth, voice or hearing having both been lost by subsequent disease, then in a case such as one have received an education, we permit him to do his own act all that in the previous case we prohibited.
3. But if this further misfortune, which so rarely occurs, is to be considered, we should allow a man who was only deaf, supposing the affliction to be from natural causes, to do everything in the nature of making a testimentary bequest, or granting freedom, for where nature has bestowed an articulate voice there is nothing to hinder him from doing as he wishes; for we know that certain jurisconsuls have made a careful study of this, and have declared that there is no one who is altogether unable to hear if he is spoken to above the back of the head; which was the opinion of Juventius Celsus.
4. But those who have lost their hearing by disease can do everything without hindrance.
5. Supposing, however; the ears are perfect, but though there is a voice the tongue is tied (although on this subject there is considerable differences of opinion among the old authors) yet supposing such a one to be well educated, there is nothing to prevent his doing anything of this nature, whether the misfortune be congenital, or the result of disease, without distinction between males and females. (p. 136)

A reading of the code reveals a number of interesting facts. First, aspects of deafness and muteness had been discussed by several Roman authors with a wide divergence of opinion and an apparently great interest. These writings are lost to us. Problems of deafness were studied closely enough to realize that complete deafness is a rarity, a fact that many twentieth-century educators of the deaf seem to find surprising. The method of speaking to individuals "above the back of the head" may refer to the first crude attempts at auditory training or the "aural method." There is sensitivity to differential impacts of adventitious deafness and partial deafness. The Romans gave full rights to those who were (1) deaf and mute, but literate; (2) deaf but articulate; (3) mute but hearing; (4) adventitiously deaf. Rights, therefore were denied those who were deaf and mute from birth who were also illiterate. Unfortunately this apparently included just about all individuals who were born deaf. Only one deaf person is mentioned by name in all the surviving Roman literature. This would be Quintus Pedius, grandson of the Consul Quintus Pedius, who with Caesar Augustus was coheir to the will of Julius Caesar (H. Peet, 1851). With the approval of Augustus, Quintus Pedius was instructed in painting and was mentioned by Pliny as among the most eminent painters of Rome.

Even with the evidence of the case of Pedius, and possibly a relatively few other individuals of noble background, it never occurred to ancient Greeks and

Romans that a person born deaf could be educated. Implicit in section 1 of the code is the belief that one born deaf would never become literate. That words could be presented without the mediation of speech directly through writing, manual spelling, and signs apparently was inconceivable to the Romans, who, ironically, had developed pantomime to its highest degree.

The Middle Ages

If the deaf may be said to have suffered from an attitude of benign neglect during classical periods, their condition following the onslaught of Rome by Germanic barbarians was even worse. The early code of nearly every nation in Europe imposed civil and religious disabilities on the deaf that were much more severe than the Justinian Code, including deprivation of rights of inheritance, restriction from celebration of the mass, and denial of the right to marry without the express dispensation of the pope (Deland, 1931; H. Peet, 1851). Except for references to miraculous cures of deafness or muteness, the deaf were either ignored or discriminated against. The most famous cure was effected by John, Bishop of Hagulstad (later known as St. John of Beverly), who worked several miracles among the Anglo-Saxons, including the teaching of speech to a deaf-mute young man. St. John first had the young man say the Anglo-Saxon *gea* (*yea*) and then taught him to repeat letters, syllables, words, and finally sentences until his speech was normal (H. Peet, 1851).

No record of an educated congenitally deaf person has been found from the time of Quintus Pedius until the fifteenth century, when Rudolphus Agricola reported the case of a deaf mute who had learned to write (Bender, 1970; H. Peet, 1851). No details were given concerning names, place, or mode of instruction, and the report was dismissed on the grounds that it was impossible to instruct one who lacked the organ of instruction, that is, the ear.

The end of the dark ages for the deaf may be marked by the writings of a sixteenth-century Italian mathematician and physician, Jerome Cardin (1501–1576), who accepted Agricola's report. He argued for the importance of teaching the deaf to read and write and believed that many abstract ideas could be explained to them by signs. He apparently was the first to realize that written words could represent ideas directly without recourse to speech, presenting his position as follows (H. Peet, 1851):

The deaf mute can conceive that the word, *bread*, for example, as it stands written, represents the object which we point out to him. Just as after having seen any object, we preserve its form in the memory and can draw a resemblance of it, so the deaf mute can preserve in his mind the forms of the written characters, and can associate them directly with ideas; for spoken words represent ideas only by convention, and written words can be made to represent ideas by convention. (p. 138)

Cardin, himself, did not treat the subject in any but a theoretical way and never put his ideas to a practical test. For the beginnings of education of the deaf, as for so many other breakthroughs during the Renaissance and at the start of the modern era, we must look to Spain for leadership.

The Beginnings of Education of the Deaf

Although there are several exceptions and considerable overlap, periods may be discerned in which the major contributions to education of the deaf may be seen as having been made primarily by one nation. National leadership in education of the deaf, interestingly enough, seems to have been related to political, economic, cultural, and military factors. Thus, the first thrust in education of the deaf may be observed in Spain during the fifteenth and sixteenth centuries, followed by a flurry of activity, partly influenced by Spanish work, in seventeenth-century Great Britain. This was followed by the introduction and spread of the "French method" (to be described subsequently) in the eighteenth century, which then was challenged by the "German method." The two remained antagonists throughout most of the nineteenth century (with the somewhat more insular British on the periphery) until the "final, complete" victory of the German method in 1880, which was coincidental with rising German political influence and the smashing German military victory in the Franco-Prussian War.

In the twentieth century, of course, the "final" victory of the German method has been shown to be not so final. One might speculate that for the remainder of the twentieth century education of the deaf in Europe might involve a struggle between protaganists of the American system of total communication and Russian neo-oralism, with the outcome being dependent as much on political as on educational considerations.

Spain

The honor of being the first teacher of the deaf is accorded to Pablo Ponce de Leon (1520–1584), a Benedictine monk who established a school at a monastery in Valladolid and tutored deaf children of Spanish nobility. It should be noted that deafness was common in the Spanish aristocracy, including even the royal family. Apparently de Leon's first student was don Francisco Velasco, the legitimate heir to the Marquisate of Berlanga and eldest son of the House of Tudor, who had been excluded from the right of primogeniture because of his deafness. Through the efforts of Ponce de Leon, don Francisco learned to speak and write, and he thus attained his lawful inheritance.

Ponce de Leon's success was acclaimed widely, including in a legal document dated August 24, 1578, in which he himself described his success (H. Peet, 1851) as follows:

I have had for my pupils, who were deaf and dumb from birth, sons of great lords and of notable people who I have taught to speak, read, write, to pray, to assist a Mass, to know the doctrines of Christianity, and to know how to confess themselves by speech. I have taught them all this. Some attained to a knowledge of Latin; others, taught Latin and Greek, acquired the knowledge of Italian. One who entered the priesthood and undertook a charge and a benefice of the Church, was also able to recite the canonical hours; and several others attained to know and to understand natural philosophy and astrology. Another, heir to an estate and a marquisate, and led afterward to embrace the military profession, learned, in addition to the knowledge above referred to, every kind of exercise and became a noted horseman. Much more, my pupils studied history, and were able to trace the annals of their own country, and also those of other lands. Better still, they proved by the use they made of them that they were possessed of the gifts which Aristotle had denied to them. (p. 141)

Ponce de Leon may be forgiven a somewhat unseeming immodesty if he indeed obtained even some of the results claimed above. If his pupils actually were profoundly deaf from birth, the results are incredible, given the circumstances and the apparent fact that methods were developed without recourse to other sources. Even allowing a certain justifiable exaggeration concerning two accomplishments previously considered impossible — teaching the deaf to read and teaching the deaf to speak — Ponce de Leon's purported work should remain a standard that present-day educators should regard with envy and that they should strive to attain.

Unfortunately, very little is known of the techniques employed by Ponce de Leon. Although he produced a written account of his work, it was either lost or destroyed, and no record of it survives its author. Other writers, including one pupil, suggest that he began with reading and writing and then moved on to speech and that he used a manual alphabet in instruction. It is unclear whether he used signs. There is a tendency for those who favor the use of signs to believe that he did (Arnold, 1879; Hodgson, 1954) and for those who oppose signs to believe that he did not (Bender, 1970).

Covarrubias, a physician to King Philip IV, reported that Ponce de Leon reversed the usual order of instruction by teaching the deaf first to write, pointing out by the finger the thing to which the written characters corresponded and then procuring them. Covarrubias is quoted by Deland (1931) as stating, "And thus as we begin by speech with those who hear, so do we as well by writing with those whose ears are closed." Covarrubias's statement preceded by four centuries the position of the American linguist Lenneberg, who argued (1967) for the use of "graphics" from the beginning in the education of the deaf.

The most complete description of Ponce de Leon's methods comes from an account written in Latin by a former student, don Pedro Velasco, younger brother of don Francisco Velasco. (The historian Monalez reported that Ponce de Leon also taught a sister of don Pedro and don Francisco.) Don Francisco's account appears below (H. Peet, 1851):

While I was a boy and ignorant, ut lapis (as a stone) I began to work by copying what my teacher had written; and I wrote all the words of the Castilian tongue in a book prepared to that purpose. Hereupon I began, adjurante Deo, to spell, and to utter some syllables and words with all my might, so that the saliva flowed from my mouth abundantly. Then I began to read history, and in ten years read the history of the whole world. Afterwards I learned Latin. All this was through the great grace of God, without which no mute can exist. (p. 149)

After the death of Ponce de Leon, there was a hiatus of more than thirty years in reported efforts to educate the deaf. This may be explained by the loss of Ponce de Leon's descriptions of his techniques and by his failure to train any successors to carry on his work. The next effort in education of the deaf again involved the Velasco family, two generations removed from Ponce de Leon's students, and two intriguing personalities, of whom very little is actually known, Juan Pablo Bonet and Manuel Rameriz de Carrion. Although they probably worked together for four years, neither referred to the other in print (nor to Ponce de Leon), and each claimed to be the originator of a new method of teaching the deaf.

The story may be pieced together as follows. In 1607 Juan Bonet, a soldier of fortune, entered into the service of Juan Fernandez de Velasco, the Constable of Castile, whose father, the previous Constable, was the brother of the three previously mentioned students of Ponce de Leon. Upon the death of Juan Velasco in 1613, his widow Duchess dona Juana de Cordoba retained Bonet as secretary to the new Constable, don Bernadino Fernandez de Velasco, then a child of 4. The duchess had two other young children, one of whom, 3-year-old Luis, had lost his hearing around age 2. Bonet took it upon himself to secure help for Luis. In 1615, he came upon Ramirez de Carrion, who was engaged as a tutor and private secretary to the deaf Marquiz de Priego, who agreed to release de Carrion temporarily to work with Luis. Thus de Carrion worked with Luis from 1615 to 1619, when he returned to the service of the Marquiz de Priego. In 1620 Bonet published the first book ever written on teaching the deaf, *The reduction of letters and the art of teaching the mute to speak.* * In the book Bonet takes complete credit for developing the system, which he described, making no mention of the previous work of Ponce de Leon or Ramirez de Carrion, stating (H. Peet, 1851) "I began to make a special study of the case, contemplating, examining and turning the matter every way to seek means of supplying the deficiencies of one sense through the remaining senses" (p. 150).

Ponce de Leon, of course, had taught three members of a preceding Velasco generation, and his work must have been known to Bonet, although it is unclear whether he was aware of any of de Leon's specific techniques. In addition, Abbot Antonio Perez, in an introduction to Bonet's book, mentions the pioneering work of Ponce de Leon (Deland, 1931; H. Peet, 1851) and criticizes

* *Reducion de las letres, y arte para ensenar a hablar los mudos.*

him for never teaching his skills to another. In the case of Ramirez de Carrion, Bonet must have either collaborated with him or overseen his work from 1615 to 1620. Because of his refusal to acknowledge the work of others, Bonet has been accused of plagiarism (Carton, 1883) or at least of a lack of generosity (Best, 1943).

An intriguing sidelight is the possible role that at least one member of the Velasco family might have played in the Spanish settlement of the present American southwest. In 1598, 22 years before the Mayflower landed in Massachusetts, don Juan de Onate established the first Spanish capital in the southwest, San Francisco de los Españoles, near the present site of Española, New Mexico (Alford, 1972, p. 40). The most notable personality in the Onate expedition was Captain Luis de Velasco, who was obviously a personage of substantial means, who was not inclined to submit to the rigor of frontier life. Alford described his belongings as follows:

Captain Luis de Velasco included among his baggage suits of blue Italian velvet, rose satin, purple Castilian cloth, chestnut colored cloth, and Chinese flowered silk. He had doublets of Castilian dressed kid and royal lion skin, gold-trimmed. He had green silk stockings with points of gold lace, linen shirts, linen breeches, forty pairs of boots, shoes, and gaiters, hats trimmed with silver cord and colored feathers; he had four saddles of blue flowered Spanish cloth bound with Cordovan leather, three suits of personal armor and three suits of armor for his horse, plus swords, daggers and a silken banner; he also carried a bedstead with two mattresses and in his retinue had servants and thirty horses and mules. (p. 39)

History does not record the reaction of the inhabitants of the Tewa village of Yugeuingge, where the capital was established, at the first sight of Captain Velasco resplendent in his sartorial glory. However, his name and obvious wealth suggest he may have been a member of the noble Velsco family of Spain, and perhaps was even the namesake of the deaf child Luis de Velasco, born in 1610, who was taught by Bonet.

Educators of the deaf who have examined Bonet's manuscript express admiration for his insight and understanding of the problems of educating the deaf (Huervas y Panduro, 1795; Tomas, 1920). Deland (1931) states, "The book shows too intimate a knowledge of the subject not to have been the outcome of actual experience, so unless Bonet worked along with Carrion, he must have preceded him in the education of the talented Luis." Peet (1851) wrote:

Considering the period at which he wrote, his views are for the most part, remarkably correct, and the course of instruction which he marks out, though little adapted for a numerous school, might, in the hands of an able and zealous private teacher, produce, if perseveringly pursued, and with subjects of good capacity, results not inferior to those ascribed to the labor of Ponce. (p. 152)

Bonet advocated initiating training through the use of a one-handed manual alphabet, which is essentially the same alphabet used today in the United

States. He attached great importance to early intervention and the provision of a consistent language environment, positions that only recently have been accepted in the modern world. For example, he insisted that everyone living in a house with a deaf person use the manual alphabet. He also advocated the early teaching of speech on the basis of the manual alphabet and the printed word, arguing that lack of early speech training is an impediment to later speech development.

Deland (1931) claimed that Bonet's ideas on sense training anticipate twentieth-century methods used in schools for the deaf. Deland quoted from a section containing suggestions for teaching similarities and differences of objects in relation to properties such as length, width, color, and weight as follows:

In this lesson he ought to be well versed; and this can be accomplished, for it is the very threshold of reasoning; and he must learn that words and concepts by which he is *to express what he thinks* [emphasis added]; and with this in view he will have to be asked many questions about different things, some of them are so similar as to demand feeling rather than sight to distinguish them, and these he must weigh in his head, so as to recognize differences in things that need some consideration. (p. 33)

The above passage is an incredible one and anticipates aspects of the work of Seguin, Montessori, Pestalozzi, and Piaget, among others. The implication that thought precedes language is a radical departure from traditional thinking and is the basis of much contemporary work in developmental psycholinguistics concerned with the semantic bases of language. The techniques are similar to those developed by Furth (1969) in his thinking laboratory for deaf children. In terms of methods, there are very obvious similarities with the Soviet system of neo-oralism (Moores, 1972a) and with the American Rochester method. Quigley (1969) has stated that essentials of the Rochester method and neo-oralism — that is, the association of fingerspelling, speech, and the printed word — had roots in the work of Bonet 350 years previously.

The third of the early Spanish educators of the deaf, Ramirez de Carrion, also was a man of genius and apparently was highly successful as a teacher of the deaf. His three most eminent pupils — Prince Emmanual of Savoy, the Marquiz de Priego, and Luis Velasco — were highly literate and successful individuals. Don Luis was named a favorite of King Henry IV, who appointed him the first Marquiz of Fresno.

Pietro di Castro (also known as Ezechiele de Castro) credited de Carrion with developing a cure for deafness. It was said that de Carrion first put his pupils through a preliminary physic and then had them shave the top of their heads and apply at night a salve consisting of brandy, saltpeter, niter, almond oil, and naphtha. Then he would speak strongly to the crown of the head, and the pupil would receive a voice and learn to speak.

Although de Carrion's "cure" has been dismissed as a fabrication, H. Peet (1851) has noted that, if it has any foundation in fact, it suggests that the subjects were only partially deaf. Nevertheless, it is interesting to note the similarity between this "treatment" and the statement in section III of the Justinian

Code more than 1,100 years before it, that no one is unable to hear if he or she is spoken to above the back of the head.

Great Britain

Interest in education of the deaf originally developed in Great Britain on the basis of a report by Sir Kenelin Digby concerning the remarkable skills of don Luis de Velasco, whom Digby met while accompanying the Prince of Wales, later Charles I, on a visit of state to Madrid. Digby reported that Velasco was so deaf that if a gun were shot off close by his ear he could not hear it (Deland, 1931) but that his speech was distinct and that he could understand so perfectly what others said that he would not lose a word in a whole day's conversation.

Digby greatly influenced the work of the English philosopher John Bulwer, who in 1648 published *Philocophus; or, the deafe and dumbe man's friend.* Bulwer made a special study of manual expression and what he considered the natural language of the hand. Deland reports that Bulwer would sign himself *Chirosopher*, or lover of the language of the hand. Bulwer's interest in deafness resulted from his friendship with two deaf brothers, Sir William and Sir Edward Gostwicke, with whom he communicated by means of a manual alphabet. Although reports of don Luis's success led Bulwer to place an emphasis on lipreading as the salvation of the deaf, Bulwer never put his ideas into practice, and the honor of being the first educator of the deaf in Great Britain must go to either William Holder (1616–1698) or John Wallis (1618–1703), each of whom actively claimed the title and denigrated the efforts of the other. Each of course claimed to have invented the art of teaching the deaf, and neither ever referred to the writing of Bulwer or Bonet.

The evidence suggests that Holder was the first to teach a deaf individual in Great Britain but that Wallis was the first to present his results to the outside world. Holder, in 1659, started to teach Alexander Popham, the son of Admiral Popham and Lady Wharton. A summary of his method was presented to the Royal Society in 1669. Holder's techniques were somewhat similar to those of his Spanish predecessors in that he advocated the use of writing as a beginning step and used a manual alphabet in the teaching of speech (a two-handed alphabet, not that described by Bonet). He developed specific techniques to teach speechreading skills, an approach different from those of Bonet, for example, who considered speechreading an art dependent on the deaf individual's own efforts. Holder relied heavily on context to differentiate between not only sounds that may look alike on the lips — for example, /p/, /b/, and /m/ — but also between meanings of the same word in varying contexts. Holder was well aware of the difficulties of speechreading and stated, "The histories of those who could discern speech by their eye are most of such as having had knowledge of language and a readiness in speaking, falling afterwards into deafness, have lost the use of speech; but still retain the memory of it."

Wallis, an Oxford professor and mathematician, began to teach Daniel Whaby, the 25-year-old son of the mayor of Northampton, in 1660. He claimed to have taught Whaby to articulate distinctly within a year.   Wallis began with the natural gestures used by his pupil and moved on to writing and the manual alphabet before introducing articulation. He differed from Holder and others in that articulation training was separate from use of the manual alphabet. Unlike Holder, but consistent with Bonet, he placed little emphasis on the teaching of speechreading.

George Dalgarno (1628–1687), a contemporary of Holder and Wallis, did not actually work with deaf pupils but produced a masterful treatise on deafness and education of the deaf in 1680: *Didascalocophus; or, the deaf and dumb man's tutor,* which was reprinted in the *American Annals of the Deaf* in 1857. Dalgarno was headmaster of a private school in Oxford. Although he was a personal acquaintance of Wallis, neither mentioned the other in print. Dalgarno advocated a more natural method for the development of language than the strong grammatical systems employed by Holder and Wallis. He believed that language could be developed in much the same way as it is in children with normal hearing. Like Bonet he placed great emphasis on early intervention and advocated continual use of fingerspelling, stating that a deaf baby could learn in the cradle as readily as any other child if the mother or nurse had "but as nimble a hand as commonly they have a tongue." Dalgarno suggested that the manual alphabet be placed in the back of the hornbook then used to teach letters to hearing children in England.

The two-handed manual alphabet recommended by Dalgarno was similar to that of Holder's. The letters were located on the fintertips and palms of one hand and were signified by touch from the finger or thumb of the other hand. Alexander Graham Bell used this system two centuries later in Massachusetts with his first pupil, who wore a lettered glove during his lessons (R. Bruce, 1973).

Dalgarno also was one of the first to emphasize that the deaf had potential for learning equal to the hearing and that the deaf could obtain the same level of functioning as the hearing if properly educated.

The first school for the deaf in Great Britain was established by Henry Baker (1698–1774), who first taught a deaf niece and, according to his own reports, developed a method of instructing the deaf to read, write, understand, and speak the English language. Following the example of his predecessors, Baker did not acknowledge — if he was aware of them — the existence of other individuals engaged in educating the deaf. Baker opened a small, very select private school and never divulged his methods. It has been reported that each pupil was required to post a bond of 100 pounds, which would be forfeited in the event that any of Baker's techniques were mentioned (Deland, 1931).

Because neither Baker's school nor his methods survived him, Thomas Braidwood (1715–1806), the first of three generations of leading educators of the deaf, who established a school for the deaf in Edinburgh in 1767, is acknowledged as the most influential early British educator of the deaf. He was joined by his son-in-law and nephew, John Braidwood, and the work was later carried on by John's widow as well as by another nephew, Joseph Watson

(1765–1829), who established the first nonprivate school for the indigent deaf, in London, around 1809.

At one time Braidwood had offered to make his methods public if financial support were forthcoming from the nobility and the gentry. Receiving no response to his offer, Braidwood continued to keep his methods a family secret. This secretiveness later was instrumental in pushing the founder of the first permanent school for the deaf in America to embrace the French method.

Although Thomas Braidwood never published anything concerning his techniques, Francis Green, a Bostonian whose son was enrolled in the Edinburgh school, published a description in 1793 of his son's education, a publication that angered the Braidwood family. Subsequently, Watson (1809) published a book based on the Braidwood method. In his program Braidwood incorporated the two-handed alphabet, gestures and natural signs, and reading and writing. His approach to the development of articulation was elemental, beginning with speech elements and gradually building up into syllables and words.

France

Because early work in the United States was influenced so heavily by French educators of the deaf, there is a tendency among Americans to believe that education of the deaf was originally a French phenomenon. Actually, organized French efforts for the deaf lagged behind the work in Spain by 200 years; and, as in the case of Great Britain, the efforts were motivated by the pioneering work of Spanish educators.

As in the case of Spain and Great Britain, we find the familiar controversy in France over who should receive recognition as the individual most responsible for the establishment of educational programs for the deaf. The two best-known claimants for the title were Jacob Rodriquiz Pereire (1715–1790) and the Abbé Carlos Miguel de l'Epée (1712–1789), two equally brilliant, but otherwise quite disparate, individuals. Consistent with other such controversies, a strong case can be made in support of either one: Pereire was the first well-known teacher in France, but his work did not survive him; de l'Epée began his work later but was responsible for establishing the first public school for the deaf in the world in Paris in 1755.

According to Deland (1931), Periere, a native of Spain, first began teaching his own sister, who was deaf, before his family migrated from Portugal to France to escape religious persecution. His work in France captured the interest of a French aristocrat, M. d'Azy d'Etavigny, who had a deaf son. Following extensive negotiations Periere and the elder d'Etavigny entered into a "performance contracting" agreement of the type popular in Great Britain at one time and similar to the performance contracting investigated by several American public schools in the early 1970s. Periere received one-third of the amount upon initiation of instruction, one-third when young d'Etavigny reached a certain level of competence, and one-third when he had completed his education.

Pereire exhibited d'Etavigny before the French Academy of Sciences in 1749, which reported (Deland, 1931):

We find that the progress made by d'Azy d'Etavigny justifies Pereire in hoping that, by his method, congenital deaf mutes cannot only learn to read, pronounce and understand common words, but also acquire abstract notions, and become capable of reasoning and acting like others. We have no difficulty in believing that the art of lipreading, with its necessary limitations, will be useful to other deaf mutes of the same class . . . as well as the manual alphabet Pereire uses. (p. 71)

Following his success with the Academy, Pereire undertook the education of Saboureux de Fontenay, the godson of the Duc de Chaulnes. de Fontenay became a noted linguist, studying not only European languages but also Hebrew, Syriac, and Arabic (Deland, 1931). He is also credited with having taught other deaf individuals manual communication (Bender, 1970). Pereire himself was careful to note that Saboureaux suffered only from a partial hearing loss (Degerando, 1827).

Pereire's students were sworn to secrecy concerning his methods, and it was his intention to keep his methods within his own family. Unfortunately, his penchant for secrecy was so strong that, at the time of his death, even his own family was not familiar with his methods, and despite the efforts of his son, mother, and daughter-in-law, his work died with him.

Most of what is known of Pereire's techniques came from a letter written by Saboureux de Fontenay, who apparently had little compunction about violating his oath. Periere employed a one-handed manual alphabet for the teaching of speech, relied on a "natural" approach to the development of language, developed auditory training procedures for those with residual hearing, and utilized special exercises involving sight and touch in sense training.

The Abbé de l'Epée apparently was less motivated to keep his methods secret than other early educators of the deaf, such as Baker, the Braidwoods, Pereire, and de l'Epée's German contemporary, Samuel Heinicke. Of course, de l'Epée also had the benefit of an independent income. Also, in defense of the above-named individuals, the methods of teaching the deaf they developed represented the most precious inheritances they could pass on to their progeny. To make the methods known to the public could detract from the economic well-being of their own families. Unfortunately, the inability of such educators to see beyond their own selfish interests could only work to the detriment of countless deaf children who were deprived of the benefits of their techniques.

de l'Epée began his work when he undertook the religious instruction of two young deaf sisters. Since he had no prior experience with the deaf, he began to develop his own system of instruction. However, his work soon was influenced by three sources. The first of these was the sign language used by the deaf in Paris. de l'Epée came to believe that sign language was the natural language of the deaf and was the only real vehicle for thought and communication for the deaf (McClure, 1969). Although he was not opposed to the teaching of speech, he regarded it as a mechanical operation and of lower priority than intellectual or spiritual concerns (Garnet, 1968). de l'Epée developed what he called "methodical" signs to supplement the natural sign language. The methodical signs represented both an expanded vocabulary and an attempt to adapt the sign language to French syntax and morphology. The second source was a copy of Bonet's original book on education of the deaf, which was donated to de l'Epée by a stranger. de l'Epée reportedly undertook to learn Spanish the very day he received the book (Bender, 1970; Deland, 1931). He also was influenced by the work of the Dutch educator Amman, who in 1692 had published *Surdos loquins* (*The speaking deaf*). Over time, de l'Epée gave decreasing attention to articulation. He was criticized severely for his position vis-à-vis articulation and speechreading (Garnet, 1968), and a great deal of confusion has been generated by seemingly contradictory statements concerning the efficacy and need of speech for the deaf.

The strongest personal attacks on de l'Epée came from Pereire and Heinicke. They were especially upset when the Austrian, Abbé Stark, was trained by de l'Epée and established the first school for the deaf in Austria in Vienna in 1789. Heinicke wrote an unsolicited letter to Stark stating, "The Parisian method of tuition is not simply of no use, but an absolute detriment to the advancement of the pupils." The distraught de l'Epée invited both Pereire and Heinicke to visit his school and observe instruction firsthand. Both refused, and the methods battle was joined for the first time. The positions of de l'Epée and Heinicke were illustrated in private exchanges of letters between the two (Garnett, 1968).

de l'Epée was succeeded by the Abbé Roch Ambroise Sicard (1742–1822) in 1790. Sicard continued the work of de l'Epée, relying on the methodical signs, writing, and the manual alphabet for instructional purposes. During his tenure a trend, which actually had begun under de l'Epée, developed toward greater reliance on natural signs. This apparently resulted from a tendency for conversation to slow down when signs were used to indicate mood, tense, number, gender, and so on. By the time of Sicard's successor, Roch Ambroise Augusta Belican, a native of Spain, the transition to natural signs and the manual alphabet was complete.

Germany*

Even though his methods have not survived, Samuel Heinicke (1729–1748) is known as the originator of the German method. A forceful, brilliant, largely self-educated man with an extensive military career, he gravitated toward education of the deaf through his experiences with deaf children as a private tutor

* The term *Germany* is used for convenience in the knowledge that during the period discussed there was no united Germany, but rather a collection of Germanic states and principalities of various sizes.

and teacher in several German cities. His success brought wide acclaim and increasing numbers of deaf students. At the invitation of the elector of Saxony, Heinicke established a school in Leipsig in 1778.

Consistent with the spirit of the time, Heinicke was secretive about the specific techniques he employed. In 1782 he wrote to de l'Epée (Garnett, 1968):

No other method can compare either in point of facility or solicity with that which I have invented and now practice, for mine is built entirely on articulate and vocal language, and upon taste which supplies the place of hearing. . . . My deaf pupils are taught by a slow and easy process to speak both their vernacular tongue and foreign languages with a clear and distinct voice from habit and from understanding. . . . The method which I now pursue as the tuition of the deaf and dumb was never known to anyone besides myself and son. The invention and arrangement of it cost me incredible labor and pains, and I am not inclined to let others have the benefit of it for nothing. By right the publication of it should be purchased of me by some prince, and I defy all the causistry in the world to argue me out of money that I lawfully and laboriously gain. Such of the deaf and dumb as are poor, I instruct gratis, while I made the rich pay in proportion to their wealth, and I often receive more than I demand. (pp. 42–44)

In his teaching, Heinicke was opposed to the use of methodical signs but not to natural signs and the manual alphabet. According to Garnet (1968, p. 43) this was not clear to de l'Epée because of difficulties in translation of Heinicke's letters.

Heinicke was opposed to the teaching of letters before the teaching of speech, arguing that this went against the natural order of learning. Influenced — as was de l'Epée in a different way and to a lesser extent — by the work of Amman, Heinicke attached a somewhat mystical quality to the spoken word. He argued that pure thought was possible only through speech, upon which everything was dependent. Operating from this premise, it was a small step for him to conclude that written language is secondary to spoken language and must follow, not precede, it.

Heinicke did seem to be somewhat inconsistent in his support of the primacy of speech in that he developed a theory that the sense of taste could substitute for hearing in the perception of sound. Thus, in his teaching, he related the taste of water to the vowel a, wormwood to e, vinegar to i, and olive oil to u.

Unfortunately, Heinicke's son Rudolf died before him, and his other two sons were not interested in the work. Although his widow and two sons-in-law attempted to carry on, they met with mixed success, and Heinicke's method did not survive him for long. de l'Epée's work began to exert an influence in Germany, and it was not until the nineteenth century that the German, or oral, method was to experience a revival in its native land.

Contrary to the popular belief, the two men much more responsible than Heinicke for the ultimate spread of the oral method were John Baptist Graser (1766–1841) and Frederick Maritz Hill (1805–1874). During the period of greatest French influence Graser had opposed the use of the French method and continued his efforts to expand the use of German techniques. He maintained that the two greatest deficiencies in education of the deaf were (1) the use of manual communication and (2) the isolation of deaf children in institutions and residential schools (Gordon, 1885a).

As the political influence of France began to decline in the early nineteenth century, an upsurge of nationalism crossed Europe. In no area was this stronger than in the German lands. Thus, Graser's arguments were accepted eagerly and put into practice in Germany. Under his influence, all teachers also were instructed in the education of deaf children so that the deaf could be integrated into regular classes with the hearing. In 1821 Graser initiated an experimental school along these lines, thus predating mainstreaming — the "latest" American conceptual breakthrough in education of the handicapped — by 150 years. Under Graser's influence the deaf were integrated into the public school programs in several German states, but because of the difficulties encountered in their academic progress, the system was abandoned after a few years (Bender, 1970; Gordon, 1885a).

Of all German educators of the deaf, the most influential was Frederick Hill, who applied the principles of Pestolozzi to education of the deaf. Hill argued that deaf children could learn language in the same way as hearing children, that is, by its everyday use in relation to the daily activities of life, as opposed to structured lessons in correct grammatical usage. He strongly believed that speech must be the foundation for all teaching and for all language, involving simple but natural interactions between the child and people in the environment. Although Hill used charts, colored pictures, and special readers, he did not allow the use of the manual alphabet or signs; natural gestures were acceptable with very young children. Hill was quite active in the training of teachers of the deaf, and his influence spread throughout Germany, eventually Europe, and finally the United States. It seemed the German, or oral, method had won the day over the French, or manual, method. The apparent high-water mark for the oral method was the famed Conference of Milan in 1880, which finally proclaimed the superiority of the oral method, a claimed superiority that was not to be challenged until after the middle of the twentieth century, in the Soviet Union and the United States.

Other Nations

Although the major advances in education of the deaf were focused in Spain, Great Britain, France, and Germany, it should be noted that work also progressed in countries such as Italy, Austria, Russia, Belgium, and Sweden and that numerous individuals in these nations contributed to improving the conditions of the deaf. In most cases educators of the deaf in these countries were influenced, and frequently trained, by the French and German leaders.

One of these individuals, Johann Konrad Amman (1669–1724), deserves special mention. Amman has the distinction of influencing the fathers of both the French and German methods, de l'Epée and Heinicke. His impact on later generations should not be ignored. Compelled to leave his native Switzerland because of his religious ideas, Amman, who had completed his M.D. at 18, settled in Holland. He became involved in deafness when he began to teach speech to a deaf child whom he was unable to cure medically. He developed his techniques independently, unaware of similar efforts in other countries. In 1692 he published the previously mentioned *Surdos loquins* (*The speaking deaf*) and followed in 1700 with *Dissertation de loquela* (*A dissertation on speech*).

Amman perceived the nature of speech in a religious sense, believing that humanity lost its "divine speech," which enabled us to effect all things merely by speaking the word. We lost this faculty at the time of the fall of Adam and Eve and retain only a mere shadow of it (Deland, 1931). Even though our spoken language is only a shadow of the original language, it is the most important characteristic that humanity possesses; therefore, according to Amman, education of the deaf must have as its primary emphasis the teaching of articulation.

Unlike most educators of the deaf of his time, Amman did not hesitate to circulate his ideas widely. In fact, he claimed to have failed with only one child, a girl whom he classified as dull of intellect. Unfortunately, despite his apparent success, Amman's descriptions of his techniques were not clear to readers, a situation he anticipated with the statement, "If I seem obscure in some parts to anyone reading this treatise, I trust that it will be imputed to him rather than to myself" (Deland, 1931).

In spite of a lack of clarity in his writing, Amman's ideas had a profound impact on several educators of the deaf, especially in Germany. It may be claimed that he, as much as Heinicke, established the foundation for what was to be known as the German method. Referring to Amman, with whose ideas he strongly disagreed, H. Peet (1851) stated:

And many later teachers, especially in Germany, influenced by his views, have strangely held that the power of articulating words was necessary to the full conception and realization of the value of words; and this idea had probably as much influence as anything else, in leading the early German educators to make articulation so prominent a part in their system of instruction. (p. 159)

Summary and Conclusion

There is no evidence of any systematic attempts to educate deaf individuals before the work of Ponce de Leon in Spain in the sixteenth century. The philosophical and practical foundations for education of the deaf, however, were developed in the seventeenth century with the brilliance of individuals such as Bonet of Spain, Dalgarno of Great Britain, and Amman of Holland setting the stage for the later establishment of schools for the deaf. The implementation of programs in the eighteenth century by leaders such as de l'Epée of France, Braidwood of Great Britain, and Heinicke of Germany was based upon the intellectual legacy of the seventeenth century.

Every issue presently facing those concerned with the optimum development of the deaf also was addressed by our predecessors. It is somewhat humbling to realize that all the issues were treated in one way or another at least 150 years ago. A partial list would include such areas as the relation of language to thought, "natural" versus "grammatical" approaches to language development, segregated education versus mainstreaming, the early teaching of reading, the efficacy of speechreading, the development of speech by elemental versus syntactic means, early home education, auditory training, sense training, and information processing via auditory and visual channels. Twentieth-century educators of the deaf have tended to treat each of these topics as something that has arisen independent of any historical context. It is hoped that the above brief overview of the work of selected individuals not only will provide an appreciation of their contributions but also will help put into perspective some of the issues as yet unresolved in the last part of the twentieth century.

3

Education of the Deaf
in the United States:
1816 to the Twentieth Century

Early Efforts

Although occasional references to deafness and education of the deaf may be found in the literature, there is no evidence of any organized attempt to provide for the deaf in America before the nineteenth century. Parents with the financial resources would send their deaf children to Europe to be educated. The Braidwoods' Edinburgh school was apparently the favorite, although Best (1943) reported that a deaf nephew of the future President Monroe was educated in Paris.

Children from two families that contributed to early attempts in education of the deaf should be mentioned. They are John, Mary, and Thomas Bolling, who enrolled in Edinburgh beginning in 1771, 1775, and 1775 respectively; and Charles Green, who began his education in 1780. The Bollings' hearing brother was to be responsible for the establishment of the first school for the deaf in the United States, which, unfortunately, was short-lived. Green's father, as previously noted, had incurred the displeasure of the Braidwoods by publication of a book on their methods.

Francis Green was an eclectic as well as enthusiastic individual. In addition to his publication on the Braidwood method he also was responsible for having much of the work of de l'Epée translated into English. Following the untimely death of his sons in 1793, Green continued his work in America, and to him belongs the credit of being the first to attempt to establish education for the deaf in the United States. In 1803, he published in the *Palladium*, a Boston based newspaper, an appeal to the clergy of Massachusetts to send him the names of all known deaf individuals in the state. In essence this constituted the first census of the deaf in America (Deland, 1931). The appeal turned up 75 names, but there was no follow-up in terms of establishment of a school.

The first person actually to work with the deaf in a capacity other than that of a private tutor probably was John Stanford, chaplain to the almshouse of New York City, who in 1810 undertook the education of several deaf children he encountered in his ministry. Stanford apparently tried to teach the children primarily by means of writing, but he experienced little success in his efforts.

48

Eventually he gave up working directly with the deaf. However, he maintained an interest in their problems and later was a founder of the New York Institution for Instruction of the Deaf and Dumb (E. Gallaudet, 1886).

The third attempt to establish an educational program for deaf children in America involved the Bolling family of Virginia and the star-crossed figure of John Braidwood, grandson of Thomas Braidwood, founder of the Edinburgh school. Colonel William Bolling, whose three deaf siblings had been educated in Edinburgh, himself had two deaf children, William Albert and Mary. In 1812, he learned that John Braidwood was in the United States, and he invited him to Virginia to establish a school.

Braidwood had been headmaster of the Edinburgh school, the most prestigious in Great Britain, for two years. Although a young man with unlimited potential, he was replaced because of intemperance and irresponsibility, and he migrated to America under a cloud. Braidwood informed Bolling that he was establishing a school in Baltimore, and Bolling sent him $600 for that purpose with the understanding that school would begin by July 1, 1812 (Bender, 1970). Apparently the school never was established, and the next thing Bolling heard from Braidwood was that he was imprisoned in New York as a debtor. Bolling paid Braidwood's debts and brought him to Virginia as a tutor for his children. Although details are lacking concerning Braidwood's work and there are some discrepancies in reports (Bender, 1970; Deland, 1931; E. Gallaudet, 1886). He returned to Virginia in 1818, and the long-suffering Colonel Bolling established a new school in Manchester, Virginia, this time with the Rever- In 1815 Colonel Bolling turned over a family estate to Braidwood and paid him a salary in return for teaching four or five students.

Braidwood disappeared from view in 1817 and went to New York, where he apparently unsuccessfully tried to establish another school (E. Gallaudet, 1886). He returned to Virginia in 1818, and the long-suffering Colonel Bolling established a new school in Manchester, Virginia, this time with the Reverend John Kilpatrick as head and Braidwood as assistant (Best, 1943). Braidwood was affiliated with the school for about six months. The school apparently was closed within a year or two. Braidwood died "a victim of intemperance" in 1819 (Doyle, 1893) or 1820 (Deland, 1931).

The Establishment of Schools for the Deaf*

The honor of establishing the first permanent school for the deaf in the United States belongs to Thomas Hopkins Gallaudet (1787–1851). A graduate of Yale at age 18, Gallaudet had completed Andover (Mass.) Theological Seminary

* In the writing of this section, I am especially indebted to Headmaster Ben Hoffmeyer and the staff of the American School for the Deaf for granting me access to the school's Historical Library, which contains a treasure of materials related to education of the deaf. Special thanks go to Jane Wilson, who copied literally thousands of pages of background material.

and was about to enter the Congregational ministry when, in 1814, he became interested in the education of 9-year-old Alice Cogswell, the deaf daughter of a neighbor, Dr. Mason Fitch Cogswell. Gallaudet undertook to teach her some simple words and sentences. His success strengthened Dr. Cogswell's determination to establish a school for the deaf in Connecticut. Following the lead of Francis Green in Massachusetts, Cogswell had conducted a census of the number of deaf individuals of educable age in Connecticut. Cogswell's efforts must have been better advertised, because he came up with 80 names, a higher total than the 75 of all ages turned up by Green in the more populous Massachusetts. Using these figures Cogswell projected a total of "upwards of 2,000" such persons in the United States, four times as great as Green's estimate of 500 (Bender, 1970).

Cogswell presented his results in 1815 to a group of community leaders in Hartford. He enlisted their support to establish a committee to raise funds to send a person to Europe to study education of the deaf. The money was raised in one day. The natural choice was Thomas Hopkins Gallaudet, who, at first, was reluctant to give up his ministerial calling. However, he was convinced by the arguments of the group, especially Dr. Cogswell's, and he agreed to undertake the journey, planning first to go to Great Britain to study the Braidwoods' method and then to Paris to learn the French method of de l'Epée and Sicard. Gallaudet sailed for Europe in the spring of 1815.* Upon arrival in Great Britain, he presented himself to the Braidwoods and John Watson, proposing that he spend a few months with them, after which he would go to Paris, thus enabling him to choose what he considered to be the most effective components from each method (E. Gallaudet, 1888).

Gallaudet's proposal was rejected by the Braidwood family, apparently because of three very strong considerations. First, the Braidwood method still was considered a family secret not to be divulged on demand. Second, the family was opposed to the French method and saw no advantage to using it in any way in connection with their system. Third, Gallaudet was dealing with the relatives of John Braidwood, who, at that time, was establishing a school for the deaf in Virginia. Since they had established a monopoly in Great Britain, there is no reason to believe they were anxious to train a rival to their family in America. The fact that the United States and Great Britain had just been at war with each other probably did not help relations.

The Braidwoods responded that it would require four or five years to learn their system, and they presented two counterproposals. Watson offered to send an assistant to America, to help establish a school, rather than train Gallaudet. Gallaudet rejected this on the grounds that he wanted to be trained and that he did not want to rely on someone wedded to one method. Gallaudet then was

---

* There are some discrepancies in dates given by various reporters. For example, E. Gallaudet (1868) reported that Cogswell and his group met on March 13, 1815, and that T. H. Gallaudet sailed on April 25, 1815. Bender (1970) sets the meeting at April 13, 1815, and the sailing at May 25, 1815. The author will not dwell on differences of this nature unless they assume major proportions.

offered a three-year residence in which he would be employed as an assistant. It called for him "To be with the pupils from seven o'clock in the morning till eight o'clock in the evening and also with pupils in their hours of recreation" (Deland, 1931). Gallaudet wasted little time in vigorously rejecting what he considered an insulting proposal. He made one final attempt, requesting that the Braidwoods release from an oath of secrecy a Mr. Kinniburgh, who had been trained by the Braidwoods and was teaching in Edinburgh. This was refused, and Gallaudet broke off negotiations to go to Paris to study with Sicard, who had met Gallaudet while on a speaking tour of Great Britain.

Gallaudet had developed great interest in the French method on the basis of the performance of two deaf men, Clerc and Massieu, who accompanied Sicard on his lectures and responded to audiences' questions on matters ranging from philosophy to the use of signs to convey abstract ideas (De Ladsbut, 1815).

Gallaudet was placed immediately in training by Sicard, and he stayed for a period of approximately four months. He prevailed upon Sicard to allow a deaf teacher, Laurent Clerc, to return to America with him. The two arrived in the United States in August 1816. Although Gallaudet had left for Europe with an eclectic orientation, circumstances dictated that he return with only a knowledge of the French system. Although he rejected Watson's offer of an assistant, he actively sought the services of Clerc, an assistant of Sicard's. Thus it was that the first teacher at the first school for the deaf in America was a deaf individual, a far different circumstance from the British system, in which deaf teachers were not employed.

In October 1816 the Connecticut legislature appropriated $5,000 for the school. Gallaudet and Clerc also traveled to several cities in the United States in the fall and winter of 1816–1817 to solicit money from private sources. On April 15, 1817, the American Asylum for the Education of the Deaf and Dumb (now the American School for the Deaf) was officially begun. The school opened with 7 students and grew to a total of 21 students by the time of the July 1817 annual report. Gallaudet served as principal until he resigned in 1830.

The permanence of the school was ensured in 1819, when the United States made a gift of a township site of 23,000 acres to the school. The land was sold by the school, and a fund in excess of $300,000 was established. The position of the American Asylum thereby was secured, and its influence was unrivaled by any other school in the first half of the nineteenth century. During that period the school provided both an education for the deaf from other states and the leadership for the establishment of new schools throughout the country. In 1819, the Massachusetts legislature decided to support the education of 20 deaf students at the American School. Similar actions were taken by the other New England states (New Hampshire, 1821; Maine and Vermont, 1825; Rhode Island, 1845). Distant states such as Georgia and South Carolina elected to send their children to Hartford until they established schools of their own.

The second school for the deaf, the New York Institution for the Education of the Deaf and Dumb, opened in 1818 and, to some extent, grew out of the unsuccessful efforts of Stanford and Braidwood. The school first survived by means of subscriptions, donations, and tuition payments, but New York City soon provided funds for 10 day students, and New York State in 1821 made permanent provision for support of an additional 32 students. In essence, it was the first day school for the deaf in the United States, although it soon evolved into a residential school. The school experienced great difficulties, according to E. Gallaudet (1886), until the appointment of Harvey Peet as principal in 1831. Peet had been an assistant of Thomas Hopkins Gallaudet in Hartford.

The establishment of the third school for the deaf is noteworthy because of the intriguing possibility that its founder, David G. Seixas, may have been distantly related to Pereire, the first teacher of the deaf in France. Seixas had found some deaf children wandering the streets of Philadelphia, and he began to educate them in his home. In April 1820 the board of directors of the Pennsylvania Institution for the Deaf and Dumb was organized, with Seixas as principal. The school was supported "by benevolent persons in Philadelphia" (E. Gallaudet, 1886) until the school was incorporated by the State of Pennsylvania, and state support for 50 students was established in 1821. In 1821, too, Laurent Clerc was hired as principal for a period of seven months to organize the school and train the teachers. Upon his return he was succeeded by Lewis Weld, another teacher from Hartford, who remained in Philadelphia until 1830, when he was appointed to succeed Thomas Hopkins Gallaudet as principal of the Hartford school.

The possibility of Seixas's relation to Pereire is suggested to the author by Deland's (1931) reference to Seixas as "a Portuguese Jew." Given his relationship to philanthropic activities in early nineteenth-century Philadelphia, he was probably a member of the prestigious and prolific Seixas family, which could trace itself back to the landing of the ship St. Charles, the "Jewish Mayflower," in New Amsterdam in 1654, and even further back to physicians and advisors of the royalty of Spain, Portugal, and England (Birmingham, 1971). Through intermarriage the Seixas family is related to all the leading original Sephardic families of America and can claim kinship to an impressive list of forebears, including Gershom Mendes Seixas, Rabbi of the Shearith Israel Congregation (the first in the United States) from 1766 to 1816 and known as the Patriot Rabbi during the American Revolution; Moses Seixas, leader of the Newport, Rhode Island, Congregation during the Revolution; Isaac Mendes Seixas Natham, a banker and one of the founders of the New York Stock Exchange; Emma Lazarus, whose words "Give me your tired, your poor/your huddled masses, yearning to be free . . ." are on the base of the Statue of Liberty; and Benjamin Nathan Cardozo, Justice of the United States Supreme Court. They are also related to the Pereira and Pereira Mendes family described by Birmingham (1971) as an "old and distinguished Sephardic family that had settled in Jamaica" (p. 121). Henry Pereira Mendes, for example, was

Rabbi of the Shearith Israel Congregation from 1877 to 1920 and was responsible for the establishment of the New York Guild for the Jewish Blind. It is intriguing to speculate whether David Seixas was aware of the work carried on in France by Pereire. Given the close-knit nature of the Sephardic communities in America, England, the Netherlands, and France, it is not beyond the realm of possibility.

The Spread of Education of the Deaf

Following the establishment of schools in Connecticut, New York, and Pennsylvania in a three-year period, only three new schools were added from 1820 to 1844. These were in Kentucky (1823), Ohio (1829), and Virginia (1839). The Virginia school was the first in which schools for the deaf and for the blind were established and placed under a single administration. From 1844 to 1860, just before the Civil War, a total of 17 new institutions were established, including the first parochial school for the deaf, St. Bridget's, in St. Louis, Missouri.

The Columbia Institution for the Deaf and Dumb in Washington, D.C., founded by Amos Kendall in 1857, deserves special mention. Edward Miner Gallaudet (1837–1917) and Sophie Fowler Gallaudet, the son and widow of Thomas Hopkins Gallaudet, were appointed superintendent and matron, respectively. In 1864 the school added a collegiate department, which was named the National Deaf Mute College (E. Gallaudet, 1886). This, of course, was later to be renamed Gallaudet College, in honor of Thomas Hopkins Gallaudet. It remains today the only liberal arts college for the deaf in the world.

The schools founded in the 50-year period from 1817 to 1867 were residential institutions, even though several schools, such as the two in New York City and Philadelphia, originated as day schools and apparently had numerous day students, that is, students who lived at home. Although the first three schools were located in the most populous areas of their states (Hartford, New York City, and Philadelphia), later schools tended to be established in areas removed from the major population concentrations. Thus schools were founded by state legislatures during that period in Danville, Kentucky; Staunton, Virginia; Jacksonville, Illinois; Cave Spring, Georgia; Fulton, Missouri; Delavan, Wisconsin; Flint, Michigan; and Faribault, Minnesota, rather than in Louisville, Richmond, Chicago, Atlanta, St. Louis, Milwaukee, Detroit, or Minneapolis/St. Paul. In addition to political reasons specific to each state, the placements probably reflected an attitude that the problems of the deaf were such that they need not be a part of the greater society. The first long-standing day schools for the deaf were not established until after the Civil War, when, in 1869, the Pittsburgh Day School and the Boston Day School (renamed the

Horace Mann School in 1877) were opened. The Pittsburgh school later evolved into a predominantly residential facility, now known as the Western Pennsylvania School for the Deaf.

The Establishment of Oral Schools

Although issues of teaching methods are dealt with more fully in following chapters, no treatment of education of the deaf in nineteenth-century America would be complete without considering the oral-manual controversy that always seemed to be operating just beneath the surface and that frequently flared into open hostility. The situation was compounded by disagreement among supporters of manual communication, with some favoring "methodical" signs following English word order, others in support of "natural" sign language with a word order different from English, and a somewhat smaller third group placing greater reliance on the manual alphabet.

Despite variations in use of the different types of manual systems, the early schools tended to place little or no emphasis on articulation or speech. Thomas Hopkins Gallaudet's plans to combine elements of the manual and oral methods were not realized at that time, and the early schools were basically manual only. Two notable exceptions were Braidwood's schools in Virginia and an oral school established by the Reverend Robert T. Anderson in Hopkinsville, Kentucky (J. Jones, 1918). The Hopkinsville school was in existence from 1844 to 1854, when it closed its doors.

Work in oral education in the United States has had its roots in two quite disparate movements. The first involved the addition of oral elements to the existing manual methods to produce a combined oral-manual system. The second has been concerned with the establishment of an oral-only system in which manual components would not be employed.

Although there were sporadic attempts to teach articulation and speechreading from the beginning, most of the effort usually was limited to the hard of hearing. In 1935 E. Boatner noted reports of successful instruction in articulation at the American School as early as 1836 with students who had lost their hearing in childhood and with adventitiously deaf students. It was believed that attempts to teach oral communication to the congenitally deaf were doomed to failure in the majority of cases. This belief was first brought into serious question in 1844 by Horace Mann and Samuel Howe, who had visited schools for the deaf in Germany and returned to the United States convinced of the superiority of the German (oral) method (Deland, 1931; J. Jones, 1918). They recommended the establishment of an oral school in Massachusetts, a recommendation strongly opposed by the American School. Mann, of course, was one of the most influential early American educators. Howe was the principal of the first school for the blind in the United States and was the person who coordinated the training of Laura Bridgeman (Lamson, 1878), a deaf-blind individual who was the Helen Keller of her age. Bridgeman's primary mode of instruction was through the manual alphabet, and it is possible that many of the techniques used by Anne Sullivan with Helen Keller were based on those previously employed with Bridgeman. Another interesting sidelight is that Howe's position was offered originally to Thomas Hopkins Gallaudet, who declined primarily because he did not want to leave Hartford (M. Boatner, 1959a).

The observations of Mann and Howe caused a sensation in the United States. Dr. Harvey Peet and Reverend George Day, from the New York Institution and the American School, were sent to Germany to observe the method firsthand. They were much less impressed with the results of the oral method than were Howe and Mann (Deland, 1931; J. Jones, 1918), declaring that the manual method produced better results and that the German method was a feeble one for education and for moral and religious instruction. However, the benefits of articulation — for at least some students — were acknowledged by at least some of the "manual" educators. Lewis Weld, principal of the American School, had made a trip to Europe before Peet and Day had. On the basis of his report (Weld, 1845), the board of directors of the American School declared (E. Boatner, 1937):

The Board of Directors will take efficient measures to introduce into the course of instruction in the school every improvement to be derived from these foreign institutions; and with regard to teaching deaf-mutes to articulate, and to understand what is said to them orally, that they give it a full and prolonged trial, and do in this branch of instruction everything that is practically and permanently useful. (p. 50)

The American School was also the first school in the United States to employ a full-time speech teacher, a Miss Eliza Wadsworth, in 1857. It was believed in many quarters that the commitment of the American School to oral education was dictated as much by political as by educational considerations and that a major goal was the prevention of the establishment of a competitive school which the State of Massachusetts would favor over the Connecticut-based American School (Report of the Joint Special Committee of the Massachusetts Legislative of 1867 on the Education of Deaf-Mutes).

The man responsible for the establishment of an oral school for the deaf, in the face of opposition from the manual faction, was Gardiner Greene Hubbard, a prominent Massachusetts lawyer of distinguished ancestry, whose daughter, Mabel, had lost her hearing through scarlet fever in 1863 at the age of 5 (R. Bruce, 1974). The Greene family was opposed to sending Mabel to the American School, preferring to have her tutored orally. Convinced of the success of their efforts, they actively sought the establishment of an oral school. They were supported in this by the parents of two other young, adventitiously deaf girls, Fanny Cushing and Jeannie Lippitt, daughter of the Governor of Rhode Island and sister of a future United States Senator from Rhode Island (R. Bruce, 1974; Deland, 1931).

When the effort to establish a school with state support was defeated, Hubbard founded a private school in Chelmsford, Massachusetts, under the leadership of Harriet Rogers, the tutor of Fanny Cushing and sister of one of the instructors of Laura Bridgeman (Deland, 1931). Hubbard persisted in his efforts at the state level and in 1867 was successful — following the endorsement of the governor of Massachusetts and a generous endowment by John Clarke — in establishing a pure oral school in Northampton, Massachusetts. Harriet Rogers was appointed the first principal.

One of the big factors in swinging the Massachusetts legislators was a demonstration given by Jeannie Lippitt, then 15, and Roscoe Greene, an 18-year-old native of Providence who had lost his hearing at age 7 (Turner; in E. Gallaudet, 1868, p. 57). They were able to discuss a variety of topics without recourse to manual communication (Deland, 1931; E. Gallaudet, 1868). The present author is unable to find any evidence indicating whether or not Roscoe Greene and Mabel Hubbard, through Gardner Greene Hubbard, were related. Although there is a difference in spelling, there is also a possibility, given their New England background, that the Hubbards were related to Charles Green, the deaf student in Scotland, and Francis Green, who had tried to establish a school for the deaf in Massachusetts more than 60 years before the beginning of the Clarke institution.

The fears that the establishment of the Clarke school would mean that the State of Massachusetts would no longer send students to the American School were unfounded. Although in his testimony before the Massachusetts Joint Special Committee Samuel Howe had recommended that after May 1867 no deaf students from Massachusetts be sent to the American School (1867, p. 11), Gardner Hubbard envisioned the oral school primarily serving those who lost their hearing at age 3 and later and those who were hard of hearing. In his testimony before the joint committee is found an interesting exchange (1867):

HUBBARD: If the child were of poor parents, I should not attempt articulation.

QUESTION: Let it grow up in silence?

HUBBARD: No, sir; I should send it to Hartford. (p. 10)

In the *First Annual Report of the Clarke Institution for Deaf Mutes*, he reiterated his position (Hubbard, 1868) that the school was primarily for the deafened and hard of hearing. Because of the attention given to the oral-manual question, two essential policies of the new school (Hubbard, 1868) representing major breakthroughs have received little recognition. First was the commitment to extend the age of admission of students downward to age 5 instead of age 10, which was common in most schools for the deaf at that time. Second was the decision to expand the usual length of instruction from six years to ten years.

Because of the drawn-out controversy involved in its establishment, many believe that the Clarke school was the first permanent oral-only school for the deaf in the United States. This is incorrect, as is the belief that the Boston Day School (now the Horace Mann School for the Deaf), founded in 1869, was the first day school. The first oral-only school was the New York Institution for Impaired Instruction, now the Lexington School for the Deaf.

The New York school, not to be confused with the New York Institution founded in 1818, grew out of a private oral school begun in 1864 by Isaac and Hannah Rosenfeld. The Rosenfelds wished to extend the benefits of the training to children whose parents could not pay. The school was reorganized, with substantial philanthropic support, and opened on March 1, 1867, seven months before the Clarke school (Deland, 1931; J. Jones, 1918). Bernhard Engelsmann, who had been a teacher in the Vienna Hebrew (oral) School for the Deaf, was appointed the first principal (Deland, 1931). The stability of the school was ensured in 1870 by the New York Legislature, which provided for the support for students on the same terms as those for the previously established school for the deaf in New York.

Edward Miner Gallaudet and Alexander Graham Bell

The history of American education of the deaf from the Civil War to World War I and the fortunes of the combined and oral methods perhaps may best be illustrated by examination of the accomplishments of their respective champions, Edward Miner Gallaudet (1837–1917) and Alexander Graham Bell (1847–1922). Over a period of decades, these two individuals were the dominant forces in education of the deaf. Originally, their relationship was a warm and friendly one (M. Boatner, 1952, 1959a, 1959b; R. Bruce, 1973), but their increasingly sharp disagreements over methodology led to a bitter antagonism that was at least partly responsible for the dichotomization of educators of the deaf into oral and combined camps.

A reading of biographies of Bell (Bruce, 1973; Burlingame, 1964; MacKenzie, 1929; Mayne, 1929) and of Gallaudet (M. Boatner, 1952, 1959a) reveals interesting insights into the two and makes it easy to understand how they eventually would come to clash. Despite apparently different interests and personalities, both were restless, dominating men of genius. Each had a deaf mother and a highly successful father, in whose work he followed. Each had achieved a full measure of success in his twenties — Gallaudet by being appointed president of the first college for the deaf (now Gallaudet College, named in honor of his father) at age 27; and Bell by receiving the patent for the telephone at age 29. Each made unique contributions to society — Bell through his inventions of the telephone and audiometer and his work on the phonograph; and Gallaudet through his book, *International Law*, which went through five printings and in recognition of which he received an honorary doctor of law degree from Yale in 1895 (M. Boatner, 1959b). G. McClure (1961), reminiscing at the age of 100 on the 1890 Convention of American Instructors of Deaf, referred to

Bell as "handsome, brilliant, aggressive" and Gallaudet as "suave, courteous, at the height of his great powers" (p. 105). Gallaudet and Bell both had achieved success early in life and had continued to be highly acclaimed individuals, accustomed to having their own ways. As will be seen, such individuals do not compromise easily.

Edward Miner Gallaudet*

The youngest child of Thomas Hopkins Gallaudet and Sophie Fowler Gallaudet, Edward Miner Gallaudet had hoped to attend Yale, as did his father, who had entered Yale as a sophomore and at age 18 was the youngest member of his graduating class. E. M. Gallaudet's hopes were smashed at age 14 on the death of his father. However, E. M. Gallaudet's early accomplishments were equally impressive. Following his father's death, he worked for two years as a bank teller to save money for college; entered Trinity College in Hartford as a junior; taught at the American School, full time for the last year; and graduated from Trinity by the age of 19. There is some indication that Trinity withheld his degree for some time, not because he did not meet the requirements for graduation but because he was able to bypass the first two years of college and complete the final two years, while employed as a teacher, with no great noticeable strain. Trinity was later to award him an honorary M.A. and Ph.D. (M. Boatner, 1959b).

E. M. Gallaudet was chosen to be principal of the new Columbia Institution for the Deaf and Dumb in Washington, D.C. Accompanied by his mother, who served as matron of the school, he assumed control of the school in 1857 at the tender age of 20. His efforts met with considerable success, and in 1864 Congress established a collegiate department, known as the National Deaf Mute College, with Gallaudet as president.

Gallaudet had followed the controversy over the establishment of an oral school in Massachusetts with interest, and he was aware of work going on in Europe. Before the establishment of the oral schools in New York and Massachusetts, he made the first of his 13 trips to Europe. In six months he visited 40 schools, and in October 1867 he reported to his board. Gallaudet disagreed with the reports of previous American educators of the deaf and advocated the introduction of articulation as a branch of instruction in all schools for the deaf in the United States (E. Boatner, 1938).

In 1868 Gallaudet called a meeting of principals of schools for the deaf (from which grew the present Conference of Executives of American Schools for the Deaf). The chief topic of concern was methodology, specifically the place of articulation and lipreading in the instruction of the deaf. The majority of par-

---

* I would like to acknowledge the contribution to this section of Dr. Maxine Tull Boatner, biographer of Edward Miner Gallaudet, who not only made available to me material on the life of E. M. Gallaudet but also graciously agreed to meet with me and answer questions concerning Gallaudet's career and relations with Alexander Graham Bell. The responsibility for any errors in this section are those of the present author and not Dr. Boatner's.

ticipants showed themselves to be open-minded and receptive to change, and a number had visited the Clarke school during its first year of operation. In a discussion on articulation Milligan made the following observations (E. Gallaudet, 1868):

I went to Northampton not believing, for physiological reasons, that those who had no audiological nerve could ever learn to speak and articulate; and it is not pleasant for me to find out that they can. (Laughter) I am willing to say that I am disappointed; but it is so that they do talk. We cannot get around it and we have got to put up with it for they won't stop talking for all our resolutions. (p. 56)

Gallaudet himself was critical of efforts to teach articulation at the American School, charging that the school did not devote enough attention to oral skills. As an example he claimed to have taught one of his college students, Samuel Greene, to speak and read lips; Greene had graduated from the American School and supposedly had received 2½ years of articulation training (E. Gallaudet, 1868, p. 70). No mention is made of any connection between Samuel Greene and either Roscoe Greene of Rhode Island or Mabel Hubbard, but again it is interesting to speculate that, given their New England background, they may have been related.

The tenor of the conference was not to abandon signs in favor of a pure oral method but rather to utilize both elements judiciously. It was noted, for example (E. Gallaudet, 1868, p. 71), that the only pupil at Clarke who was observed to read from a printed book was a girl who previously had attended the American School. Turner (E. Gallaudet, 1868) reflected the majority view in his statement that "Dactology and signs, instead of being a hindrance would, if properly used, be decidedly advantageous" (p. 71).

Out of the conference came a resolution stating that all institutions for the deaf had the duty to impart instruction in lipreading and articulation to all pupils who might profit from it. Undoubtedly E. M. Gallaudet played the key role in establishing oral education in schools for the deaf in the United States and was instrumental in gaining acceptance of a combined oral-manual philosophy. J. Jones (1918, p. 16) pictures the young Gallaudet standing as the single champion of speech and lipreading in the American schools in the midst of a number of older superintendents wedded to their philosophies. A reading of the proceedings of the meeting suggests this is an exaggerated view, but it is obvious that Gallaudet was forced to use his considerable persuasive powers to win the conference to his viewpoint. Even then there were difficulties. W. McClure (1969) reports Gallaudet was called the degenerate son of a noble father for his actions. However, his efforts were successful. If Thomas Hopkins Gallaudet is the father of education of the deaf in the United States, Edward Miner Gallaudet is the father of oral education. While ensuring the future of oral instruction, E. M. Gallaudet was unaware that sign language was to come under strong attack and that the question for the future would revolve around whether education of the deaf should be combined oral-manual or oral only.

Thus the man who in 1871 argued that sign language was used to excess (E. Gallaudet, 1871) felt constrained to defend the value of sign language in 1887 (E. Gallaudet, 1887) and, clearly on the defensive, before the end of the century wrote an article entitled "Must the Sign Language Go?" (E. Gallaudet, 1899). It has been pointed out (J. Jones, 1918) that Gallaudet's position was consistent over the years. In 1868 he was in opposition to the prevalent manual-only system, and in 1899 he was speaking out just as strongly against the dominant wave of the oral-only method. To place this movement in perspective, it is helpful to examine the career of Alexander Graham Bell, Gallaudet's contemporary and long-time adversary, who was acclaimed by Deland (1931) as the man who broke the death grip that the sign method had upon Americans.

Alexander Graham Bell

Alexander Graham Bell was born in Edinburgh, Scotland. His father was Alexander Melville Bell, a noted teacher of diction and elocution whose dreams of fostering a universal language led him to develop the system of Visible Speech, a method of teaching articulation that was used, among others, with the deaf (Bender, 1970; R. Bruce, 1973, 1974). Alexander Melville in turn had been influenced by his father, Alexander Bell, who started out as a shoemaker (Burlingame, 1964), became an actor, and finally a teacher of speech (R. Bruce, 1973, 1974). In all three generations may be perceived a dedication to the teaching of speech. The grandfather is quoted (R. Bruce, 1974) as stating, "Perhaps, in no higher respect has man been created in the image of his Maker, than in his adaptation for speech and the communication of his ideas" (p. 3). Alexander G. Bell's mother had been deaf from scarlet fever from age 4, and he used a manual alphabet to communicate with her (Bender, 1970; R. Bruce, 1974).

In 1868, A. G. Bell introduced Visible Speech at a private school for the deaf in London (Bender, 1970). This was not his first position. As a teenager, he had been a teacher of elocution at a boy's school in Scotland (R. Bruce, 1974).

Bell moved to Canada with his parents in 1870 for health reasons. Two of his brothers had died of tuberculosis (Mayne, 1929), and his parents were afraid the same fate would befall him if he remained in Great Britain.

In 1871 Bell went to the Boston Day School to teach Visible Speech. The following year he demonstrated his methods at the Clarke school and the American School (Bender, 1970). It is reported that he addressed the graduating class of the American School in sign language (R. Bruce, 1973).

Bell returned to Boston, where he established a school of vocal physiology, taught at Boston University, conducted electrical experiments, and tutored, all at the same time. One of his students was Mabel Hubbard, who had been among the first pupils at the Clarke school. The Hubbards had some reservations about the romantic interest that developed between their daughter and the impoverished young inventor (MacKenzie, 1929). Bell also tutored a young deaf boy by the name of George Sanders and lived with Sanders in the home of the boy's grandmother, where he conducted his experiments. Mr. Thomas Sanders, along with Gardner Greene Hubbard, provided Bell with financial support for his experimental work (Burlingame, 1964). Bender (1970) reports that Bell used a lettered glove by which he communicated in some way with George Sanders. The lettered glove was of the type originally recommended by Dalgarno (1680).

Bell received the patent on the telephone in 1876, at the age of 29, where-upon the Hubbards withdrew their opposition to their daughter's marrying a still young but no longer impoverished inventor. From that time on, although he would continue to think of himself as "a teacher of deaf-mutes" (Bruce, 1973), Bell would find himself forced to devote his attention to other questions, the most time-consuming and draining being a series of legal actions that were necessary for him to verify his claim upon the invention of the telephone.

In 1879 Bell moved to Washington, where he first met E. M. Gallaudet. Apparently they were brought together by Gardner Greene Hubbard (M. Boatner, 1959a). In 1880 Bell received an honorary Ph.D. from Gallaudet College (M. Boatner, 1959a).

Bell established a small private school for the deaf in Washington in 1883 (Montague, 1940), and it had a number of interesting and innovative features. For example, he used "whiteboards" instead of blackboards and charcoal instead of chalk (Montague, 1940). All objects were labeled. The floors had rugs, and the children clustered around a low table. Hearing children as well as deaf attended the school. Unfortunately, because of the challenge of rival claimants to the invention of the telephone, Bell had to turn his attention elsewhere and, in 1885, closed the school. From that time he was destined to provide leadership to the cause of education of the deaf in a less direct manner.

The split between Bell and Gallaudet was precipitated by two papers written by Bell: *Memoir upon the formation of a deaf variety of the human race* (1883a) and an article entitled *Fallacies concerning the deaf* (1884). Bell's position basically was that the American system of education of the deaf had the effect of isolating deaf people from society, increasing the number of marriages of deaf people with other deaf people, and thereby inadvertently contributing to increases in the numbers of deaf people. He saw the major contributing factors being the system of residential schools, which brought the deaf together, and the sign language, which Bell believed hindered English, causing the deaf to associate with and marry each other, thus propagating their physical defect.

Bell believed that a law forbidding congenitally deaf persons from intermarrying "would go a long way towards dealing with the evil" (1884, p. 45) and that an even more practical step might involve legislation forbidding the intermarriage of persons "belonging to families containing more than one deaf-mute" (p. 45). Acknowledging the doubtful advisability of legislative interference, Bell recommended the elimination in programs for the deaf of (1) educational segregation, (2) the "gesture language," and (3) deaf teachers.

Bell noted that in 1883 nearly one-third of the teachers of the deaf in

America were themselves deaf. He stated (1884): "This must be considered as another element favorable to the formation of a deaf race — to be therefore avoided" (p. 48).

Bell's position was in opposition to the combined oral-manual philosophy of Gallaudet, who immediately responded (E. Gallaudet, 1884). Gallaudet was answered not by Bell but by his father-in-law, Gardner Hubbard (1884). The battle was soon joined, and the issues have come down into the latter part of the twentieth century still largely unresolved.

The Battle Is Joined

On the face of it, one would have expected Bell and his supporters to have swept the field with ease. Opposing Gallaudet was an array of seemingly overwhelming forces. Chief of these, of course, was the brilliant, aggressive Bell himself, who, in addition to his own ability was able to draw upon his well-deserved international reputation and prestige as the inventor of the telephone and who had at his disposal a personal fortune from which he was willing to establish, endow, and support organizations dedicated to pursuing his goals. Outside of the education of the deaf, Bell enjoyed an unbroken string of victories in his confrontations with rivals, including a smashing defeat of the giant Western Union Telegraph Company, which Bell and his associates drove out of the telephone business (R. Bruce, 1973; Burlingame, 1964). In addition, the oral-only position had just triumphed in Europe, and the 1880 International Convention in Milan (which Gallaudet attended) represented an overwhelming victory for the "pure oral method." Among the resolutions passed were those declaring: (1) given the incontestable superiority of speech over signs in restoring deaf-mutes to society, and in giving them a more perfect knowledge of language, that the oral method ought to be preferred to signs; and (2) considering that the simultaneous use of speech and signs has the disadvantage of injuring speech, lipreading, and precision of ideas, that the pure oral method ought to be preferred.

The conflict was not so uneven as it might have seemed, however, and the pure oral method never achieved the hegemony in the United States that it did in Europe. Bender (1970, p. 168) reported that the United States was the only real stronghold for the silent (sic) method after the Conference at Milan, that "other countries made sincere efforts to incorporate the recommendations of the Congress into their schools" (p. 68), and that the oral method was adopted as the preferred mode in all countries except the United States (p. 167).

Edward Miner Gallaudet was the individual most responsible for the survival of combined oral-manual education, albeit in very reduced circumstances. The man who challenged and defeated the predominant manual-only philosophy early in his career was the one who in the later stages of his career found himself involved in a much more difficult struggle to prevent the domination of an oral-only system (E. Gallaudet, 1907). His success in these efforts represents, in the author's opinion, the two most outstanding contributions to education of the deaf made by an American.

Gallaudet presented Bell with a protagonist at least as determined and single-minded as himself. Gallaudet did not hesitate to confront Bell directly, both in print and in public debate — tactics that Bell found it difficult to deal with, preferring to work through organizations or second parties.

In 1887 Bell founded the Volta Bureau in Washington, D.C., with an endowment of $200,000 for the increase of diffusion of knowledge concerning the deaf (Bender, 1970). With Bell's support, a journal, the *Association Review* (now the *Volta Review*), was first published in 1889. In 1890 the establishment of the American Association to Promote the Teaching of Speech to the Deaf was complete, supported by a $25,000 endowment by Bell (Bruce, 1973), who continued to make up for the association's deficit each year (Deland, 1931). In 1909 the association took over the Volta Bureau, and in 1956 the association's name was changed to the Alexander Graham Bell Association for the Deaf, Incorporated.

Relations between Bell and Gallaudet flared into open hostility in 1890–1891 and centered on Gallaudet's efforts to establish a normal, or teacher training, component to Gallaudet College aimed at training teachers with normal hearing in the use of the combined method. Gallaudet had mentioned his plans to Bell, who accepted an invitation to lecture the class upon the establishment of the program (Boatner, 1959a, p. 132). After the U.S. House approved a $5,000 appropriation, Bell, without informing Gallaudet, requested a hearing before the Senate Appropriations Committee to oppose the program. He secured petitions from oral-only schools (Boatner, 1959a) and presented to Congress a list of principals of 21 oral schools who were opposed to appropriations for teacher training at Gallaudet College (Ferreri, 1908, p. 81).

Bell's major expressed fear was that deaf graduates would be admitted to the training department (R. Bruce, 1973; Ferreri, 1908). Although plans at that time did not call for deaf students in the projected department, Gallaudet argued that the oral schools could not legitimately oppose the employment of the deaf (Ferreri, 1908, p. 82). The Senate cut the $5,000 appropriation, and Bell wired friends that the manual department was defeated (Boatner, 1959a), whereupon Gallaudet mounted a counterattack. When Bell modified his position to support an appropriation of $3,000 to be earmarked specifically for oral teaching in the college, Gallaudet noted in his diary, "Bell has heard from the back districts" (Boatner, 1959a, p. 134).

Gallaudet accepted the $3,000 appropriation, set up an articulation schedule, and then set out to raise additional money. Gallaudet's board of directors approved six fellowships at $500 each to provide training in oral and manual instruction, thus defeating Bell's efforts and setting the foundation for teacher training in the combined method.

In commenting on Bell's role in the affair, Gallaudet wrote (Boatner,

1959a), "It is a pitiful spectacle to see a man of naturally generous impulses given over to partisan spite" (p. 134).

In an apparent response, the Clarke school expanded its training program in 1892 to provide teachers of articulation for other schools (Ferreri, 1908). Bell and the Hubbard family had always kept a close relationship with the Clarke school, which Hubbard had been instrumental in establishing.

The second major source of friction was the relationship between the American Association to Promote the Teaching of Speech to the Deaf and the older Convention of American Instructors of the Deaf, which had been established in 1850. Although Bruce (1973) claims it was Gallaudet's intransigence that led Bell to found a new independent organization, Boatner reported (1959a) that in 1893 and 1894 Gallaudet had made overtures to Bell to merge the two organizations and received what he thought were positive responses. When his suggestion was rejected, Gallaudet felt Bell once again had misled him. It is logical to conclude, given the strength of mind of the two, that each was willing to merge only on his own terms. At the 1895 Convention of American Instructors of the Deaf in Flint, Michigan, Gallaudet launched a strong attack on Bell that, despite a perfunctory handshake at the end of the convention to wild applause (W. McClure, 1969), spelled the end of attempts to join the two groups. Gallaudet was elected president of the conference and was to remain so until 1917 (Boatner, 1952). When Bell attempted to become an active member, in Gallaudet's words, "His money was refused" (M. Boatner, 1959a, p. 139). As a result, education of the deaf split into two warring camps, the oral-only and the combined, and the schism has persisted for almost 100 years, with each faction having its own professional organization, journal, and parent affiliate. In the present author's opinion, the split precipitated an educational dark age lasting well past the middle of the twentieth century. Although it is wasteful to dwell too long on missed opportunities, one can imagine what benefits might have accrued to the education of deaf individuals if only Bell and Gallaudet had joined forces.

Summary

The establishment of educational facilities for the deaf in the early nineteenth century set the pace for services to the handicapped in the United States. The number of schools and the quality of programs increased throughout the century. The major obstacle to progress was intense and often acrimonious disagreement between advocates of oral and manual systems of instruction. The goal of Thomas Hopkins Gallaudet to combine the best elements of the English (oral) and French (manual) methods was not realized. The legacy of two bitterly hostile camps was passed on to the twentieth century, and only in recent years has there been a strong movement toward reconciliation of the two views.

4
The Causes of Deafness

Introduction

Parents and professionals frequently are hampered in their efforts to provide adequately for deaf children because of a lack of information concerning etiology. This is especially unfortunate because the residua and sequelae of many known causes of deafness — for example, maternal rubella, mother-child blood incompatibility, cerebro-spinal meningitis — may include heart defects, vision problems, brain damage, and mental retardation in addition to hearing loss.

Vernon (1968) has pointed out that the void in etiological data (1) hinders the development of a constructive approach to the prevention of deafness, (2) leaves researchers without knowledge of the base populations with which they are concerned, and (3) in individual cases prevents differential diagnosis where factors such as site of lesion and possible central nervous system involvement need to be determined. The present lack of etiological information, then, is harmful both on an individual and a programmatic level.

It may be somewhat surprising, and more than a little frustrating, to find that for over a century the single largest etiological category for deafness has been *cause unknown*, accounting for as much as 30% of the deaf population even in recent surveys. One reason for the paucity of information has been a lack of research activity on medical and genetic aspects of deafness. For example, the relationship betwen maternal rubella — perhaps the most common nongenetic cause — and congenital deafness was not described until 1944 (Bordley, Brookhauser, Hardy, & Hardy, 1967), and it was not until 1949 that a group of deaf children were identified (Goodhill, 1950, 1956) with a common history of erythroblastosis fetalis as a result of Rh factor incompatibility. In the genetic sphere more attention has been devoted to the study of exotic syndromes related to deafness that, however fascinating clinically, account for only a small proportion of the deaf population.

The greatest problem in identifying etiology is that the procedure typically is retrospective in nature and, as discussed in Chapter 5, usually involves parents with little or no previous contact with deafness and for whom the process of diagnosis of hearing loss was probably traumatic. In such a situation the chances of making an incorrect judgment about etiology are great.

66

One factor is the tendency of parents to abscribe a child's deafness to external forces beyond their control. Parents may believe that the child had normal hearing during the first stages of development but then lost the ability to hear. This tendency is strengthened in the majority of cases in which there is no history of deafness on either side of the family. Since it is not unusual for the final diagnosis of deafness to be made until 2 years of age or later, the mother's recollection of the early stages of her pregnancy may be somewhat blurred. Because it is common for the first trimester of pregnancy to entail a certain amount of physical stress, most mothers can recall discomforts that could be symptomatic of rubella or flu. A misdiagnosis of an etiology of maternal flu or rubella is made in an unknown, but probably significant, number of cases in which the actual cause is genetic in nature. The author is aware of several cases in which parents, after having a deaf child, were told that the cause was not genetic, whereupon they had another child who was also deaf. Even when the cause is genetic, the next child need not be deaf. As will be shown, when the cause of deafness results from recessive genes, the chances of any one child being deaf would be 1 in 4. Also, in a relatively small number of cases, the deafness may be sex-linked, appearing only in male offspring.

Countervailing the tendency to attribute etiology to external factors is the opposite tendency among many professionals to make a diagnosis of genetic etiology when no other cause can be determined. The extent to which such diagnoses are incorrectly made obviously is impossible to ascertain. However it probably is relatively common, especially in cases involving maternal rubella. For example, Bordley et al. (1967), working with a study group of 47 children who exhibited positive virus cultures, found that in 15 of the cases there was no history of prenatal rubella or maternal exposure to rubella, leading them to the obvious conclusion that prenatal rubella can damage a child while manifesting no clinical symptoms in the mother.

In view of the above, it must be concluded that the assignment of etiology is fraught with inaccuracy at present. A substantial number of children classified as deaf by genetic causes probably have lost their hearing through disease. On the other hand, many children have been diagnosed with an etiology of disease, usually rubella, when the real cause has been genetic. There is no way of knowing which misdiagnosis is more common.

Early Investigations of Causality

From the time of Green's first census of the deaf in Massachusetts, educators of the deaf in America have been interested both in the prevalance and causes of deafness in the population. Analysis of the annual reports of the American School for the Deaf reveals consistent early attempts to identify and to classify as precisely as possible causes of hearing loss in students at the school. Similar efforts were made at other schools for the deaf in Europe and in the United

Table **4.1**   Causes of deafness in students at the American School, 1817–1844

| Category | Student status | | Total |
	Former students	In attendance in 1844	
Congenital	270	71	341
Unknown	87	9	96
Acquired			
Fever (140)	(107)	(31)	(140)
Spotted fever	45	1	46
Scarlet fever	20	22	44 (sic)
Fever	29	6	35
Typhus fever	11	1	12
Lung fever	1	1	2
Yellow fever	1	0	1
Sickness	76	8	84
Inflammation in head	24	6	30
Ulcers in head	14	8	22
Accidents	10	12	22
Measles	11	1	12
Whooping cough	8	4	12
Dropsy	5	0	5
Fits	2	2	4
Small pox	2	0	2
Palsy	2	0	2
Croup	1	0	1
Total *Acquired*	262	72	336
Totals	619	152	773

SOURCE: Adapted from L. Weld, *Twenty-eighth Annual Report of the American Asylum at Hartford for the Education of the Deaf and Dumb,* 1844, p. 38.

States, especially at the schools in New York City, Philadelphia, and Columbus, Ohio.

In an analysis of the records of 773 former and then current students at the American School, Weld (1844) reported that deafness was congenital, present at birth, in 341 cases (44%) and acquired in 336 cases (44%). For 96 individuals, or 12% of the total, there was insufficient information on which to make a judgment. Examination of Table 4.1 indicates that the two most commonly cited cases in the *acquired* category were *fever* of some kind ($n = 140$) and *sickness* ($n = 84$). Spotted fever was identified and was responsible for deafness

Table **4.2**   Causes of deafness in students at the American School, 1848

Category		Number		Percentage of total
Congenital		110		55.0
Acquired		86		43.0
Scarlet fever	41		20.5	
Ulcers	8		4.0	
Hooping cough (sic)	6		3.0	
Inflammation	4		2.0	
Dropsy of brain	4		2.0	
Scrofula	3		1.5	
Other	10		5.0	
Unknown		4		2.0
Totals		200		100.0

SOURCE: Adapted from W. Turner, "Causes of Deafness," *American Annals of the Deaf*, 1848, 125–132.

in 45 of 262 former students with acquired deafness, but for only 1 of 72 students with acquired deafness attending in 1844. This appears to be the only category with great difference between former and "current" students. Although no data are presented regarding age of onset of hearing loss, it may be assumed that the majority of students in the *acquired* category had achieved some level of proficiency in speech and language before losing their hearing, leading to the conclusion that the "deaf population" of the American School from 1817 to 1844 had a different composition than schools for the deaf in the present day, which consist of a large majority of students who either were born deaf or lost their hearing before the acquisition of language.

In a follow-up to Weld's report, Turner (1848) presented data on 200 deaf individuals who had been pupils at the American School (Table 4.2) and speculated on possible causes of deafness. There is probably some overlap between Turner's data and the "current" student data presented by Weld in 1844, but since the maximum term was six years, it is probably less than might be expected. Turner's data indicate that deafness was congenital in 55% of the cases ($n = 110$) and acquired, or accidental, for 43% of the students ($n = 86$). In 4 cases it was unclear whether the loss was congenital or acquired. Scarlet fever accounted for almost one-half of those with acquired deafness (41 of 86) and more than 20% of the entire student population. It is interesting to note that scarlet fever was the named cause of deafness for only 20 of 619 students at the school before 1844 (Table 4.1).

Turner's discussion of possible causes of deafness provides fascinating reading and contains evidence of great insight as well as some speculation that comes close to superstition. Among the latter is the somewhat diffidently advanced possibility that deafness might be caused by mental impressions of the mother before the birth of her child. In support of this possibility Turner reports the case of a woman who, attending a funeral while pregnant, was frightened by the scream of a deaf girl as the coffin was lowered. The image and sound stayed with the mother and, as she feared, her child was born deaf (p. 28). She and her child similarly influenced neighbors, and 4 families eventually produced 11 deaf children in a neighborhood where no deaf people previously had lived. To further buttress his case, Turner also pointed out several families with both acquired and congenital deafness, concluding:

If then, there be any connection between the accidental deafness of the first child and the congenital deafness of the next, it must be in the way already supposed; and the one event must be regarded as the cause of the other through the impression so sad an occurrence would naturally make upon the mother's mind. (pp. 29-30)

Given Turner's statement, it is quite possible that many of the cases classified as accidental or acquired by Weld and Turner were in actuality congenital in nature. Those cases cited in which the first child in a family was judged to have acquired deafness and a later child was born deaf might reflect the fact that deafness is not suspected in a child for some period of time but, given the presence of one deaf child in a family, parents are sensitive to the possibility of its occurrence and are more likely to diagnose it at an early age.

Although he believed a classification of congenital or accidental could be made with little room for doubt in most cases, Turner acknowledges that it was sometimes impossible to ascertain when or how a child became deaf. He described the process as follows:

Probably in a majority of instances the attention of parents is first called to the subject by the child's not beginning to articulate at the usual age. It is suggested that deafness may be the reason of this inability. A series of experiments is instituted, the result of which, is a clear conviction, in the minds of the parents, that such is the fact. They next inquire into the cause of deafness in their child; and if they can recall any severe sickness in its infancy, they conclude that this must have been the case, however unlikely to produce such a result. On the other hand, in some cases of accidental deafness, the true cause, having been less noticeable is overlooked, and the child is said to have been born deaf. (p. 26)

Turner also mentioned the intermarriage of near relations as a possible cause of deafness. Although he suggested that judgment be withheld pending future examination, he reported a widespread impression that there was a relationship between consanguineous marriages and deafness.

Perhaps the most extensive early analysis of the causes of acquired deafness was performed by a physician, Dudley Peet (1856),* who reported on the as-

* Dudley Peet, a physician, is not to be confused with Harvey Peet, the principal of the New York school.

Table **4.3**   Reported causes of acquired deafness in 13
schools for the deaf in Europe and the United States,
1856

Reported cause	Number
Diseases and accidents unknown	398
Scarlet fever	44
Fever (not named)	38
Measles	35
Colds	26
Convulsions	24
Inflammation in the head	20
Falls	19
Gatherings in the head	15
Scrofula	12
Whooping cough	12
Other	111
Total	754

SOURCE: From D. Peet, "The Remote and Proximate Causes
of Deafness," *American Annals of the Deaf*, 1856, 8,
129–130.

signed causes of acquired deafness in a total of 754 students from 13 schools for
the deaf, 9 in Europe and 4 in the United States (Table 4.3). It is interesting
to note that Peet classified approximately 50% of the cases of acquired deafness
under the heading *diseases and accidents unknown*, in contrast to Turner, who
classified only 4 cases as *unknown*. Except for that, no single cause or group
of causes appears to predominate.

D. Peet also presented information on the age of onset of deafness for 284 of
the cases (Table 4.4). If this group was representative of deaf students in general in the nineteenth century, the figures would seem to suggest that the
proportion of students who became deaf after age 3 was lower than most present-day educators assume. Peet's figures suggest that in more than half the
cases of acquired deafness the students lost their hearing by age 2, and almost
three-quarters lost their hearing by 36 months. Given the data of Turner and
Weld, which show that somewhat less than half the students in their studies
had acquired deafness, it may be stated that the postlingual population of nineteenth-century schools for the deaf might have been as small as 20%. For the
present, *postlingual* will be defined as 36 months or later.

Peet discussed in passing the possibility of hereditary transmission of deafness
by deaf parents, noting that there was a certain degree of danger, but emphasizing that the children of most marriages of deaf individuals had normal hearing.

Table **4.4**   Age of onset of deafness in 284 students, 1856

Age of onset	Number	Cumulative percentage
Birth to 12 months	94	33.1
12 to 24 months	73	58.8
24 to 36 months	41	73.2
36 to 48 months	19	79.9
48 to 60 months	27	89.4
60 months and older	30	100.0
Total	284	

SOURCE: From D. Peet, "The Remote and Proximate Causes of Deafness," *American Annals of the Deaf*, 1856, 8, 129–130.

He also mentioned the possibility of a predisposition to deafness resulting either from parental dissipation before gestation or from dissipation in youth.

Peet also commented on how a hereditary predisposition might manifest itself in what he termed *alternation*, where some children will be deaf and others hearing; he cited one family in which the second, fourth, sixth, eighth, tenth, twelfth, and fourteenth children were born deaf.

Sharing Turner's concern, Peet stated that of all the known causes, intermarriage was the most prolific cause of predisposition to deafness, stating:

It has been settled beyond a shadow of doubt, that intermarriages affected by cousins, and even some of second cousins, give rise to offspring which are generally either of small size, imperfect health, or of imperfect development in some part; they are either idiots, blind, clubfooted, or deaf and dumb. And those offspring of cousins who are not, are rather the exceptions than the rule. (pp. 132–133)

It is possible to examine trends in etiology in a 100-year period by comparing the data presented in the above-cited studies with census information for the United States from 1880 to 1920, bearing in mind that the data are incomplete, partially inaccurate, and subject to widely diverse interpretation.

Best (1943, p. 86) presented data on etiology of deafness from the five census investigations from 1880 to 1920. The most striking aspect of the census data is the by-now-familiar situation in which the largest single category includes those classified as *unknown and all other*, a category that appears to grow as a function of the drop in the percentage of individuals in the *scarlet fever* and *meningitis* categories. The census data really had only three major categories: *scarlet fever*, *meningitis*, and *measles*. The relative incidence of scarlet fever dropped from 26.5% in 1880 to 15.6% in 1920. Since scarlet fever accounted for only about 3.9% (20 of 619) of the students at the American School before

1844 (Table 4.1), 14.5% of current students in 1844 (Table 4.1), and 20.5% of students in 1848 (Table 4.2), it appears that the impact of scarlet fever on hearing in the United States was minor at the beginning of the nineteenth century and consistently increased, as the century progressed, reached a peak before the beginning of the twentieth century, then steadily declined, until at present it is of relatively little importance in childhood deafness.

The impact of meningitis is more difficult to ascertain, because the term was not employed in early investigations. It is probable that significant numbers of cases classified as *fever, sickness, inflammation,* and *unknown* would fall within this category, but it is impossible to estimate how many. The census data, however, report a drop from 28% of the total in 1880 to 13.8% in 1890, with the incidence figures remaining fairly constant thereafter.

Measles was named in less than 2% of the cases (12 of 773) by Weld (Table 4.1) and was identified in only 2 of 190 cases by Turner (1848). Those cases are included in the *other* category in Table 4.2. The census data list measles as a cause consistently in about 5% of the cases in each census from 1880 to 1920. The category refers to childhood measles, not maternal rubella.

Early Issues on Heredity and Deafness

As previously noted, early investigators into causes of deafness were greatly concerned with the possible influence of heredity on deafness, or at least the tendency toward deafness. As investigators searched for the causes of deafness, they did not operate in a vacuum, but rather were influenced by a number of forces operating in society at large. As the nineteenth century unfolded, more and more attention was given to consideration of the implications of Darwin's theories for human society. Toward the end of the century the question of the inheritability of intelligence, or of the relative influences of heredity and environment on human behavior, assumed the proportions of a great issue.

Coupled with the growing influence of Mendellian principles of genetic inheritance, the tenor of the times was definitely on the side of heredity, even in the United States, which might be expected to have exhibited more of an environmental bent. However, the initiation of land-grant colleges in the United States in the 1860s introduced principles of scientific experimentation on a widespread basis and, among other things, revolutionized agriculture across the world. Not only were old strains of food improved and new, more hardy, and productive strains developed, but also the selective breeding of livestock produced continuous and unexpected improvement. It is not surprising therefore to observe a growing interest in applying the concept of eugenics to human beings, that is, to improving the human race by influencing its breeding habits.

It is not surprising either that many individuals involved in animal breeding were also interested in human breeding and vice versa. Of those related to the field of education of the deaf, Alexander Graham Bell is best known. A member of several eugenics groups and of the American Breeders Association — his son-in-law was its president — one of Bell's many experiments involved attempts to induce multiple births in a mutant strain of sheep with multiple sets of nipples, reasoning that the mothers then could be responsible for doubling the economic yield of an investment in a flock (R. Bruce, 1973).

Despite the success of animal breeding techniques, eugenics has been a discredited concept — not completely justifiably — primarily because of its association with Hitler's racist policies in Germany. In the United States there has been a continued public reaction against it because of its identification with controversies over the possible existence of differences in intelligence among races.

Consanguinity

The comments about consanguineous marriages by Turner (1848) and D. Peet (1856) were part of a general concern about the apparent tendency of marriages of relatives to produce defective children to a much greater extent than marriages of unrelated individuals. Apparently the most influential mid-nineteenth-century study was conducted by Bemiss (1858), who investigated the extent to which 833 consanguineous marriages in the United States produced handicapped children. Bemiss found a total of 3,942 children produced from these marriages, of whom 1,134 were defective in one way or another, the largest categories being *idiotic* ($N = 308$), *scrofulous* ($N = 300$), *deaf and dumb* ($N = 145$), *deformed* ($N = 98$), and *blind* ($N = 85$). The results of his investigations in various state institutions led Bemiss to state: "Over 10% of the deaf and dumb and over 5% of the blind and near 15% of the idiotic in our State institutions for such subjects of these defects are offspring of kindred parents or of parents themselves the descendents of blood intermarriage" (p. 14).

Morris (1861) argued that the marriage of relatives was a violation of natural laws and that blindness, insanity, idiocy, lunacy, and other defects of mind and body were their legitimate consequences. In advocating the elimination of consanguineous marriages, Morris (1861) stated: "In all countries where there is a commingling of races, and where we find residents from every corner of the globe and employment for all, there it is that congenital deafness falls least heavily . . ." (p. 31). Morris quoted from a paper presented by Buxton in 1858, relating to his investigations in the British Isles as follows:

As regards the marriage of blood relations, there can be no question now as to the great influences which this cause exercises in the production of congenital deafness, as well as of every other physical and mental defect. In an inquiry which I made some time ago, — from a large number of persons, I found that about every tenth case of deafness resulted from the marriage of cousins. (p. 31)

The sensitivity toward consanguineous marriages apparently was influenced by a belief that heterogeneous populations were superior to homogeneous ones;

that the more alike parents were genetically, the greater the possibility of having affected children.   This position was strengthened by investigations show-ing tremendous variation in incidence figures for various handicaps in the countries of Europe, and sometimes even within different parts of the same country.

In relation to deafness H. Peet (1852, 1854) reported an incidence figure for congenital deafness in Europe of approximately 1:1,500 for the general popula-tion, stating that 615 of every 1 million children were born deaf, more than twice the rate of the United States.   Peet noted that the range was from 1 per 200 in the isolated Swiss canton of Bern to 1 per 2,180 in Saxony.   He pointed out (1854, p. 20) that in areas of Europe with stable populations, and therefore frequent intermarriage, the proportion of children born deaf was high.   The more heterogeneous the population, the lower was the rate of deafness re-ported.

In a report to the Paris Academy of Medicine, Maniere is reported (Morris, 1861) as arguing:

Marriage between near relatives is never met with more frequently, than in the localities where deaf-mutes are born in the greatest numbers; as in some of the valleys of Swit-zerland, where the inhabitants are almost shut out from communication with the neigh-boring countries, and present all the conditions favorable to those alliances among rela-tives. (p. 30)

Buxton (1858), using 1851 United Kingdom census figures, reported that the incidence of congenital deafness in the British Isles was highest in relatively isolated Scotland and lowest in England.   He is quoted by Morris (1861) as stating:

In Cornwall, Derbyshire, the northern counties of Scotland, among the stationary pop-ulation of Hertfordshire, in the mountainous parts of Ireland, in remote Norway and Al-pine Switzerland, the proportion of children born deaf is very large; for here the native intermarry among each other, age after age; from the cradle to the grave, the same peo-ple are found fixed to the same spot, pursuing the same occupations; no enterprise leads them abroad; nothing tempts the native of other locales to come and cast his lot among them; it is a continual process of transmitting the same blood and sinew, from genera-tion to generation; and the lowering of the healthy standard of the race is natural and in-evitable. (p. 31)

Despite the great interest in the effects of consanguinity during the nine-teenth century, a relatively large number of deaf children continue to be the products of the unions of blood relatives.   In a study of the deaf population of New York State, Sank and Kallman (1963) reported that 12% of the sample were the offspring of marriages of near relatives.   Referring to data over more than 40 years, Hudgins (1973) reported that approximately 5% of the students at the Clarke School for the Deaf were the offspring of consanguineous parents.

Marriages of the Deaf

Although educators of the deaf were aware early along that deaf parents have a greater likelihood than hearing parents of producing deaf children, marriages of the deaf were not treated with the same degree of concern as consanguineous marriages, at least not for the 50 years following the establishment of the first school in 1817. There were probably several reasons for this. First, it was well known that the majority of children produced from marriages of deaf individuals would have normal hearing. The proportion of children with normal hearing from such marriages probably was even higher in the nineteenth century than today because of the relatively high number of individuals whose deafness was not caused by genetic factors.

There also appeared to be a consensus that the marriage of blood relatives, with the indirect dangers of so many different kinds of disabilities surfacing in their children, was by far a more serious concern. Such a consensus was strengthened by the evidence that the deaf population in general in mid-nineteenth-century America was a self-sufficient, productive, contributing segment of society (Moores, Harlow, & Fisher, 1974). The feeling of the times was summed up by Turner (1848), who stated that, while it was not a surprise for congenital deaf parents to have deaf children, it was more likely their children would hear. Concerning marriages of deaf individuals, he believed that the possibility of having deaf children was so slight that

it need not deter them, when other circumstances render it proper, from entering the married state; especially when the fact is kept in mind that educated deaf-mutes generally manage their affairs judiciously; bring up their children well, and become useful and respectable members of the community. (p. 32)

For hearing educators of the deaf the presence of large numbers of deaf educators served as a constant reminder that the levels of sophistication and intellectual achievement which deaf individuals may attain are equal to those of the hearing. The esteem in which competent deaf educators were held may be illustrated by the fact that, at the time of his retirement, Thomas Hopkins Gallaudet, the acknowledged father of education of the deaf in America, was teaching a full load of classes in addition to his responsibilities as the chief administrative officer of the American School, yet he received a lower salary than Laurent Clerc, the first deaf teacher of the deaf in America (M. Boatner, personal interview, 1974).

The positive attitude toward deaf people in general and the role of deaf teachers began to change in the late 1860s, concomitant with the spread of the oral-only method. As the sole criterion for acceptability came to be the understandability of a person's speech, the influence of deaf individuals — especially those who were congenitally deaf — on the education of the deaf eroded quickly. It was only a short period of time until deaf teachers were excluded from teaching in many schools for the deaf and serious consideration was being given to mechanisms for restricting marriages of congenitally deaf adults.

However, this turn of events had not been anticipated by midcentury. Although the early schools for the deaf kept records of their graduates and attempted to maintain contact, the efforts do not appear to be as comprehensive as those involving questions of etiology. Of course, this is not an unusual situation even today. Most educational programs, of any nature, tend to possess more information on current students than on graduates. Gathering follow-up information is more time-consuming, tedious, and expensive, and it was especially so in the agrarian society of nineteenth-century America.

The information available seemed to provide little cause for alarm. Turner (1848, p. 32) reported that nearly 100 families of former students at the American School had been found who had married and that in about half the cases both parents were deaf. There were deaf children in only five families, while in the others — even of six to eight children — all were hearing. D. Peet (1856) reported that there was not enough evidence to form definite conclusions concerning the amount of transmission of hereditary deafness when one or both parents were deaf. He stated (p. 132) that he knew personally of only two families in which both parents were deaf and there was direct transmission of hereditary deafness, although he acknowledged that he had heard of several other instances.

H. Peet (1852) reported that deaf parents are more likely than hearing parents to have deaf children. He reported that in the marriages of two deaf individuals, approximately 5% (1 out of 20) of the children would be deaf. In cases of marriages of deaf and hearing individuals, the number of deaf children fell to less than 1% (1 out of 135) of the children. In this context, Peet also investigated the hearing status of the children of the hearing siblings of his deaf subjects and came to the following conclusion: "The brothers and sisters of a deaf mute are about as liable to have deaf mute children as the deaf mute himself, supposing each to marry into families that have or each into families that have not shown a predisposition toward deaf dumbness" (p. 21).

Twenty years after he had reported deafness in only five families of married graduates of the American School, Turner (1868) reported a far greater incidence of deafness in the offspring of the school's graduates (Table 4.5). The incidence figures for the latter report probably present a more accurate picture of the situation.

Approximately one-half of the marriages (56 of 110) involved a hearing partner, a higher proportion than might be anticipated, and far in excess of current figures for marriage of deaf and hearing individuals. Also, the average family size would seem to be smaller than the norm for that period, with a total of 275 children in 110 families, or 2.5 children per family.

In 1883 Bell published his *Memoir on the development of a deaf variety of the human race,* in which he argued that the educational system then set up for the deaf in America was inadvertently contributing to an increase in the incidence of deafness. Bell stated (1883a): "The production of a defective [sic] race of human beings would be a tragedy. Before the deaf were educated intermarriage was so rare as to be almost unknown. Intermarriages have been

Table 4.5   Hearing status of children of graduates of the American School for the Deaf, 1868

Marriage patterns		Number of children		
Hearing status of parents	Number of families	Deaf	Hearing	Total
Deaf × deaf	30	15	77	92
Deaf × hearing	56	6	120	126
Congenital deaf × incidental deaf	24	17	40	57
Totals	110	38	237	275

SOURCE: Compiled from data collected by W. Turner, "Hereditary Deafness," *Proceedings of the National Conference of Principals of Institutes for the Deaf and Dumb*. Washington, D.C., 1968, pp. 91–96.

promoted by our methods of instruction"* (p. 41). Among the forces he saw as contributing toward the formation of a deaf variety of the human race were:

1. Segregation of children into institutional schools for the deaf

2. Reunions of graduates of these institutions, and organizations of the deaf into societies, including national associations of the deaf

3. Development by deaf groups of their own periodicals and newspapers

4. Instruction of the deaf by the "gesture language," which interferes with English and therefore forces the deaf to associate with each other

5. Widespread employment of deaf teachers

In Bell's opinion (1883a, 1884) the above factors increased the chances of deaf people's marrying each other and therefore propagating deafness. In his arguments, he placed great reliance on data from six schools for the deaf in America, with the most extensive data being provided for students from the American School for the Deaf. Bell noted that of 2,106 pupils who had attended the American School, 693, or nearly 33%, were known to have had deaf relatives (p. 9) and that of 5,823 pupils from the six schools all together,

---

* The term *defective* as used by Bell and other authors is a term with which the present author disagrees.

1,719, or 29%, had deaf relatives (p. 11). The percentages were even higher when only those students who were known to be congenitally deaf were considered.

Bell discussed a number of possibilities for reducing the incidence of deafness, stating that "a law forbidding congenitally deaf persons from families from intermarrying would go a long way towards dealing with the evil" and that "legislation forbidding the intermarriage of persons containing more than one deaf mute would be more practical" (p. 46). Bell, however, concluded that it was doubtful whether legislative interference would be advisable (p. 46) and proposed that the marriage of deaf people to other deaf people could be done away with by (1) the elimination of educational segregation, (2) the elimination of gesture language, and (3) the elimination of deaf teachers. In other words, if deaf children were educated in integrated, oral-only environments without exposure to deaf adults, there would be little or no motivation to marry other deaf individuals when they came of age.

Although Bell's desire to reduce the incidence of deafness is understandable, his interpretation of data was inconsistent, and he had no justification to believe the marriage of deaf people would produce "a deaf variety of the human race." A case in point is his treatment of the data for former students of the American School (p. 9). While it is true that 693 of 2,106 had deaf relatives, Bell's own tables indicate that only 2% (43 of 2,100) had deaf parents. Of this number only 25 had both a deaf mother and a deaf father, and 18 had one hearing and one deaf parent. Thus the elimination of the marriages of deaf people with other deaf people would have reduced the American School's student population over more than 60 years by a total of 25, that is, reducing it from 2,106 to 2,081.

It is puzzling why Bell chose to concentrate on marriages of the deaf to the exclusion of other causes of deafness. For example, he must have been aware of the literature indicating that deafness was caused far more frequently by consanguineous marriages of hearing individuals than by marriages of unrelated deaf people, yet he never addressed this problem. Even more mystifying is his lack of expressed concern over the most common cause of acquired deafness of that period, the disease that deafened both his mother and his wife in early childhood, scarlet fever.

Bell expounded his ideas forcefully, especially his opposition to sign language, which, according to R. Bruce (1973, p. 393), he considered to be ideographic, imprecise, inflexible, and lacking in subtlety and power of abstraction; it was a narrow prison intellectually and socially. In 1887 Bell presented his position in a talk on inheritance to the Gallaudet College Literary Society, during which E. A. Fay provided a running translation in sign language (R. Bruce, 1973, p. 411). There is no indication that any part of the translation suffered from imprecision, inflexibility, or lack of abstraction.

Bell graciously turned over his data to Fay, who at the time was vice president of Gallaudet College, and helped him conduct an expanded and more complete version of his own investigation, the final results of which were published by the Volta Bureau (Fay, 1898). The major conclusions may be summarized as follows:

1. Deaf individuals are less likely to marry than hearing individuals.

2. Those deaf individuals who do marry tend to have fewer children.

3. Deaf people tend to marry deaf people.

4. When both parents are deaf, the marriage is more likely to be a happy one, with a lower incidence of divorce or separation.

5. Despite Bell's arguments for integration and elimination of sign language, those who attend day schools and exclusively oral schools still tend to marry deaf people. This is true even of those who attend *no* program for the deaf.

6. Deaf Americans marry more often than deaf Europeans.

7. The large majority of offspring were hearing even when both parents were deaf.

   a. When both parents were adventitiously deaf, 2.3% of the children were deaf.

   b. When both parents were congenitally deaf, 25.9% of the children were deaf.

   c. When both parents were congenitally deaf but had no deaf relatives, 4% of the children were deaf.

Fay's comments concerning the position of the European deaf suggest they continued to suffer from the same deprivations at the turn of the century that had existed more than 50 years. Fay stated (p. 6) that almost half the deaf adults in Europe were dependent upon others for their support. The highest rate of marriage was reported for Denmark, where 23.7% of deaf adults were married. In the German states the figure was around 10%.

Publication of Fay's findings tended to mute some of the more outspoken opposition to marriages of deaf individuals, although it has never died out completely. Even though Bell was instrumental in disseminating Fay's *Marriages of the deaf in America*, his own *Memoir* remains widely known and quoted, perhaps partially because of its provocative title.

Much definitive work on hereditary childhood deafness has grown out of Bell's support of research on hereditary deafness conducted at the Clarke School for the Deaf. In summing up what is known to date on the effects of the marriages of deaf individuals on the incidence of deafness in the population, Brown, Hopkins, and Hudgins (1967) conclude:

In evolutionary terms, hundreds of generations, the frequency of genes causing deafness will rise if all other conditions remain the same. In the short run, say the next ten generations, it is to be expected that there will be no noticeable increase in the frequency of identified genetic deafness that cannot be attributed to factors other than increase in gene frequency. The effect of individual decisions about reproduction among the deaf will not be significant in terms of the population because most genetic deafness results from matings of hearing parents. (p. 101)

Contemporary Identified Causes of Deafness

In many cases, determining the causes of deafness in children remains a difficult process, and it is not surprising that, even today, *etiology unknown* accounts for a sizable proportion of the deaf school-aged population. In general, however, a number of major causes of early-childhood deafness may be identified that would be acknowledged by a majority of observers, even though there might be a great diversity of opinion about the relative incidence of deafness attributed to those causes. The most common presently identified causes of childhood deafness are: heredity, maternal rubella, meningitis, prematurity, and mother-child blood incompatability.

In a survey of the reported causes of hearing loss for 41,109 students enrolled in programs for the deaf during the 1970–1971 school year, Reis (1973a) reported that causes were identified for 21,193 students, or only 51.6% of the total. In 9,784 cases (23.8%), programs reported that the cause had never been determined. In an additional 10,132 cases (24.6%), either the information was not available or the schools left the item blank on the reporting form (Reis, 1973a, p. 2). It is probable that in a substantial number of such cases the cause was not determined. Table 4.6 presents etiological data on reported causes of deafness of the total 41,109 students. Examination of Table 4.6 reveals that the most commonly reported cause of childhood deafness was maternal rubella, with an incidence of 147.8 per 1,000, or approximately 1 in every 7 students. The only other causes accounting for more than 3% of the population were heredity (7.48%), prematurity (5.37%), meningitis (4.91%), and Rh incompatibility (3.41%). All except meningitis are prenatal causes. Further examination of Table 4.6 reveals relatively little fluctuation across the age groups, with the exception of the incidence figures for rubella, which accounts for 36.19% of all causes in children 5 to 7 years old and only 2.87% for those 14 to 16 years old. The cyclical nature of rubella is observed easily, and the results of the 1958–1959 and 1964–1965 epidemics are apparent for two age groups: 11 to 13 and 5 to 7. Reis (p. 4) also notes that the rate for rubella for those under age 5 (21.21%) is accounted for mostly by those born in 1966 and also reflects the effects of the 1964–1965 epidemic.

Two other sources should be discussed which, although they did not draw from as large a sample, probably are more accurate to the extent that each one relies on a systematic program of data collection and analysis from a single school and therefore does not have to rely on a variety of sources of uneven quality. The first source (Vernon, 1968) consists of information on all children ($n = 1,468$) for whom application was made for entrance into the California School for the Deaf, Riverside, from 1953 to 1964. The second source is

Table **4.6**   Reported causes of deafness for students enrolled in educational programs in the United States, 1970–1971

	Number of students						
	All ages	Under 5 years	5–7 years	8–10 years	11–13 years	14–16 years	17 years & older
	41,109	2,527	10,216	7,529	9,509	6,749	4,569
Causes[a]	Number per 1,000 students[b]						
Prenatal							
Maternal rubella	147.8	212.1	361.9	57.9	106.2	28.7	44.6
Heredity	74.8	79.1	53.5	81.8	74.6	92.6	82.1
Prematurity	53.7	52.2	45.4	54.7	58.1	66.4	43.3
Rh incompatibility	34.1	34.4	22.6	35.1	34.3	44.1	42.9
Other[a]	79.8	85.0	64.6	89.2	81.2	90.3	76.1
Unknown	188.3	230.3	149.7	196.7	189.5	193.4	227.6
Not reported	112.5	92.2	83.6	121.5	126.4	127.2	122.6
Postnatal							
Meningitis	49.1	72.4	40.8	59.1	44.1	45.6	53.6
Other[a]	132.3	83.9	84.5	147.7	141.7	176.2	162.6
Unknown	49.7	37.6	36.9	56.4	53.2	55.9	57.3
Not reported	134.0	79.9	115.0	156.3	144.5	142.5	134.8

[a]Only etiologies with an incidence of more than 30 per 1,000 (3%) are included. Remaining etiologies are classified in the *other* category.

[b]Each column sums to more than 1,000 because, for about 5% of the students, more than one cause of hearing-impaired loss was reported (Reis, 1973a, p. s).

SOURCE: Adapted from P. Reis, *Reported Causes of Hearing Loss for Hearing Impaired Students*, Washington, D.C., Annual Survey of Hearing Impaired Children and Youth, Ser. D, No. 12, Washington, D.C., Gallaudet College, 12, 1973, pp. 3–4.

information on students enrolled at the Clarke School for the Deaf during the 1972–1973 academic year (Hudgins, 1973), a school that traditionally has devoted more attention to investigations into causes of deafness than any other school in the United States.

Vernon (1968) presented both minimum and maximum incidence figures in order to provide an understanding of the possible range within categories (Table 4.7). Thus, for example, if only children with deaf parents are included, the incidence of hereditary deafness is 5.4%. If the definition is expanded to include children with any family history of deafness, the percentage rises to

Table **4.7** Minimum and maximum incidence rates for major etiologies of deafness, California School for Deaf, Riverside, 1953–1964

	Incidence estimate			
	Minimum		Maximum [a]	
Etiology	*Number*	*Percentage*	*Number*	*Percentage*
Prematurity	175	11.9	257	17.4
Rubella	129	8.8	139	9.5
Meningitis	119	8.1	128	8.7
Heredity	79	5.4	384	26.0
Rh factor	45	3.1	54	3.7
Other	474	32.3	142	9.6
Unknown	447	30.4	447	30.4
Total	1468	100.0	1551	105.3

[a] *Number* and *percentage* columns for the *maximum* category sum to more than 1,468 and 100% of the sample because in approximately 5% of the cases more than one possible cause was listed.

SOURCE: Adapted from M. Vernon, "Current Etiological Factors in Deafness," *American Annals of the Deaf*, 1968, *113*, 106–125, 108–110.

26%. The other major etiological category showing a large discrepancy between the minimum and maximum rates is *prematurity*, accounting for 11.9% when no other known cause of deafness was present, rising to 17.4% when it was combined with such other factors as rubella, Rh factor, family deafness, and meningitis.

Vernon claimed that his data provide more accurate and comprehensive information than other studies because his sample includes all children who applied to an educational program, not just those students who were admitted. Because a significant percentage of deaf children are not admitted into existing school programs, limiting an investigation only to those in school restricts its comprehensiveness.

Vernon's incidence figures are similar to those reported by Reis (1973a). The same five major categories are identified: *prematurity, rubella, meningitis, heredity,* and *Rh factor*. They account for 37.3% of all causes in Vernon's minimum incidence estimates and 42.95% for Reis's data. Vernon reports 30.4% of subjects as *etiology unknown*, and Reis reports 38.4%. Within the major categories the biggest differences are in *rubella*, to be expected because Vernon's data did not include children from the 1964–1965 epidemic, and in *prematurity*, where Vernon's percentages are two to three times as great.

Hudgins (1973) reported on the causes of deafness for students enrolled at the

Table 4.8   Reported causes of deafness among students at the Clarke School for the Deaf, 1972–1973

Category	Number	Percentage total
Acquired deafness	95	45.03
Rubella	51	24.17
Blood incompatibility	14	6.64
Prematurity	12	5.69
Meningitis	8	3.79
Other	6	2.84
Questionable	4	1.90
Congenital (deaf parents or siblings)	48	22.75
Unknown	68	32.23
Total	211	100.01 [a]

[a] Percentage exceeds 100% because of rounding.

SOURCE: From R. Hudgins, *Clarke School for the Deaf 106th Annual Report*, Northampton, Mass., 1973, pp. 59–60.

Clarke School for the Deaf during the 1972–1973 school year. Consistent with other investigations, the five major reported etiologies were rubella, blood incompatability, prematurity, meningitis, and heredity. The terminology employed by Hudgins is somewhat different. Her two major categories are *congenital*, which included only those with deaf parents of siblings, and *acquired*. This is similar to the criteria for the maximum incidence classification of *heredity* used by Vernon in Table 4.7. Hudgins includes all other major etiologies under the *acquired deafness* category, whereas Reis (Table 4.6) differentiates between prenatal and postnatal causes. Therefore Reis's prenatal and postnatal incidence figures cannot be compared directly with Hudgins's *congenital* and *acquired* categories.

Examination of Table 4.8 reveals that for 32.23% of the students (68 of 211) etiology was unknown, a figure similar to the 30.4% reported by Vernon for the California School for the Deaf, Riverside. The tendency for investigators in different parts of the country to come up with almost identical figures placing so many children in the *unknown* category is impressive, especially given the care with which the Clarke and Riverside schools approached the task. It illustrates how inadequate present knowledge concerning etiology is. In a recent longitudinal evaluation of seven preschool programs throughout the United States, Moores, Weiss, and Goodwin (1973a) reported that etiology was unknown in 32.4% of the children, a percentage almost identical to those reported by Vernon and by Hudgins.

In terms of the major etiological factors, incidence figures appear to be consistent with those previously presented. The somewhat higher rubella rates probably represent the incorporation of the full brunt of the 1964–1965 epidemic into the school population. The number of cases involving prematurity are close to those of Reis and much lower than Vernon's, again possibly because Vernon's data include school applicants who had been rejected as well as those who had been accepted. The somewhat higher figures for the *blood incompatibility* category may reflect the inclusion of ABO and Rh factor blood complications in the Clarke data.

Discussion: Major Contemporary Causes of Deafness

Evidence has been presented to document five major identified causes of childhood deafness in the United States today: heredity, maternal rubella, prematurity, meningitis, and mother-child blood incompatibility. Of these, only heredity and meningitis were identified as major etiological factors during the nineteenth century. This, of course, does not mean that the others were not major factors — just that they were not identified as such.

A short discussion of each etiology is in order. It is most appropriate to begin with a discussion of hereditary childhood deafness because it possibly accounts for more deafness than any other cause, is so inadequately understood, frequently is so difficult to diagnose, and therefore provides such difficulty in making future projections.

Hereditary Childhood Deafness

The term *hereditary deafness* is a generic label for a wide variety of conditions. For example, Konigsmark (1969a, 1969b, 1969c, 1972a, 1972b) identifies over 60 types of hereditary hearing loss that may be differentiated by *type of transmission* (dominant, recessive, sex-linked), *age of onset* (congenital, adolescence, adulthood), *type of loss* (conductive, sensorineural) and *frequencies affected* (low-frequency, midfrequency, or high-frequency hearing loss). The present discussion is limited to those individuals with severe, congenital sensorineural losses, that is, children who are likely to be served by educational programs for the deaf. Causes of hereditary hearing loss in the teens (e.g., Alport syndrome) or later life (otosclerosis) will not be considered.

Although it has been acknowledged that a high proportion of the incidence of congenital deafness is hereditary, reasonably accurate estimates have not been established. It is obvious that Vernon's (1968) minimum estimate of 5.4% and Reis's (1973a) 7.1% are low. When Vernon's criteria were expanded to include all children for whom family deafness existed, the percentage rose to 26%. Using the same criteria for Reis's data, the percentage would rise to 19.9% (1973, p. 16). This percentage itself must be considered a minimum because for approximately one-third the students family history was not reported. Hudgins (1973) reported that 22.75% of students at the Clarke school had deaf parents and/or siblings. Unlike Vernon and Reis, she did not include other relatives. Vernon (1968, p. 109) reported an incidence figure of 6.2% of children having deaf relatives other than parents or siblings. If a similar ratio held for the Clarke population, then a prevalence figure of 28 to 30% (22.75 + 6.2) of students at the Clarke school having deaf relatives seems reasonable. Thus incidence figures from the California School for the Deaf (Vernon, 1968), and from the Clarke School for the Deaf (Hudgins, 1973), and from 555 educational programs for the deaf in the United States (Reis, 1973a) reveal that from 16 to 30% of deaf children have deaf relatives, suggesting that for those children, the cause of hearing loss is related to, if not caused by, genetic factors. Reis reports (1973a, pp. 13–14) that 17% of students with an etiology of Rh incompatibility had another family member with a hearing loss and that 87% with an etiology of meningitis had a family member with a hearing loss. Reis notes: "In the absence of other information, geneticists usually assume that if a hearing impaired person has a parent or sibling who is hearing impaired, the hearing loss is due to genetic factors. This assumption may sometimes be incorrect" (p. 14).

It is interesting to compare the estimates from the three studies—that 26 to 30% of the deaf school population in the United States in the 1960s and 1970s had deaf relatives — with Bell's figures for the nineteenth century. He reported (1883, p. 9) that 33% (693 of 2,106) of students who had enrolled at the American School had deaf relatives. For six schools studied (p. 11) the figure was 29%, or 1,719 out of a total of 5,823 students. The evidence suggests that the proportion has remained remarkably stable over a period of time.

On the other hand, there are large numbers of congenitally deaf children whose loss was caused by recessive transmission and whose family histories show no evidence of deafness. The extent to which this factor contributes to the population of deaf children is unclear, but it probably is large.

Konigsmark and McKusick (1966) reported that at least one-third of the students at the Indiana, Ohio, and Maryland schools were hereditarily deaf. Other studies have placed the percentage in excess of 50% (Sank & Kallman, 1963).

Recessive congenital deafness   Recessive deafness typically is transmitted to a child by clinically normal parents, that is, by parents who themselves have no hearing loss but who are carriers of genes for deafness. In a simplified example, the case may be presented as follows:

Let H = gene for normal hearing
h = recessive gene for deafness

If each parent has the gene pair Hh, each will have normal hearing but be a carrier. The possibility of having a deaf child (hh) would be 1 out of 4:

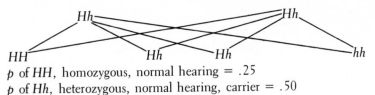

p of HH, homozygous, normal hearing = .25
p of Hh, heterozygous, normal hearing, carrier = .50
p of hh, homozygous, deaf = .25

In this case, 25% of children would have normal hearing and carry no genes for deafness; 50% would have normal hearing and, like their parents, would be carriers; 25% would be deaf.

This type of recessive transmission of deafness accounts for as much as 40% of early profound childhood deafness, (K. Brown, 1967; K. Brown, et al., 1967; Konigsmark, 1972a, 1972b). However, it is clear that several different genes may produce congenital recessive deafness; that is, genes causing deafness may exist at different genetic loci. From an examination of records, Chung and Brown (1970) concluded that four or five relatively common recessive genes produced most of the cases of congenital deafness in students at the Clarke school. K. Brown et al. (1967) estimated the existence of 30 to 150 recessive genes for deafness in the general population. These same investigators pointed out that the marriage of two hereditarily deaf individuals may involve persons whose deafness results from different genes and whose children therefore would have normal hearing. Regarding incidence figures of this type of marriage, they reported: "About half of the marriages of hereditary deaf reported at Clarke School are of this type in which both partners are hereditary deaf but due to different genes so that they run no higher risk of having a deaf child than does a couple with normal hearing" (p. 98).

Related to questions of consanguinity, several investigators (Hudgins, 1973; Konigsmark, 1972; Sank & Kallman, 1963) have noted that the pedigrees for recessively transmitted deafness, as well as for a wide spectrum of diseases, frequently involve the offspring of consanguineous marriages.

K. Brown et al. (1967, p. 101) postulate that mutation and/or other factors may be maintaining the gene frequency for deafness, estimating a mutation rate of 4×10^{-5} (0.00004) for both dominant and recessive loci. If correct, this would mean that 1 out of every 4 hearing persons in the general population is a carrier for at least one of the recessive genes causing childhood deafness.

Dominant congenital deafness   Estimates of dominant transmission of heredi-tary deafness usually range from 10 to 15% of the cases of early-childhood deafness (K. Brown et al., 1967; Konigsmark, 1972a, 1972b). In this situation a single gene can produce the deafness. For example, if A = dominant gene for deafness, and B = gene for hearing, the heterozygous combination AB would produce deafness. In a marriage involving a heterozygous AB with a homozygous BB, one-half the offspring would be deaf (AB). The other half, BB, would have normal hearing and would not be carriers, as shown below:

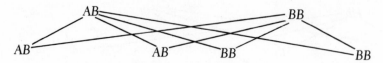

It should be stressed that hereditary hearing loss, as well as inheritance of other traits, is affected by the penetrance of the gene. *Penetrance* may be defined as a statistical concept referring to the frequency with which a genetic abnormality is manifested among those possessing the genes involved. For example, in the Waardenburg syndrome only 20% of those with the dominant gene are deaf. K. Brown et al. (1967) estimate the penetrance, or "expressivity," when referring to the severity of the disorder in a particular individual to be 80 to 100% for dominant genes and 100% for recessive genes. Davis (1970), on the other hand, states: "With the recognition of the low penetrance of some genes that produce deafness it becomes reasonable that the majority of cases of unexplained severe congenital hearing loss and deafness are actually sporadic hereditary deafness" (p. 26).

Sex-linked congenital deafness   Males and females differ genetically in that females have two X chromosomes and males have one X and one Y chromosome. The sex of a child is determined by whether the father contributes an X chromosome or a Y chromosome. XX children will be female, and XY children will be male, as follows:

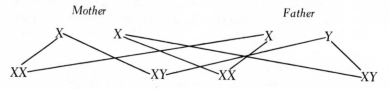

The X chromosomes also carry other genes, some of which may be abnormal. In the XX pairing they may function as recessive, making the mother normal, but a carrier. In the XY pairing the abnormal gene would not be inhibited, thus affecting the male offspring. In cases of sex-linked disease, males but not females are affected. The most widely known disease of this type is hemophelia. Transmission is as follows:

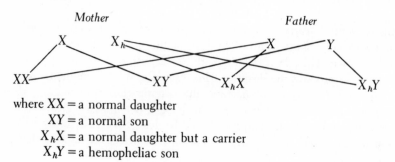

where XX = a normal daughter
    XY = a normal son
    $X_h X$ = a normal daughter but a carrier
    $X_h Y$ = a hemopheliac son

Another example of sex-linked transmission involves certain types of color blindness that are much more common in males than females. Sex-linked congenital deafness appears to be a factor in a relatively small number of cases. Konigsmark (1972) quotes studies showing it to be involved in about 3% of the cases of early-childhood deafness. K. Brown et al. (1967) report sex-linked genes or other segregating genes with sex influence as accounting for less than 2% of the cases of childhood deafness.

Future projections   The evidence seems to suggest that hereditary deafness, especially of a recessive nature, will continue to be a major etiological category for some time to come. Given the apparent low penetrance of some genes, the numbers of different genes that may cause deafness, mutations, and the high proportion of hearing individuals who are carriers, the prevention of hereditary deafness is extremely difficult.

In discussing the general question of genetic health and transmission of disease, Lappe (1973) put the question into perspective and in doing so mirrored the thinking of nineteenth-century investigators who have been quoted earlier in this chapter. He argued:

One of the emerging concepts of genetics is that genetic diversity — per se — is itself of great value for species survival. . . .   While there is no way for everyone in a freely marrying population such as ours to become, or remain, heterozygous for any one gene, the survival of the population is reinforced by many people being heterozygous for different genes. . . .   As long as this diversity exists, there will be genetic disease and disability due to the chance coming together of the same deleterious recessive genes. . . . Thus the greatest paradox of the concept of genetic health is that, while from a population point of view, the "healthiest" individuals are those who carry the greatest number of genes in the heterozygous state, they are also the ones at greatest risk for transmitting genetic disease. (p. 9)

Maternal Rubella

While it was not associated with hearing loss until World War II, maternal rubella was identified as the greatest cause of hearing loss in the middle 1960s and has been recognized as the major nongenetic cause for school-aged deaf children well into the 1970s. The effects of the 1964–1965 epidemic continue to be felt and will do so throughout the lives of those affected. Unlike hereditary deafness, rubella frequently is associated with other handicapping conditions, ranging from blindness to heart defects.

Rubella is a common virus disease, frequently benign and difficult to diagnose clinically. Approximately 20% of women of childbearing age have had it and therefore have developed an immunity (Masland, 1968). If they have rubella during the first trimester (3 months) of pregnancy, and sometimes later, it may kill or cripple their unborn children by crossing the placental barrier and attacking the fetus. The virus is capable of killing growing cells, and it attacks growing tissues of the eye, ear, and/or other organs.

The fact that a "rubella epidemic" on the scale of the 1964–1965 epidemic, or even the 1958–1959 epidemic, did not occur in the early 1970s suggests that procedures such as immunizations and therapeutic abortions have had some effect. However, although the means to do so apparently exist, deafness that results from maternal rubella has not been eradicated. Unfortunately, even when aware of the dangers, many people simply do not bother to get vaccinated. While in the long run the prognosis is favorable, some problems raised by Chenoweth (1969) must still be considered:

1. How can the spread of the disease by "rubella babies," who may excrete the virus for as long as three years, be prevented?
2. Women being vaccinated should not become pregnant for at least 2 months, because of danger to the fetus from the attenuated virus.
3. Pregnant women should not be vaccinated because of danger to the fetus. (p. 5)

Mother-Child Blood Incompatibility

Although other types of blood incompatibility have been associated with deafness (e.g., ABO), Rh-factor complications represent the major cause of this type. The difficulty arises in a woman who is Rh− (she does not have the factor) carrying an Rh+ fetus. The mother's system develops antibodies that may pass into fetal circulation and destroy the Rh+ cells of the fetus. Although there is less danger in the first or second pregnancy, sufficient antibodies may be developed by the third pregnancy or later to endanger the fetus. The result is known as *erythroblastosis fetalis*, a breaking down of fetal blood cells. If the pathology affects the brain in a certain way, it is known as *kernicterus*. The mortality rate for this condition is quite high. Of the survivors, the incidence of deafness, cerebral palsy, aphasia, and retardation is high. Vernon (1967a) reports that over 70% of Rh-factor deaf children had multiple handicaps.

Given the presence of widespread additional residua of Rh-factor involvement in addition to deafness, it is heartening to know that we have the means to eliminate Rh deafness (Goodhill, 1967, 1968). Today the Rh− mother suspected of having an Rh+ fetus can be studied through transabdominal amniocenteses. Thus delivery timing, fetal transfusions, and exchange transfusions can be based on biochemical information. The possibilities of an anti-Rh gamma globulin are great. However, all of this depends on good prenatal care, something that many mothers do not receive. Thus Rh factor remains a cause of deafness.

Meningitis

Meningitis usually involves a bacterial invasion of the labyrinths by way of the air-cell systems in the middle ear or by way of the meninges (Lindsay, 1967). It remains the most common cause of postnatal deafness in the school-aged population. Best (1943) reported that it accounted for 28% of all deafness in 1880 and approximately 15% from 1890 to 1920. More recent incidence figures (Hudgins, 1973; Reis, 1973; Vernon, 1967b) range from approximately 5 to 7%, reflecting perhaps a decrease resulting from the development of antibiotics and chemotherapy (Lindsay, 1967).

Vernon (1967a) has pointed out that changes in treatment have also lowered the age of onset for those who do have a residuum of deafness. As an example, he cites the case of tuberculous meningitis, which historically had a 100% mortality rate but which Fisch (1964) reported as an etiology of 106 cases in a British sample of 1,509. Vernon noted 5 cases in his California sample, among whom there was a wide variety of handicaps other than deafness. It seems clear that, although the proportional contribution of meningitis to deafness has decreased, those whom it afflicts tend to have other severe handicaps in addition to deafness.

Prematurity

Evaluation of the impact of prematurity, per se, on the incidence of deafness is extremely difficult. Although it is evident that prematurity (defined as a birthweight of 5 pounds, 8 ounces or less) is more common among the deaf population than among the normal hearing, the degree to which it is a causative factor is debatable. An additional complication is the fact that it also occurs in conjunction with other identified major etiologies. For example, in Vernon's data (1967c), 43% of the rubella and 14% of the Rh factor cases were also premature.

It is reasonable to speculate that, as improved medical techniques save premature children, the number of children with severe handicaps related to prematurity will increase. The lower the birthweight, the greater will be the danger of damage from, for example, intracranial bleeding and anoxia. Thus, an increase in the number of deaf children with additional handicaps related to prematurity is predicted.

Conclusion

Of the five major known etiologies of early-childhood deafness, hereditary deafness is the most common, occurring in as many as 50% of all cases. It is also the only major etiology not associated with high prevalence of other handicapping conditions. The incidence of deafness that results from heredity, especially recessive inheritance, is expected to remain at its present level for the foreseeable future.

Deafness from etiologies of rubella and Rh-factor incompatibility should decline markedly. A decline in the incidence of deafness related to meningitis has been observed and should continue, but in those children affected the condition may be associated more commonly with other severe handicapping conditions. The incidence of deafness related to prematurity will probably rise, with those affected, again, being susceptible to other handicapping conditions. In sum:

1. The incidence of genetic early-childhood deafness should remain stable.

2. The incidence of nongenetic early-childhood deafness should decrease, though a higher percentage of this group will have multiple handicaps.

3. Even if the overall incidence decreases, relative to the general population, the numbers of children in educational programs may very likely remain stable or increase because of an increasing tendency, as noted in Chapter 1 for programs: (a) to extend services to time of identification, (b) to serve minority children, (c) to provide for children with mild and moderate losses, and (d) to develop programs for children with multiple handicaps who presently are not receiving an education.

5

Families and Deaf Children: Interpersonal Relations from Diagnosis to Adulthood

Introduction

Nuclear family units may be viewed as organisms with relatively uniform life cycles possessing identifiable periods of growth, change, and decline. Typically, they may be conceived of as moving from the original dyadic unit — the husband and wife alone — through stages involving the bearing of children, the education of children, and the preparation of adolescents and young adults for independent existence. Finally, the process comes full cycle, ending in the aging family, in which the original family members — the husband and wife — once again constitute the nuclear family unit.

Based on Duvall's (1970) criteria, the following family stages may be identified for the purposes of this chapter:

1. The childless married couple
2. The childbearing family
3. The family with preschool children
4. The family with school-aged children
5. The family with adolescent children
6. The family launching young adults
7. The aging family

When a family moves from one stage to another, the roles and functions of its members are subject to change. During periods of change there is a greater degree of tension, and the possibility of role conflict and family disintegration is increased. Available evidence suggests that the presence of a handicapped child tends to exacerbate normal family strains and frequently hinders a smooth transition from one stage to another. In this chapter, we will examine what is known about family dynamics when a handicapped child is present and draw the implications for the adequate development and functioning of families that have one or more deaf children.

In order to provide a framework in which families and their individual members might be studied, the following assumptions have been made (Aldous, 1969):

1. Family behavior is a resultant of past experience of family members as incorporated in the present as well as their goals and expectations for the future.
2. Families develop and change over time in similar and consistent fashion.
3. Humans initiate actions due to maturational and social development as well as react to environmental pressures.
4. The family and its members must perform time specific tasks set by associations in the broader society and their own selves.
5. The individual in a social setting is the basic autonomous unit. (p. 709)

Although all the above assumptions are important, two points about assumption 1 are of overriding concern and should constantly be borne in mind. First, if family behavior is a result of *past* experience of family members, then the presence of a deaf child may be accompanied by extreme trauma, because most parents of deaf children have had minimal prior exposure to deafness. Second, the presence of a deaf child raises uncertainty and calls into question goals and expectations about the future, not only for the deaf child but also for the mother, father, and siblings.

As noted by Moores (1972b), it is imperative that professionals begin to study the impact of deafness in the family as well as on the child. Much more than just a loss of hearing is involved. The family's whole world is changed, and feelings of guilt, confusion, and helplessness are both common and natural. Professionals must develop ways of dealing effectively with these feelings if the whole family is to be helped.

In this context, it is of limited benefit to consider the deaf child, or the family, as separate entities. The reciprocal nature of parent-child and child-child interactions cannot be overemphasized. The deaf child is a member of a social group. As such, he or she exerts considerable influence on the role and function of each member of the group. In turn, as a participating member, the deaf child is influenced by the group as a whole and by its individual members. The complex interactions operative in the overall family constellation cannot be ignored if we are to gain insight into the developmental process as it involves deaf children and their families.

The Impact of a Deaf Child on a Family

At present, no comprehensive study using a developmental approach in family analysis has been undertaken on an actual family with a deaf child. According to Hersch and Solomon (1973), conceptualization of what deafness means to the child, the family, and the society has not been explored thoroughly from a psychological viewpoint. Until such desperately needed work is accomplished, it is necessary to rely on available evidence on "normal" families and on families with children suffering from handicaps other than deafness (e.g., Farber, 1957, 1959, 1960; Ross, 1964). Some of the following must remain conjecture when applied to deafness, but all efforts have been made to keep the discussion consistent with present knowledge about family form and function.

For most families, the greatest adjustment usually involves moving from the *childless married couple* dyad into the *childbearing family* stage. Parents typically remember their prechildbearing period as the happiest time of their marriage (Hill, Foote, Aldous, Carlson, & MacDonald, 1970). The immediate impact of a first child is to disrupt previous family routines and to modify the values of parents. Frequently, the family has had two sources of income in the *childless* stage and has enjoyed relative freedom of movement. The birth of the first child may serve to remove the wife and mother from the labor market, at least temporarily, and place her in a more dependent financial position relative to the husband and father. Her freedom of movement is constrained, and the demands of motherhood are both physically and emotionally tiring. The husband may be faced for the first time with complete responsibility for the financial well-being of the family and may suffer from reservations about his ability to function as provider. Both he and the wife may have some difficulty in accepting the fact that the child is receiving a large amount of attention that previously was devoted entirely to the spouse.

Most families adjust adequately to the birth of the first child, and the family enters upon a new stage of functioning. The birth of additional children usually is not perceived as quite so traumatic as that of the first child. Since the birth of a child causes changes in role and function and by itself can be a catalyst of change, it is logical to assume that strain is increased at the birth of a deaf child or, more specifically, upon identification of the child as deaf. Effects of the strain, in turn, will affect the child. The deaf child presents the family, if it has not received adequate counseling, with specific problems in the form of shame, guilt, parental recriminations, and restricted communication.

Periods of Stress

Moores (1973a) has postulated that families go through four periods of extreme stress during the development of their deaf child. The periods are defined as follows:

1. Process of identification of loss
2. Entrance into the school situation
3. Beginning adolescence
4. Early adulthood (p. 115)

Process of Identification

The periods may be perceived as corresponding to family stages 3 through 6, which were identified on the basis of Duvall's work (1971). The final identification of deafness might represent the culmination of a long, emotionally draining process. Typically, the mother has known for some time that something is wrong with the child, but she is not exactly sure what it is. Frequently, a pediatrician has offered assurances that the mother is overconcerned and that the child is merely a late bloomer (Meadow, 1967, 1968a, 1969). The final diagnosis may even be a relief — at least the parents now know what is wrong — but the feeling of relief is quickly followed by overwhelming complications. Parents wonder whose fault it is, the father's or mother's. Some interpret a child's deafness as God's way of punishing parents for past sins.

On a somewhat different plane, more practical considerations emerge. Because of the parent's lack of knowledge about deafness, there is uncertainty about whether the child will ever be self-sufficient and eventually assume a productive role in society or whether the child will constitute a lifelong burden, emotionally and financially draining the resources of the family. The extent of the financial problem for families with young deaf children is immediate and extensive and should not be minimized. Medical care, consultation, and the almost-mandatory immediate fitting of the child with a hearing aid — which usually costs hundreds of dollars — can quickly erode a young family's financial resources and plunge it into debt. They must react and cope with the shock immediately. The child needs their attention — usually there are no professionals to help them work through their grief.

Finally, in their desire for the child to be an extension of themselves, parents ask, "Will our child be normal? Above all, will speech be possible?" It is at this point that professionals first fail deaf children and their families. If parents receive inaccurate and misleading advice at this time, the negative effects may never be overcome. It is only natural for parents to think that the basic problem of the deaf child is an inability to speak, when, in reality, the basic problem is an inability to hear. Professionals have the responsibility to ensure that — as gently as possible, but also as firmly as possible — parents are made to understand this.

Another fact of life that is difficult for parents to accept is the irreversibility of deafness (Meadow, 1968b). For most children we deal with, there are no cures, and none are projected for the foreseeable future. Parents, however, are not aware of this. Once the child is diagnosed, they expect remedial medical treatment. Raised in a society with a "disease" orientation to deviancy, parents naturally assume that deafness can be treated in much the same way as appendicitis, tonsillitis, pneumonia, or the common cold. Surely there must be some medicine or surgical technique to help the child. It takes a great amount of adjustment for a parent to realize that the child, and the family, must be prepared for a lifetime of deafness.

Parents who never work through the trauma and grief to achieve a mature acceptance of the deafness are forced to assume a double burden of unacknowledged (and therefore unexpiated) grief and pretense. Mindel and Vernon (1972) have treated the denial of deafness in detail. For some, the word *deafness* itself is anathema. Slogans such as "Happiness in a hearing world," and "Talk, Talk, Talk" proliferate. The term *deafness*, with all of its harsh implications, is replaced by *auditorily handicapped, hearing handicapped*, and *soft of hearing*. Legitimate terms such as *hearing impaired*, which has been used to refer to the complete range of hearing loss from mild to profound, have been perverted in such a way as to constitute a denial of deafness.

Some organizations in the field of deafness function primarily to facilitate the development of speech in deaf children. This is a commendable undertaking, but certainly not the only — or even most important — goal for young deaf children. One can only guess how many thousands of families have been harmed by the counseling of well-meaning but misinformed individuals whose advice has not really been aimed at the healthy development of the deaf child but rather at the neurotic selfish needs of parents who want their children, as psychological and physical extensions of themselves, to be "normal," that is, speaking. Mindel and Vernon (1972) make the point, and the present author agrees, that the fixation on normalcy (speaking) prevents parents from working through their grief to the mature acceptance of deafness that is a prerequisite for adequate psychological and social development. Without such acceptance, parents will not develop healthy mechanisms to cope with the outer reality of a child with a hearing loss and the inner reality of adjusting to the feeling of loss of a desired normal child.

In relation to the denial of deafness Schlesinger and Meadow (1972a) noted that some parents abhor any vestige of difference between a hearing child and a deaf child. They may forgo the use of hearing aids and prohibit gestures and vocalization from their deaf children.

The feelings of most parents include considerable ambivalence as they work through the outer and inner realities of what it means to have a deaf child. The establishment of family equilibrium cannot take place in a vacuum. Parents cannot plan for the needs of one member of the family without considering the total needs of the whole family. For example, should an entire family move to a place where there is a school or program for the deaf child? In a multichild family, it is disruptive to concentrate on one child alone. Research on families with retarded children suggests that normal sisters frequently are expected to assume responsibilities toward the handicapped sibling that they are not prepared to handle (Farber, 1959). This sometimes leads to personality problems for the normal child. Although no comparable data exist for families with deaf children, it is possible that the presence of a deaf child in a family presents a potentially disruptive situation for a normally hearing sister.

The effects of deafness, or the effects of communication limitations growing from deafness, have an early and profound impact on families and on parent-child communication. Schlesinger and Meadow (1971, 1972a) reported that, in comparison with mothers of young hearing children, mothers of young deaf children are rated as more controlling, more intrusive, more didactic, less flexible, and less approving or encouraging. Goss (1970) found that mothers of deaf children are less likely to show verbal antagonism. Collins (1969) reported that 40% of the behavior of mothers of preschool deaf children was "directing." In his study, 13 of 16 mothers could communicate with their children only about things or events that were present in time and/or space.

Schlesinger and Meadow (1972a) report that parents of deaf children reported a constant concern over whether they were being overprotective or underprotective. They used a more narrow range of discipline techniques, with more reliance on spanking, and exhibited more frustration concerning children.

A factor that has received little or no consideration in the literature is the role of the extended family unit in times of stress. Hill et al. (1970, p. 304) report that the vertical kinship network of three generations (child-parent-grandparent) is turned to, predominantly for giving and receiving help in time of trouble, compared with the horizontal network of siblings and cousins, the network of friends and neighbors, and helping agencies. In a vertical extended family network of three generations, each generation turns to the network for help in solving problems it cannot solve itself. It would be logical to assume, then, that with the occurrence of disability there would be an increase of vertical, or cross-generational involvement. Although there is little evidence in this area, it is interesting to note that Mindel and Vernon (1972) commented on the influence of grandparents on families with deaf children. They reported that often mothers who were frustrated and aware of their children's inability to communicate refrained from using manual communication because of grandparental opposition. If possible, grandparents, as well as siblings, should be involved when helping families adjust to deafness.

Parents and preschool intervention programs Schlesinger and Meadow (1972a) report that because the deaf child's problem has been viewed as an educational problem, the mother is trained by educators to become a teacher. Thus, to the strain of communicative frustration is added the strain of extended demands on the mother's time and attention. In commenting upon the dangers inherent in placing too great a strain on parents, Meadow (1967) said:

The press from educators who begin to work with deaf children and their parents very early leads to over-expectations for verbal achievement and over-emphasis on the training that may or may not lead to verbal competence. This encourages in some matters a didactic, intrusive over-anxious surveillance of the deaf child's oral progress, with accompanying reduction in the relaxed playful creative happy interaction that may be necessary for normal growth and development. (p. 432)

Entrance into the Formal School Situation

A second period of potential stress appears when the child is 5 or 6 years old and about to enter first grade. The life cycle of a family involves changes in family relations and in individual roles over a long period of time. Although the deaf child probably has received some preschool training, parents perceive entrance into the formal elementary school years as a critical point. In essence this constitutes the first substantive change in roles of the deaf child. Successful development of the family life cycle entails the management of status changes in such a way that each of the family's several careers are mutually supportive of the style of life the family is seeking to achieve (Hill et al., 1970). Farber (1957, 1968) claims that family integration depends to a large extent on a lack of role tension in interpersonal relationships among family members.

The choice of educational program that parents make for the child at this juncture is critical. It is essential for family integration that the child make a successful adjustment to the new role as student. Failure may arrest part of the life cycle of the family and alter individual and familial expectations for later stages.

At this time, goals and expectations probably have been influenced greatly by the advice of outside professionals as well as by direct experience. Moores, McIntyre, and Weiss (1972a, p. 72) found differences in parents of deaf children as young as 4 years of age, as a function of the type of preschool program the child was attending. For example, fathers and mothers of deaf children in oral-only programs believed the primary function of an educational program of hearing-impaired children was to develop speech and speechreading skills. Parents of children in programs utilizing both oral and manual communication believed the primary function was to provide appropriate instruction in academic skills such as reading, language, and writing.

During this period parents often are expected to make decisions on such matters as day or residential schooling, integrated or segregated classrooms, and oral-only or combined oral-manual instruction. Decisions typically are made in the face of conflicting professional opinion, appeals to emotionalism, predictions of failure, and threats if the "right" advice is not followed. Options usually are presented in either-or terms, and the earlier-sown seeds of guilt, shame, and recrimination may come to fruition during the process.

Beginning Adolescence

When a child in our culture enters adolescence, the possibility of role tension in the family is increased. Frequently it is a time of uncertainty for the adolescent, who is undergoing physical and emotional changes and is no longer a child but not yet an adult. The strain is greatly intensified for a deaf child, who may experience greater difficulty in establishing a personal position within the family structure. Schlesinger and Meadow (1971) report that adolescence is a time of particular stress for deaf children and their parents. In many ways, the gap between the deaf child and the hearing is widening. Socialization patterns may be different from those of siblings with normal hearing. The child's speech has probably not come along as well as parents expected, or were led to expect. Parents who were told their child would develop normal speech if only they would talk, talk, talk to the child now realize this has not happened and will not happen. As different patterns of boy-girl interaction develop, the parents notice that the child has fewer hearing friends than he or she once did and that the friends are less patient than they were. If the child is not in school with other deaf students, he or she begins to search them out in church and social groups.

It is at this time that many parents see their hopes smashed, their dreams for "normalcy" crushed (Mindel & Vernon, 1972). Because they were not helped to work through the confict when the child was young, the final realization unleashes a tide of frustration, resentment, and hostility which is vented on the system of professionals that has misguided them and failed to prepare them for reality.

Stinson (1972) reported that mothers of adolescent hearing boys tend to react to task pressures by increasing demands on children, while mothers of adolescent deaf boys react under the same conditions by relaxing demands.

While this is happening, the position of the deaf child in the family may be eroding relative to hearing siblings. Jenne and Farber (1957) report that retarded children came to be treated as more immature than even younger brothers and sisters. To some degree the situation of the deaf child may be similar. Parents may feel that the deaf adolescent is generally not as mature as a younger sibling. They are unaware that the immaturity may be explained by their failure to help the child develop to full potential. They forget that the hearing sibling probably has had more leeway in dating, driving, and staying out late as well as having more responsibility for chores around the house. An example of differential expectations parents may have is provided by Meadow (1967) from an interview of a mother of two adolescent boys, one hearing and one deaf:

They tell us he (the deaf boy) has the potential but we've always been told he doesn't apply himself. His younger brother is a straight A student. This makes it hard for the others because we expect the same from all of them. (How does he get along with his brother?) All right. Though there's a little conflict. His younger brother is given more privileges, that makes a little tension. We let his brother take the car anywhere. Fred being deaf, I felt he couldn't be quite as capable, not as responsible. Careless. We wouldn't let Fred stay out as late. (p. 145)

Early Adulthood

The final point of stress to be considered comes when the deaf individual prepares to leave the nuclear family and begin an independent existence. This step probably is a more traumatic one for deaf persons and their families. Parents probably are more overprotective, and deaf children more dependent. The occupational outlook is more limited for deaf individuals. Boatner, Stuckless, and Moores (1964), for example, reported that salaries of young deaf adults in New England were on the average 22% lower than those of their hearing siblings.

Deaf individuals tend to marry at somewhat later ages than the hearing, with most of the marriages being with other deaf individuals. The great majority of the offspring have normal hearing. An area in need of study is the development of hearing children of deaf parents and the types of adjustments made by such families. For example, is the situation perceived by normally hearing grandparents as a continuing crisis? Are they more involved in the families of their deaf children than in the families of their hearing children? Are hearing children expected by their deaf parents to assume adult roles at an early age? If the children act as go-betweens on the telephone and interpreters in face-to-face situations, how does this affect the roles, functions, and expectations of the family and its individual members? The answers to these and similar questions must remain conjecture at the present time and are in need of immediate investigation.

Facilitating Satisfactory Growth and Development

It is wrong to paint a completely depressing picture of the situation. Despite the fact that deaf individuals usually receive inadequate instruction in language, speech, and school subjects; that their parents are miscounseled and misled; that they face prejudice, distrust and discrimination — in spite of all of this, the majority of deaf people make an adequate adjustment to the world. They marry, raise children, pay taxes, contribute to the good of the community, fight, watch television, and entertain themselves in much the same way as everyone else. Most of their problems are caused by the dominant society. Deaf people have survived and endured in the face of an indifferent world that must be dealt with daily.

Instead of approaching the topic with the question of what is deviant, wrong, or pathological about families with deaf people, one might wish to ask, "What are the characteristics of families with deaf children making satisfactory adjustments?" Given the presence of a deaf child in the family, it may be assumed that factors such as age and sex of the deaf child, age and sex of siblings, hearing status of other family members, religious affiliation, and familial socioeconomic status will affect family integration. Very little is known about the impact of such factors with one exception — the hearing status of parents.

The Need for Observational Data
in Naturalistic Settings*

Within the past 10 years educational programs for deaf children have extended the age at which children are served. Now most large metropolitan areas provide some type of educational service to deaf children and their families from the time of identification of a hearing loss. Educational interventions for the deaf, then, must be perceived as extending into the home and involving not only the deaf individual but also the complete family unit. However, except for the work of Meadow and Schlesinger (Meadow, 1968a, 1968b, 1969; Schlesinger & Meadow, 1971, 1972), there have been few efforts to observe systematically the impact of deafness on a child and his or her family.

Because of a lack of information about the interaction of deaf children and their environment, interpretation of differences found between deaf and hearing children or various categories of deaf children must be tentative. The most obvious case would involve research consistently suggesting that deaf children of deaf parents are superior to deaf children of hearing parents in academic achievement and English language abilities (Meadow, 1968a; Moores, 1971, 1976a; Quigley & Frisina, 1961; Stevenson, 1964; Stuckless & Birch, 1966; Vernon & Koh, 1972).

There is an obvious need for careful, detailed observation of the behavior of deaf children in naturalistic settings to determine whether environmental challenges for them are different from those for hearing children and the extent to which such differences require different modes of adaptation. In applying an ethological approach to the study of human beings, we need to describe the individual's intelligent behavior as well as the cognitive demand characteristics of the environment (Charlesworth, 1974). The cognitive demand characteristics not only daily challenge the individual to act intelligently but also influence the development of intelligence. Therefore, we not only must study deaf individuals, if we are to understand the nature of their abilities and how they use them, but we also must have a better understanding of what the environment requires of them.

Intelligent behavior, then, may be seen as a mode of adaptation to everyday environmental demands, requiring naturalistic observation of such behavior relative to such demands (Charlesworth, 1973). Within this context, Hinde

* I would like to acknowledge the contribution to this section of William Charlesworth, colleague in the Research, Development and Demonstration Center in Education of Handicapped Children, Professor in the University of Minnesota Institute of Child Development, and member of the Humanethologie Arbeitsgruppe, Max Planck Institute für Verhalten Physiologie, West Germany. His work in the Research, Development and Demonstration Center in Education of Handicapped Children on applications of ethological principles to observations of retarded children and their families has led the present author to begin to acquaint himself with the discipline of ethology and to consider the use of ethological methods in the study of deaf children and their families.

(1966) has argued that if a species appears to be deficient in some faculty, as defined by a particular type of test, one must refer to the natural situation to assess the extent to which this is compensated for by the development of other faculties. Applying similar reasoning to the study of human beings, Charlesworth (1974) argues that if psychologists or anthropologists go into a section of town with a lower socioeconomic status, or into a ghetto, or into the jungles of the Amazon, or even into the back wards of a mental institution, they should assume that the individuals in these places have already made their adaptations.

By extending such reasoning to research in the area of deafness, it should be possible to (1) identify those environments which further maximum development of deaf children and (2) identify those areas, if any, in which deafness, per se, has implications for the development of the individual. The most important theoretical and practical issue deals with the nature of human communication and language and lies at the base of the oral-manual (now oral–total communication) controversy. In its simplest terms, the question may be put: Is the core of human language auditory-vocal, or does it lie deeper, with the auditory-vocal channel being merely the most convenient and most common mode of communication? Phylogenetically we have acquired elaborate acoustic and articulatory mechanisms that enable our species to develop spoken language. We remain uncertain of the extent to which a nonfunctioning or partially functioning acoustic mechanism, per se, blocks children from realizing the linguistic competence which is theirs by nature of genetic inheritance. The use of observational techniques in naturalistic settings could contribute to the resolution of this issue to a greater extent than our present state of knowledge permits.

Applications of ethological principles might help us identify what it is in the deaf child's environment that requires adaptation by means of cognitive skills and help us determine how frequently such demands occur. Such an approach would be tedious and time-consuming, involving the use of minute categorical and episodic observations that would lead to the construction of ecologically valid test items or situations capable of tapping basic skills only after much trial and error. However, we must move beyond the laboratory and consider how individuals function in nontest situations if we wish to identify basic cognitive skills and fundamental problem-solving processes that are significantly related to successful adaptation. The potential benefits to be realized are such to justify a major commitment in this direction.

Conclusion

In conclusion, if the growth of a healthy personality and the maintenance of family integrity is dependent on complex action, reaction, and interaction among family members, what are the implications for a family with a deaf child who cannot communicate even with the parents because they insist upon communicating only in a medium that is convenient to them—speech? If the development of an adequate concept of self is contingent upon the ability to express needs, wants, and desires (Mead, 1934), what is the self-concept of young adults who cannot describe to their parents the movie they saw the previous night? Do deaf children who grow up with the slogan "Happiness in a hearing world" feel that, by definition, they can never be happy? Are we by inference setting inappropriate goals for these persons and setting the stage for family disintegration? Instead of encouraging and enabling deaf individuals to develop to the limits of their potential, their world has been structured in such a way that they usually come to believe they are acceptable to society, to their families, and to themselves only when they are an imperfect copy of a hearing sibling. For the benefit of deaf individuals and their families, this destructive cycle must be broken.

6

The Acquisition
and Use of English

Introduction

In considering the phenomenon of language acquisition in children, a number of characteristics of the process, and of language itself, should be considered. First is the fact that all children, given a linguistically "normal" environment, learn the language of their society in a consistent, relaxed, almost unconscious manner, in a very short period of time. The major landmarks in the process of acquisition seem to be similar regardless of the language involved. For example, children first begin to put two words together around the age of 18 months and have mastered the basic elements of a language by 4 years of age.

One of the most important aspects of language is the "creativity" involved in its acquisition and use. The young child is not a passive organism into which language is poured. Rather the child is the catalytic agent: Language does not merely develop, it is acquired by the child. Also, for both the child and adult it is not essentially a process of imitation or memorization. Language systems are marked by their openendedness and productivity. The linguistic ability of the normally fluent users of a language is such that, given a finite vocabulary and an internalized knowledge of the rules of a language, they can generate a potentially infinite* number of grammatical utterances, all of which would be perceived as such by other normally fluent users of the language. Put another way, we may say that one of the most salient characteristics of language usage is that it is novel, yet appropriate.

Language may be said to function simultaneously at the three levels of sound, shape, and sense—or phonology, morphology, and semiology—presenting us with a system that is highly structured yet at the same time highly unpredictable. The slow rate of development of a science of verbal behavior lies in part in the unique nature of language. It is so simple and so complex at the same time.

Considering the above characteristics of language acquisition and usage, and

---

* Whether a language may be considered "infinite" as opposed to "incalculably large" is a moot point. Because the term *infinite* has been more prevalent in discussing language, it is used here.

then attempting to relate them to the acquisition of language, or the teaching of language, in children who do not master the language of the home and community, one must be aware of a quintessential paradox. The issue may be stated as follows: If young children in all societies of which we have evidence are able to develop their language abilities quickly and without apparent strain, then the process must be a simple one—at least for young human beings. As such, it must be consistent and rule-bound. On the other hand, if the language is infinite, it must be (in an ideal sense) unpredictable or (in a practical sense) highly complex. The complexity of language is attested to by the fact that no technique has yet been devised to *teach* any language satisfactorily, and no scientist has yet developed a satisfactory complete description of any language. Since it is widely acknowledged that children learn even a second language much more efficiently than adults do, it would appear that language acquisition is not related to "intelligence" as it is commonly understood.

For those interested in the development of language skills in deaf children it is informative to be aware of recent developments in the study of language acquisition by children with normal hearing. With this foundation, perhaps a delineation of necessary and sufficient conditions for the fostering of language growth can be undertaken. If no final answers are forthcoming, at least some modifications of present techniques and emphases might be suggested.

Communication, Language, and Speech

Before considering the field of psycholinguistics, it is necessary to make a distinction among the terms *communication*, *language*, and *speech*, labels that all too often have been used interchangeably. Communication is one of the most important, if not the most important, aspects of behavior, both human and nonhuman. Communication, broadly defined, involves any interaction between living organisms and can be observed up and down the phylogenetic scale from the amoeba to the most complex forms of primate life. Mating, fighting, and the specialized signaling systems of organisms such as birds, bees, and fire ants are all covered under this general category. Not only can the same species communicate with each other, but there is abundant evidence of interspecies communication. Human beings communicate with dogs, with chimpanzees, and with a wide variety of wild and domestic animals. It is possible that even plants and animals can communicate. For example, certain plants project an unmistakable, even if false, message to bees.

For human beings the most important sub-category of communication must be language. Language is something that apparently is uniquely human and that transcends the animal limitation to the here and now, or to some instinctive innate patterns of behavior. Language is dependent on learning and is modifiable by experience. One of the most noticeable aspects is the very fact that it must be learned. It is not passed on through germ plasm. Although all

children have the capacity to acquire one or several languages, the process must proceed within a linguistic environment; it does not develop naturally, as studies of feral children attest.

If for human beings the most important aspect of communication is language, then the most important category of language for most people must be speech. In all societies the vast majority of children learn their language through an oral medium. There is no society in which individuals who have possessed both normal hearing and normal vision have failed to develop a vocal communication system. Most children acquire language during the first five or six years of life by means of speech input and production. For them, other potential aspects of language, such as reading or writing — or even fingerspelling, the language of signs, or Morse code — are secondary and are learned on the basis of the primary system, speech. It is possible that human beings have evolved in such a way as to make the vocal mechanism uniquely adapted to language. It obviously requires the expenditure of less energy than a system involving the hands and utilizing the space from the waist to the top of the head.

There are two basic realities of which educators of the deaf must remain aware. First, speech is the most common mode of communication in our society. However, it is not necessarily the only mode.

A sharp distinction, therefore must be made between language and speech. A typical individual, being exposed infrequently to deaf individuals, is usually most acutely aware of their poor speech. Unfortunately, because this inadequate speech is so noticeable, most people, including some educators of the deaf, erroneously conclude that this is the major problem of deafness. Speech, although important, is only one aspect of a more fundamental problem. A large number, perhaps the majority of deaf children, even if able to articulate perfectly, still would have difficulty in communication because their syntax, morphology, and vocabulary would differ from those used by hearing individuals with whom they came into contact. From the viewpoint of the hearing observers, the deaf children would put words in incorrect order, would add unnecessary words and subtract necessary ones, would use inappropriate word endings, and would be limited by a restricted vocabulary.

Developmental Psycholinguistics*

The term *psycholinguistics* rightfully includes all aspects of the study of language acquisition and usage. It is concerned with speech, grammar, and semantics and necessarily touches on and overlaps areas such as psychoacoustics, descriptive linguistics, transformational grammar, articulatory phonetics, communication theory, and behavioristic and neobehavioristic psychology. As such, the compleat psycholinguist does not exist; no one could ever be proficient in all these areas. Instead, there are individuals whose interests lead them to work under this broad umbrella.

In essence psycholinguistics represents an attempt to provide a common meeting ground between the two quite disparate disciplines of psychology and linguistics. In the United States psychologists have concentrated for the most part on prediction and control of behavior with specific emphasis on the role of reinforcement. The field of linguistics has been more concerned with grammar without respect to control or meaning. Language has been perceived as something uniquely human and transcending other kinds of behavior. The role of reinforcement has been minimized.

The differences in viewpoint reflect a much broader social issue that has existed for centuries. In one group we find a tendency to look at the human mind as almost completely plastic and flexible. This position is exemplified by

---

* Anyone aware of the recent explosion of interest in the study of language acquisition must realize that one section of a chapter cannot begin to do justice to the subject and of necessity can provide only a cursory introduction to the field. The topic, "language and deafness" itself should be dealt with in book length, but unfortunately no such book exists. For interested readers who wish to pursue the subject, Appendix C contains a list of books on language that the author has found useful.

the claim of John Watson (1924), a father of American behavioristic psychology, that given a normal, healthy child at random, he could train it to become any type of specialist desired — doctor, lawyer, artist, merchant, beggar, or thief — regardless of the child's talents, penchants, tendencies, abilities, parents, or race.

On the other side are those who attach much more importance to biological factors. In the field of language acquisition more and more interest is being devoted to innate predispositions, to the idea that the tendency to develop language is programmed within each child. This position may be summed up by the argument that the tendency of human children to acquire language is as deeply ground into their constitutions as is the tendency to use their hands, and that the environment merely triggers a process which has been anticipated by millions of years of evolutionary development.

Traditionally, in the United States, it was believed that the process of imitation was the primary factor in the learning of a language. Language was seen as developing by gradual increments, with the parents playing a central role by providing a model and shaping increasingly "grammatical" utterances by means of selective reinforcement. The stimulus-response paradigm was of paramount importance, and the operant conditioning model was invoked to explain verbal behavior (Skinner, 1957). A child's utterances were judged for "correctness" in terms of how closely they approximated the standards of adult usage. Development of language proficiency was assessed in relation to vocabulary growth; increase in length and complexity of utterances, relative to frequency of usage of different parts of speech; and gradual elimination of errors.

A major divergence from this emphasis may be traced back to the 1950s, to the seminal investigations of children's understanding of English morphology originated by R. Brown (1958), emphasizing the ability of children to apply generalized rules to "words" never encountered before; such investigations have influenced an entire generation of psycholinguists. Increasingly, since that time, the trend has been toward perceiving the language of children not in terms of an adult model but as a system that in many ways possesses characteristic rules and structures not found in the language used by adults. Children's language, then, may be approached with no preconceptions and may be considered to some extent sui generis, of its own kind, unique within itself.

A second major development has been the more recent movement away from purely formal or structural descriptions of language acquisition toward more of an effort to take motivational and situational factors into account. Thus not only language structures but also underlying intentions and semantic functions are considered within the framework of developmental psycholinguistics. The impetus for this shift may be seen in the work of Bloom (1970) and Bowerman (1973). For a complete discussion of the issues, readers are referred to the integrative work of R. Brown (1973).

One of the most significant contributions of developmental psycholinguistics has been the evidence that language does not develop in children solely by means of parental selective reinforcement. Language explodes. Children make great inductive leaps to realize grammatical proficiency in an amazingly short period of time. They learn a language by interacting with it, by actively coping with and manipulating their environment. They do this on the basis of unplanned input on the part of their parents. Children also may master their language through a number of successive, increasingly complex stages. There is also evidence to suggest that the process of language acquisition, which apparently is based on essential cognitive characteristics shared by all human beings, is similar across all languages. In an examination of material available on the acquisition of 40 different native languages, Slobin (1973) has identified several similar developmental processes existing across languages that, superficially, appear to be widely divergent.

Levels of Language

Part of the difficulty experienced in past attempts to resolve the simplicity–complexity paradox of language lay in the inability to understand that language exists simultaneously, in an intricately interrelated manner, on the three levels of sound, shape, and sense, characterized by Joos (1964) as phonology, morphology, and semiology, respectively. The sound system, or *phonology*, usually is mastered by age 4. This does not mean that children produce all the phonemes (sounds) of the English language by this time. They might not be able to produce a distinct *y, w, l,* or *r*. They might substitute a *v* for a *th* in the medial position. However, they do have these sounds under passive control. They can distinguish and react to them when spoken by someone else.

By the shape of a language is meant its *grammar* (syntax plus morphology). *Syntax* refers to word order in a language, and *morphology* deals with word forms. For example, ways of illustrating differences in number (*boy-boys, goose-geese*), tense (*walk-walked, fly-flew*), and form class (*happy-happily, slow-slowly*) are treated within the context of morphology. Similar to the learning of the sound system, children have acquired mastery of the shape of their language in a short period of time. The major part of grammar is learned by children in an English-speaking environment by age 5. They have learned the most common, and therefore most useful, elements of morphology by this time (Berko, 1958) and are able to apply them on a systematic basis to new situations and words when appropriate. For example, 4- and 5-year-olds were shown two illustrations and were told: "Here is a *wug*. Here is another one. Now there are two _____." The children would supply the appropriate plural form *wugs*, although they had never heard it before.

Of course, children still make mistakes in terms of adult language. Just as surely as they produce *boys, girls, played,* and *walked,* they also will come up with such consistent but grammatically unacceptable combinations as *mans, foots, goed,* and *runned.* However, even these "mistakes" are indications of an ability to apply rules or generalizations systematically to language, and usually they are eliminated quickly. Joos (1964) claims that children will have acquired all the grammar they will ever have by age 8.

Semiology has to do with the meaning and vocabulary of language. Joos (1964) states that the bulk of words which people know are learned before age 20. Although they may continue to add new words to their vocabulary throughout their lives, the new words typically are learned in the context of proper nouns. It should be understood, however, that the size of an individual's vocabulary is not necessarily a reflection of his or her language ability. Young children with limited vocabularies may be considered grammatically competent if they demonstrate an understanding of the morphological and syntactic structure of their language. It is not uncommon, on the other hand, for deaf adults to possess a relatively large number of nouns and verbs in their repertoires but still be considered grammatically or linguistically retarded in English because of their inability to use the words in proper order or to produce the correct morphological form.

Nouns and verbs, the *content words* of English, are no more important than *function words*, which are the words that establish the structure of a language. The primary role of function words is to connect other words in discourse. The more meaningful content words are set with the skeleton or framework provided by the function words. Included as function words, in terms of traditional grammar, are articles (*a, an, the*), conjunctions (*and, but, or*), and prepositions (*to, for, among*). There exist a relatively small number of such words in the English language, and they are mastered quite rapidly.

Very few words are added to the list of noncontent words in a language. In contrast, the set of content words in our language is enlarging constantly and is potentially infinite. Words of this nature are introduced to keep pace with developments in areas such as industry, science, education, and politics. Thus, the content of a language is modified more rapidly than its structure.

Although nouns and verbs make up the bulk of an adult's vocabulary, they are not the most commonly used words in a language. A Lorge-Thorndike (Thorndike & Lorge, 1944, pp. 259–263) count of more than 4½ million words from popular American magazines revealed that only 25 words accounted for approximately 33% of the total usage, appearing more than 1½ million times. Each of the 24 most commonly used words was a pronoun or function word; 8 were pronouns, 7 were prepositions, 4 were auxiliaries, 3 were conjunctions, and 2 were articles. *The, and*, and *a* account for more than 10% of word usage. Only 8 small words, none larger than 3 letters, are used 20% of the time. The 13 most common make up more than one-fourth (25%) of the total corpus. Obviously, people who do not have control over these "interstitials" of a language would be limited severely in their understanding of messages, no matter how large their vocabulary. The advantage that hearing children possess over deaf children is their unconscious mastery over the first two levels of language, phonology and grammar. They handle these almost automatically and can concentrate on meaning, or content, both in sending and receiving messages. Deaf children, because of a history of insufficient input in their environment, typically cannot approach communication in the same way. They must try to filter meaning from English messages through inadequately developed phonological and grammatical systems. The result is frequently a distortion of the original message. The situation produces children whose intellectual potential must be normal but whose achievements are limited because of a failure to provide them with the basic tools of standard English grammar.

Stages of Language Development

It has been noted that in the development of grammatical competence children move through a number of stages. At first they produce holophrastic, one-word utterances. They might, for example, combine the word *milk* with some appropriate intonation and/or gesture to indicate that they wanted some milk, liked the milk, or spilled the milk. Sometime around the age of 18 months children begin to use two-word combinations (Braine, 1963; Brown & Bellugi, 1964). Braine analyzed the first combinations produced by children and suggested two distinct word classes, pivot and open. The *pivot class* is made up of a small number of words whose position in grammatical sequence has been learned. The *open class* contains all other words and accounts for most of children's vocabularies. Open words occur in relatively fewer combinations than pivot words, and they also may be used alone, that is, as holophrases. Braine stated (1963) that in the initial state of acquisition the language expands rapidly in vocabulary by adding new members to the open class and that it develops structurally by singling out at intervals new pivot words: He cited the parallel in the distinction between open and closed words in adult language (nouns, verbs, and adjectives versus pronouns, prepositions, auxiliary verbs, etc.) to that between open and pivot words in children's language. For one child, Braine reported that of 89 recorded word combinations, 64 followed the pivot–open (PO) sequence.

Children rapidly move from two-word utterances into structures that come more and more to approximate the language of the adult community, a process that essentially is completed before entrance into school. Within the context of language development, two important considerations of child grammars must be made. First, the sequence is constructed by an individual child and may or may not follow adult word order. For example, although Braine's subject was able to produce "allgone milk" or "allgone plane," it is not likely that the child's parents used the same sequence; they probably said, "The milk is all gone" and "The plane is all gone." This sequence of words illustrates that more is involved in the production of utterances than simple imitation. A second factor of importance is children's ability to produce novel, for them, combinations. Thus, a child who first said "see boy" also would be able to produce "see rock," "see boat," and "see mommy" in some appropriate situation.

The importance of the concept of pivot grammar has come into question with the increased attention being directed to functional aspects of language.

Bowerman (1973) reported that the pivot grammar model did not apply to the acquisition of Finnish in her study. Bloom (1970) examined the two-word constructions of children learning English in her study and concluded that pivot grammar was inadequate as an explanatory device and provided only a superficial description of the child's competence. In the by-now-classic example, Bloom reported how one child (Kathryn) uttered the same string, "mommy sock," under two different circumstances. In one situation, Kathryn picked up her mother's sock, and in the other her mother was putting Kathryn's sock on Kathryn. Braine's system would assign the same structure to each "mommy sock" utterance and therefore does not reflect the underlying relations being expressed by the child. Using a "rich" interpretation of the child's utterances, Bloom would assign different grammatical structures depending on the situation. Although such an approach is less parsimonious and more subject to error, it probably provides a more adequate representation of the child's grammar and enables the investigator to accommodate to situational variables.

Process of Language Acquisition

The problem narrows down to this: (1) can the necessary and sufficient conditions for learning language be delineated and (2), if so, can the environment of deaf children be structured so as to expose them to such conditions? No consensus exists concerning the processes of language development, and most findings are tentative. The processes described below — which, in the author's opinion, reflect minimum requirements for the development of language — have been discussed by Brown and Bellugi (1964) in greater detail and have received wide attention.

Imitation Although it has been established that children don't learn by imitation alone, imitation evidently is an important factor in the acquisition of language. It is an imitation by reduction. A child may copy an adult's utterances and retain adult word order but, for a number of reasons, may leave out parts of the original. Thus "Daddy went bye-bye in the plane" is imitated as "Daddy bye-bye" or "Bye-Bye plane." It is interesting to note that in spontaneous imitation children tend to verbalize in terms of their own level of syntactical development. For example, if they do not have the present progressive form under control, they might follow "The baby is playing in the bed" with "Baby play" or "Play bed" but probably not with "Playing bed" unless a parent specifically demands that construction. In contrast to pivot grammars, children, when imitating, preserve the word order of the model but omit some words and omit or alter some inflections. The following exchange reported by Gleason (1967), taken from a conversation with her 4-year-old daughter, is an example of how children speak and produce imitations in terms of their own structures:

Very recently, I had a conversation about baby rabbits with a four year old named Cynthia Gleason. It went like this:

Table 6.1   Typical expansions of child's speech by mother

Child	Mother
Daddy plane	Daddy went on the plane
Mark ice cream	Mark is eating ice cream
Sock gone	Sheila's sock is gone
Throw ball	Throw the ball to Eric
Drop ball	Kevin dropped the ball
Climb tree	She climbed the tree

She said, "My teacher holded the baby rabbits and we patted them."
I asked, "Did you say your teacher held the baby rabbits?"
She answered, again, "She holded the baby rabbits and we patted them."
"Did you say she held them tightly?" I asked.
"No," she answered, "she holded them loosely." (p. 1441)

Expansion   The second process described by Brown and Bellugi (1964) was *expansion*, a kind of reverse imitation by which parents help children test their hypotheses about language. The parent will take a child's utterance, echo it, and change it back into acceptable adult language. In the Brown and Bellugi study approximately 30% of the utterances were expanded. In most expansions the word order of the child's utterances is preserved, and words and inflections are added. Table 6.1 lists some typical expansions. McNeill (1966) claims that an expansion sequence may be considered a controlled experimental observation by which children try out various patterns, incorporating the acceptable ones into their repertoire and dropping the unacceptable ones.

The exchanges presented in Table 6.1 suggest that parents provide a "rich" interpretation to children's utterances, much as Bloom (1970) did in her study. Brown and Bellugi (1964) saw the process of expansion as a parental training device, but an experimental study by Cazden (1965) that used expansion training failed to produce significant results.

Induction   The third and perhaps most important process described by Brown and Bellugi is the *induction* of the latent structure of a language, by which children are able to understand and construct sentences that they have never heard but that are well formed in terms of general rules implicit in the sentences to which the children have previously been exposed. Children's tendency to overgeneralize has been well documented. Such expressions as "He runned" or "Two mans" do not represent adult speech — it is unlikely that children have heard adults use these combinations — but rather are the result of "inappropriate" generalization of common morphological constructions. Along with progressive differentiation of syntactic classes by which the overgeneralizations are gradually eliminated, there exists simultaneously an integrative process by which children increase their ability to deal more efficiently and flexibly with more complex patterns of language.

Implications for Education of the Deaf

The insights into language development of normally hearing children are fascinating by themselves, but the issue is: What are the practical implications of such findings toward the development of language skills of deaf children? It is crucial that continuing growth of knowledge about the phenomenon of language development exert influence on programs for the deaf. Five major areas deserving special attention from professionals in deafness are described in the following sections.

Optimal Period

In view of the evidence that children learn their language quite rapidly and that children are superior to adults in learning a second language, Moores (1970) has reviewed the possibility that a critical period, or at least an optimal period, exists for language acquisition. The specific ability to develop language appears to peak around ages 3 and 4, and it tends to decline steadily thereafter. Perhaps any language program that is initiated after age 5, no matter what methods are used, is doomed to failure for the majority of deaf children. Although hearing children do not begin to put words together until about 18 months, they have received language input from birth. It seems imperative, therefore, that all deaf children receive language instruction not at age 6, or 5, or even 4; but as soon as their hearing loss has been diagnosed. Implicit in this is the need for more systematic procedures for early identification of hearing-impaired children.

The lack of effective communication for the first five years has tremendous implications for later psychoeducational development. Normally hearing children have obtained much of their factual knowledge of the world and set the basis for their personality development. They are able to cope with and manipulate their environment. They interact with peers and adults. They can ask: Why? When? Where? How? Who? They can talk about the present, the past, and the fanciful. Children who are disciplined but not reasoned with, who have no answer to their questions, who have no control over and little understanding of their environment start with a deprivation that may never be overcome.

Teaching and Learning

The possibility must be faced that language cannot be taught but must be learned by the children. If, as now appears feasible, children in all cultures learn languages by progressing similarly through a number of stages, or a similar process, the implication is that this sequential process is mandatory. If so, attempts to teach language by direct imposition of an adult grammatical model will be unlikely to succeed.

In the final analysis, the most efficient approach is to provide young deaf children with a language environment in the home that is as close as possible to the environment enjoyed by hearing children. If language cannot be taught, and if it is learned before age 3 or 4, it should be possible to structure the environment in such a way as to enable deaf children to learn it. The focus should be shifted from the school to the home. This in no way implies that all mothers of deaf children should function as teachers. Mothers of hearing children do not operate in this manner. The language development of normally hearing children is not achieved on the basis of formal parental instruction but by providing children with the tools and setting — that is, the exposure — for learning. In this respect the role of parents of a deaf child should be that of learning facilitators, not teachers. This significant distinction must be understood.

Language and Speech

There has been a tendency for teachers of the deaf to treat speech and language as synonymous and to use the terms interchangeably. The result of failing to distinguish between the two has been an unfortunate emphasis not on the basic problem, the English language, but on its outward manifestations, speech. In a paper presented to the International Conference on Oral Education of the Deaf, Lenneberg (1967a) stressed the point that the primary goal of education must be language, not its subsidiary skills. He then developed the argument that the establishment of language is not inseparably bound to phonics, and he urged that graphics (reading and writing) be introduced at the earliest possible time. Lenneberg included fingerspelling and signs within his definition of graphics.

Sentence Generation

Another example of an inadequate approach to language learning and remediation is the tendency to attack deficiencies not at the base from which the inappropriate utterances are generated but on the surface, where they are manifested either in speech or in writing. The difficulties encountered in changing patterns of usage can be illustrated by some of the "deafisms" encountered in the spoken and written language of deaf children. Statements such as "I went to swimming" or "I went to home" are familiar to most teachers of the deaf and, despite herculean efforts, frequently remain in strength in the children's corpus of utterances, probably because the focus of remediation has been misplaced. Faced with the string "I went to swimming," most teachers would provide the more acceptable "I went swimming" and perhaps have the child imitate or produce it. For that particular utterance at that particular time, the mistake has been corrected; but in the next breath the child next comes out with "I went to skating," "I went to shopping," or "I went to fishing." The harried teacher then can go on to change each one of these, only to have others pop up.

The point has been made strongly by Chomsky (1959, 1967) and Lenneberg (1967b) that language competency lies in the ability to generate novel yet appropriate utterances on the basis of a limited vocabulary and a knowledge of the rules of the language. By restricting themselves only to the surface behavior, teachers lessen their likelihood of accomplishing the final goal — the ability of the children to provide the appropriate structure any time they have to in any future utterance. What must be altered are the rules by which children produce the patterns, in this case a *to plus verb plus -ing* sequence. The inappropriate generative patterns must be supplemented by more commonly accepted ones. To develop methods for accomplishing this is a forbidding task fraught with pitfalls, but it must be done.

Imitation and Expansion

Even though research on the relative importance of imitation by children and expansion by parents is inconclusive, it seems logical that both are necessary to some extent in the development of language proficiency. The problem comes down to developing some means for mothers to provide good clear forms for children to imitate, and to enable children to express themselves in a manner understandable to the mothers, who then can provide appropriate expansions. The absence of such a mutually intelligible communication system greatly limits or even precludes the development of linguistic abilities in the mother tongue.

Summary

In recent years conceptions of functional aspects of language and of how language is acquired by children have been altered radically. Programs designed to assist deaf children in the acquisition of language will have to accommodate to new advances and insights. The various methods of teaching language to the deaf, presented in Chapter 11, should be evaluated within the framework of current knowledge of the language acquisition process.

7
Deafness and Intellectual Functioning

Introduction

Interest in and speculation about the essence of humanity and the nature of human intellectual processes may be traced back through the writings of antiquity and, assuming ancient oral traditions to be reliable, provided part of the framework by which legal, moral, and cultural codes were developed. The philosophical issue may be expressed by the question: In what way(s), if any, are human beings different from (other) animals? The topic probably has been a subject of discussion since human beings first possessed the ability to communicate with each other using an abstract symbol system, that is, language.

Language and Humanity

It is obvious that the present supremacy of the human race cannot be explained in purely physical terms. Although human beings are relatively large, powerful, and swift, several examples of larger, more powerful, and swifter animals come readily to mind. Although specialized developments such as the thumb, or opposable digit, indubitably have provided us with unique capabilities for advancement, it is obvious that we most differ from animals in our intellectual abilities and in our use of language.

Still, the acknowledgment of differences does not provide an adequate resolution to the issue of whether the differences are quantitative or qualitative. In other words, are we like other animals, only more highly advanced? Are our brains like those of other primates, only more complex? Are the presence of language and the development of religion, culture, and science a logical outgrowth of an evolutionary process that may be operating on other members of the animal kingdom; or are human beings qualitatively different from all other beings? Do different laws apply to us to the extent that language and at least some types of mental functioning represent characteristics limited to one species?

The issue probably will continue to occupy the human race for centuries. Of course, it can never be proved conclusively that human beings are unique,

122

it can only be disproved. It is possible that chimpanzees have religious beliefs (or the potential to have them), that dolphins have fully developed linguistic systems, and that earthworms have rich fantasy lives. However, until it is demonstrated that animals are capable of functioning at the "human" level, most individuals will continue to believe that we are somehow, in some way, unique. This position is represented by Lenneberg (1973), who notes that the size of the human brain is not what differentiates us from animals. Neither is it general cognitive ability, since even severely retarded individuals show signs of language development. Lenneberg states:

Thus our capacity for learning language is not due to special brain connections between sight and hearing; nor is it due to a simple increase in the size of the brain or in general, intelligence. Something must be going on in our brain that is just lacking in the brains of other species. (p. 54)

Lenneberg's views are shared by a majority of investigators who have investigated animal communication systems such as the songs of birds, dances of bees, and — closest to Homo sapiens — the communication systems of primates. While acknowledging the complexity of such systems, most scientists argue that they are different in quality from human language. Lancaster (1968) summarized the predominant argument as follows:

The interest in human evolution and in the origin of human language has distorted the study of the communication systems of non-human primates. These systems are not steps toward human language and have much more in common with the communication of other mammals than with human language. The more that is known about the communication systems of non-human primates the more obvious it is that these systems have little relationship with human language, but much with the ways human beings express emotion through gesture, facial expression and tone of voice. (p. 239)

Thus it seems that human beings can and do employ mechanisms paralinguistically to express states of emotion in much the same way as higher primates do; but the higher primates, apparently, are incapable of stating propositions, of talking about the not-here and not-now, or of producing and understanding novel yet appropriate utterances.

It should be stressed that a substantial number of psychologists, especially American psychologists, would not subscribe to the position that human communication and thought is qualitatively different from animal varieties. This is due to the influence of behaviorism, which has had such a profound effect on twentieth-century American psychology, as exemplified by Watson (1924) and later by Skinner. It represented a break with the European tradition, in which psychology was closely related to philosophy, and reflected a conscious attempt to pattern psychology after the "hard" sciences such as chemistry and physics. In this way psychology in America shifted its emphasis from the study of the mind to the study of behavior. "Mentalistic" approaches were rejected, and the domain of problems deemed amenable to investigation was limited to the observable and quantifiable. The search for powerful, encompassing laws of behavior led psychologists to concentrate increasingly on more and more tightly conceived and conducted experiments. This in turn led to an increased emphasis on animal experimentation, especially concerning basic paradigms of learning involving operant conditioning, with special attention devoted to the effects of differential patterns of positive reinforcement, negative reinforcement, and punishment on learning.

The assumption was, and is, that one may generalize from the behavior of mice in contrived situations in the laboratory to the complex behavior of human beings in social situations. The same factors that control bar-pressing and maze-running behavior are seen as controlling linguistic functioning. Manipulation of contingencies of reinforcement develop and maintain verbal behavior as well as other behavior in strength. This school of thought was presented in its most ambitious form by Skinner in his book *Verbal behavior* (1957).

Animal Communication

If the nature of language acquisition and usage in actuality is not qualitatively different from other behavior, it is logical to assume that, given the proper environment and reinforcement schedules, the most intelligent nonhuman primates should be capable of developing languagelike behavior, at least at the same level as very young children. The assumption has been tested on several occasions. The experiments typically have involved a husband-and-wife team of psychologists raising a chimp in a homelike atmosphere. The efforts to develop spoken language have met with a consistent lack of success. Given evidence that chimpanzees do not possess the physiological structure to produce articulate speech, Gardner and Gardner (1969) undertook to teach American Sign Language to one named Washoe. The results have been impressive (Gardner & Gardner, 1969, 1971), with Washoe developing a relatively large sign vocabulary that she was able to use appropriately in multisign combinations. Washoe's success has caused a stir in the scientific community. Although she apparently did not use signs in the way a human child might to develop language (Brown, 1973; Klima & Bellugi, 1973), she was able to use them in a far more sophisticated manner than most psycholinguists and psychologists would have predicted. As a result, many scientists now are far less emphatic in their rejection of an evolutionary link between primate communication and human language.

A perhaps even more impressive demonstration of the cognitive, if not linguistic, potentials of primates may be found in the work of Premack (1971, 1973; Premack & Premack, 1974) with the chimpanzee, Sarah. Working with plastic "words" and magnetized boards, and utilizing conditioning procedures, Sarah's trainers successfully developed a vocabulary based on a "give" transaction; that is, Sarah received a particular fruit when she placed the appropriate plastic disk on the board. Then she was introduced to simple sentences, interrogatives, compound sentences, and complex sentences — all of which she apparently mastered. She was able to exhibit "linguistic" knowledge of perceptual "same-different" distinctions; that is, she would label two apples *same* and an apple and a banana *different*. She also was able to perform at 80% accuracy on conditional sentences of the following type (Premack & Premack, 1974):

Mary take red	if then	Sarah take apple.
Mary take green	if then	Sarah take banana. (p. 352)

In this situation, if Mary took a red card, Sarah was to take an apple. If Mary took a green card, Sarah was to take a banana. This was accomplished through contingency or reinforcement training.

In discussing Sarah's accomplishments, Premack and Premack (1974), state:

With a slim vocabulary of 130 words, Sarah learned to name persons, objects, verbs, etc. She progressed to a series of simple sentences, in which she learned properties, classes, quantifiers, plurals, the copula, and so on. And she comprehended compound sentences, reaching finally the complex sentence. The training was accomplished by simply mapping language elements to an already existing perceptual structure. (p. 362)

It is Premack's position, then, that the beginnings of language have their foundations in the presence of certain perceptual and conceptual abilities. Without these abilities language cannot develop. Not only human beings, but at least chimpanzees, possibly other primates, and perhaps some lower forms of animals possess these abilities. The extent to which language then can be used to teach new distinctions and to develop logical operations or be used as a metalanguage is unknown. This is a matter for investigation.

The idea that the development of language in children is based on existing perceptual and conceptual abilities is accepted widely at present. Premack's departure results from his position that these abilities are not necessarily restricted to the human species. Although it is possible that the tests of comprehension used with Sarah inadvertently produced spuriously high results (R. Brown, 1973), it is undeniable that the work of Premack and his associates with Sarah has shaken the complacency of many developmental psycholinguists and caused them to reconsider a number of their unquestioned assumptions.

Thought and Language

Moving past the animal realm, it is obvious that the study of human thought is complicated by the existence of human language. If we were to ask people how they think and they were to respond, our interchange would take place through words; that is, we would think and then translate the thoughts into language. What the essence of thought is must remain speculation. It is possible that we think in words, that language raises thought to new heights, or that language distorts thought. The limitations of present research techniques and the unreliability of introspection prevent us from reaching any definite conclusions. Chomsky (1968) has stated that perhaps the one thing the human mind is incapable of comprehending is the human mind.

In the past there was some optimism that it might be possible to study the evolution of language by investigating its nature in "primitive" societies and following its development in presumably more complex cultures through its full realization in industrial society. However, the evidence suggests (R. Brown, 1958) that the languages of so-called primitive cultures are every bit as complex as those of other cultures. In addition, no society has ever been found that does not have a fully developed language. Therefore, it is impossible to rank languages on a scale of complexity or along a "concrete–abstract" continuum.

Related to the above is the growing awareness that all societies are organized into extremely complex structures and that the individual members of these societies function in a highly complex manner, again suggesting that the concept of intellectual development unfolding as human beings live in more and more technical environments is erroneous. For a comprehensive treatment of the subject, interested readers are referred to the writings of the French anthropologist Claude Levi-Strauss, especially his work *The savage mind* (1966).

Linguistic Relativity

Related to the above question has been speculation about the question of linguistic relativity. On one hand may be found the Whorfian, or Sapir-Whorfian, hypothesis (Whorf, 1956), which suggests that the structure of the language an individual habitually uses influences one's *Weltanschauung*, one's view of the world, implying that language either determines thought or greatly influences the manner by which an individual perceives and organizes the environment. Whorf developed his hypothesis as a result of his investigations of American Indian languages and their apparent lack of congruence with traditionally studied Indo-European languages.

Although it cannot be denied that languages vary in numerous ways, there is a tendency to reject the Whorfian hypothesis, at least in its strong form, and to contend that artificial surface differences mask a remarkable uniformity across languages in the deep structure (Chomsky, 1965, 1968). It appears that, despite their many differences, certain basic psychological and linguistic commonalities are exhibited by all languages. Greenberg, Osgood, and Jenkins (Greenberg, 1963) state: "Underlying the endless and fascinating idiosyncrasies of the world's languages there are uniformities of universal scope. Amidst infi-

nite diversity, all languages are, as if it were, cut from the same pattern" (p. 255).

Cross-cultural studies utilizing semantic differential techniques developed by Osgood, Suci, and Tannenbaum (1957) tend to support such a position. Results have shown with remarkable consistency across cultures that evaluative, potency, and activity factors constitute the underlying dominant dimensions in the affective meaning system (Kumata & Schram, 1956; Mackay & Ware, 1961; Rosen, 1959; Suci, 1960). The findings support the contention (Osgood, Suci, & Tannenbaum, 1957) that although people who speak different languages may vary in reactions to specific concepts, human beings share a common framework for the process of differentiating meaning.

In a review of the literature on childhood language acquisition involving 40 languages, Slobin (1973) reported that the initial processes were consistent across such apparently diverse languages as Japanese, Russian, Yarubu, and English. The results reported by Osgood and by Slobin, and supported by Chomsky's theoretical arguments, lead to the conclusion that there are great similarities across language and that these similarities result from cognitive processes and experiences which are shared by all human groups. This conclusion finds additional support in the work of Piaget, who, in extensive studies of the development of children, has concluded in essence that language depends more on cognition than cognition depends on language (Piaget, 1962, 1969; Sinclair-de-Zwart, 1969).

Nineteenth-century Views on Deafness and Thought

Given that deaf people do not acquire language primarily through the auditory-vocal channel, and given the common belief that deaf people are linguistically deficit, it is not surprising that much interest has been expressed over the nature of intellectual processes in deaf people.

In the nineteenth century, educators of the deaf were interested in the nature of deaf children's thought before instruction (Ballard, 1881; H. Peet, 1855). Such a concern was natural, because a large number of deaf children did not begin their education until age 10 or later. Before that age, for the majority of deaf children the major source of information had to come from the children's own observations and participation in their environment. Communication usually was dependent on a primitive gesture system developed by the children and their families.

Given the emphasis on moral and religious training, a great amount of attention was given to whatever value systems or religious insights children developed in the absence of instruction. Several attempts were made in different schools to encourage students to recall through introspection the nature and extent of their experience and thought before beginning their education.

In an intriguing treatise on the notions of deaf children before instruction, H. Peet (1855) dealt with the nature of man, the origin of language, and the relationship of language and thought in a highly insightful way. Beginning with Humboldt's statement (H. Peet, 1855), "Man is man only by means of speech, but in order to invent speech he must be already man" (p. 8), Peet developed the position that the language of gestures mixed with instinctive cries was the language of the first man. Arguing that "the possession or capacity of acquiring a language is one of the surest tests of humanity" (p. 19), he noted that all human languages, including those of primitive tribes, were fully developed, and that languages were not at different stages of development — an insight ahead of his time. In discussing the similarities found between the languages of Europe, Peet rejected the idea that one of them constituted the original language and suggested instead that "a primitive language may have provided the stem from which all languages of the Caucasian race have branched" (p. 19). Although Peet does not make specific reference, he must have been familiar with the work of William Jones, who in 1786 related Sanskrit, Greek, Latin, Gothic, Celtic, and Persian and postulated a common descent from an earlier language no longer in existence (Waterman, 1970).

Concerning the notions of the deaf before instruction, Peet reported that without instruction deaf children had no conception of God, the Creation, or the soul, and that they had a terror of death. He concluded that there was no religious thought without instruction.

In an earlier investigation, Ray (1847) reported that before instruction deaf children tended to interpret parts of their environment in anthropomorphic terms. For example, the sun and moon frequently were personified. In one form or another, of course, this is not unknown in modern society or even in modern religion.

The American psychologist William James (1890) and the French psychologists Binet and Simon (1910) argued that thought processes were developed before language in deaf persons. Referring to reports of two deaf individuals concerning their thoughts before instruction, James noted the presence of abstract and metaphysical conceptions, even when the only language was that of pantomime.

Booth (1878) argued in essence that concern over the relation between thought and language was misdirected. His position was not only that thought was independent of the various modes of expression but that thought and language were separate and distinctive processes. As such it was possible to employ one or the other alone and independently. According to Booth (p. 224) the point is not whether deaf people think in words or in gestures, but which — words or gestures — comes first to mind when thought seeks expression.

The Assessment of Intelligence

It is commonly accepted that the assessment of intelligence — whether accomplished through traditional IQ tests, aptitude tests, or Piagetian-based measures — constitutes an inexact science. The problem lies in the necessity of "measuring" small incidences of behavior in a short period of time in an artificial situation and then making generalizations about how an individual will function in the real world. Even assuming adequate assessment instruments — an overoptimistic assumption — results may be considered valid and reliable only to the extent that the motivation and experience of the testee matches that of the population on which the test was standardized.

Dissatisfaction with psychometric practices in the schools — especially the use of IQ scores to decide placement in classes for the retarded — is widespread. Children who are not white, middle-class speakers of standard English are discriminated against by such tests and tend to be placed in special classes in disproportionate numbers.

The situation for deaf children can be even more severe. In many cases they possess minimal speech skills and have difficulty understanding what is expected of them unless the psychometrist is experienced in dealing with deaf children. As a rule the scores of deaf children may be depressed if a test requires proficiency in speech or speechreading or in knowledge of standard English. Because of communication difficulties, scores in timed tests also may be depressed. It is a safe operating principle to suspect any low scores. This is true of the testing of all individuals, but it is even more applicable in relation to deafness. For a treatment of the most appropriate tests of intelligence for use with the deaf, see Vernon and Brown (1964).

It is beyond the scope of the present chapter to review the hundreds of investigations of the intelligence of deaf individuals. The purpose, rather, is to illustrate how perceptions of the intelligence of deaf people have changed over the years. This will be done by examining the work of researchers who have studied the question (Pintner, Eisenson, & Stanton, 1941; Myklebust, 1953; Rosenstein, 1961; Vernon, 1967) at different periods of time and by attempting to illustrate how we have arrived at our present position.

Stage I, The Deaf as Inferior: Pintner

As a culmination of his own decades of research in deafness, Pintner (Pintner, Eisenson, & Stanton, 1941) reviewed and summarized all available data on the intelligence of the deaf. Although the results of different investigations frequently were confusing and even contradictory, Pintner concluded that deaf children were inferior in intelligence. He set the average retardation at 10 IQ points as compared to hearing norms. He reported a relatively small variation across different types of tests (1941, pp. 126–128), listing mean IQs for deaf children of 88 on the Draw-a-Man Test, 91 on performance tests, and 86 on drawing-on-paper tests. In each case the hearing norm was 100.

Stage II, The Deaf as Concrete: Myklebust

Reviewing work done from the time of Pintner's summary, Myklebust (1953, p. 351) concluded that the evidence indicated deaf children were *not* generally inferior in intelligence. However, Myklebust qualified his stand by arguing that even if deaf children were *quantitatively* (in terms of IQ points) equal to the hearing, they were not necessarily *qualitatively* equal. He went on to claim (p. 35) that the qualitative aspects of the perceptual and conceptual functioning of deaf individuals, and their reasoning, seemed to be different. Myklebust concluded that it was difficult for the deaf child to function in "as broad and in as subtle and abstract a manner as the hearing child."

Myklebust's interpretation of the results of research led him to the following statement (1953):

Deafness causes the individual to behave differently. The entire organism functions in an entirely different manner. This shift in behavior and adjustment is compensatory in nature. . . . Deafness does not simply cause an inability in human communication. It causes the individual to see differently, to smell differently, to use tactile and kinesthetic sensation differently. And perhaps more important than all of these, but because of them, the deaf person perceives differently. As a result of all these shifts in functioning, his personality adjustment and behavior are also different. To say that the deaf person is like the hearing person except that he cannot hear is to oversimplify and to do an injustice to the deaf child. His deafness is not only in the ears, it pervades his entire being. (p. 347)

Although Myklebust represents a welcome improvement over Pintner's summary, in essence he perceives the deaf as being quantitatively equal to the hearing but qualitatively inferior. He attributes the qualitative inferiority to the more "concrete," and therefore less "abstract," nature of the intelligence of deaf people. Myklebust and Brutton (1953) comment on "the overall concreteness which has been attributed to the deaf" and state that deafness "restricts the child functionally to a world of concrete objects and things" (p. 93). Unfortunately, largely because of the influence of Myklebust, it has become a cliché among educators of the deaf that deaf children are more "concrete." It is doubly unfortunate because of the somewhat pejorative nature of the term and because neither *concrete* nor *abstract* are ever defined. R. Brown (1958) has treated the subject in detail, especially the tendency to use *concrete* to categorize without explaining or defining terms. Brown remarks:

There is a beautiful simplicity in the notion that all departures from ourselves are basically the same kind of departure. *Abstract* is the word that has been chosen to name the special quality of our mind and *concrete* the word for all other minds. The words have been used to maintain the master preconception rather than with referential consistency. The result is that *concrete* and *abstract* name all sorts of behaviors having no clear common properties. These unwitting shifts in reference are responsible for the general agreement that all kinds of sub-human mind are concrete, as opposed to the abstract mind of the healthy, civilized adult. (p. 297)

Stage III, The Deaf as Intellectually Normal: Rosenstein and Vernon

In a review of the literature of perception, cognition, and language in deaf children, Rosenstein (1961) remarked on the lack of agreement on terminology. He noted (p. 276) for example, that the label, *abstract ability* has been used to refer to a visual memory task, a test of nonverbal reasoning by analogy, and an arithmetic reasoning task. In other contexts the same tasks have been assigned different labels; for example, a figure-ground relations test was interpreted by one writer as representing a *perceptual* ability and by another as representing a *conceptual* ability (p. 276).

Rosenstein reviewed several studies conducted with deaf subjects and reported that no differences could be found between deaf and hearing subjects in conceptual performance when the linguistic factors presented were within the language experience of the samples of deaf children. He concluded that the sphere of abstract thought is not closed to the deaf. In a survey of the literature on language and cognition, Furth (1964) reached essentially similar conclusions and reasoned that the poorer performance of deaf individuals on some tasks may be explained parsimoniously either by lack of general experience that is no longer manifest by adulthood or by specific task conditions that favor linguistic habits.

Using a somewhat different approach, Vernon (1967d) reviewed a total of 31 research studies conducted on more than 8,000 deaf children ranging in age from 3 to 19. Those represented all studies of intelligence of the deaf conducted from 1930 to 1966 that Vernon could locate and involved 16 different performance tests on intelligence. Vernon reported (p. 330) that in 13 of the experiments, the deaf had superior mean or median scores to either test norms or control groups, whichever was used. In 7 studies the scores were not significantly different, and in the remaining 11 studies the deaf were inferior. Vernon summarized the results as follows:

When one examines the high mass of data and the comparisons made with it, keeping in mind the aforementioned higher incidence of neurological impairment of and the lower socioeconomic background of the deaf group, it is clear that these language-impoverished [sic] youths do as well in a wide variety of tasks that measure thinking as do youngsters of normal language development. (p. 331)

Thus, by the 1960s leading researchers in the area had come to the conclusion that deaf people are not intellectually deficient. Obviously, however, the consensus remained that deaf people — on the basis of poor skills in standard English — were language deficient or linguistically impoverished. This consensus will be challenged in the following section.

Relationship of Thought, Language, and Deafness

The activities of Furth (1964, 1966a, 1969, 1971, 1973, 1974) have made educators of the deaf aware of the work of Piaget and have been influential in modifying the perceptions of educators toward language, thought, and deafness. Of greatest impact, perhaps, has been Furth's assertion that although deaf children receive inadequate instruction in English, speech, and school subjects, and although their parents are miscounseled and misled; and although they face prejudice, distrust, and discrimination — in spite of all this — the majority of deaf individuals make an adequate adjustment to the world.

Furth, among others, has contributed to a move away from the tendency to view deafness and deaf individuals on the basis of deviancy, deficiency, or pathology, substituting for these the much healthier and more positive approach of searching for strengths and fostering optimal development. He has affirmed the independence of thinking from language, at least up to concrete operatory thinking, and has advocated a reordering of priorities in education of the deaf (as well as general education) in which education for thinking would take priority over language instruction. Without denying the importance of language, especially for the developed mind, Furth argues that the appropriate medium for helping the developing mind is not verbal language, but rather experience in concrete situations (1971). As a result of this position, projects such as a thinking laboratory for deaf children (Furth, 1969) and a book of games without words (Wolff & Wolff, 1973) have been developed.

If one were to play devil's advocate, however, it should be noted that many of Furth's statements tend to be categorical assertions of fact instead of more appropriate presentations of hypotheses, which, at best, are debatable. Frequently many of these assertions are unqualified or qualified only in other writings, thereby causing confusion in unwary readers. Some examples are provided in the direct quotes below:

The simple fact is that Piaget is the one great psychologist who holds a theory of thinking that makes sense of the fact that deaf children can grow up into thinking human beings even though they do not know much language. (1971, p. 9)

The inferior performance of the deaf on some tasks is parsimoniously attributed to either lack of general experience which is no longer manifest by adulthood or to specific task conditions which favor linguistic habits. (1964, p. 145)

Language refers to the living language as heard and spoken in our society. (1964, p. 147)

We use the term experiential deficiency to describe the intellectual poverty in which deaf children grow up. (1973, p. 259)

Sign language is the natural language of the deaf. (1974, p. 267)

Language is a principal and preferred medium of thinking for a developed mind, for a mind that has reached, as Piaget calls it, the formal operative stage. (1971, p. 11)

Where deaf persons in general fall short is at the formal operative level. More precisely what happens is that they barely reach formal operative thinking, and then they cannot develop their minds much further because they do not have the tool of language. (1971, p. 12)

The above statements contain several inconsistencies and unquestioned assumptions that should be challenged. Of primary importance is the belief, implicit and explicit, that deaf individuals typically do not know much language. Furth has referred to the extensive literature regarding low levels of reading achievement to justify his position that deaf individuals tend to be linguistically deficient. However, reading achievement scores do not necessarily reflect linguistic functioning. Considering his reliance on reading achievement scores and his reference to living language as that heard and spoken in our society, it appears that Furth means that deaf people tend to be deficient in standard middle-class American English usage. Given his statement that sign language is the natural language of the deaf, it would seem that his statements on the lack of language in the deaf be qualified pending intensive investigations on the nature and functions of sign language. For example, when the author was a classroom teacher beginning to learn to sign and to teach through the use of simultaneous signs and speech, he found that in the case of difficult concepts—or, rather, concepts difficult for him to communicate — if one student could get the concept, the idea could be conveyed easily and efficiently through sign language, no matter how seemingly difficult. In his own readings of studies of intellectual functioning of the deaf, the author has come to the conclusion that in those cases where the deaf have shown inferior performance, the most parsimonious explanation may be neither lack of language nor experiential deficiency, but rather the very real possibility that *the experimenters were unable to communicate effectively with the deaf subjects*. Therefore, the author believes serious reservations must be entertained concerning Furth's position because: (1) he has not demonstrated that the deaf lack language; and (2) he has not demonstrated that deaf persons "fall short" at the formal operative level. Given the above position, the author also must question claims that only Piaget's theory of thinking can explain the existence of thought without language in the deaf, not because of any basic disagreement with Piaget, but because the deaf, as a group, cannot be considered to be without language.

It also should be pointed out that, despite Furth's claims, Piaget is not the only theorist who does not consider intelligence to be based on language. As Furth himself acknowledges (1964, p. 145), William James in 1890 and Binet and Simon in 1905 suggested that thought processes were developed in a deaf person before language. As the present chapter demonstrates, a review of articles in the *American Annals of the Deaf* suggests a consistent interest in the relationships between thought and language, beginning with an article in the first volume by Ray (1848) titled "Thoughts of the deaf and dumb before instruction." As may be expected, opinions were diverse, and there were frequent exchanges of a very active nature, sometimes running over several issues of *Annals*. The most ambitious undertaking was a translation from the German of Schneider's, "The thought and language of the deaf-mute," which was published in nine installments of the *Annals* from 1908 to 1911.

Outside of the field of education of the deaf, it is inaccurate to state that Piaget's is the only theory that does not consider intelligence to be language-based. Osgood (1963, 1966, 1968), for example, consistently has argued for the primacy of meaning. Furth's statement also ignores the extensive recent work dealing with semantic bases of language and attention given to the primacy of cognitive development (e.g., Antinucci & Parisi, 1973; Bloom, 1970; Bowerman, 1973; R. Brown, 1973; Clark, 1973; MacNamara, 1972; I. Schlesinger, 1971; Slobin, 1973).

In his survey of cognition in handicapped children Suppes (1972, p. 41) commented that Furth does not really make a strong theoretical point because his analysis is concerned entirely with command of a standard natural language. Noting Furth's acknowledgment that the processes deaf children use are not clear, Suppes reasoned that process-oriented approaches to cognitive skills seem to argue strongly that some sort of language is being used internally, even if the language is not that of the society in which the children live.

Suppes goes on to state that the experiments on logical reasoning, on which Furth bases his conclusions, are all extremely elementary. Suppes summarized his position as follows:

It seems to me that the real test will not be successful efforts to transform more sophisticated forms of inference into nonverbal contexts, because this seems prima facie impossible, but rather to test the ability to communicate and handle such inferences in sign language. These more developed forms of inference are not primarily auditory in nature but visual; for example, there is very little development of mathematical proofs in purely auditory fashion. (p. 41)

An Alternate Approach

Since the present chapter is oriented to educational implications for the deaf, it is most appropriate to turn to the position of a theorist whose work influenced educational procedures with deaf children, as Furth's already has. This would be Lev Vygotsky, whose book *Thought and language* first appeared in 1934 and was translated into English in 1962. Vygotsky was yet another theorist who did not consider intelligence to be language-based. In discussing the genetic roots of thought and language, he concluded:

1. In their ontogenetic development, thought and speech have different roots.
2. In the speech development of the child, we can with certainty establish a preintellectual stage, and in his thought development, a prelinguistic stage.
3. Up to a certain point in time, the two follow different lines, independently of each other.
4. At a certain point, these lines meet, whereupon thought becomes verbal and speech rational. (p. 44)

Because Vygotsky's work has been so influential with Soviet educators of the deaf, who have in turn been critical of Furth's position (Shif, 1969), the author will outline some areas in which Soviet techniques differ from Furth's, which primarily involve thinking activities based on Piagetian principles (Furth, 1969) and placing relatively little reliance on language and communication. It is suggested that fruitful areas of study might involve examination of the effects of the different procedures on the general development of deaf children.

It should first be noted that in the Soviet Union it is customary to address the complex dialectical interdependence of thought and language rather than to treat them separately. Shif (1969), for example, has criticized Furth for studying language and thinking interaction outside of the developmental changes that occur in the course of deaf children's acquisition of language. Shif argues that behind grammatical activities which occur so quickly in hearing children are complex mental processes. Another characteristic is the belief that complex mental processes, or complex functional systems, are formed during the child's associations with adults (Luria, 1969). Third, it is believed that the child from the beginning is a social being who must develop a means of communication as quickly as possible.

To a large extent, the type of activities utilized are similar to those advocated by Furth. Instruction concentrates on practical activities to encourage independence (Moores, 1972a). There is extensive use of manipulative toys and materials such as paper, plastic, textiles, papier-mâché, and plexiglas. Emphasis is placed on arts and crafts to develop concepts of position and color as well as creativity. Activities with practical application include work with illustrations and figures. There are numerous measuring and continuing experiences. A large portion of children's early education is devoted to organized observation of the environment.

Despite the above similarities, the goals of Soviet educators of the deaf represent a different set of priorities (Moores, 1972a). They are:

1. To give the child tools of communication, especially expressive communication, at an early age.
2. To change a passive youngster to an active one with initiative in learning.
3. To free the child and his language from the immediate situation. (p. 380)

To illustrate the principle of communication, Zukov, during a discussion with the author (Moores, 1972a), represented the interdependence of language and subject matter by showing language as the hub of a wheel with spokes radiating out to the circumference (Figure 7.1). Language is considered the most important dimension of the first stage of education and is included in all subjects. Without language, Zukov argued, other subjects cannot be taught effectively. Language is a means of communication in itself and must be taught as such. Just as language can be used to teach all subjects, all knowledge can also be used to enrich language developments. Because early education is centered on everyday needs, the first words taught to children are those through which they can influence their environment. Typically, the first word taught is *give* (note the similarity to Premack), and it is introduced in the context of toys. Initial emphasis is on such action words as *come, go, eat, drink, sleep, sit,* and *walk.*

The above material is a response to the assumption implicit in Furth's, and others', approach that deaf individuals can develop either their language or their thought, but not both. Many psychologists are interested in studying the nature of thought without language. In the author's opinion, deaf individuals are not appropriate candidates for such investigations, because they *do* have language. The outline of an approach based on Vygotsky's work is an attempt to illustrate briefly that there are alternatives to the present systems of educating deaf children which involve different conceptions of language/thought interactions that are worthy of consideration and investigation.

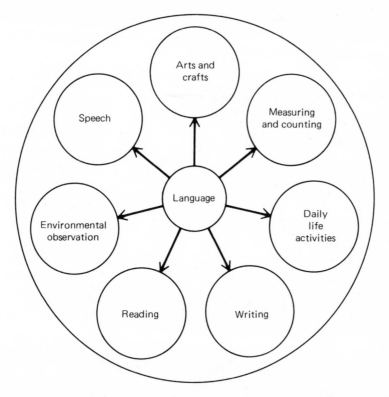

Figure 7.1 The principle of communication (Zukov). (From D. Moores, "Neo-Oralism and Education of the Deaf in the Soviet Union," *Exceptional Children*, 38 (1972), 377–384. Used by permission.)

Conclusion

The available evidence suggests that the condition of deafness imposes no limitations on the intellectual capabilities of individuals. In addition, there is no evidence to suggest that deaf persons think in more "concrete" ways than the hearing or that their intellectual functioning is in any way less sophisticated. As a group, deaf people function within the normal range of intelligence, and deaf individuals exhibit the same wide variability as the hearing population.

It is concluded finally that the efforts to use deaf subjects in order to study language/thought interactions is misdirected. Deaf people do not lack language abilities — no matter what scores are obtained on standardized tests of reading achievement — and in no way can they be considered alinguistic.

8
Deafness and Mental Health

Introduction

There have been two basic approaches to the question of social-emotional, or "psychological," adjustment of deaf individuals. The first, and most commonly used, assumes what might be called a *deviancy model*. Within this model the emphasis is on identifying ways in which deaf persons are different from a norm or standard established for a hearing population. Difference is equated with deviance — with all its negative connotations — and *deviance* comes to be used interchangeably with *deficiency*. The deviance model has been the basis for various "psychologies of deafness" that have been promulgated over the last several generations. Implicit in the term *psychology of deafness*, of course, is a belief that the impact of deafness is so overwhelming that general psychological principles are inadequate to deal with the condition.

A second approach, more healthy and more realistic, is beginning to receive attention and support from professionals concerned with the social-emotional development of deaf individuals. Rather than searching for that which is different, deviant, or deficient, emphasis is placed on the conditions necessary for the development of a healthy, whole, well-integrated person. Implicit in this approach is the assumption that the basic needs of all human beings, hearing or deaf, are essentially similar and that the development of a healthy personality is based on meeting those needs satisfactorily.

The trend toward a more positive model of human nature held by those concerned with the impact of deafness on development reflects a general movement away from the deviance models, especially those based on Freudian principles that were dominant in psychology in the nineteenth century and most of the twentieth century. The developmental theories of Maslow (1954) and Erikson (1959, 1963, 1968) have been especially influential in laying the foundations by which the growth of the individual may be perceived within a more balanced framework.

Schlesinger and Meadow (1972a) place the issue in the following perspective:

Does the absence of early auditory stimulation, feedback and communication in itself create a propensity toward a particular adaptive pattern? Or, alternatively, does early

140

profound deafness elicit particular responses from parents, teachers, siblings and peers that contribute to developmental problems referred to above? These are questions that are difficult to resolve in an either/or way, since the concomitants of organic deafness and the social expectations it arouses in others are intertwined from the very beginning. Rather than belaboring the nature/nurture controversy, it is more fruitful to look instead at the entire life cycle, examining instances of optimal and minimal adjustment and seeking out the antecedents, correlates and consequences of these patterns. (pp. 2–3)

The Limitations of Research in Social-Emotional Development of Deaf Individuals

Before addressing representative research, it is necessary to establish an appropriate set by which results may be interpreted. Two overriding factors cannot be ignored. First is the extremely difficult nature of the task of assessing what we will call "personality," and second is the fact that the impact of deafness, per se, on an individual can never be measured in isolation but only within the context of complex social variables.

If the measurement of intelligence is an inexact science, then the measurement of personality is an inexact art. For all the difficulties that have faced the field of intelligence testing, it must be acknowledged that wide varieties of reliable and empirically validated tests have been developed and used extensively. Examiners have at their disposal individual and group tests, verbal and performance tests, oral and paper-and-pencil tests, and tests that provide either quantitative or qualitative results. With only a few notable exceptions — for example, the Minnesota Multi-Phasic Inventory (MMPI) — similarly reliable and valid measures of personality do not exist. The process is much more subjective, and interpretation of results is susceptible to a much greater degree to the bias of interpreters. Because most of the more commonly used measures either require a relatively high level of reading (e.g., the MMPI) or should involve substantial communication between tester and testee (e.g., the Rorschach and the Thematic Apperception Test, or TAT), their applicability to deaf individuals may be limited. An exceptional degree of caution must be reserved for interpretation of results obtained through utilization of procedures such as the TAT and Rorschach. It is essential that the examiner have experience communicating with deaf individuals with a wide range of oral and English skills, including some who may rely completely on manual communication.

Results of investigations of social-emotional adjustment of deaf individuals also may be influenced by factors only incidentally related to deafness itself. The most obvious example relates to commonly observed familial stresses caused by inadequate adjustment to the presence of a deaf child. As detailed in Chapter 5, the presence of a deaf child in a family can be a traumatic, emotionally draining experience, beginning with the process of identification and continuing into adulthood. Feelings of guilt, recrimination, and hostility are common. Because the majority of parents of deaf children have normal hearing and have had little contact with deaf individuals, deafness constitutes a mysterious, threatening force difficult to confront. Communication with the child is often minimal, and normal two-way communication between parent and child may not exist.

In such a situation a deaf child, reacting to a lack of effective communication and to other negative aspects of the environment, may develop patterns of behavior that may be classified as "immature," "hyperkinetic," "autistic," "egocentric," and so on. However, to attribute this behavior to deafness is to miss the point entirely. It more appropriately may be attributed to unsatisfactory environmental conditions that developed because a child's parents were not helped to adjust to the fact of deafness and therefore did not provide the child sufficient environmental support to develop to his or her potential.

Another factor that is commonly overlooked — and is of special concern in evaluating studies comparing groups of deaf individuals to groups of hearing individuals — is the fact that some of the major causes of deafness such as rubella, meningitis, and mother-child blood incompatibility may involve harmful sequelae and residua in addition to hearing loss. To take a hypothetical example, researchers might compare a group of deaf and hearing children born in the early 1960s on a number of variables and find that the hearing children were more robust, better coordinated, and less impulsive. However, unless the researchers controlled for etiology, the extent to which they might generalize their findings would be limited severely. Lower group scores might be explained by the presence of substantial numbers of deaf children with an etiology of rubella with involvements, however mild, in addition to deafness. Low scores also might have resulted in part from a tendency of some mothers of deaf children to restrict the children's activities so that they do not develop physical skills to the same degree as their hearing siblings.

A useful rule of thumb in evaluating research of this nature is to examine the *upper* range of scores of the respective groups. If the highest scores obtained by individuals in the deaf groups are similar to the highest scores in the hearing group on a particular measure, then it would be a mistake to conclude that deafness itself influences functioning in that area, even if group mean scores were lower for the deaf group.

To summarize, results of investigations of social-emotional adjustment of deaf individuals, Levine (1960, pp. 51 and 52) reported that all studies found the

1. Many of the instruments used assume a level of communicative interaction that may not exist between hearing testers and some deaf testees.

2. Adequate development of a deaf individual may be inhibited not by deafness itself but by inadequate coping behaviors of significant others in the environment.

3. The residua and sequelae of some of the major etiologies of deafness may involve impairments in addition to hearing loss.

Nominalism and Reification

A final cautionary note is in order. In the behavioral sciences, it is a common failing of practitioners to neglect to define their terms. One widespread phenomenon is the recourse to *nominalism,* which may be defined as equating the naming, labeling, or categorizing of a behavior or characteristic with a description or definition of the behavior or characteristic. Thus, it may be simple or convenient to label a child as *schizophrenic, aphasic, autistic,* or *learning disabled.* The terms themselves may be useful and even may convey specific information among professionals sharing a particular jargon or argot, but their abuse is much more frequent than their proper use. To say that a person behaves in a certain way "because he is schizophrenic" or "because she is aphasic" is a periphrastic — and paraphrastic — exercise. For example, an individual may be classified as *autistic* on the basis of certain behaviors. Then the term is used in such a way as to suggest an explanation of the behaviors that originally were the basis for the label. A classical example of nominalism is the misuse of the term *dyslexia* by many educators. Children may be labeled dyslexic on the basis of their failure to learn to read (a seldom acknowledged alternative is that the school never taught them to read). If an observer were later to inquire why the children could not read, the answer would be, "Because they are dyslexic." A perfect tautology: (1) They are dyslexic because they have not learned to read; (2) They have not learned to read because they are dyslexic. Unfortunately, it is doubtful whether such exercises in semantics help to understand and ameliorate the condition of nonreaders.

Related to nominalism is *reification,* which may be defined as the tendency to believe that just because a label or term is used, it refers to something that actually exists. The most obvious examples of such misuse of terms relates to Freud's concepts of *id, ego,* and *superego* — constructs that he developed as efficient mechanisms to aid in his examination and explication of various aspects of human functioning. Unfortunately, the concepts in many cases have been distorted to the extent that the terms are interpreted as referring to actual components or aspects of an individual, or of personality. Pressing further, one might argue that the use of the term *personality* also constitutes a resort to reification. It should be remembered that the spread of American behavioristic psychology may be attributed in large part to the overreliance of "mentalistic" psychology on nominalism and reification in place of tough-minded, empirically based experimentation. However, it also should be remembered that the counterreaction against behaviorism may be attributed to reluctance, or inability, to come to terms with issues of complex human behavior.

Research on Personality Characteristics
of Deaf Individuals

In a review of personality studies conducted with deaf groups, Donoghue (1968) presents the major issue in the following manner:

Psychological research indicates, as is so often the case in our discipline, that over the years professional opinions concerning the effects of auditory failure on the adjustment pattern of the deaf have polarized to some extent. In one division of this dichotomy of opinion there are those who maintain the loss of hearing, whether fully or partially, leads to an increasing number of atypical behavioral symptoms which suggest at least a graduated degree of emotional maladjustment probably is present. At some variance with this form of ontological metaphysics, there are those who maintain that that functional loss of any part of the physique, be it motor, sensori-neural, or some other variety, need not necessarily be pinpointed as a probable etiological source of observed abnormalities. (pp. 39–40)

A cursory reading of the most commonly cited studies of personality characteristics of deaf individuals would suggest that the first position is the more prevalent: that the loss of hearing leads to atypical behavior symptoms. Pintner, Fusfeld, and Brunswig (1937) reported that the deaf are more neurotic, introverted, and less dominant than the hearing. Soloman (1943) reported deaf subjects to be immature, submissive, and dependent. Deaf subjects also tended to be more insecure, apathetic, anxious, and suspicious. In a study of teenage deaf girls utilizing the Wechsler Adult Intelligence Scale (WAIS) and the Rorschach test, Levine (1956) reported that the deaf subjects were egocentric, irritable, impulsive, and suggestible and that for them controls were external. Myklebust (1964) noted an immaturity in caring for others and stated that responses of deaf subjects to the MMPI suggested psychotic reactions. Springer and Roslaw (1938) reported a higher incidence of neurotic tendencies among the deaf as well as a greater degree of repressive behavior.

Baroff (1955) reported that the deaf exhibit lack of anxiety, introspection, and impulse control. Levine (1948) reported similar findings but suggested such behaviors reflect normal adjustment mechanisms, given the environment deaf individuals face. Altshuler (1962, 1963) has characterized the behavior of deaf subjects in terms such as "egocentric," "lack of empathy," "gross coercive dependency," "impulsivity," and "absence of thoughtful introspection."

In summarizing research results obtained utilizing projective techniques with deaf individuals, Levine (1960, pp. 51 and 52) reported that all studies found the following characteristics: emotional immaturity, personality constriction, and deficient emotional adaptability. More than a decade later, Schlesinger and Meadow (1972a) arrived at the same conclusion: "Psychologically, the most frequently stated conclusion about deaf individuals is that they seem to reflect a high degree of 'emotional immaturity' " (p. 2).

However, the situation is not so clear-cut as a summary of the literature might suggest. Almost every one of the above researchers felt constrained to qualify his or her findings. The lack of confidence in the results, or at least the reluctance to generalize from the findings, may be attributed to a number of factors. First is the questionable suitability of the instruments used. Heider and Heider (1941), for example, decried the practice of studying deaf individuals primarily by means of instruments developed for individuals with normal hearing. They expressed particularly strong reservations toward the comparison of deaf and hearing groups based on tests designed to measure adjustment to the life faced by normally hearing individuals. Grinker (1967) advocated the development of instruments directly devised and applicable to the deaf and suggested a TAT could be devised to elicit the specific emotional problems of the deaf.

Although Myklebust reported that scores on the MMPI were deviant from hearing norms, he also pointed out the extroverted social feeling of the deaf, a condition which is not common in individuals exhibiting psychotic behavior. Therefore, the usual psychopathological categories delineated by the MMPI were not appropriate to his subjects. Best (1943) also has commented on the gregariousness of deaf people, as a group, and has expressed his admiration for their optimism and ability to cope with an indifferent or hostile world.

It also should be emphasized that behavior which might be considered maladaptive, neurotic, or psychotic in one situation might be healthy and realistic in another. For example, people classified as paranoid might have delusions of prosecution. They might believe incorrectly that people talk about them or dislike them or are hostile to them. However, for many deaf people such beliefs are not delusions, they reflect reality. In too many cases, deaf persons have faced rejection and hostility from their families. Their sense of worth has been denigrated because of unclear speech patterns. People *do* talk about them — teachers of the deaf seem especially prone to tell visitors at length about the limitations of their students in front of the children as though they had no sense of what was occurring — and they *do* face social and economic discrimination. Within this context, Knapp (1968) and Zeckel (1953) challenge the negative conclusions of many of the studies on personality adjustment of deaf individuals and argue, for example, that because deaf people have good reason to be aware of the derogatory behavior of others toward them, a feeling of mistrust is a healthy — not a psychopathological — reaction.

In addition, the testing situation must be a threatening situation for many deaf subjects. In all the above studies, the tester had normal hearing. The vocabulary frequently was unfamiliar, and the deaf subjects usually had to rely completely on oral communication. Even when manual communication was employed, the situation tended to be artificial. For example, in a review of the literature, Mangan (1963) noted that Levine's (1956) investigation of responses of deaf girls to the Rorschach involved manual as well as oral communication, and he concluded that the study provided for excellent communication between examiner and subjects. However, there is reason to question this conclusion. The subjects were all students at the Lexington School for the Deaf, an oral-only school that does not allow signs in the classroom. Although it has been reported that the students use signs as their preferred mode of communication outside of the school grounds (Kohl, 1966), they probably were reluctant to do so with hearing adults. Also, in the research study under consideration, manual communication was a one-way street. The examiner never resorted to signs but, rather, relied completely on speech. Only the subjects were free to respond by speech, signs, and gestures. In discussing the use of projective techniques, Donaghue (1968) stated:

Language is not an insurmountable barrier to a test such as the Rorschach; it can be given in English, German, Urdu or the language of signs used by deaf persons. The only really important criterion, aside from the examiner's professional proficiency, is the determination of whether the language employed is the one the client and examiner can adequately use in discussing the percept seen. This is a most important consideration where the deaf are concerned. (p. 43)

Seen in this light, the study reported by Levine (1956) does represent an advance over other studies referred to, in that the subjects at least were permitted to use manual communication. Still, tester and testee used different modes. Given the oral-only philosophy of the Lexington school at that time, the hearing status of the examiner, and the complete reliance of the examiner on oral communication, it is safe to assume that the testing situation was not an optimum one.

In sum, it appears that, in regard to deafness, efforts at the assessment of personality variables are at about the same level as intelligence testing was 30 years ago. For the most part, inappropriate tests have been administered under unsatisfactory conditions, and results have been compared with unrealistic norms. An impressive number of competent researchers with experience in the area of deafness (Donoghue, 1968; Heider & Heider, 1941; Levine, 1948; Myklebust, 1964; Schlesinger & Meadow, 1972a) have questioned the results obtained and/or the extent to which the findings reflect actual deviancies in the deaf population.

The Establishment of Psychiatric and Mental Health Services for the Deaf

Major initial advances in research and provision of services to the deaf in the fields of psychiatry and mental health have been made essentially by professionals in four institutes: the New York State Psychiatric Institute; Michael Reese Medical Center Psychiatric and Psychosomatic Institute, Chicago, Illinois; St. Elizabeth's Hospital, Washington, D.C.; and the Langley Porter Neuropsychiatric Institute, San Francisco, California. Although the organization and objectives of each of these institutes vary somewhat, their combined efforts have been such as to exert a profound impact on educational, rehabilitative, and social programs for the deaf throughout the world. Contributions have been made in the development of models for the provision of services to deaf individuals on inpatient and outpatient bases, in clinical and incidence research, in parent counseling, and in the training of professional personnel to work with deaf individuals. Each of the programs also has begun, at least, to study techniques by which the optimal development of deaf individuals might be facilitated. Each of the institutes has been involved in training, research, and service. As such, they form a unique group. For example, in 1970, outside of the United States, there was only one psychiatric service unit for the deaf in the world, the Wittingham Hospital Department of Psychiatry for the Deaf in Preston, Lancashire, England (Denmark & Eldridge, 1971).

The New York program, which was begun in 1955, preceded the other three by approximately ten years. Because the State of New York has taken a leading role in making commitments to the development of mental health programs for the deaf, the statewide system of services is a model that should be emulated in other areas. A short description of the evolution of the New York system may provide some insight into the conditions and procedures necessary for the development of mental health services on a state or regional basis. For complete details on the system readers are referred to the reports written on the various projects connected with it (Altshuler & Rainer, 1968; Rainer & Altshuler, 1966, 1967, 1970; Rainer, Altshuler, & Kallman, 1963).

The first major activity involved a statewide census of the deaf, the gathering of basic statistics and interviews of randomly selected deaf individuals and families. All deaf patients in New York State mental hospitals were identified and followed, and a psychiatric outpatient clinic for the deaf was established. The outpatient clinic, although little publicized, served more than 200 patients, even though it was open only two days per week (Rainer, Altshuler, & Kallman, 1963). Information on deaf patients scattered throughout the state's 21 mental hospitals suggested that they frequently were isolated, misdiagnosed, poorly evaluated, and virtually untreated. For example, original figures suggested that the incidence of schizophrenia among the deaf was higher than would be predicted on the basis of population figures. However, on closer examination it was shown that schizophrenia was not more common among deaf *admissions* than among hearing admissions. The discrepancies were traced to the fact that to a greater degree hearing patients received treatment and were released, whereas deaf patients more frequently were untreated and tended to be institutionalized longer. Because of the lack of trained professional personnel capable of communicating with them, deaf patients frequently became custodial cases.

The first phase — gathering data and establishing outpatient services — extended over a seven-year period, from 1955 to 1962. The second phase, from 1963 to 1966, developed as a demonstration project a special inpatient unit for the deaf at Rockland State Hospital (Rainer & Altshuler, 1966). The outpatient services were expanded, and consultative relationships were established with the New York School for the Deaf in White Plains.

The third phase, from 1966 to 1970 (Rainer & Altshuler, 1970), had a number of different objectives. First was the development of a halfway house to facilitate reintegration into the community. Related to this was further development of close cooperation between the total state psychiatric program and the various state rehabilitation agencies. A new aspect of the system was the development of a program of preventive psychiatry in the New York City metropolitan area. In somewhat of a departure from previous activities, this effort was concerned with a wide range, from early school age through the adult years. Services included group therapy for students, group counseling for parents, and discussions with teachers and cottage personnel at a school for the deaf.

Recommendations for Rehabilitation and Preventive Services for the Deaf (Rainer & Altshuler, 1970)

Relying on the knowledge and experience gathered from their efforts extending from 1955 to 1970, Rainer and Altshuler (1970) advanced the following recommendations and observations:

1. Mental illness and emotional difficulty are no less prevalent among the deaf than among the hearing. Diagnosis and treatment are more difficult and take longer.
2. Experienced mental health personnel (psychiatrist, psychologist, social worker, rehabilitation worker, nurse) must and can be recruited and trained in manual communication and special problems of the deaf. A teacher of sign language is an early and prime requisite.
3. Psychiatric treatment methods (individual and group psychotherapy and pharmacotherapy) can be adapted and applied to the deaf patient.
4. A clinic can be established once the personnel are available and will draw referrals from schools, rehabilitation agencies, families, physicians and the deaf themselves.
5. The deaf community can be made aware of the value of mental health facilities and will give aid by educational and volunteer programs, once the stigma of mental illness is removed.
6. For the acute or more seriously mentally ill deaf person, inpatient hospital facilities are the most efficient means for concentrating therapeutic efforts. A ward for patients of both sexes, with a specially trained staff is most effective, and 30 beds have been found adequate to deal with the needs of the adult deaf population of a state as large as New York. Patients with illness of recent onset have the best prognosis, but chronic patients transferred from other hospitals to such a special ward often do strikingly well.
7. Such a ward ought to offer as a minimum, medical and nursing care, individual and group psychotherapy, drug and other somatic treatments and an occupational therapy workshop. Group therapy is particularly effective in fostering deaf patients' insight into their own behavior.
8. For the most effective results of a comprehensive treatment program, it has to be supplemented by a rehabilitation approach as described in the present report. Psychiatric case finding, diagnosis, and treatment of the deaf patient only bear full results when a rehabilitation team paves the way back to the outside world. This is especially important for the deaf where many needed facilities must be built or strengthened.
9. The rehabilitation counselor can function best as part of the mental health team,

working in regular liaison with state agencies to open case files while patients are still under treatment. Exploration of patient's vocational skills and interests must begin before discharge and the lag between discharge and placement kept at a minimum.

10. Through occupational therapy workshop and other voactional training shops, new skills can be developed. Group and individual teaching in the hospital can improve patients' abilities in the 3R's; for this an experienced teacher of the deaf is essential.

11. Housing is of prime importance; by adding an experienced social worker who knows the problems of the deaf and can communicate well, it is possible to arrange for such placement (family, individual, home, foster care, as the case may be) and to teach the patients how to go to and from work and organize their lives in the most healthy way.

12. Halfway house facilities in the community can be used for interim housing and reintegration of the deaf hospital [sic] into the community. A social worker at the halfway house specifically assigned to the group of deaf persons can effectively show them the upward path of increasing independence. Deaf and hearing ex-patients work together well at this halfway house level.

13. Turning to prevention of psychiatric disturbance, schools for the deaf can make effective use of a mental health team — psychiatrist, psychologist and social worker. Trouble shooting with early psychiatric intervention is but one approach. Group therapy with adolescent students encourages greater awareness of interpersonal relations and forestalls problems in this area. Discussions with teachers and cottage personnel alert them to difficulties and assist them in proper handling of their pupils.

14. Since mental health begins at home, early contact with parents of deaf children and counseling, individually and in groups can help these parents to overcome their guilt and shame, avoid the extremes of over-protection and rejection, and encourage them to communicate with the children by all means available. Social worker and psychiatrist can both work in bringing parents together for this purpose.

15. Deaf professional personnel can be of great value at all levels and should be recruited or trained whenever possible. (pp. iii–iv)

Rainer and Altshuler's comprehensive recommendations can provide the foundations for the establishment of effective state and regional programs. With only a few notable exceptions, they have yet to be utilized systematically and, for the present, constitute ideals to be pursued. It is hoped that the situation will improve in all states and regions in the near future.

The Facilitation of Optimal Development

Consistent with the findings of the New York Psychiatric Institute, the staffs of the Langley-Porter, St. Elizabeth, and Michael Reese institutes have emphasized that the incidence of emotional disturbance in deaf adults would be much lower if effective programs could be established to reach parents of deaf children and help them deal with their children in more effective ways. In discussing the Michael Reese program, Stein, Merrill, and Dahlberg (1974) stated:

Many of the mental health programs of the adult deaf can be traced to inadequacies of early parent-child relationships, unrealistic expectations on the parts of parents, and the inability of parents to ever accept the fact that their growing child is different and to a certain extent always will be different. Basically we were interested in developing programs to prevent or at least moderate the occurrence of mental health problems in the adult deaf population by fostering a more healthy, early parent-child relationship. With this in mind, staff child psychiatrists, clinical psychologists, and psychiatric social workers established individual and group psychotherapy sessions to explore the feelings of parents who enrolled in our preschool program. (p. 3)

It is interesting to note that the above-mentioned program conducted by the Siegel Institute for Communicative Disorders, Michael Reese Medical Center, was the first preschool program in the Midwest to use manual communication. It was initiated in 1966 in the face of strong opposition from some of the public school programs in the Chicago area. In some cases parents were informed that their children would not be allowed to enroll later in public schools because of the danger that other deaf children would be contaminated by their signs.[*] Since that time the situation has changed radically, and the public schools in the area have followed the lead of Michael Reese in implementing more flexible educational programs.

Work actually was begun at St. Elizabeth's Hospital by Robinson in 1963, when he initiated a group psychotherapy class for six mentally ill deaf patients (Bowe, 1971b). The first full-time staff member was added in 1968, and the hospital now serves individuals on both an inpatient and outpatient basis.

Meadow, a sociologist, and Schlesinger, a psychiatrist, in their work affiliated with the Langley-Porter Institute (Schlesinger, 1969; Schlesinger & Meadow, 1971, 1972a, 1972b) also have stressed the importance of the early years for satisfactory development and have devoted a great amount of effort to facilitate the adjustment of parents toward a realistic acceptance of deafness in their children.

Meadow and Schlesinger utilized the developmental approach of Erikson (1959, 1963, 1968), who perceives the development of the individual as progressing through a sequence of critical stages or phases. Each stage presents the individual with a crisis, or task, that must be met successfully. The individual has at his or her disposal parental and societal resources. Erikson identifies the following eight phases in the life cycle of the individual:

1. Basic trust versus mistrust: infancy
2. Autonomy versus shame and doubt: early childhood
3. Initiative versus guilt: childhood
4. Industry versus inferiority: school age
5. Identity versus identity confusion: adolescence

[*] Personal communication, McCay Vernon, November 1966.

6. Intimacy versus isolation: young adulthood
7. Generativity versus stagnation: parenthood
8. Integrity versus despair: old age

For each phase, the outcome is usually some balance between the extremes. Schlesinger and Meadow (1972a) examined influences on the deaf child's development within an Eriksonian perspective for each of the eight stages in order to provide an understanding of the means by which parents might help their deaf children develop in spontaneous and joyful ways. Schlesinger and Meadow noted that successful passages through the life cycle were found most often in deaf children of deaf parents. Since the majority of deaf children have hearing parents, Schlesinger and Meadow presented their account in the "hope that it will help hearing parents to ponder, to increase the acceptance of deafness in their children, and with this acceptance help their children to meet and master the challenges of each life crisis" (p. 29).

Conclusion

In his book *Deafness and the deaf in the United States,* Best (1943) expressed his admiration for the way in which most deaf individuals coped with deafness and managed to live healthy, productive lives. He dedicated his book in part as follows: "the most misunderstood among the sons of man, but the 'gamest' of them all."

The present author has the same sense of admiration that Best felt. When one considers the obstacles faced by deaf individuals in their lives, the fact is that as a group they make up a well-adjusted, healthy, productive, stable, contributing segment of society. Even professionals working with deaf individuals — who should know better — have accepted unquestionably myths, distortions, and half-truths about deafness and deaf individuals. Supposed authorities on deafness have stated that deaf people are not capable of abstract thought, that they have no language, and that their personalities are deviant. All of these glib generalizations — which are supported by *no* evidence — have influenced the development of harmful stereotypes concerning deafness that are held by hearing people who have little or no contact with deaf individuals.

When the author was in a training program to become a teacher of the deaf, he was taught that the major problem of the deaf was poor speech. A few years later the consensus changed to the position that the biggest problem was language, a position the author could not accept fully because of his belief that while most deaf individuals may have difficulty with standard English usage, they obviously possess language skills. While the indictment might sound overharsh, the author's view has evolved to the extent that he believes the major obstacle facing deaf people is well-meaning but misinformed hearing individuals. This includes hearing parents who, no matter what their intentions, reject or overprotect their deaf children and fail to provide them the security of knowing love with no strings attached. It also applies to the hearing people who reject, ignore, or otherwise inappropriately react to deaf individuals.

In the final analysis, the blame cannot be attributed to parents who were miscounseled or to the lay public, which is ignorant of the nature of deafness. Parents restrict communication not because they want to but because they have been told it is in the best interests of the child. Speaking to this topic, Altshuler (1967) stated:

Another thing which is important in the relationship of parent to child in the presence of deafness, is the misguided advice that parents often get, to the effect that they should not use any type of language with the children except speech. In the end this amounts to what you might call a sort of double bind, where the message is "I want to communicate with you (the child) because I love you and ultimately want you to be able to learn to speak." Actually, however, this attitude can make for separation between parent and child if carried to an extreme. (p. 66)

The problem lies in the misuse of power exerted by so many professionals over the lives of deaf individuals from the time of diagnosis through adulthood. There are guilty practitioners in all fields — pediatricians, audiologists, otologists, psychologists, educators, social workers, counselors, and myriad others. There is little chance for improvement until the insensitivity of hearing professionals is reduced and the paternalistic — and maternalistic — attitudes of such people, with their assumptions of superiority, are obliterated.

9
American Sign Language and Manual Communication

Introduction

This chapter provides a background for the consideration of linguistic systems that apparently meet all criteria traditionally considered necessary for true languages, with one exception — they involve the visual-motor channel as the primary means of communication rather than the auditory-vocal. Manual sign languages employed by deaf individuals do indeed constitute legitimate language systems. The nature and use of sign languages will be discussed, and an overview of structural and functional characteristics of what is known as American Sign Language (ASL) will be treated. Suggestions will be made for the educational use of manual communication, and an attempt will be made to dispel some common misunderstandings. Although the major portion of this chapter deals with American Sign Language, related work in Europe is incorporated.

Although some variation of American Sign Language probably is used by a majority of deaf adults in the United States and Canada, American Sign Language remains an exotic language. It is subject to less scientific analysis than many dialects spoken by isolated tribes in the most primitive, inaccessible areas of the world. There are a number of explanations for such neglect. Of primary importance has been the tendency of many educators of the deaf to treat any form of manual communication as behavior that must be repressed. During the twentieth century, until the 1960s, programs for the deaf in the United States followed an oral-only philosophy of education, at least until age 11. After this age, some programs would allow their "oral failures" to be exposed to signs in the classroom. Children were considered failures because they did not meet the one criterion for success — speaking well enough to become part of the hearing world. Because the goal of education was "normalcy" — that is, speaking — a prejudice developed against signs as alinguistic, concrete, and inflexible. Signs were confused by some with "natural" gestures, reflecting their ignorance of the arbitrary, learned nature of a true language of signs.

A second factor that inhibited the study of manual communication systems was the tendency of many linguists, especially those heavily influenced by

Bloomfield (1933), to assume that all languages were primarily spoken and that other forms of communication — for example, written — were imperfect outgrowths of a basic spoken system. This position was challenged by the pioneering work of Stokoe (1958), who brought the tools of linguistic analysis to bear on American Sign Language and demonstrated that it is a linguistic system with all the important characteristics of a spoken language.

In addition to the work of Stokoe, other recent developments have increased interest in the function and structure of sign language systems. The input of theoreticians and researchers concerned with the biological bases of language has been considerable. Lenneberg (1967a) has advocated the use of graphics, under which he includes signs, with very young deaf children. Bellugi-Klima and her associates at the Salk Institute are conducting a series of investigations on the development and use of American Sign Language by deaf children and adults. In a presentation at the University of Minnesota in February 1972, Chomsky described as "barbaric" the educational practices in the State of Massachusetts that did not allow the use of signs with deaf children.

Another source of interest is generated by ethologists and researchers interested in investigating the growth of communication systems in animals. The work of Gardner and Gardner (1969) in teaching signs to the chimpanzee Washoe is well known. Although the theoretical orientations and research objectives of individuals such as Lenneberg and the Gardners are dissimilar, and even in opposition, it is apparent that, as emphasis has shifted from learning to built-in propensities for language, more attention is being paid by various researchers to human nonvocal communication and to animal communication.

A final liberalizing influence, which should not be underestimated, is the growing societal awareness and acceptance of cultural pluralism and the increasing willingness to accept differences. There is less of a press toward conformity to a standard, whether it be the white standard, the Anglo standard, or the hearing standard. In this context, deaf people can be judged as human beings rather than on the basis of the extent to which they have mastered articulation skills.

American Sign Language

The difficulties of dealing with any language are complex. For example, researchers attempting to develop a comprehensive definition of the English language would have to come to terms with the wide variety of dialects spoken in England, the United States, South Africa, and Australia. They would have to decide at which point two dialects of a language differ so much that they become two separate languages. Pushing further, they would find differences in English usage not only between countries but also between regions of the same country. To complicate matters even more, there are observable class differences in the use of English that cut across regional and national lines. The final compounding factor is the fact that individuals themselves easily move from one dialect to another, depending upon circumstances. The style and vocabulary that professors use in teaching a class or preparing a paper need not approximate in any way the manner in which they express themselves when their role changes to that of a spectator at a hockey match or a parent on a canoe trip with the children.

Historically, the problem of definition might have been solved by reference to a standard dialect. For example, for a number of reasons, mostly political, the English spoken around London assumed a dominant status. Questions of correctness of usage were decided by the prescriptions of the King's English. Most early English-speaking settlers of the American Colonies, however, came from the midlands and from the north of England; they spoke different, and therefore "inferior," dialects.

There is a present tendency to treat dialects as equals. There is no reason to perceive London English as more correct than any other dialect. Its ascendancy reflects political and economic, not linguistic, supremacy in much the same way as the French around Paris and Castilian Spanish became standards.

By making dialects respectable, the problem of definition obviously becomes much more difficult and ambiguous. The English language must be redefined to encompass enormous diversity, an almost impossible task. Most people eventually would be satisfied to conclude that although they cannot define and describe English, they do have the ability to recognize it when encountered and to understand and use it when circumstances require.

The difficulties inherent in dealing with the term *sign language,* or even *American Sign Language,* are still more complex. There are deaf children and adults across the United States and Canada using a variety of visual-motor communication systems. At the lowest level a system might consist of home-made gestures invented and understood perhaps by only one group of six or seven students in a classroom excluding parents, teachers, and even other deaf students in the same program. At the other end of the continuum would be an arbitrary, abstract, somewhat standardized system capable of expressing all levels and nuances as well as a spoken system. A complicating factor is that signs usually have not been passed down from parents to children; rather, they are suppressed by most adults with whom children have contact. Young deaf children usually are not allowed more than minimal contact with deaf adults. Typically the children develop a sign system surreptitiously, against the wishes of the adults in their environment. At a conference on communication, Falberg (1971) suggested that sign language, in its broadest sense, is the only extant language which has been passed down from child to child.

At one time it was believed that there was a standard of correctness, which was the relatively formal system used in classroom instruction at Gallaudet College, the world's only college for the deaf. Gallaudet Sign was, and is, to the American Sign Language as London English was, and is, to the English language. As a graduate student with normal hearing at Gallaudet, the author

learned formal sign language in a classroom situation. However, attempts to use the newly learned skills in informal situations quickly demonstrated there are differences between how some concepts "should" be signed and how they actually were signed. An example would be the formal sign for *animal*, which illustrates a beating heart and movement on four feet. Although deaf students recognized the sign in formal use, they seldom, if ever, used it themselves. Other examples might be the formal and informal signs for *father* and *mother*.

Recently American Sign Language has attracted investigators from a number of disciplines. As representatives of areas such as linguistics, anthropology, developmental psycholinguistics, and psychology have brought their specialized skills, and esoteric dialects, to bear on the phenomenon of manual communication, they have generated, along with some fascinating results, a plethora of terms that are confusing to lay people. A quick survey of recent literature would turn up such examples as the following: Sign, sign language, Manual English, Linguistics of Visual English, High Sign, SEE 1 (Seeing Essential English), SEE 2 (Signing Exact English), and Ameslan. Working definitions of the most commonly used of these terms will be presented below.

Definition of Terms

The roots of American Sign Language do not lie in the English language but can be traced back to a variant of French Sign Language used by deaf individuals in Paris, which was modified by de l'Epée to reflect French syntax. The modified French Sign Language was brought to the United States by Laurent Clerc, who became the first teacher at the American School for the Deaf in 1817. The system underwent further modification in America. Still, although a competent user of English can sign and spell in grammatical English patterns, and a competent user of French can do the same in French, many basic American signs remain cognates with the original French ones.

Popular folklore to the contrary, there is no universal sign language. A sign language, as any other language, has many arbitrary characteristics that must be learned. For example, Stokoe (1972a) reported that in England — because of the relative lack of mutual intelligibility of signs between regions and because a two-handed alphabet is employed — signs learned in Canterbury were of little use in communicating with deaf persons in other parts of Britain. However, in Dublin communication was easier because the manual alphabet was similar to the American (and French), and because Irish Sign Language, which also stems from French Sign Language, has many cognates with American signs. Stokoe (1972a) also reported that at the 1968 meeting of the World Federation of the Deaf in Paris as many as six manual interpreters were used at one time to translate speeches into various sign languages. Obviously, then, there is no one language of signs. The potential number of sign languages, like spoken languages, clearly is unlimited.

Manual communication encompasses gestural systems from primitive, small-group, even idiosyncratic subsystems limited to the here and now up to highly complex forms that in every way may be considered legitimate language systems. For purposes of convenience, we shall refer to *American Sign Language* (ASL) as including those systems in use throughout the United States and Canada which have a high degree of mutual intelligibility, although regional and class variations may exist. Within ASL, as within other languages, there exist different types of linguistic codes that may be considered either formal or standard* variants. In this context the *standard* system may be thought of as a linguistic system possessing its own rules that do not necessarily follow the same constraints as the formal English system. The more a system accommodates itself to English, by this definition, the more it moves toward being in the *formal* category. At the extreme might be complete reliance on the manual alphabet without resorting to any signs to provide a one-to-one correspondence with the printing word.

Note that the above is merely one way of classifying manual communication systems. It could be argued that what are called *standard* and *formal* here are, in reality, two languages and that a deaf child of deaf parents first might learn ASL and later in school learn English as a second language. In essence, this is the position taken by Cicourel and Boese (1972) and by Stokoe (1972b).

---

* In a linguistic sense, one could refer to *high* (H) and *low* (L) variants, rather than to *formal* and *standard*, respectively. The author did this in a previous work (Moores, 1972). Because the terms *high* and *low* may be interpreted as prejudicial, they are not used in this chapter.

Manual Alphabets and Signs

Using manual communication, it is possible to present a word in two different ways. One involves the use of *fingerspelling*, or spelling the word letter by letter using a manual alphabet that consists of 26 letters with a one-to-one correspondence with traditional orthography. In fingerspelling, the hand is held in front of the chest, and letters are represented by different hand configurations. The rate of presentation is equivalent to a comfortable rate of speech somewhat faster than the rate of an accomplished typist.

The one-handed American manual alphabet may be traced back to the work of Bonet in Spain in 1620, and at least one educator believed that it was in use in Italy a century earlier (Best, 1943, p. 518). Farrar (1923, p. 39) reported the existence of a manual alphabet in common use in the Middle Ages, and Best (1943, p. 518) noted that pictures of dactylology are to be seen in tenth-century Latin bibles. These alphabets apparently were used by individuals with normal hearing rather than for instruction of the deaf.

Bonet's one-handed alphabet essentially is the same as that currently in use

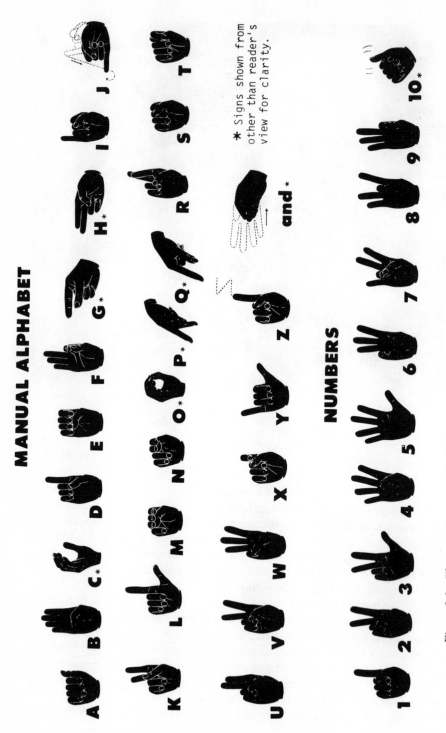

Figure 9.1   The American manual alphabet. (Used by permission. Copyright © 1976, Kathryn A. Licht.)

in Europe and the United States. The Spanish manual alphabet was introduced into France by Pereire, who modified it somewhat to conform to French orthography, and who, like Bonet, used it as a means of teaching speech (Abernathy, 1959).

The Abbé de l'Epée, and later Sicard, adopted Pereire's alphabet and incorporated it with the use of signs rather than as a means of teaching speech. It was brought to the United States, with minor modification, by Gallaudet and Clerc in 1817 (Abernathy, 1959). Figures 9.1 and 9.2 illustrate the manual alphabets in use in the United States and Russia. The similarity between the two is striking.

Other manual alphabets have been developed but have never been accepted so widely as the one-handed Spanish alphabet. As previously noted, Alexander Graham Bell used a manual alphabet (A. Bell, 1883a, 1883b) that may be traced back to the work of Dalgarno (1680). Bell's alphabet is presented in Figure 11.1.

Farrar (1923) reported that many alphabets have been developed which were phonetic or syllabic in nature but that none of these ever achieved any permanency.

A two-handed alphabet is used in Great Britain and some of its erstwhile commonwealths and possessions. Abernathy reported (1959, p. 238) that it is similar to an alphabet first mentioned in 1698. At that time it apparently was used only by hearing individuals.

A second way of presenting a word or concept is through a *sign*, which represents a complete idea. Each sign has three elements: (1) the position of the hands, (2) the configuration of the hands, and (3) movement of the hands to different positions. As an illustration, the concept *good* is signed in the following way: the left hand, in the *B* configuration, is held palm up before the chest. The right hand, in the *B* configuration touches the lips. The right hand then is brought down so that the back of it rests on the palm of the left hand. A more complete description of the components of signs will be presented in a following section.

Proficient practitioners of manual communication, then, have a variety of options open to them. They may communicate completely with signs, using no spelling, or they may communicate completely through fingerspelling. Most individuals tend to use both signs and fingerspelling in their conversations. As a rule of thumb, the more informal a situation, the more signs tend to dominate. As a situation becomes more formal and "Englishlike," there is a tendency to use spelling to a greater extent.

Opponents of the use of signs have been critical, arguing, "the sign language has no copula," or "the sign language has no sign for *the*." As we have established, there is no such thing as "the sign language." It should be stressed that anything that can be expressed by speech also can be expressed by the hands. Formal systems force the use of just such elements. If there are elements that cannot be signed, they can be spelled. In passing, one might observe that Russian lacks a word for *the* and at least a present-tense copula. No

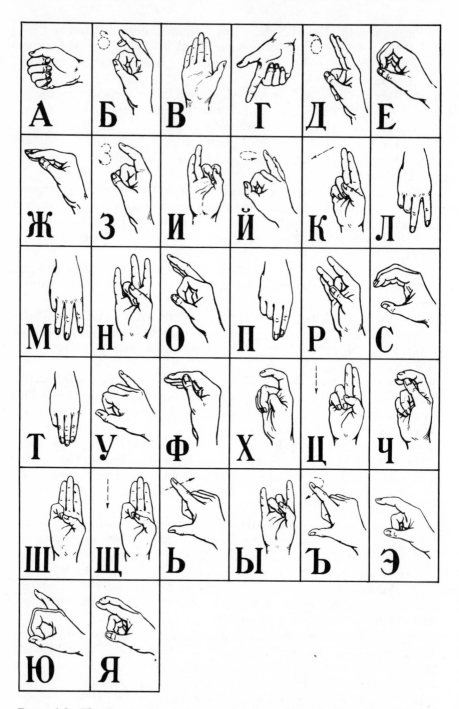

Figure 9.2 The Russian Sign Language alphabet. (From A. Gerankina, *Practical Work in Sign Language*, Moscow, Institute of Defectology, 1972.)

Table 9.1   Major systems of manual communication presently in use in the United States

Standard	Formal	Pedagogical (prescriptive)
Native Sign Language	Signed English	SEE 1
Ameslan	Manual English	SEE 2
		Linguistics of Visual English
		Cued speech

one has ever suggested on this basis that Russian does not qualify as a legitimate language.

Referring to Table 9.1, *Native Sign Language*, or *Ameslan* (Fant, 1972), represents a system in which a minimum of spelling is employed, the copula is omitted, and word order does not necessarily follow English. Much information is presented through context, facial expression, and body posture. This is "the sign language" that has been criticized so frequently. It is classified here as the standard form of ASL. *Signed English*, a formal variant, expresses all aspects of English, including the copula, bound morphemes, and English word order. Notice that Native Sign Language and Signed English are not dichotomous, in the author's opinion, but represent two ends of a continuum.

Independent of Signed English, which uses a mixture of signs and fingerspelling, would be *Manual English*, which is pure spelled English without the benefit of any signs.

A number of systems have been developed recently for pedagogical purposes. The best-known are Seeing Essential English (SEE 1), Signing Exact English (SEE 2), and Linguistics of Visual English.

Linguistic Analysis of American Sign Language

If ASL is to be considered a true language, it must be demonstrably accessible to linguistic analysis; the visual system would have to possess elements similar to morphemes, the smallest units of meaning in a language. Although it is relatively simple to show equivalence between a sign and a morpheme, little attention has been paid to isolating the distinctive building blocks from which signs are developed in much the same way that spoken morphemes are seen as clusters of consonants and vowels.

Stokoe (1958) developed the concept of a *chereme* /KERIYM/ as a motor analogue to a phoneme. Cheremes constitute the visible distinct elemental units of a sign language much as phonemes constitute the auditory distinctive units of a spoken language.

Table 9.2   Tab symbols for writing the signs of American Sign Language

1.	Ø	zero, the neutral place where the hands move, in contrast with all places below
2.	⌒	face or whole head
3.	⌢	forehead or brow, upper face
4.	⌷	midface, the eye or nose region
5.	⌣	chin, lower face
6.	Ʒ	cheek, temple, ear, side-face
7.	π	neck
8.	[ ]	trunk, body from shoulder to hips
9.	↳	upper arm
10.	⌄	elbow, forearm
11.	α	wrist, arm in supine position (in its back)
12.	Ɒ	wrist, arm in prone position (face down)

SOURCE: From W. Stokoe, C. Croneberg, & D. Casterline, A *Dictionary of American Sign Language*, Washington, D.C., Gallaudet College, 1965. Second edition © 1976 William C. Stokoe, Linstok Press, 9306 Minkwood St., Silver Spring, Maryland 20901.

There are three classes of cheremes, identified as *tab* (*tabulator*), *dez* (*designator*), and *sig* (*signation*). Briefly, the three are defined (Stokoe, 1958) as follows:

TAB — Tabulator; the position marking aspect of sign language activity; specifically the position in which a significant configuration (dez) makes a significant movement (sig).

DEZ — Designator; that configuration of the hand or hands which makes a significant motion (sig) in a significant position (tab).

SIG — Signation; the motion component or aspect of a sign language activity; specifically motion of a significant configuration (dez) in a significant position (tab).

The three aspects of any sign, therefore, are: (1) the place(s) where it is made, (2) the distinctive configuration(s) of the hand or hands making it, and

Table 9.3   Dez symbols for writing the signs of American Sign Language

1.	A	compact hand, fist; may be like 'a,' 's,' or 't' of manual alphabet
2.	B	flat hand
3.	5	spread hand; fingers and thumb spread like '5' of manual numeration
4.	C	curved hand; may be like 'c' or more open
5.	E	contracted hand; like 'e' or more clawlike
6.	F	"three-ring" hand; from spread hand, thumb and index finger touch or cross
7.	G	index hand; like 'g' or sometimes like 'd'; index finger points from fist
8.	H	index and second finger, side by side, extended
9.	I	"pinkie" hand; little finger extended from compact hand
10.	K	like except that thumb touches middle phalanx of second finger; like 'k' and 'p' of manual alphabet
11.	L	angle hand; thumb, index finger in right angle, other fingers usually bent into palm
12.	3	"cock" hand; thumb and first two fingers spread, like '3' of manual numeration
13.	O	tapered hand; fingers curved and squeezed together over thumb; may be like 'o' of manual alphabet
14.	R	"warding off" hand; second finger crossed over index finger, like 'r' of manual alphabet
15.	V	"victory" hand; index and second fingers extended and spread apart
16.	W	three-finger hand; thumb and little finger touch, others extended spread
17.	X	hook hand; index finger bent in hook from fist, thumb tip may touch fingertip
18.	Y	"horns" hand; thumb and little finger spread out extended from fist; or index finger and little finger extended, parallel
19.	Ȣ	(allocheric variant of Y); second finger bent in from spread hand, thumb may touch fingertip

SOURCE: From W. Stokoe, C. Croneberg, & D. Casterline, A *Dictionary of American Sign Language*, Washington, D.C., Gallaudet College, 1965. Second edition © 1976 William C. Stokoe, Linstok Press, 9306 Minkwood St., Silver Spring, Maryland 20901.

Table 9.4   Sig symbols for writing the signs of American Sign Language

1.	∧	upward movement
2.	∨	downward movement
3.	∿	up-and-down movement
4.	>	rightward movement
5.	<	leftward movement
6.	Z	side to side movement
7.	T	movement toward signer
8.	⊥	movement away from signer
9.	I	to-and-fro movement
10.	α	supinating rotation (palm up)
11.	ɒ	pronating rotation (palm down)
12.	ω	twisting movement
13.	ɳ	nodding or bending action
14.	☐	opening action (final dez configuration shown in brackets)
15.	#	closing action (final dez configuration shown in brackets)
16.	⌐	wiggling action of fingers
17.	e	circular action
18.	)(	convergent action, approach
19.	X	contactual action, touch
20.	ꭓ	linking action, grasp
21.	⧲	crossing action, grasp
22.	⊙	entering action
23.	÷	divergent action, separate
24.	↔	interchanging action

SOURCE: From W. Stokoe, C. Croneberg, & D. Casterline, A *Dictionary of American Sign Language*, Washington, D.C., Gallaudet College, 1965. Second edition © 1976 William C. Stokoe, Linstok Press, 9306 Minkwood St., Silver Spring, Maryland 20901.

(3) the action(s) of the hand or hands. Tables 9.2 through 9.4 present the cheremes of American Sign Language. A sign may possess one or more of each of the three classes of cheremes. Any sign, then, is a unique combination of 3 or more of the 55 cheremes of American Sign Language. The order of writing the symbols follows a tab, dez, sig sequence.

A *Dictionary of American Sign Language* has been developed (Stokoe, Croneberg, & Casterline, 1965) using the tab, dez, sib cheremic system. In this system, the previously described sign for *good* would be written in the following way:

$$\smile \; B_T{}^x \; \text{::}\} \; B_T{}^x \; \} \; B_T{}^{xtx}$$

Sociolinguistic Considerations

The work of Bernstein (1960, 1964) in England at the intersection of sociology, psychology, and linguistics has provided new insights into the relationships between social class membership and the function of linguistic codes. From his research Bernstein has posited the existence of two different types of language codes, which he labeled *restricted* (or *public*) and *elaborate* (or *formal*).

In Bernstein's scheme, which was concerned with class differences, middle-class individuals learn both an elaborate code and one or more restricted codes, and they can move back and forth between codes at will. Lower-class children are limited to a restricted code, which has serious implications for school advancement and later success. Other forms of language might not be comprehended directly but may have to be mediated through the children's own system. In the classroom the children must translate the code of the teacher through their own structures to make it personally meaningful.

Because Bernstein's work was concerned with class differences in the use of language, it is of only limited applicability to the situation in relation to American Sign Language, per se, especially if one attempts to equate ASL only with a public, or restricted, code. As a legitimate language, ASL would have both formal and restricted codes.

One must further be cautious in applying Bernstein's conclusions from work in England to systems of language usage in the United States. Bernstein himself (1972) has decried the misinterpretation of his work, especially in the United States, to the detriment of politically disadvantaged populations. There has been justifiable criticism of attempts, for example, to treat Black English as a restricted, and therefore inferior, dialect that must be eliminated. Recent evidence suggests that it is a legitimate complex variant of the English language and that it provides its users with tools of communication as well as any other dialect (Baratz, 1969; Baratz & Shuey, 1969; Labov, 1966). It should be noted that users of Black English can make some distinctions not easily made in Standard English. For example, the distinction between "He workin' " and "He be workin' " is a difficult one to make in the standard dialect.

In discussing the role of standard and nonstandard dialects, Baratz (1968) concludes:

He must be able to maintain his non-standard language because it is necessary for him for the majority of his experiences which occur outside the middle class culture. To devalue his language, or to presume standard English is a "better system" is to devalue the child and his culture and to reveal a shocking naivete towards language. Our job then is to teach the child a second language system (dialect if you wish) without denying the legitimacy of his own system. (p. 145)

The goal, then, is not to stamp out Black English, Native Sign Language, or Spanish dialects of the southwest. It is to give children the skills by which they can move from one system to another, from a standard system to a formal one, when the situation requires it. This is desirable not because the formal system — the relatively formal, prestigious middle-class American English — is inherently better, but because it is the system shared by a majority of Americans and therefore provides a meeting ground of commonality for communication and participation in the broader culture.

The analogy between deaf children and black or Spanish-speaking children should not be pushed too far. True, all may be subject to the scorn of teachers who may denigrate their methods of communication, but, at least on the outside, black children or Spanish-speaking children have access to an already-developed language system used by parents and peers alike. Deaf children, except for the relatively few with deaf parents, usually do not even have a shared linguistic system with their parents and are subject to repression at home as well as in school. Deaf children even are denied the support and identification that other linguistically different children find at home and in the neighborhood.

The Learning of Esoteric Manual Communication Systems

When children with normal hearing set out to learn the language of the adult community, the basic process is a rapid one and usually is completed without observable difficulty before the children enter the educational stream (Brown & Bellugi, 1964; Lenneberg, 1967b, 1970; McNeill, 1966). The beginning of deaf children's education, on the other hand, involves an attempt to *teach* a language system to them (Moores, 1970b). Spurred by a need to communicate and lacking mastery over the auditory-based system, the children will develop small-group gesture systems to help them communicate in some basic way (Tervoort, 1961). The existence of these gesture systems is a fact of life and may be observed even in programs that adhere to the so-called "pure" oral method (Kohl, 1966; Lenneberg, 1967a; Moores & McIntyre, 1971; Moores, Weiss, & Goodwin, 1974; Stafford, 1967).

It is noteworthy that these systems usually are constructed by the children. This is in no way analogous to the situation of children who constantly are exposed to spoken English (or Signed English) and who move steadily toward the acquisition of adult linguistic proficiency. We are talking about children who are developing methods of communication on their own in the face of a frequently hostile world. These children in a sense are rediscovering or reconstructing the wheel.

A primary concern must be the effect that such a system has on the later learning of American English, whether in a spoken, written, or signed form. Tervoort (Tervoort & Verbeck, 1967; Tervoort, 1975; Moores, 1970d) studied intensively the development of communication structure patterns in deaf children over a period of years in the United States, the Netherlands, and Belgium in order to assess the relationships between the in-group systems, which he termed *esoteric*, and the out-group, *exoteric* systems of adult Dutch and American English. Although the term *exoteric* may be equated with our previous use of the term *formal*, the esoteric systems would not be considered standard because of the lack of mutual intelligibility between groups.

In this study, Tervoort and Verbeck reported that children of all ages tended to use signs as the preferred means of communication in their private conversations. There was a consistent growth of grammatically correct usage as a function of age until age 14. After this age, American students continued to improve (show closer approximation to adult English patterns), while European students leveled off. Tervoort attributed the superiority of the American students, in part, to the positive influence of the educated adult deaf with whom they had contact. Tervoort and Verbeck (1967) stated:

> The sign language of the American adult deaf is a source from above, strongly influencing the interchange of the deaf teenager, on campus too, and on the contrary the fact that no such source from above is available for their mates across the ocean with whom they are matched. Once the esotericity of at least part of the subjects' private communication is established as a fact (whether this is a fact that should have been prevented, should be corrected, or even denied, is not the issue here), it is evident that normal need for communication finds a better outlet in an adult arbitrary system, than in uncontrolled and half-grown symbolic behavior not fed from above in education terms: — it seems clear that the choice has to be: either well controlled, monitored signing tending towards an adult level, semantically and syntactically, or no signing whatsoever; but no signing that is uncontrolled and left to find its own ways. (p. 148)

The impact of the continued restriction of students to an esoteric system is illustrated dramatically by the fact that only 2% of the utterances of American children consisted of completely esoteric imitative gestures, as compared to 10% of the European total. Some educators of the deaf believe that the English usage of deaf people is poor because of the influence of sign language, which is "ungrammatical." Tervoort's results show that such a position is naive and that a causative role cannot be attributed to gestures or signs. It is more logical to conclude that many deaf individuals have difficulty expressing themselves in spoken, written, or Signed English because of the imposition of an early linguistically deprived environment. Charrow (1974) has treated the subject of a nonstandard deaf English, and Bonvillian, Charrow, and Nelson (1972) have examined the nature of American Sign Language in detail.

If such a thing as nonstandard English does exist, its existence may be attributed not to signs but to the influence of inadequate instruction in Standard English. In many cases the restrictive factors are provided by the gesture systems unconsciously employed by oral-only teachers. An example of this may be provided by the experiences of a deaf graduate student at the University of Minnesota. She began instructing deaf junior high students in Minneapolis in the use of Signed English in a program that previously had been "pure" oral but found that the students had developed habituated signs which were difficult to modify. The most ingrained one happened to be a gesture that covered the use of all interrogative forms. It consisted of holding both upper arms tightly against the body with hands face up, and away from the body, at chest level about 18 inches apart. Tracing back her own school experiences, she realized, of course, that this was the common body stance of teachers of the deaf when asking questions of their students. She was struck by the irony that teachers, who have slapped the hands of students for gesturing, unconsciously provided a model of limiting, restrictive gestures. As a result, rather than having at their disposal the means of expressing *how, who, what, why,* and so on, the children are forced to lump them all together into one undifferentiated mass.

From his observations of deaf children in "pure" oral programs in Massachusetts, Lenneberg (1964) reported the following occurrence:

Recently, I had occasion to visit for half a year a public school for the congenitally deaf. At this school the children were not taught sign language on the theory that they must learn to make an adjustment to a speaking world and that absence of a sign language would encourage the practice of lip reading and attempts at vocalization. It was interesting to see that all children, *without exception* [emphasis added], communicated behind the teacher's back by means of "self-made" signs. I had the privilege of witnessing the admission of a new student, eight years old, who had been *discovered* by a social worker who was doing relief work in a slum area. The boy had never had any training and had, as far as I know, never met with other deaf children. This newcomer began to "talk" sign language with his contemporaries almost immediately upon arrival. The existence of an innate impulse for symbolic communication can hardly be questioned. (p. 589)

Perhaps, in establishing evidence for the existence of an innate impulse for symbolic communication, Lenneberg overstated the case in his reference to the child who immediately began to "talk" sign language. It would seem as logical to have him begin almost immediately to talk Spanish or Hebrew. American Sign Language possesses many of the properties of spoken languages, including a structure and a relatively abstract, arbitrary, referential vocabulary. No one learns to use it almost immediately.

It is also questionable whether a child could pick up "self-made" signs so rapidly. In building communication systems, as Tervoort (1961) noted, groups of deaf children develop esoteric manual "languages" that are unintelligible not only to deaf children in other schools but also frequently to deaf children of other age groups in the same school.

A more parsimonious explanation of the interaction observed might be to assume that, in the course of his eight years of family interaction, the child learned a limited number of "transparent," easily interpreted gestures which served as the basis for his initial contact with other deaf children.

Structural and Functional Characteristics of Sign Systems

Although the study of use of sign languages in adults and the development of sign language proficiency in children is still in beginning stages, there is enough evidence to make some tentative statements concerning the similarities and differences between auditory and visual systems. As previously mentioned, Bellugi and associates at the Salk Institute are devoting great attention to this area.

Three characteristics of manual communication systems — at least, of those used in the United States — that are of potential pedagogical importance are: (1) the iconic nature of many common signs; (2) the motoric, or enactive, nature of many signs; and (3) the use of spatial dimensions. Because of the transparent, or easily interpreted, nature of such signs, it is possible that many children are able to receive and express some information at a younger age than children who rely primarily on the auditory-vocal channel. For example, the commonly used signs for *eat, sleep, drink, drive, cry, fight, hug,* and *wash* clearly represent the respective actions. Not only are they relatively easy for children to understand, but the children make the appropriate signs at an age when most children probably cannot articulate the appropriate words. The advantage is not limited to "verbs," or action words. Signs such as those for *milk* (the motion for milking a cow), *water* (touching the lips with the W configuration), and *table* (an iconic representation of the top of a table) are understood and presented easily. Work in progress by Moores and associates suggests that the first word appears among deaf children of deaf parents at an earlier age than it does among normally hearing children. This "iconicity" and transparency of some aspects of sign languages was probably what led Lenneberg (1964) to his previously cited report on the deaf boy who began using sign language upon his first contact with other deaf children.

Within this context, it is logical to conclude that there may be more understandability across signed languages than across spoken languages, at some levels. For many of the earliest learned signs — for example, *eat, sleep,* and so on — there are probably a limited number of powerful salient characteristics to choose from, and we might expect similar signs to develop in different communities. However, a distinction should be made between primitive gestural communication and true communication by sign language involving arbitrary learned systems. Even the most iconic signs illustrate only aspects of objects or actions and are arbitrary even when readily understood. It is also possible that the older a sign system is, the higher the proportion of opaque signs (*opaque* is used here to refer to an unclear connection between a sign and referent). For example, in ASL the sign for *female* is made by running the right hand in an A configuration along the jawbone to the front of the chin, apparently referring to strings on the bonnets females wore in bygone days. Similarly, *coffee* is signed by imitation of the motion of grinding coffee beans in a coffee grinder. Over the years the signs have remained constant, while the connections to referents have become obscured.

Along the same lines, the proportion of opaque signs probably increases as a sign language is utilized for formal as well as standard functions. The sign for *psychology* is represented by forming a semblance of the Greek letter ψ with two hands, and the sign for *psychiatry* is an outgrowth of the sign for *psychology*. *Religion* is signed by touching the right shoulder with the right hand in the R configuration and then pointing straight ahead, keeping the same configuration.

The use of space also provides different dimensions to a sign system and may enable an individual to communicate complex linguistic relationships in a relatively simple way. In other words, if we assume the primacy of cognition over language, a signed language can convey concepts that in spoken American English would be acquired only at a relatively late age. As an illustration, the strings "I give you" and "You give me" may be differentiated simply by changing the direction of the sign. In the first case the sign *give* moves from the signer to another individual. In the second it moves toward the signer. The same relationships can be expressed for other actions, such as *help, hit, tease,* and so on, and for nominal and pronominal designations. One project investigator has remarked, not altogether facetiously, that it is a shame that formal English possesses no such power and efficiency.

American Sign Language also shows some relationships that spoken English does not. Signs for polar pairs such as *good-bad, open-close,* and *same-different* are made in such a way as to indicate that they are related but differ along some dimension. For example, the sign for *bad* is made in the same way as for *good,* except that as the right hand comes away from the face, it is turned palm down before touching the left hand.

Results of investigations by Bellugi (Bellugi, 1972; Bellugi & Fisher, 1972) involving hearing adults who had deaf parents and who were proficient in ASL as well as in spoken English indicated that different rates of speech are employed when using speech alone, signs alone, and speech and signs simultaneously to tell stories. Under the three conditions, approximately the same amount of time was required to tell the stories, and the amounts of information conveyed were equal. The total number of signs was reported to be less than the total number of words. This finding indubitably may be explained at least in part by their definition of what a sign is. For example, the previously mentioned string "I give you" is coded as one sign and three words. Of primary importance is the fact that the one sign conveys a complete subject-verb-object relationship as clearly as three words do. Hoffmeister, Moores, and Ellenberger (1975) have developed translation and definition rules for the glossing of signs into English.

Changing Uses of Signs

The extent of the lexicon of signs in ASL is unclear, and estimates vary widely. For example, the Stokoe et al. (1965) *Dictionary* has approximately 3,000 entries. Klima (1975) estimated a lexicon of 25,000 signs, based on work at the Salk Institute. As signs are used in a variety of settings and as signs have become respectable, the number of signs in use has increased. In many cases varieties around a basic sign will develop. As an illustration, although the verb *to be* is used infrequently in informal conversation, it may be expressed by touching the lips with the forefinger and moving the hand straight out. This sign also may be used to express the concepts *true, real,* and *sure.* When individuals wanted to differentiate between different parts of the verb *to be,* they would rely on fingerspelling. Now there is a growing tendency to differentiate by using signs. *Be, am,* and *are* are signed in the same manner as the generic *to be;* they differ only in their initial configurations, which are *B, A,* and *R,* respectively. *Was* and *were* are differentiated only by their final configurations, *S,* and *R.* An even more powerful example of how a family of signs may develop is given by the fact that, except for hand configurations, the following words are all signed in the same manner: *association, class, department, family, group, organization, society, team, union,* and *workshop.*

The proliferation of new signs and the development of variations around commonly used signs are reflections of the growing acceptance of manual communication and its increasingly important role in educational settings. No longer are signs being passed on only from child to child. They now are being used educationally with children in a majority of programs serving deaf children. As the demands on and for manual communication have increased, there has been a corresponding growth in the development of pedagogical systems closely related to formal variants of English. The two most widely known of these developing programs are *Seeing Essential English (SEE 1),* developed by David Anthony (Washburn, 1971), and *Signing Exact English* (SEE 2), developed by Gustason, Pfetzinger, and Azwolkow (1972). Readers are referred to the original sources for complete descriptions of the systems.

Essentially, both systems have a number of characteristics in common. They are being developed for use of normally hearing parents of deaf children as well as for teachers. Conscious attempts have been made to generate new signs for elements that in the past would have been fingerspelled. Thus, signs have been developed for pronouns (*he, she, it*, etc.), affixes (*-ly, -ness, -ment*), verb tenses, and articles (*an, the*) that previously were fingerspelled or omitted.

Both systems use existing signs as a base. However, there are differences. Gustason, Pfetzinger, and Azwolkow (1972) especially emphasize that signing should be by word rather than by concept. They offer the word *run* as an example of a word that has a variety of meanings, as in to *run* for office, *run* up the flag, *run*ning water, and so on (p. 4). If signing by concept, each of these meanings for *run* would be signed in a different way. Gustason et al. recommended one sign for all meanings, arguing that this approach is more compatible with the English spoken by native speakers and, therefore, easier to learn. Because both systems are relatively new, there is no indication at present of the effectiveness of SEE 1 and SEE 2 in relation to each other and to the more commonly used Signed English. Stokoe (1975) has argued that these systems are merely codes for English and should not be confused with the real American Sign Language, that is, with the language used by deaf Americans in their everyday lives.

Another system that briefly attracted interest was the *cued speech method* developed by Cornett (1967, 1969), in which the manual component is incomplete and not understandable by itself. This is similar to the hand-mouth and phonetic alphabet systems in use in Europe during the nineteenth century. Because the child must simultaneously speechread in order to decode the complete message, Cornett advanced his method as a compromise between oralists and manualists. Moores (1969a, 1969b) pointed out that cued speech represented only one of numerous such compromises, and he enumerated both theoretical and practical shortcomings of the system. Moores concluded that Cornett had treated the terms *speech* and *language* as equivalent, and he suggested that the system might be beneficial to the development of articulatory skills without necessarily proving to be of benefit in language development.

Pedagogical Uses of Manual Communication

In a paper presented to the International Conference on Oral Education of the Deaf, Lenneberg (1967a) stressed that the primary goal of education must be language, not its subsidiary skills. He went on to criticize educators of the deaf for not distinguishing between speech and language. Stressing that the key is to get as many examples of English into the child as possible, Lenneberg developed the argument that the establishment of language is not inseparably bound to phonics, and he urged that graphics be introduced in addition to oral methods at the earliest possible time. Lenneberg included fingerspelling and signs within his definition of graphics. Lenneberg's theoretical position is consistent with Tervoort and Verbeck's (1967) finding that manual communication had no deleterious effects on speech. It should be emphasized that both Lenneberg and Tervoort recognized the primary importance of oral communication in our society. They advocate balanced — as opposed to rigid manual or rigid oral — communication.

Recent Trends

As previously noted, the ascendency of oralism may be traced as far back as the International Congress on Deafness in Milan, Italy, in 1880, at which a resolution was passed stating that the use of manual communication of any kind would restrict or prevent the growth of speech and language skills in deaf children.

In view of the frequent bitterness involved over manual communication, it is somewhat surprising to find that until 1965 objective research was almost nonexistent. Most of the available literature still consists primarily of position papers in favor of one or another of the various methodologies. A situation worthy of note is the fact that while most educators of the hearing impaired have preferred straight oral methods, many psychologists, psychiatrists, and "outside" educators who, for one reason or another, have become interested in the problems of limited hearing argue for some form of manual communication (Moores, 1971).

Studies of Deaf Children of Deaf Parents
Who Use Manual Communication*

Because there have been no educational programs involving the use of manual communication with young children until recently, many investigators have turned to the study of deaf children with deaf parents who use manual communication in the home. If the use of manual communication is harmful, then deaf children of deaf parents would be expected to be inferior in academic achievement, in psychosocial adjustment, and in all aspects of communication, including speech, speechreading, reading, and writing. Table 9.5 summarizes completed studies of deaf children of deaf parents compared with deaf children of hearing parents. Stevenson (1964) examined the protocols of pupils of deaf parents enrolled at the California School for the Deaf at Berkeley

* This and the following section are adapted from D. Moores, *Recent research on manual communication*. Research, Development and Demonstration Center in Education of Handicapped Children, University of Minnesota, Occasional Paper No. 7, April 1971.

Table **9.5**   Studies of deaf children of deaf parents receiving manual communication

Investigator	Comparison
Stevenson (1964)	134 deaf children of deaf parents with 134 deaf children of hearing parents
Stuckless & Birch (1966)	38 deaf children of deaf parents matched with 38 deaf children of hearing parents
Meadow (1966)	59 deaf children of deaf parents matched with 59 deaf children of hearing parents
Quigley & Frisina (1961)	16 deaf students with deaf parents out of a population of 120 deaf students
Vernon & Koh (1970)	32 deaf children of deaf parents matched with 32 recessively deaf children of hearing parents
Brasel & Quigley (1975)	18 students whose deaf parents signed approximating English (*Manual English*); 18 students whose deaf parents signed using forms other than Manual English (*average manual*); 18 students of hearing parents with early intensive oral training (*intensive oral*); 18 students with no special preschool training who used oral-only communication with hearing parents (*average oral*).

SOURCE: D. Moores, *Recent Research on Manual Communication.* Occasional Paper No. 7, April 1971. Research, Development and Demonstration Center in Education of Handicapped Children, University of Minnesota.

Programs	Results
California School for the Deaf, Berkeley	Those with deaf parents were educationally superior in 90% of pair matchings; 38% of students with deaf parents went to college, 9% of those with hearing parents.
American School for the Deaf Pennsylvania School for the Deaf Western Pennsylvania School for the Deaf Martin School for the Deaf Indiana School for the Deaf	Children with deaf parents superior in reading, speechreading, and written language; no differences in speech or psychosocial development.
California School for the Deaf, Berkeley	Children of deaf parents ahead 1.25 years in arithmetic, 2.1 years in reading, 1.28 years in achievement; superior in written language, fingerspelling, signs, willingness to communicate with strangers; more mature, responsible, sociable; no differences in speech or speechreading.
Kansas School for the Deaf Michigan School for the Deaf Pennsylvania School for the Deaf Texas School for the Deaf Rochester School for the Deaf California School for the Deaf, Riverside	Children of deaf parents superior in fingerspelling and vocabulary; no differences in speechreading and achievement; children of hearing parents superior in speech.
California School for the Deaf, Riverside	Children of deaf parents an average of 1.44 years superior on academic achievement and superior in reading, vocabulary, and written language; no differences in speech and speechreading.
Programs across the United States	*Manual English* group scored highest on all 10 measures of achievement, reading, and grammatical ability; *average oral* group scored lowest on all 10 measures; *average manual* group consistently scored higher than *intensive oral*.

from 1914 to 1961 and matched them to deaf children of hearing parents. He reported that 38% of those with deaf parents went to college, as compared to 9% of those with hearing parents; and that of the 134 paired comparisons, students with deaf parents had attained a higher educational level in 90% of the cases.

Stuckless and Birch (1966) compared 38 deaf children of deaf parents who had used the language of signs with their children from birth with 38 deaf children of hearing parents who never used signs. Children were matched on the basis of IQ scores, age, sex, age of school entrance, and extent of hearing loss. Deaf children of deaf parents were superior on measures of written language, reading, and speechreading. There were no differences on teachers' ratings of psychosocial adjustment or in speech intelligibility.

Meadow (1966) reported that a group of 59 deaf children of deaf parents scored higher than a matched group of deaf children of hearing parents in self-image and academic achievement. Relative superiority in academic achievement increased with age, reaching 2.2 years in senior high school. The children of deaf parents were rated as being (1) more mature, responsible, and independent; (2) more sociable and popular; (3) more appropriate in exhibiting sex-role behavior; and (4) able to react more appropriately to situations. The two groups were rated similar in speech and speechreading. The group with deaf parents were rated higher in written language, fingerspelling, signs, willingness to communicate with strangers, and absence of communicative frustration. In discussing the qualitatively different reactions to deafness by hearing parents and deaf parents, Meadow noted that hearing parents had a tendency to view their children's major difficulty as an inability to *speak* rather than an inability to hear (p. 306).

Vernon and Koh (1970) compared 32 deaf children of deaf parents with a group of 32 recessively deaf children of hearing parents. The groups were matched for sex, IQ, and chonological age. Those with deaf parents had been exposed to manual communication from birth. Academically they were superior in reading, vocabulary, and written language, with an average general achievement level 1.44 grades superior to the group with hearing parents. No differences were found in psychosocial adjustment, speech, or speechreading.

Quigley and Frisina (1961) in a study of the effects of institutionalization reported that deaf children of deaf parents—who were 16 among 120 day students — were superior in vocabulary and fingerspelling but that there were no differences in speechreading and academic achievement. Their speech was poorer than that of the deaf children of hearing parents.

In a study directly comparing children of deaf parents with children of hearing parents who had completed an intensive oral preschool program, Vernon and Koh (1970) reported that the children of deaf parents exhibited a superiority of approximately one full grade in all areas over the Tracy Clinic oral preschoolers. Children of deaf parents were rated superior in reading, with no differences in speech and speechreading.

Brasel and Quigley (1975, 1977) investigated the development of two groups of deaf children of deaf parents and two groups of deaf children of hearing parents.   The four groups were identified as follows:

1. Manual English. This group included deaf children whose deaf parents signed and fingerspelled in approximation of Standard English syntax with their children from infancy.

2. Average manual.   This group was made up of deaf children whose deaf parents used forms of manual communication other than Manual English with their children from infancy.   This includes "the form of MC [manual communication] commonly used by the large number of deaf persons who have inadequate English syntactic skills" (Brasel & Quigley, 1975, p. 2).

3. Intensive oral.   This group of deaf children had hearing parents who provided them with early and intensive oral training in communication and language and who used exclusively oral means of communicating with the children during the first five years.

4. Average oral.   These deaf children had hearing parents who provided no special training during preschool years but who used exclusively oral methods of communication during the first five years.

There were 18 subjects in each group, and the average age was 14.8 years. Subjects were tested on four subtests of the Stanford Achievement Test, on six syntactic structures, and on written language.   On every test measure employed, the two groups with deaf parents were significantly superior to the two groups with hearing parents.   The *Manual English* group scored highest in each of the 10 measures, and the *average oral* group scored lowest.

The *Manual English* group was superior to the *intensive oral* group. Perhaps the most startling result was the finding that there were no significant differences between the *average manual* and *intensive oral* groups, although the former group consistently obtained higher scores.   The results may be considered startling because the *average manual* group was characterized as consisting of subjects "whose parents' written language was grossly deviant from Standard English" (Brasel & Quigley, 1975, p. 122).   The children in the *intensive oral* groups started school earlier and came from families with higher educational backgrounds and socioeconomic status.   The average gross family income was $17,569 for the *intensive oral* group and $9,306 for the *average manual* group (Brasel & Quigley, 1975, p. 50).

Brasel and Quigley describe the situation in the *intensive oral* (IO) families as follows:

The IO group was composed of Ss whose parents reported they expended every effort toward obtaining the best and most intensive training they could find for their children; all mothers and some of the fathers as well sought and received training in oral methodology and used this training to implement and augment [sic] school training in the home — sometimes to the extent where the home became, in effect, an extension of the school, and the parents surrogate teachers. From the reports it would appear that the parents of the IO Ss lost no opportunity to bombard the Ss with language through oral and written means, labelling the furniture, taking pictures and pasting them in scrapbooks with labels underneath, cutting out different colored objects and requiring Ss to match them with the spoken description, etc. Fixing up a special learning area in a corner of one of the rooms in the family home was a frequent tactic employed by parents who worked daily with their children. At the same time, however, when questioned about the efficacy of their methods . . . the answers revealed an underlying despair in most cases. The Ss could understand and be understood by *only the mother* in the majority of cases. (pp. 122–123)

In the studies presented above it must be emphasized that the children of hearing parents in no way represent multihandicapped, disadvantaged, or "nonoral" children. Average IQ's for the control groups were reported as 109 by Meadow, 104 by Stuckless and Birch, and 114 by Vernon and Koh. In each case, the socioeconomic status of those with hearing parents was higher; for example, Meadow matched children of deaf fathers who were skilled craftsmen with children whose hearing fathers were professional, managerial, and sales workers.

The results reported by Stevenson, Quigley, and Frisina; Stuckless and Birch; Meadow; and Vernon and Koh are interesting in themselves. They take on even greater significance in view of advantages that supposedly accrue to children with hearing parents. The socioeconomic status of children with hearing parents is superior. The English and spoken language of deaf adults tend to be nonstandard. Deaf children of hearing parents more frequently are enrolled in preschools and receive individual tutoring. Meadow reported that only 40% of the children with deaf parents received preschool training, as compared with 82% of those with hearing parents. Almost 90% of the hearing families interviewed had had some involvement with the Tracy Clinic correspondence course. Not one of the deaf families had sent for it.

Vernon and Koh emphasize that their sample from the Tracy Clinic represents a select group: An IQ of 114 places a person in the upper 20% of the population; the children received intensive oral instruction and auditory training in a three-year preschool program; and their parents received professional group counseling and, in some cases, private psychotherapy to help them adjust to deafness in their children.

Children of hearing parents then, have more preschool experience and tutoring and come from families with higher socioeconomic levels and more standard English patterns. Yet the children of deaf parents exhibit educational, social, and communicative superiority. One only can speculate on the attainments of deaf children of hearing parents if — in addition to familial, social, educational, and economic advantages — they had benefited from some form of early systematic communication with their parents.

Preliminary findings in a series of studies being conducted at the University of Minnesota on the language development of deaf children of deaf parents by Moores and associates suggest that deaf children go through the same stages as hearing children in the acquisition of linguistic abilities. The types of linguistic structures produced vary across children, apparently largely dependent in part on whether the mother uses signs in both formal and standard variants. Of the three mothers studied most closely, two use both variants, and their children have been observed using different signs for different forms of the verb *to be* and employing bound morphemes such as *ing*, *-s*, and *-ment*. As such signs are used more and more with young children, it will be interesting to observe the extent to which they stay in informal conversations.

At this point, perhaps it is appropriate to mention the role of deaf teachers in the education of deaf children. Traditionally, deaf teachers have been excluded from day programs for the deaf. Although they have taught in many residential schools, they usually are limited to teaching either older or retarded children. These restrictions usually are related to the belief that deaf children will not develop good speech and language skills if exposed to deaf adults. Based on the evidence gathered indicating the superiority of deaf children of deaf parents in language functioning, academic achievement, and psychosocial adjustment, there is no reason to accept such a position. Newman (1971) has suggested that in many situations a deaf teacher might indeed be superior to a hearing one. Not only has discrimination against deaf teachers been harmful to deaf adults, but also their absence may have adversely affected the educational and psychological development of a large number of deaf children. There is no evidence to support a policy that refuses deaf adults the opportunity to teach deaf children across all ages and levels of intellectual ability.

Direct Methodological Comparisons
in Academic Settings

Examination of Table 9.6 indicates that very few comparative studies have been conducted. Because of the predominance of oral-only methods of instruction in the classroom, especially with younger children, there were almost no comparative data on the various methodologies in the United States before 1960. The only exception would be a survey of 43 day and residential programs conducted in 1924-1925 (Day, Fusfeld, & Pintner, 1928), which reported that students at the Rochester School for the Deaf enjoyed the highest academic achievement, relative to their ability, of all programs assessed.

For the most part, manual communication has not been considered appropriate for "normal" deaf children. In a study (Education of deaf children, 1968) in Great Britain, some schools volunteered the following circumstances in which teachers use manual media in class:

Children not developing well orally, from one cause or another
With dull children
With children with brain damage or severe language disorders
With children with cerebral palsy

Table 9.6 Direct methodological comparisons

Investigator	Comparison	Programs	Results
Morozova (1954)	Oral-only programs versus neo-oralism (Rochester method)	Schools in Soviet Union	Children with fingerspelling master in 2 years material requiring 3 years under oral-only method.
Quigley (1969)	Oral-only preschool versus Rochester method preschool	American School for the Deaf Indiana School for the Deaf	Rochester method students superior in fingerspelling, speechreading, 5 of 7 measures of reading, 3 of 5 measures of written language; oral-only students superior in 1 of 5 measures of written language.
Quigley (1969)	Rochester method elementary and secondary programs versus programs of simultaneous method	Rochester School for the Deaf New Mexico School for the Deaf California School for the Deaf, Riverside White Plains (N.Y.) School for the Deaf Colorado School for the Deaf Oregon School for the Deaf	Rochester method students superior in all subtests of Stanford Achievement Test and fingerspelling; no differences in speech or speechreading.

With maladjusted children

With dually handicapped children

With children of deaf parents

With immigrant children

With children transferred from other schools

To impart information quickly

To satisfy children's needs for expression

Experimental use of fingerspelling to help young children to speak (p. 343)

The predominantly negative connotations toward manual communication held by many teachers of the deaf are revealed in this list. It is almost as though good, "normal" deaf children must be protected from contamination so that their oral-aural skills will not be affected.

The pioneering work in development and evaluation of combined methods of instruction in this century can be traced to the efforts of Russian educators over a 15-year period beginning roughly in 1950. As early as 1938 Russians had decided that the pure oral method was a dismal failure. According to Zukov (Moores, 1972a), the majority of children by eighth grade could not communicate effectively in any way, whether by speech, speechreading, reading, or writing. They had deficiencies in every aspect of expressive and receptive language, with inadequacies found in the use of prepositions, pronouns, tense, gender, number, and noun declensions. They confused morphological rules and produced the equivalents of *donuted* for *donuts*, *dragonflied* for *dragonflies*, and *interests* for *interesting*. In other words, they exhibited linguistic weaknesses almost identical to deaf students in American programs. Zukov argued that the rigid pure oral method itself was the major factor in the production of children who were unable to speak or speechread. The restriction of language to articulation made the entire education process too inefficient.

To provide children with tools of communication—especially expressive communication — at an early age, the Russians began experimenting with the combined use of fingerspelling and oral communication, a system they labeled *neo-oralism*. Morozova (1954) reported that 3- and 4-year-old children using fingerspelling could acquire in two years that which previously required three years to learn under the pure oral method.

Quigley (1969) attempted to assess the effects of the Rochester method on achievement and communication in two studies. In the first he compared two preschool programs for the deaf in the United States, one using the Rochester method and one using a traditional oral approach. After four years of instruction, students of the Rochester method were superior in fingerspelling, in one of two measures of speechreading, in five of seven measures of reading, and in three of five measures of written language. The control group was superior in one of five measures of written language.

The second study involved a comparison over five years of students in three residential schools receiving instruction in the Rochester method matched with three control groups in contiguous states being taught primarily through the simultaneous use of signs, fingerspelling, and oral means. In all the schools, the students had been taught by oral-only means when younger. At the end of five years, the experimental groups scored higher on all subtests of the Stanford Achievement Test. There were no differences at the beginning of the experiment. Applications of Moores's cloze procedures (Moores & Quigley, 1967) revealed the experimental group to be superior in form class or grammatical functioning with no differences in vocabulary. The experimental group was superior in fingerspelling, but there were no differences in speech and speechreading. Quigley reported that the Rochester method was not introduced until age 12 in two of the schools. The school that used the method at a younger age was the one which enjoyed the greatest advantage relative to its control (p. 77).

Quigley drew the following implications from the two studies:

1. The use of fingerspelling in combination with speech as practiced in the Rochester Method can lead to improved achievement in deaf students particularly on those variables where meaningful language is involved.
2. When good oral techniques are used in conjunction with fingerspelling there need be no detrimental effects on the acquistion of oral skills.
3. Fingerspelling is likely to produce greater benefits when used with younger rather than older children. It was used successfully in the experimental study with children as young as three and a half years of age.
4. Fingerspelling is a useful tool for instructing deaf children, but it is not a panacea. (pp. 94-95)

Beginning in 1969, a growing number of programs for young deaf children have initiated the use of simultaneous oral-manual communication. For the first time researchers are able to investigate the relationship between manual communication and oral language development. Moores and his associates (Moores, 1970c; Moores, 1974; Moores & McIntyre, 1971; Moores, McIntyre, & Weiss, 1972a, 1972b; Moores, Weiss, & Goodwin, 1973, 1974) have been conducting a longitudinal evaluation of seven preschool programs for the deaf in the United States that differ along a number of dimensions, including methodology, extent of integration of deaf and hearing children, amount of parental involvement, and emphasis on early academic skills. Results are treated in detail in Chapter 11.

Summary

The manual communication systems employed by deaf individuals have thrived for centuries in the face of prejudice, hostility, and attempts of repression by the dominant hearing community. It was argued 200 years ago that the teaching of speech and lipreading (now more commonly called *speechread-*

ing) would spell the doom of signs and that the system would fade away and die an unmourned death as children acquired oral skills. Since that time periodic waves of enthusiasm have developed for panaceas in the guise of auditory training, integration, early intervention, and parent training. For some reason each of these, worthy in itself, has been viewed as obviating the need for manual communication.

Based on experience with deaf children and adults, this author's view is somewhat different. Manual communication systems have shown a great resilience and ability to endure. This suggests that the systems are meeting an unmet need. The author is impressed particularly by the number of highly educated deaf adults who have excellent receptive and expressive oral skills but who also use manual communication in their everyday activities. As long as it retains its power of expression and its utility, manual communication will continue to survive its detractors. In all probability its increasing public exposure on television, in public school systems, and in the theater will extend its use to populations other than the deaf.

10
Early Intervention Programs

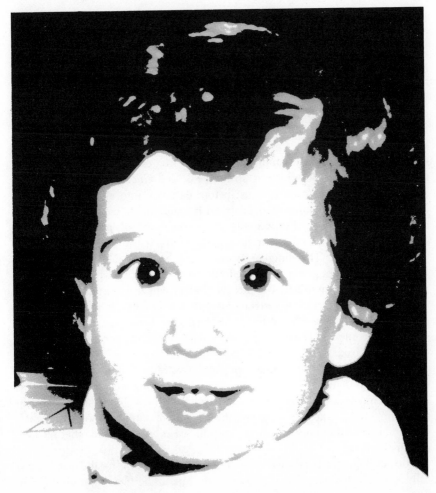

Introduction

In discussing programs for deaf children below the traditional age of entrance into a formal educational program, which for the sake of convenience may be placed at age 6, it is necessary to establish some operational definitions of terms, if confusion is to be eliminated. Examination of the literature on early intervention programs for the deaf reveals a wide variety of descriptors applied to the programs. As more and more programs have been developed to serve children at increasingly younger ages, the number of terms has proliferated accordingly. Thus at the present time one may read about *preschool, nursery, kindergarten, prekindergarten, pre-preschool,* and *infant* programs. There are some obvious distinctions among the terms. For example, *infant* programs usually are designed for children up to age 3, and *kindergarten* is commonly accepted as referring to an age just before entrance into elementary school. However, a great amount of overlap exists, and much confusion has been engendered as a result. For example, the terms *preschool, pre-preschool, nursery, prekindergarten,* and *infant* have all been applied to programs serving 3-year-old children. The different terms would be justifiable if they actually represented different programmatic efforts, but in most cases they do not.

For purposes of simplicity the present chapter will use the term *early intervention* to refer to programs designed to serve deaf children from birth, or time of identification, to age 6. When other terms are used, they will be defined within the context of their usage, particularly with reference to the ages of children involved.

Early intervention incorporates not only services to children but also those programmatic activities designed for parents of young deaf children. This would include educating parents on causes of deafness, individual and group counseling and therapy sessions, and the training of parents to work with their deaf children in the home situation. In some cases, siblings and other relatives also are involved.

The development of effective early intervention programs for the deaf historically has been hampered by a number of factors. The two major obstacles to the development of comprehensive services have been: (1) that deafness is a low-incidence condition and (2) that deafness imposes such severe communication limitations that specially trained personnel are required to deal with the problem.

Most residential schools, cognizant of the importance of the home during the early years, have hesitated to extend the residential components of their programs below age 4. Until the late 1960s, public school programs typically did not offer services to children below ages 5 or 6 because of restrictive state laws. In cases where lower age limits were set, the legislation usually was permissive, not mandatory; that is, school systems were permitted to establish programs for younger children, but they were not mandated to do so, and no state support funds were appropriated.

As a result, most early intervention programs for the deaf were established within the context of private schools, university clinics, and speech and hearing centers. Not only was there frequently a lack of coordination, even communication, between these programs and the public and residential schools in which the children eventually would enroll, but there were differences in orientation and goals that only could prove detrimental to children and parents involved. These unfortunate circumstances in many cases have carried over to the present and continue to impede the development of comprehensive, well-integrated programs.

Meeting the Problems of Early Intervention: The Nineteenth Century

Despite the self-conscious tendency of many recent programs to label themselves *exemplary, innovative, model, demonstration,* and so on, few, if any, elements of these programs were not employed, or at least considered, generations and centuries ago. Thus Meier's (1961) proposal to train mothers to use the manual alphabet with deaf children as young as 1½ years old was anticipated by Dalgarno (1680), who developed the outlines of a training program for young children in the home and who advocated fingerspelling to children in the cradle. The supposedly new concept of integrating young deaf children and hearing children was advocated in England by Arrowsmith (1819) and was widespread in Germany in the middle third of the nineteenth century (Gordon, 1885a). Although the Santa Anna, California, program rightfully is acknowledged as the first public school program to teach manual communication to hearing children (Holcomb, 1970), neither the idea nor the practice is new. Signs were used along with speech in many of the common schools that integrated deaf and hearing children in Germany in the nineteenth century.

In fact, the first early intervention program for the deaf in the United States, established by Bartlett in New York City in 1852, possessed many of the elements of recent "innovative" programs. After more than 20 years' experience as a residential school teacher, Bartlett established a "family" school "adapted to the physical, mental and moral wants of children of an early and tender age" (1852, p. 32). He proposed

not so much to confine the little ones to a regular routine of exercises in school hours, as to teach them and accustom them at the table, in their little plays, walks and amusements, and in the ordinary every-day occurring incidents of juvenile life, to express their thoughts and learn to think in alphabetic language, thus making the acquisition of language a matter of early imitation, practice and habit, as nature plainly indicates it should be. (p. 35)

Bartlett also accepted hearing children, usually siblings of deaf children, into his family school. The hearing children acquired facility in the language of signs and the manual alphabet. Bartlett believed the system to be mutually beneficial to deaf and hearing children. Echoing Dalgarno and Thomas Hopkins Gallaudet, both of whom believed that the manual alphabet would help hearing children master English orthography, Bartlett argued (Gordon, 1885b):

We find this beneficial to both classes — to the deaf mutes in enlarging their scope of thought by bringing their minds into contact to those of their more favored companions; beneficial yet more variously to those who hear and speak, quickening their perception and improving their mental development by presenting to their minds language under entirely new forms; by the use of the manual alphabet in spelling words; and also by no means inconsiderable advantage of improved ease and expressiveness of manner, induced by practice in the use of gesture language. (p. 249)

Bartlett's program, then, was modeled along the lines of a family unit. It integrated deaf and hearing children. Language learning was by a natural process, and all modes of communication were used by both deaf and hearing children. The program apparently was a success (Gordon, 1885b), but it did not survive its founder. Many of its innovative features were lost, only to be "reinvented" in the latter part of the twentieth century.

One other early intervention program deserves mention: the Sarah Fuller Home for Little Children Who Cannot Hear. This was established in West Medford, Massachusetts, in 1888 to serve very young children before entrance into school programs (Adams, 1928). The home was closed in 1925 because of rising expenses. As an alternative, a home visitation program was established in cooperation with the Horace Mann School for the Deaf. A trained teacher of the deaf visited the homes of deaf children to train mothers and to teach children the oral method. A mother, aunt, or grandmother would be present at each lesson and would be given instructions in procedures to follow with the child until the next visit.

The home visitation program appears to be a prototype for the home visitation components of many contemporary programs. However, most of these actually are modeled on family-oriented programs developed in Great Britain and Scandinavia. Like Bartlett's family school, there is no direct line of progression from the Fowler home visitation program to present early intervention programs for the deaf in the United States.

For the most part, except for a few privately financed programs such as the above, early education for deaf children was limited to those whose parents had financial means that enabled them to retain tutors. Educators in the residential and day school programs, although unable to initiate early intervention programs, were painfully conscious of the importance of early education and the development of communication between deaf children and their families. The first issues of the *American Annals of the Deaf* contained articles about early instruction and suggestions for parents of young deaf children (Ayres, 1849; Woodruff, 1848). This emphasis was continued with consistency throughout the nineteenth century (e.g., Crouter, 1885; Gordon, 1885b; Hirsch, 1887; H. Peet, 1886; Pettengill, 1874; Ray, 1852; Waldo, 1859). Also, many schools developed instructions and procedures for parents to use with their young children (Gordon, 1885b). The use of signs, the manual alphabet, and pictures for instruction were common components.

For the most part the advantages of living at home for very young deaf children was emphasized. Pettengill stated (1874):

The very best way, in my opinion, to educate a deaf-mute, is for the parents of the child, as soon as they discover he cannot hear, to commence to make efforts to open and enlighten his mind by means of natural signs, and at the same time to endeavor to make him utter sounds and read from the lips. (p. 1)

Pettengill noted that deaf individuals originally were educated by their parents or by private tutors, with instruction and training being addressed directly to the individual. It was Pettengill's position that it was only through tutoring that the highest results could be obtained and that schools, which through necessity dealt with groups of children, could hope only to approach this ideal. In order to maximize the effectiveness of schools, Pettengill (1874) wrote:

A school for young children, in my opinion, is rightly constituted and likely to subserve the end of its establishment just in proportion as it conforms to its prototype — the well ordered family. If we accept the family as the model school, it settles some disputed questions in education, and establishes the principles, first that both male and female teachers should be employed — females especially — in the more tender years; second, that boys and girls should be trained together; third, that the monitor system is a good one, the elder pupils assisting in the education of the younger; and fourth, that each individual pupil should receive special instruction according to his personal requirements, peculiar deficiencies, particular gifts and prospective work, and not be taught in large classes. (pp. 6–7)

Pettengill's approach, at the first stage, was similar to that of Ayres (1849), an earlier educator who also had addressed himself to techniques of early home training. Ayres, however, saw the processes as being more complex, especially in consideration of the role of natural signs during children's development.

Asserting that education, to be complete, must begin and end at home, Ayres attempted to show parents how to begin the intellectual training of deaf children before they entered school. Stating that communication is the children's primary need, he reasoned that the natural language of signs is the foundation of all language. Of these natural signs, Ayres (1849) states:

This language of signs — and we shall not be understood here to speak of the system-atized language of signs used in our Asylums for the deaf and dumb, or as they are called by the French, signs of reduction — is the foundation of all language. It is just as necessary to the child who hears, as to the child who is deaf. It is the first vehicle of thought, the first means of intellectual or soul communion. But its range is limited, its capacity small, and its use, but for a brief period. Upon this stock is grafted, in the case of the child who can hear, language or speech. . . . Yet the first lessons in language, provided by nature, are the same for the deaf and dumb child and the child who enjoys the faculty of hearing. (p. 180)

It is interesting to note in passing that Ayres presents a position concerning the foundations of language that is consistent with Piaget's, especially as it relates to the importance of the sensorimotor stage for later learning.

Ayres argued that the utility of natural signs was limited for the most part to the very early stages of development and that deaf children would cease to prog-ress past a certain point if the signs continued to be the major mode of com-munication.

In order to unfold for children "the mystery of speech in the home" (p. 181), Ayres suggested that parents use the manual alphabet, which, he claimed, could be learned in one or two hours. Ayres preferred the manual alphabet to the use of systematic signs at this point because of his belief in its superiority to help deaf children acquire a first knowledge of English.

Ayres's approach was consistent with that of his contemporary Bartlett in his emphasis on the manual alphabet in early instruction and in his conviction that the acquisition of language should develop along natural lines. Antici-pating the motto "Talk, talk, talk" by more than a century, Ayes exhorted parents:

The great secret of success is practice. Teach the child to talk at all times. Talk to him and talk with him. Let all the household do the same. It is not by lessons; it is not by systematic instruction that any child learns language well. It is by conversation, here a little and there a little, as his necessities, his inclinations, or his circumstances prompt. (p. 183)

In an article by an unidentified author ("The Kindergarten Method," 1875), the desirability of the kindergarten method was argued, based upon Froebel's concepts of early education with orderly, "unstructured" activities designed for children from ages 3 to 7. The use of the manual alphabet was seen as provid-ing the child with a means of communication. Consistent with the reasoning of previously mentioned educators of the time, the primacy of home influence was emphasized:

There can be no doubt that the most favorable circumstances for the development of a deaf-mute child would be a training at home, according to the Froebel method, conducted by the mother, or by a competent kindergartener, with six or eight hearing and speaking children of the same age as comparisons. (p. 123)

Acknowledging that such a program realistically could not be developed for the majority of young deaf children, the author suggested alternative plans, presenting as the most preferable a system by which a kindergarten would be established for the deaf in every large city. The kindergartens, although physically separate, would be affiliated with state residential schools for the deaf, and they would enroll children between 2 and 3 years of age. The proposed system was never developed.

There is also substantial evidence that nineteenth-century educators of the deaf in the United States and Europe were aware of the ways in which even slight amounts of residual hearing facilitated speech development (E. Gallaudet, 1868), of the difficulties faced by parents in the diagnostic process, and of the initial tendency of parents to regard as the major problem the child's inability to speak, instead of the inability to hear. Describing the difficulties of ascertaining deafness in a young child, Hill (1868) wrote:

The child gives the father the hand asked for, goes to him at his call, looks at the striking clock, turns about when the door is shut hard, notices the ball rolling behind it. Are these not unmistakable signs of the ability to hear? The father thinks so and the other will cherish this belief. That a deaf mute child could do all this they have no idea. The deaf mute child does it all, but with this distraction — it does not obey the spoken order or the call, but the outstretched hand of the father and the nod; it turns its eye to the clock because it sees its brother look in that direction; the shut door, the rolling ball, the passing wagon, the clapping of the hands act upon the child's sense of feeling. The father and the mother moreover, easily and willingly allow themselves to be deceived. (p. 72)

In a sensitive article printed in a report of the Royal Wurtemberg Institution for the Deaf and Dumb ("Early Home Training," 1869; translation, 1879) it was stressed that the cause of speechlessness is to be found not in the organs of speech but in the lack of hearing. Reporting on parents' difficulty in understanding this, it was noted (1879):

That the dumbness of the child, which in many cases is discovered first, is only the consequence of deafness, they seldom take into consideration. They regard the dumbness as the real infirmity, and instead of getting at the root of the evil, instead of attacking the cause (the deafness) with which the effect (the dumbness) would cease, they try to cure the dumbness. (p. 15)

The article from the Wurtemberg Institution revealed several additional similarities with the prevalent attitude toward early intervention procedures for the deaf in the United States. These, of course, must be reflections of the influence of prominent German educators of that time on American educational thought, certainly not vice versa. The desirability of initiating training at birth, or at time of identification of deafness, was emphasized. Parents were encouraged to use signs along with speech in communicating with their child, and a liberal use of pictures for instructional purposes was advocated. It was stated that deaf children should be sent to the village schools for little children and that the teacher and pastor had a moral obligation to meet their special needs in order to prepare them for entrance into formal programs for the deaf around age 8 or 9.

In summary, although nineteenth-century educators of the deaf did not have at their disposal the means to implement widespread early intervention programs, they were united in their convictions of the importance of early communication between the child and his or her family and the necessity of facilitating intellectual development as early as possible. The recommendations of various educators were highly consistent with each other and contained progressive components lacking in most early intervention programs for the deaf before 1970. Some of these components were:

1. Use of the family unit as the organizational model
2. Use of natural signs and gestures to establish a basis of communication
3. Reliance on simultaneous oral-manual communication
4. Heavy reliance on the manual alphabet
5. Early introduction of reading and writing in the education of the deaf child
6. A commitment to a natural, informal, relaxed atmosphere for facilitation of the development of speech and language
7. Early integration of deaf and hearing children, to the mutual benefit of both

Early Intervention Programs in the Twentieth Century

As previously noted, most early intervention programs for the deaf before the 1960s were not affiliated with either public school programs or state-supported residential schools for the deaf. They were supported primarily through private means, and they did not reach the general population of deaf children. Typically, they were conducted under the leadership of otologists and audiologists, with speech therapists bearing the responsibility for actual work with the children. Teachers of the deaf were not involved. In such programs educational considerations received low priority, and the problems of deafness were perceived within a medical framework or as involving an inability to speak, which could be remediated simply by proper fitting of hearing aids and training in articulation. This naivete was compounded by the fact that those affiliated with such programs usually had no knowledge of the programs for the deaf in which the children eventually were enrolled, nor did they know what happened to their former pupils ("clients," "patients"), and they had no social or professional contacts with deaf adults. This situation did not start to change until the late 1960s, when a new generation of audiologists and speech pathologists began to appear who were much more attuned to problems of language and communication (as well as speech) than their predecessors.

It should be noted that the situation was just as dismal in the early 1970s, when educators of the deaf "took over" to a large degree. During that period, in many programs, teachers of the deaf assumed the responsibilities of parent counselors, social workers, child development specialists, educational audiologists, and psychologists — roles for which they were completely unqualified.

Those few programs which were established in connection with public day and residential school programs for the most part consisted of extension of entrance requirements down to ages 4 and 5. They seldom dealt in a systematic way with younger children or with family dynamics. Although some of the programs were housed in separate buildings or even were "off campus," the actual practices represented no major departures from tradition; instead, they usually consisted of watered-down activities originally designed for 6- and 7-year-old deaf children. The programs shared with private clinics and centers a fixation on the development of articulation and oral-aural receptive skills to the exclusion of social, cognitive, and linguistic factors. They were usually less successful than their private counterparts in utilizing residual hearing, probably because (1) they did not have the same sophisticated equipment, (2) they did not have the same trained specialists, and (3) they did not work with as many children with mild and moderate hearing losses. Before the methods revolution in the 1960s, only one early intervention program in America allowed the use of any form of manual communication along with oral. This was the New Mexico School for the Deaf, which employed the Rochester method (Hester, 1963).

Mention should be made of a unique service provided by the John Tracy Clinic, which was established in Los Angeles in 1943. The clinic has developed a correspondence course for parents of preschool deaf children that is free of cost to all parents. In addition, staff members of the clinic respond personally to all letters. Enrollments have come from 114 countries, and the course has been printed in 16 languages, involving more than 32,000 families (Thielman, 1970).

The correspondence course has been particularly valuable to parents in areas where no services existed for their children. In many cases, the course and personal letters from the clinic provided the only sources of support and guidance for parents suddenly faced with the task of raising a young child who could not hear.

The Spread of Early Intervention
Programs

According to enrollment information presented in the annual Directory of Services editions of the *American Annals of the Deaf,* the greatest increases in
early intervention programs for the deaf occurred between the years 1963 and
1973, to the point where probably a majority of deaf children in urban areas
are identified and receive some services before the traditional age of school entrance. Unfortunate exceptions are Chicano, black, and Native American
children, who are diagnosed at early ages less frequently and who do not receive equal services from some programs even when diagnosed.

The impetus for early intervention programs during this period came from
several sources. First, there was a widespread dissatisfaction with the results
obtained by educational programs for the deaf and a consensus that sweeping
changes of some sort were necessary. The evidence accumulated that intellectually normal deaf adolescents and adults in North America and Europe were
unable to read at the fifth-grade level (Furth, 1966b; Norden, 1970; Wrightstone, Aranow, & Moskowitz, 1963), they lacked basic linguistic skills in the
language of the normal hearing community (Moores, 1970e; Simmons, 1962;
Tervoort & Verbeck, 1967), and they were incapable of receiving and expressing oral communication on anything but a primitive level despite the commitment of most schools to exclusively oral instruction (*Education of deaf children,*
1968; Montgomery, 1966). One position held that the educational retardation
of deaf students who leave school could be reduced by establishing early intervention programs.

A second major factor was the influence of the movement in general education toward "compensatory" education and increasing emphasis on the importance of the early years to later functioning, which resulted in the federally
sponsored Head Start system. In the same way that many idealists perceived
Head Start as compensating for all the handicaps of poverty, malnutrition, and
discrimination visited upon politically and economically disadvantaged seg-
ments of the population, some educators of the deaf foresaw the early intervention programs for the deaf as overcoming all the linguistic, social, and academic difficulties with which deafness so frequently is related.

The rubella epidemic of 1964–1965, the worst recorded rubella epidemic to
hit the United States, also played a major role in the establishment of early intervention programs. In its aftermath, educators of the deaf nervously anticipated a "bulge" of deaf children inundating elementary school programs by
1970 and taxing existing facilities beyond their capacities. Estimates of the
number of children varied widely. All that was known for certain was that it
consisted of the biggest single wave of deaf children in the nation's history and
that a large proportion of the group would suffer from additional handicaps.
Early intervention programs were established across the country not only to
prepare these children for eventual entrance into school programs but also to
allow programs to understand the needs of these children and plan for them.

Research on Effectiveness of
Early Intervention Programs

Unfortunately, there were few models by which the new programs could be organized. Although early intervention programs for the deaf had been in existence for generations, individuals interested in the development of new programs or the modification of ongoing ones quickly discovered that almost no educational guidelines existed for effective intervention programs for the deaf. In view of the strong opinions prevalent in the field it is somewhat surprising to find a lack of comparative data. Most of the literature cited as research involves description, defense, and praise of a program by a person who has developed it or in some way is closely related to it. With the exception of a possible audiogram or tape accompanying a lecture, no data are presented.

The lack of data may be traced to two causes. First is the fact that the extreme difficulty of evaluating effectiveness of early intervention programs is confounded by the addition of the dimension of deafness, not only because deafness is a low-incidence handicap, reducing the efficacy of usual statistical procedures, but also because of the frequent lack of communication between child and evaluator. Second, and perhaps even more inhibiting, is the highly emotional nature of the question of metholodogy with deaf children, especially young deaf children. There are educators who firmly believe that the use of any kind of manual communication will prevent children from developing speech and language and doom them to lifelong existence in a mute subculture. Others just as firmly believe that depriving children of just such a system will cause them irreparable linguistic, educational, and emotional damage. Given such a climate, most researchers prefer to investigate other questions. In the author's opinion, neither concern should be sufficient to deter a search for objective analysis. Educational decisions must be made daily. If no information exists, the decisions will be made on the basis of other, less desirable, factors.

The relatively few studies for which data exist have presented results consistent with research activities in other fields. In many respects, investigations of programs for the deaf parallel the research into early intervention programs for the "disadvantaged." In spite of all the enthusiasm and subjective reports of success, there is little to suggest that the programs have had much lasting effect on children. Table 10.1 presents the studies of effectiveness of such programs. Phillips (1963) compared children receiving preschool training from age 3 with others receiving no preschool training at six schools for the deaf. By 9 years of age there were no differences between experimental and control groups on language arts, arithmetic, and socialization. Craig (1964) matched children who had preschool training (over age 3) with those who had no preschool training at two schools for the deaf; no differences were reported in lipreading and reading skills.

McCroskey (1967, 1968) evaluated the effectiveness of a preschool home-centered program with auditory emphasis by comparing children who had gone

Table 10.1 Studies of the effectiveness of preschool programs

Investigator	Comparison
Morozova (1954)	Oral-only preschool versus neo-oralism (Rochester method)
Phillips (1963)	Oral preschool versus no preschool
Craig (1964)	Oral preschool versus no preschool
McCroskey (1968)	Oral preschool versus no preschool
Quigley (1969)	Oral-only preschool versus Rochester method preschool
Vernon & Koh (1972)	Oral preschool versus no preschool
Vernon & Koh (1972)	Oral preschool versus deaf children of deaf parents with no preschool

Preschool programs	Results
Schools in Soviet Union	Children with fingerspelling plus oral instruction master in 2 years material requiring 3 years under oral-only method
Lexington School for the Deaf White Plains School for the Deaf Illinois School for the Deaf Pennsylvania School for the Deaf American School for the Deaf New Jersey School for the Deaf	No differences in language, arithmetic, and socialization
Western Pennsylvania School for the Deaf American School for the Deaf	No differences in reading and speechreading
Atlanta Speech School	No differences
American School for the Deaf Indiana School for the Deaf	Rochester method students superior in fingerspelling, speechreading, 5 of 7 measures of reading, 3 of 5 measures of writing language; oral-only students superior in 1 of 5 measures of writing language
Tracy Clinic	No differences in speech, speechreading, general achievement, and reading
Tracy Clinic	Students with deaf parents and no preschool superior in reading and general achievement; no differences in speech and speechreading.

through the program with children who received no training. The few differences found between the groups tended to favor the children who received no preschool training. McCroskey postulated that perhaps those children who received early training had more severe problems and thus were identified at an earlier age. Because no pretreatment data were gathered on the children, this must remain speculation.

Vernon and Koh (1972) reported the Tracy Clinic graduated 123 students from its three-year preschool program from 1944 to 1968, of whom 56 percent had attended the California School for the Deaf at Riverside. Children from the Tracy program at the Riverside school were matched with children receiving no preschool training on the basis of age, IQ, and sex. There were no differences between the children trained at Tracy Clinic and those with no preschool training in speech, speechreading, academic achievement, or reading. A third group, consisting of deaf children of deaf parents, was superior in academic achievement and reading. There were no differences in speech and speechreading between the children of deaf parents and either of the other two groups.

Neo-oralism

Shortly after World War II, educators of the deaf in the Soviet Union concluded that education of the deaf was a complete failure that could be traced to two basic misperceptions. The first was an inability to recognize that speech and language are distinct entities. Equating the two led educators to emphasize articulation skills at the expense of linguistic and cognitive development. The second mistake was an unfortunate tendency to consider the child a relatively passive organism. As a result, classrooms were structured in such a way that almost all conversations and activities were initiated by the teacher. A new system, labeled *neo-oralism*, was developed. It had three basic goals:

1. To give children tools of communication, especially expressive communication, at an early age
2. To change passive youngsters into active ones with initiative in learning
3. To free children and their language from the immediate situation

From the beginning, instruction concentrates on practical activities that encourage independence. There is extensive use of toys such as paper, plastic, textiles, papier-mâché, and plexiglas. Emphasis is placed on arts and crafts to develop concepts of position and color as well as creativity. Activities with practical application include work with illustrations and figures. There are numerous measuring and counting experiences. A large portion of the children's early education is devoted to organized observation of the environment. Morkovin (1960a) and Moores (1972a) have described the system in detail.

According to the position of Soviet educators, the Russian language can be expressed in three separate modes: oral speech, written speech, and dactyl speech (fingerspelling). Each one is considered a separate form of the Russian language, and each is used as soon as possible.

Because oral and written speech are so difficult for very young children, fingerspelling is introduced and used from the beginning; even children who cannot speak or write can fingerspell. Both parents and teachers are expected to spell complete sentences at all times. For many children, as they develop mastery over spoken and written forms of Russian, the use of fingerspelling is phased out.

Morozova (1954) reported that 3- and 4-year-old children could acquire in two years that which previously required three years under the pure oral method. Moreva (1964) replicated Morozova's study and reported that 3-year-olds could master fingerspelling in from two to eight weeks and that 2-year-olds required five to six months. Martsinovskaya (1961) and Titova (1960) found that fingerspelling facilitated the separation of words into their phonetic composition and accelerated vocabulary growth. It did not hinder articulation or formulation to syllabic structure. Korsunskaya (1969) reported that if everyone around the child fingerspells, the language mastery process becomes like that of a hearing child. However, children do not rely on fingerspelling exclusively, even though it is easier. She reported it aids in the development of speechreading and appears to affect speech neither positively nor negatively.

Addressing himself to teachers' reservations that children might depend on fingerspelling and not attempt speech, Shif (1969) conducted electrophysiological research which showed close simultaneous coordination of hand and tongue muscles, suggesting that fingerspelling can be part of a coordinated integrated system forming auditory-visual and vocal-motor bonds in the production and reception of speech.

Of greatest surprise to many American educators is the claim that children educated under neo-oralism end up being more oral than those trained under the traditional pure oral method, because they have a language base and a vehicle of communication from a very early age. This is in direct opposition to the American system, in which only older children have been exposed to combined oral-manual instruction. In this regard Morkovin (1968) noted:

The author [Morkovin] spoke with a group of profoundly deaf children who were graduates of the new type of kindergarten at Malokhova, near Moscow. The children were eight years old and in the second grade of elementary school. They were able to express themselves orally and to ask questions about life in America. (p. 197)

Programs for the deaf in the Soviet Union were visited also by officers of the British Department of Education and Science who were charged with investigating the possible place of signs and fingerspelling in the education of the deaf in Great Britain. Following are their reactions (*Education of deaf children*, 1967):

The children of four, five and six years old who we saw in class certainly understood their teacher well, and mostly spoke freely and often with good voice although they were regarded as being profoundly deaf and were unselected groups. We could not judge the intelligibility of the speech, but our interpreter (who had never previously seen a deaf child) said that she could understand some of them. The children were also very lively and spontaneous, and did not appear to be oppressed by methods used, which might strike someone accustomed to English methods as unsuitable for young children.

It appeared to us, from what we were shown, that the Russians are more successful than we are in the development of language, vocabulary and speech in deaf children once they enter the educational system. This seemed to us a strong point in favor of their method (use of fingerspelling from the very start as an instrument for the development of language, communication and speech), the investigation of which was the main object of our visit. (pp. 44–45)

Zukov (1962) claimed that under traditional methods children entering school at age 7 would learn 200 words and 8 sentence patterns. Now, 550 to 600 words and 80 patterns are learned the first year. Zukov reported that children who have gone through preschool now have as many as 2,000 words in their vocabulary upon entering the elementary program. More important, their language has achieved control over their behavior. They have words to control and direct their own actions.

Research on neo-oralism has been conducted in over 70 programs in the Soviet Union. By the early 1960s its superiority over the traditional pure oral method had been established to the satisfaction of researchers at the Moscow Institute of Defectology, and neo-oralism was established officially through the Soviet Union.

In an attempt to test the generalizability of the findings of the Soviet research, Quigley (1969) compared preschool children (ages 3½ to 7½) taught under the traditional oral-only method with a group taught simultaneously by speech and fingerspelling, the Rochester method in the United States. Although it had been used in the United States for 100 years, it had never been tried, with one exception (Hester, 1963), with young children in the twentieth century, for fear that fingerspelling would inhibit very young children's oral development. Quigley found that children taught by the Rochester method were superior in fingerspelling, speechreading, written language, and reading, thus supporting the results reported by the Russians.

Choosing Among the Methods

The crux of the methodology issue for an individual comes down to this: What type of stimulation should be recommended for newly diagnosed deaf children? The diagnosis for very young children often is confused, and in many cases it is uncertain how much sound they receive and how it is processed. This is an especially relevant concern for children with etiologies such as rubella, meningitis, and prematurity, where other complicating factors may exist. For children with whom it is difficult to predict a potential for developing language

auditorilly, educators have two alternatives. If they believe the base of language lies in the auditory mode and that visual presentation inhibits this, they will recommend a straight auditory emphasis. The auditory failures later would be programmed into multisensory systems. If they believe the base of language lies deeper, they would consider modality to be relatively unimportant and, when in doubt, would provide simultaneous auditory-visual presentation.

If the base of language really is auditory, the first approach would serve the auditory children educationally and lose the others. The second approach would lose all children. If the base of language goes deeper, the first alternative would save the auditory children and lose the others. The second alternative would save all children. Given the present state of knowledge, educators making decisions regarding methodology must do so in the face of great uncertainty. In thinking through the problem, they must be aware that if their orientation is wrong, their decisions will have lasting detrimental effects on children.

Program Orientation

The methods controversy traditionally had dichotomized the field to such an extent that other substantive issues have not received adequate attention. For example, the content of early education programs has been all but ignored. The majority of programs have been in the mold of the traditional nursery school, with emphasis on socialization. Parent guidance may be the major aspect of such a program, and placement contiguous to hearing peers is usually an essential component. Stress is placed on the spontaneous development of speech and language skills. Descriptions of such programs may be found in the writings of Knox and McConnell (1968), Pronovost (1967), Reed (1963), and Van Uden (1970).

A somewhat later development has been observed toward child-centered intervention programs with emphasis on the development of cognitive and academic skills (Moores, 1976b). The impetus grew out of work with retarded and Head Start children which suggested that the more successful early intervention programs contained some structured components with specific academic and/or cognitive training. Prereading programs may be introduced as early as 2 to 3 years of age (Clark & Greco, 1973; Clark & Moores, 1973). Reports of investigators such as Bereiter and Engelmann (1966); Di Lorenzo (1969); Karnes, Hagens, & Teska (1968); Spicker (1971); and Weikert (1968) had the greatest impact.

It should be noted that a program may be considered cognitive without being academic. For example, activities may be planned according to Piagetian concepts of child development and may not reflect traditional academic emphases such as prereading skills and arithmetic drills. The *Games without words* activities developed by Wolff and Wolff (1973) in an illustration of this type of program.

A Longitudinal Evaluation*

A longitudinal evaluation based on a modification of Cronbach's (1957) characteristics by treatment interaction model was conducted in cooperation with seven early education programs† by Moores and associates (Moores, 1970c, 1975; Moores & McIntyre, 1971; Moores, McIntyre, & Weiss, 1972, 1973; Moores, Weiss, & Goodwin, 1973a, 1973b, 1974; Weiss, Goodwin, & Moores, 1975).

The model is based on the thesis that when results of educational research consist entirely of comparisons between groups, they are of limited value. Such investigations may be neat and may produce results, but they frequently mask important interactions between individuals and different types of treatments or educational programs. The search should not necessarily be for the "best" method for all children but rather for the preferred method for a particu-

---

* This section is an expansion of a similar section that appeared in D. Moores, A review of education of the deaf. In L. Mann & D. Sabatino (Eds.), *The third review of special education.* New York: Grune & Stratton, 1976, pp. 19–52.
† The American School for the Deaf, West Hartford (Conn.); Callier Hearing and Speech Center, Dallas (Texas); Maryland School for the Deaf; Minneapolis (Minn.) Public Schools; New Mexico School for the Deaf; Rochester (N.Y.) School for the Deaf; St. Paul (Minn.) Public Schools. An eighth program, The Bill Wilkerson Hearing and Speech Center, Nashville (Tenn.) withdrew after the first year.

lar child at a particular stage of development. A detailed explanation of the rationale is presented by Moores (1970c).

The programs were selected to represent a number of important components of various early intervention systems. The programs differed as to methodology (auditory, oral-aural, Rochester method, total communication); setting (day, residential); orientation (traditional nursery, academic, cognitive); emphasis (parent-centered, child-centered); and placement (integrated, self-contained). Each participating program was considered a strong representative of a particular early intervention mode.

The evaluation was designed to avoid what had been perceived as weaknesses in previous evaluations. Among the steps taken were the following:

1. Programs were involved that provided services from time of identification.

2. Programs were chosen that served complete, not select, populations.

3. Programs had no role in the evaluation itself.

4. Measures of use of residual hearing were employed.

5. Decisions about inclusion of pupils in the study were made by an audiologist on a "blind" basis; that is, data presented to the audiologist did not identify the program from which a child came.

6. Investigators were able to follow children who entered neighborhood schools, that is, those who were mainstreamed.

7. Measures of expressive and receptive communication abilities were developed and administered in addition to tests of articulation and receptive vocabulary.

Complete results are presented in detail in the reports themselves, and interested readers are referred to original sources. Subjects were tested during spring of 1971, 1972, 1973, and 1974. Since all subjects were born between March 1966 and March 1968, by the final testing the average age was 7 years with a range from 6 to 8 years.

Academic achievement   Achievement of the sample, as measured by the Metropolitan Achievement Test, Primer Battery, is comparable to that of hearing children of the same age in reading and below hearing children in arithmetic. The relatively poor achievement in arithmetic was noted in 1973 and 1974, suggesting a general weakness in all programs involved, in that reading is emphasized to the detriment of computational skills. The high reading scores suggest that the programs have provided children with the skills for basic reading. However, since there is evidence that the children lack knowledge of more complex English linguistic structures (such as passives, interrogatives, verb tenses, and negatives), it is probable that the children will show less progress over the years in reading than the standardization hearing population.

Table 10.2   Receptive communication scale (core items), percentage scores obtained in 1972, 1973, and 1974

Subtest	1972	1973	1974
Printed word	38	56	76
Sound alone	34	43	44
Sound and speechreading	56	63	68
Sound, speechreading, and fingerspelling	61	72	75
Sound, speechreading, and signs	72	86	88
Total percent correct	50	62	69

SOURCE: D. Moores, A Review of Education of the Deaf. In L. Mann & D. Sabatino (Eds.), *Third Review of Special Education.* New York: Grune & Stratton, 1977, p. 44.

In terms of program comparisons, the mean raw scores for reading ranged from 22.69 to 29.50; for arithmetic, from 17.15 to 22.38; and overall, from 39.85 to 51.87. In each case the lowest score was from program D, and the highest was from program F. Program D was a traditional auditory, parent-centered program with emphasis on socialization and integration. Program F was a Rochester method program with a cognitive academic orientation.

Illinois Test of Psycholinguistic Abilities (ITPA)   In 1972, 1973, and 1974, the average scores of the subjects on the five visual-motor subtests of the ITPA were almost identical to norms established for children with normal hearing, suggesting normal functioning in these areas. The deaf subjects consistently have exhibited superiority on one subtest, Manual Expression. The ITPA scores with this population do not correlate with scores on expressive and receptive communication, suggesting that, for young deaf children, visual-motor tests of the ITPA may assess underlying cognitive abilities rather than psycholinguistic abilities per se.

In the beginning years of the study, mean scores were quite sensitive to the amount of structure and academic orientation of a program. These differences seemed to disappear by 1974, indicating that previous program differences on the ITPA were spurious.

Receptive communication   Subjects were assessed in their receptive abilities across five modes: printed messages; sound alone; sound and speechreading; sound, speechreading, and fingerspelling; and sound, speechreading, and signs. Table 10.2 indicates that for 1972, 1973, and 1974, excluding understanding of the printed word, the least efficient mode was sound alone. Understanding

Table 10.3   Percent correct on receptive communication scale (core items), by program and mode of communication

Program		N	Printed word	Sound alone	Sound & speech-reading	Sound, speech-reading, & fingerspelling	Sound, speech-reading, & signs	Total % correct
A		6	90	40	53	77	83	68
B		12	67	40	65	51	80	63
C		8	77	37	65	75	93	69
D		13	65	58	67	55	85	64
E		7	80	34	51	80	94	68
F		9	90	35	83	89	—	75
G		6	77	53	90	97	93	82
Totals	N		60	60	60	48	40	60
	$\bar{X}$		76	44	68	75	88	69
	σ		29	27	31	28	21	19

SOURCE: Moores, D., Weiss, K., & Goodwin, M., *Evaluation of Programs for Hearing Impaired Children, 1973–1974*, University of Minnesota Research, Development and Demonstration Center in Education of Handicapped Children. Research Report #81, 1974, p. 63.

increased with the addition of each element — speechreading, fingerspelling, and signs — with the combined use of sound, speechreading, and signs representing the single most effective means of communication. Scores on the printed word increased dramatically from 1973 to 1974 as a function of increased attention to reading in all programs.

Programmatic comparisons of scores in 1974 reveal a number of interesting patterns (Table 10.3). Scores on understanding the printed word range from 65% for program D to 90% for programs A and F. It is significant to note that program D also was the lowest on the MAT reading tests, while program F was highest.

In terms of the four measures of person-to-person communication, the situation becomes much more complex. Programs D and G, at 58% and 53% respectively, are far superior to the other programs in reliance on sound alone. As previously mentioned, children in program D were trained in the auditory method. Those in program G all started in the Rochester method and later were tracked into oral-aural or total communication classes; all children were exposed to signs. The results suggest that manual communication has no effect, either positive or negative, on use of residual hearing.

The addition of speechreading to sound provides different patterns. Scores on this measure probably are more important than sound alone, because the daily face-to-face contact of most deaf individuals with hearing people involves understanding by means of simultaneous speechreading and use of residual hearing. The range of scores for this mode is 53% for program A to 90% for program G. Analysis of increases in scores from sound alone to sound plus speechreading reveals the least improvement to be 9% in program D (from 58 to 67%), a program with an auditory emphasis; the greatest improvement was 48% in program F (from 35 to 83%), followed by 37% in program G (from 53 to 90%). Since the two highest-scoring programs employ manual communication, it is obvious that manual communication does not detract from the use of either residual hearing or speechreading.

The addition of the fingerspelling component reveals a wide range of scores. The scores for program B (51%) and program D (55%) are depressed because program B was changed from an oral-aural program only during the 1973–1974 year. In 1974 program D began to permit manual communication with a few of its children who were classified as *nonoral*. The score of 97% correct for students in program G represents the highest single score for any program on any subtest, and the 89% for program F also suggests a high level of functioning. Both programs are above the overall mean score obtained for sound and speechreading and signs.

The final addition — signs — represents the most efficient overall mode, at 88% correct; no program, even including programs B and D, scored below 80%.

Scores on understanding of passives, negatives, and verb tenses suggested that the deaf students tended to process all sentences as simple, active declaratives and to ignore indications of tense, mood, and negation, regardless of the mode of communication; the exception was that performance was better when dealing with the printed word.

Expressive communication　Consistent with their superiority on the sound-alone receptive test, pupils in Programs D and G scored highest in articulation of one- and two-syllable words with no context. However, when rated on spontaneous description and story-telling across three groups of raters (hearing graduate students, interpreters for the deaf, and deaf adults), their scores fall below the overall average. For these measures the range of intelligibility was from 29.90% for program B to 45.11% for program C, a total communication program. For all programs the most efficient raters were interpreters (56.66%), followed by deaf adults (31.41%) and graduate students (19.54%).

Cognitive development　Tests of classification, conservation, and seriation reveal no differences between programs in 1974 on any of the measures. Previous difference in favor of a "Piagetian" preschool program G disappeared, suggesting that the activities themselves had no lasting effect on cognitive development, as measured in the above three areas.

Communication patterns　Classroom observation consistently revealed that the least communication occurred in oral-aural classes, and that the most took place in total communication classes. To a large extent, teachers and children in oral-aural classes relied on gestures, apparently unconsciously; this tendency was so strong that one program could properly be classified as oral-gestural. Similar discrepancies were found in some total communication classes in which only a small proportion of the spoken words were signed. This was especially true in programs that recently had switched methodology.

Parental attitudes   At the beginning of the evaluation, parents of children in oral-aural programs saw the goals of early intervention programs to be the development of speech and speechreading skills, whereas parents of children in combined oral-manual programs placed greater emphasis on academic skills such as reading and mathematics. By 1974, the attitudes of parents in oral-aural programs had changed to essentially the same as those in combined programs.

The findings of the longitudinal evaluations are the basis for guidelines for early interaction programs for the deaf presently being developed.

Summary

Although the number of early intervention programs has increased significantly since 1960, interest in education of very young deaf children may be traced back to the nineteenth century. Recent trends suggest that the majority of programs are now found in schools, rather than in traditional clinics or speech and hearing centers.

Research in the 1960s indicated that little or no measurable benefit resulted from exposure to early intervention programs. More recent work suggests improvement in the efficacy of programs that have moved away from the traditional preschool model. Factors identified as associated with the improvement include: (1) cognitive and academic training, (2) more parental involvement, (3) use of combined oral and manual communication, and (4) improved utilization of residual hearing.

11
Teaching and Training Techniques

Although the present book is not designed as a curriculum methods course, it is helpful to have some understanding of techniques and methods traditionally and currently employed in teaching deaf children. Material in this chapter could have been presented throughout the book in various chapters such as "The Acquisition and Use of English," "Early Intervention Programs," and "Elementary and Secondary Education." However, topics such as language, speech, speechreading, and auditory training for the deaf have an internal consistency and interrelation that justify treatment in the same section.

Each topic in this chapter, as in many other chapters, would require a full book to do justice to it. Interested readers are encouraged to investigate all areas more completely through additional readings.

Methods of Teaching Language to the Deaf *

Basically, there have been two approaches employed in helping deaf children acquire mastery of the language of society. The first, known as the *natural method,* is concerned with helping children acquire idiomatic usage of a language. This type of approach has also been labeled variously as the *synthetic, informal,* and *mother's method.* As the names imply, an effort is made to follow the "normal" course of language acquisition as closely as possible. The term *method* in this context has nothing to do with the oral-manual-combined–total communication methods controversy.

The second approach, originally known as the *grammatical method* (Nelson, 1949), has also been referred to as the *scientific, philosophical, logical, system-*

* Much of the information contained in this section, especially that relating to methods used in the nineteenth century, was obtained from the Historical Library of the American School for the Deaf. I would like to thank Dr. Ben Hoffmeyer, Headmaster of the American School, for granting me free access to the library, for allowing me to borrow several of the library's rare publications, and for approving the duplication of what ended up to be thousands of pages of material.

atic, formal, analytical, and *artificial method.*   The major aims of this approach are to provide students with simple and correct language structures. For reasons of convenience, the present chapter will use the terms *natural* and *analytical* to identify the two systems.

The discussion in Chapter 2 about the origins of education of the deaf in Europe reveals that both approaches have long and respectable historical antecedents.   The techniques developed in sixteenth- and seventeenth-century Spain obviously represent analytical approaches to the teaching of language by Bonet and de Leon.   Dalgarno's (1680) contention that children would develop language normally if their mothers would fingerspell to them in the crib presages the development of the natural method.

It should be noted that most teachers, and programs, for practical reasons, are somewhat eclectic in their approaches.   Although they may orient toward one or the other method, they usually incorporate both to some extent.   The issue was highlighted in 1876 in the course of an exchange between Pettengill and Fay (the editor of the *American Annals of the Deaf*) in an article entitled, "The Natural Method of Teaching Language" (Pettengill, 1876).   Pettengill took exception to a previous statement of Fay's that "nature's method" was attractive in theory but it had never really been practiced in any institution for the deaf.   Pettengill claimed that he had indeed put the theory into practice with good results.   Fay responded (Pettengill, 1876):

We are very glad to learn that the experiment in question has been tried by Mr. Pettengill and Mr. McWhorter with satisfactory results. The article in the *Annals* was written for the purpose of urging teachers to follow the methods of nature more closely than had generally been done. But then, as now, we believed that in this attempt to follow nature, the average teacher, especially when charged, as in the case of most of our institutions, with the instruction of a large class, needs the guidance of some prearranged plan, system and order. (p. 1)

Thus, spokesmen for both the natural and analytical methods acknowledged the desirability of a natural type of language acquisition process.   The disagreement remains over the extent to which this is posssible without conscious "artificial" techniques and the extent to which the natural method becomes unnatural in a clinical or classroom situation.

Analytical Methods

The major analytical systems used in the United States are listed in Table 11.1. The method was brought to the United States from France by Laurent Clerc and Thomas Hopkins Gallaudet and was established in this country before the introduction of the natural method (Farrar, 1923).   Originally instruction was based on the work of de l'Epée in France (T. Gallaudet, 1817), in which complete sentences were learned at the outset with signs associated with printed words.   Signs were employed for function words, as well as content words, and

Table 11.1 Major analytical systems used to teach language to the deaf in the United States

System	Year introduced
Sicard's theory of ciphers	Developed in France in early 1800s; demonstrated in United States by Clerc in 1851
Barnard's symbols	1836
Peet's language system	1844
Jacobs' primary lessons	1858
Hartford (Storrs) symbols	1860
Wing's symbols	1883
Barry five slate system	1893
Fitzgerald Key	1926
Streng's applied linguistics	1972

for bound morphemes such as those that signify person, number, and tense (H. Peet, 1859). Emphasis was on memorization rather than on original composition. Sicard, de l'Epée's successor, believed that the deaf could learn to construct sentences by means of a grammatical system, and he developed his *theory of ciphers* (Clerc, 1851; Wing, 1887). He divided the sentence into five basic "parts" — nominative case, verb, objective case, preposition, and object of preposition — and used these to develop basic "correct" word order. At one time, the system was in wide use in the United States and probably was the model for the Barry five slate system, which was developed later (Nelson, 1949).

Frederick Barnard, a teacher at both the American and the White Plains schools, and later president of Columbia University, developed a comprehensive system of grammatical symbols based upon notions of being, assertion, attribution, and influence (Barnard, 1836). Although quite well developed on a firm theoretical base, the system never achieved popularity because of its complexity and the difficulty of using it with small children (Wing, 1887).

A course of instruction that was the model for primary training in schools for the deaf for several years was introduced by H. Peet (1845, 1860, 1868), who advocated that ideas should precede words and that difficulties should be presented to children one step at a time. Lessons were developed as a series of carefully designed progressions through increasingly difficult grammatical principles.

The *Hartford*, or *Storrs, symbols* (Porter, 1868, 1869; Storrs, 1880) were developed by Storrs in the belief that the natural method was confusing to deaf children. It was his contention that for deaf children language should involve a step-by-step process of principle construction, and he argued that through the

Table 11.2   Sentence representations used in the Storrs system

Sentence	Representation

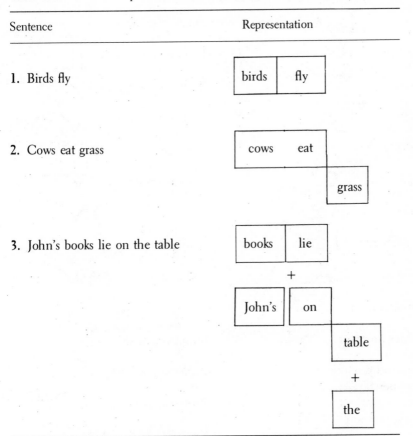

1. Birds fly

2. Cows eat grass

3. John's books lie on the table

SOURCE: Adapted from S. Porter, Professor Porter's Paper on Grammer. *Proceedings of the Sixth Convention of the American Instructors of the Deaf*, Washington, D.C.: U.S. Government Printing Office, 1968, p. 145.

analytical method ("scientific method" in his terms) children could memorize 300 conversational formulae which would serve their everyday needs.

Storrs's symbols were designed to provide visual representations of syntactic relations, and sentence "pictures" were presented in boxlike form. In Table 11.2 examples are presented of the three sentences. "Bird's fly," "Cows eat grass," and "John's books lie on the table." Table 11.3 presents the different symbols used to represent various aspects of English grammar. It illustrates the complexity of the Storrs symbols and perhaps provides some insight into the reasons for the decline of the analytical method relative to the natural method at that time.

The next major analytical system was *Wing's symbols*, developed in 1883 by

Table 11.3   Storrs symbols

Noun		Singular number	
Pronoun		Plural number	
Adjective		Verb transitive	
Adverb		Verb intransitive	
Verb		Verb passive	
Preposition		Verb progressive	
Conjunction		Indicative mood	
Interjection		Subjunctive mood	
Proper noun		Potential mood	
Common noun		Imperative mood	
Relative pronoun		Infinitive mood	
Noun and pronoun in the nominative case		Participle	
Possessive case		Participle as a noun	
Objective case		Present tense	
Independent case		Past tense	
Masculine gender		Future tense	
Feminine gender		Present perfect tense	
Common gender		Past perfect tense	
First person		Future perfect tense	
Second person		Verb singular	
Third person		Verb plural	

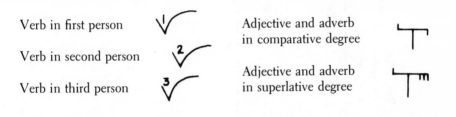

Verb in first person		Adjective and adverb in comparative degree	
Verb in second person			
Verb in third person		Adjective and adverb in superlative degree	

SOURCE: From M. Nelson, "The Evolutionary Process of Teaching Methods to the Deaf with a Survey of Methods Now Employed." *American Annals of the Deaf,* 1947, 91, 230–294, 249.

George Wing, a deaf teacher at the Minnesota School for the Deaf ("Minnesota Course of Study," 1918). The symbols consist of numbers and letters placed over words, phrases, or clauses. The system is different from others in that it is designed to show forms, functions, and positions of parts of sentences, rather than being limited to traditional parts of speech. The symbols are grouped into four categories: (1) *the essentials,* (2) *modifying forms,* (3) *correctives,* and (4) *special symbols.*

Barry developed a *five slate system* (Barry, 1899; Pope, 1935) that apparently was based on Sicard's theory of ciphers (Nelson, 1949). As may be implied by its name, the system utilized five large slates on the blackboard that were reserved for five categories: (1) *subject,* (2) *verb,* (3) *object,* (4) *preposition,* and (5) *object of preposition.* The similarity to Sicard's five basic sentence parts is obvious. Children also had small slates similarly divided, and great attention was paid to careful analysis of sentences and their component parts. The system was quite popular, and, according to Long (1918), it was used in every school for the deaf in the United States by 1918.

The Barry five slate system was supplanted by the *Fitzgerald Key,* developed by Edith Fitzgerald, a deaf teacher. The Key, as it is commonly known, was developed to provide children with rules by which they could generate correct English sentences as well as final and correct their own errors in compositions (Fitzgerald, 1929). Instruction in the Key usually begins by placing individual words under appropriate headings, such as *Who, What,* and *Where,* for example. The systems employ the following six visible symbols:

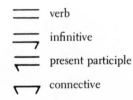

verb

infinitive

present participle

connective

Table 11.4 Sample of exercises using the Fitzgerald Key

Whose:	Who: / What:	What did ___ do?	What: / ( ) / Whom:	Whose:	Whom: / What:	Where:	From___: / For___: / With___: / How: / Why:	How far: / How often: / How long: / How much:	When:
	Mary	Went				Home			Yesterday
	Bob	Rode		His	Bike				
	Sue	Gave	Her Dog		Bone		With Sally		
	Molly	Played		A					
Bill's	Mother	Drove				To St. Paul			
	He	Played				Outside			Last Night

⊤   pronoun

⊓   adjective

Words at first are combined in a simple manner under appropriate headings such as *Who* or *What*. Practice is undertaken on proper word order. For example, the sequence of modifiers preceding nouns is presented as: *How many, What kind, What color, What.*

The complexity of the utterances is increased gradually to include transitive verbs and objects, possession, phrases of place and time, and so on, following definite procedures until the children are able to work with the complete Key, which may be found on the blackboard along a wall in most classrooms for the deaf. Children also work exercises in their seats with "Key paper" containing the various elements of the Key. Table 11.4 presents some simple sentences organized according to one version of the Key.

In a comparison of the Barry five slate system and the Fitzgerald Key, Buell (1931) argued that the Key was more comprehensive, flexible, and grammatical. Her opinion apparently was shared by a majority of educators of the deaf. In an investigation of language methods used with the deaf in the United States and Canada, Nelson (1949) reported that the Fitzgerald Key was utilized in 84 of 132 schools and programs surveyed. In 66 cases it was employed exclusively, and in 18 it was used in combination with another method. The Barry five slate system was used exclusively in 12 programs and in combination with other methods in an additional 13 programs — 11 of which involved some use in coordination with the Fitzgerald Key. Since Nelson's survey, the five slate system has further eroded in popularity, and the Key continues to be by far the most widely used analytical approach.

A final analytical system should be mentioned. This is the method developed by Streng (1972). It is based on principles of generative-transformational grammar and, as such, represents significant advances over previous analytical methods. The more sophisticated systems — such as the Barry five slate, the Wing symbols, and the Fitzgerald Key — may appropriately be classified as generative grammar systems. By this is meant that they provide the tools by which a majority of the most commonly used English structures may be generated. However, they are handicapped in that they produce essentially linear, left-to-right strings and are unable to illustrate some logical relations between utterances which would be intuitively obvious to a native user of a language. An example might be relationships between active and passive transformations such as *The girl pushed the boy* and *The boy was pushed by the girl*. A generative-transformational grammar is more efficient for a number of reasons, including its ability to demonstrate logical and syntactic relations between such utterances.

However, there are no illusions that any analytical approach, by itself, will provide all deaf children with a knowledge of standard English. Analytical methods are necessary to the extent that "natural" approaches have failed to provide breakthroughs. In discussing the limitations of our understanding of language as it relates to teaching language to deaf children, Lenneberg (1967b) stated:

From these examples it is clear that the construction of proper sentences is not facilitated by telling a child how to do it. It must be admitted that no one knows how it is done. . . . No grammar, old or new, furnishes us with a recipe of how to speak grammatically. There is no grammatical system available that could be used to help an essentially language-deficient person to put words together to form good sentences. So far, grammars merely specify the underlying structure of sentences and explain how sentences of different structure are related to each other. (p. 324)

The most sophisticated grammars now in existence are models of a language, not of a user. For example, constraints imposed by such factors as limitations, situational variance, motivation, and distortion of the communication channel are not considered in dealing with a model of a language, but they certainly influence a user of a language. This important distinction must be acknowledged in considering the teaching of language or the language functioning of an individual subject to constraints not placed on a language model of competence. Chomsky (1967) discussed the pitfalls as follows:

We noted at the outset that performance and competence must be sharply distinguished if either is to be studied successfully. We have now discussed a certain model of competence. It would be tempting, but quite absurd, to treat it as a model of performance as well. Thus we might propose that to produce a sentence, the speaker goes through the successive steps of constructing a base-derivation, line by line from the initial symbol S, then inserting lexical items and applying grammatical transformations to form a surface structure, and finally applying the phonological rules in their given order, in accordance with the cyclic principle discussed earlier. There is not the slightest justification for any such assumption. (pp. 435–436)

Natural Methods

The major force for the introduction and spread of the natural method in education of the deaf was provided by the German educator Hill, a follower of Pestolozzi (Nelson, 1949; Schmitt, 1966). Hill advocated that natural language could be developed in deaf children just as it was with the hearing. Hill's *mother's method* placed great emphasis on children's experiences. The teaching of grammar was delayed until a relatively late age.

Interest in the natural method grew in the United States after the Civil War, apparently because of widespread dissatisfaction with results obtained through adherence to a strictly analytical approach. Pettengill (1876, 1882) argued that a natural method was theoretically sound and could be employed in schools for the deaf. In his initiation of the *Rochester method* (simultaneous use of speech and the manual alphabet) at the Rochester School for the Deaf in 1878, Westervelt (Scouten, 1942; Westervelt & Peet, 1880) embraced the natural method, with special emphasis on "instruction" during play situations.

Another powerful advocate of the natural method during the same period was Greenberger, principal of the Lexington School for the Deaf, who argued (1879) that so long as deaf children were taught language in an artificial manner, they would never transfer their knowledge into actual use. He advocated supplying words to deaf children on the basis of need; that is, rather than teaching vocabulary in any systematic way, words should be introduced in natural situations. Following Greenberger's leadership, the Lexington school has been known ever since as a leading exponent of the natural method. At one period, the natural method was sometimes referred to as the *Lexington method* (Nelson, 1949).

A final factor in the spread of the natural method was the influence of A. G. Bell, in particular the publication of the methods he employed in tutoring young George Sanders (Bell, 1883). Following Froebel, Bell utilized play to a great extent, organizing lessons around toys and games. He combined this with the ideas of Dalgarno (1680) concerning the early introduction of reading and writing, which Bell attempted to use in a "conversational" manner. Bell's approach seemed to be a reasonable combination of natural and analytical systems as well as of oral and manual methods. In order to enable the child to communicate ideas to others, Bell once again resorted to Delgarno and used a finger alphabet in which the letters were written on a glove (Figure 11.1). Messages were spelled by pointing to the appropriate spot on the hand with the index finger of the other hand. By 6 years of age, Sanders had mastery over English to the extent that he was able to communicate effectively by writing with hearing persons.

In spite of the claims of proponents of the natural method and its unquestioned advantages, at least in theory, it was not established as the predominant method in the United States. In fact, the results suggested that a pure natural method was no more effective in meeting the needs of deaf children than a pure analytical method. The similarities with the oral-manual controversy, in which the evidence suggests limited benefits from either a "pure" oral or a "pure" manual system, should be obvious. A reaction quickly set in. Two influential analytical systems, Wing's symbols and the Barry five slate system, were developed before the turn of the century and were in use in programs for the deaf in the United States until replaced by another analytical system, the Fitzgerald Key. In her survey of methods, Nelson (1949) reported that the natural method was used exclusively in only 10 of 132 programs surveyed. In 9 other programs it was used in combination with an analytical method.

Since that time, the use of the natural method, or at least of natural methods, has increased. The work of Groht (1933, 1958), who, like Greenberger, was a principal of the Lexington School for the Deaf, has been particularly influential in this area. Groht argued that language principles are best taught in

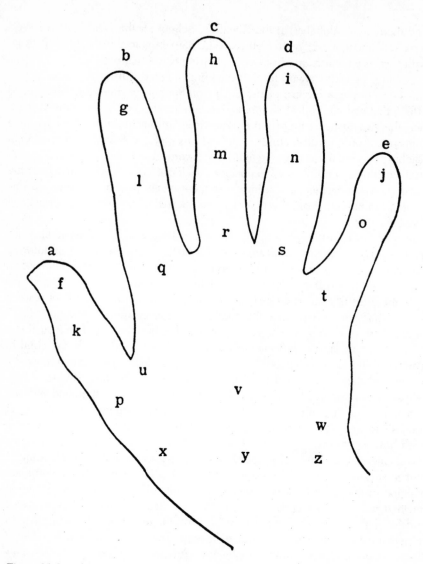

Figure 11.1   Alexander G. Bell's finger alphabet.

natural situations and then practiced through games and stories. Drill and
textbook exercises are seen as far less effective than repetition in meaningful situations.

   At present most programs appear to be eclectic mixtures of natural and analytical approaches, with the emphasis varying from one program to another. If
anything the natural method is somewhat more prevalent. To a large extent
this may be attributed to the inability of teachers to instruct children effectively

in an analytical method. Unlike their predecessors, present-day teachers of the deaf have little or no background in formal English grammar and have little grasp of the principles upon which the study of grammar is based.

Summary

Despite advances over the last 200 years, the teaching of language to the deaf remains an inexact science. Progress has been gradual through a process of small improvements. Although deaf children do develop language skills, they usually do not acquire proficiency in the Standard English dialect used by a majority of hearing persons with whom they come into contact. Even if the "final breakthrough" is not in sight, recent advances in the study of childhood language acquisition are of great potential benefit for the education of deaf children. For the present, a judicious blend of natural and analytical techniques appears to have the best potential for success in bringing to deaf children the language of the community at large.

The Teaching of Speech

Given the lip service paid to the development of speech by all educators of the deaf and the dominance of the field by oral-only proponents until recent times, one might be inclined to expect that the teaching of speech to deaf children would be a well-researched, empirically based systematic process. Anyone so inclined would be sadly disappointed. With the exception of an excellent presentation of techniques used to develop speech at the Lexington School for the Deaf by Vorce (1974), and an overview of speech and deafness by Calvert and Silverman (1975), the contemporary literature is scarce. The situation in teaching speech to the deaf is analogous to that of the weather — everyone talks about it, but very few seem to do much about it.

Although the terms *speech* and *articulation* have been used interchangeably by some individuals, it must be understood that human speech incorporates a number of complex processes, of which articulation is only one. Articulation involves the generation of speech sounds by modifications of the vocal tract, which consist basically of the mouth, nasal, and pharnygeal cavities. Changes in placement and manner of articulators such as the lips, teeth, tongue, palate, and pharynx cause changes in speech sounds.

In addition to articulation one must have an understanding of the power source for human speech. Respiration, which relies on the lungs and various muscular and skeletal elements, provides the basic air stream from which speech is developed. *Phonation*, dealing with vocal tone production, is provided by the larynx, which produces a vibrating air stream.

It is interesting to note that all the mechanisms involved in speech production originally were developed in human beings to serve biological functions.

Most obvious, of course, would be the mechanisms involved in breathing, such as the lungs and larynx as well as the nose, mouth, and pharynx.

A complete treatment of the anatomy and physiology of the human speech and hearing mechanism is provided by Zemlin (1968), *Speech and hearing science: anatomy and physiology*. A highly readable and helpful presentation on the use of hearing aids is provided by Berger (1970), *The hearing aid: Its operation and development*. Those interested in pursuing the subjects of speech and hearing more fully might begin with Wever (1949), *Theory of hearing*, and Ladefoged, *Elements of acoustic phonetics* (1962).

Techniques and methods currently in use here have been in existence for 50 years or more. This, in itself, would not be a cause for alarm if there were evidence that the approaches had met with consistent success, but there is none. Although most programs view their approach to the teaching of speech as eclectic, a better descriptor might be haphazard. After 100 years of oral-only education, the state of the art may be summarized as follows:

1. Knowledge about the processes by which deaf children acquire speech is virtually nonexistent.

2. Information on the use of speech by deaf individuals in natural situations is almost completely anecdotal.

3. Educators of the deaf, as a group, make no distinction between speech development and speech remediation.

4. No valid reliable diagnostic speech tests have been developed for the deaf. Those most commonly used have been designed for hearing individuals.

5. There is inadequate understanding, in qualitative and quantitative terms, of the speech of deaf children. The classic study of speech intelligibility (Hudgins & Numbers) was reported in 1942, and results are based on the reading of 10 simple sentences.

6. To the best of the author's knowledge *no* study has ever been conducted comparing the effects of different techniques or methods of teaching speech to the deaf.

7. As a general rule, methods of teaching speech to the deaf in the United States have neither a theoretical nor a pragmatic base.

Hudgins and Numbers (1942) analyzed the speech of 192 deaf pupils from two schools for the deaf. Each subject read ten unrelated simple sentences, and intelligibility was rated by individuals familiar with the speech of deaf individuals. Two major types of errors may be identified: articulatory and rhythmic. In articulation, seven categories were developed for consonant errors, and five for vowels that were articulated incorrectly. However, articulation, per se, was of only secondary importance in the intelligibility of the speech of the deaf subjects as compared with other aspects of speech. For example, sentences spoken with correct rhythm were understood correctly four times more frequently than those with incorrect rhythm. In general, the speech of the subjects was characterized by arhythmic patterns, poor phrasing, monotonic expression, and lack of pitch.

In a review of the status of speech curricula in programs for the deaf in the United States, Vorce (1971, pp. 223, 224) states that there has been little or no experimentation in speech content and methodologies and that few models exist from which a curriculum might be adapted. She acknowledges the existence of a substantial literature dealing with various aspects of speech teaching, such as voice quality, pitch variations, breath support, durational aspects, abutting consonants, color coding for breath-nasal-voice concept, speech charts, orthographic systems, spectrographic analyses, and so on. However, she points out that not one well-controlled study of deaf speech was conducted over large populations from the time of the Hudgins and Numbers study in 1942 to the publication of her overview in 1971. She further notes that there are only a few books in existence which are relevant to the planning of speech programs. A case in point is the monograph in which the Vorce chapter appears, *Speech for the Deaf Child: Knowledge and Use* (Connor, 1971). Although there are many interesting and useful background chapters, overviews, and descriptions of speech aids, only the chapters by Vorce (1971) and Magner (1971), in the author's opinion, have direct applicability to the classroom. All too frequently, the other writing consists of panygerics on the benefits of good speech and attacks on the perceived enemy of entrenched oral-only advocates — manual communication (Connor, 1971; Hardy, 1971; Simmons, 1971).

Vorce concluded that, given the paucity of materials, the responsibility for initiating changes rested on the coordinators and teachers of individual programs. This unfortunate reliance on local sources leads to a large degree of inconsistency. Vorce received responses from 21 programs on questionnaires developed to elicit information about speech curricula. The results gave little indication of agreement, and Vorce reported that the range in philosophy and/or methods varied not only from program to program, but often within programs themselves. The results are summarized (Vorce, 1971) as follows:

Most include systematic or routine teaching of speech skills (although speech methods and content vary with the age and individual needs of the children and many indicate that skills "are taught only as needed"); most children of elementary school age have daily speech periods, but at other levels specific daily work is often not provided in the overall plan; most speech work is group work at least some of the time, with a few programs providing individual tutoring at specific levels; less than half employ special speech teachers (the majority of these being at the upper levels where pupils "rotate" among subject matter specialists); no consistent system for planning speech work emerges (some decisions are made jointly by the classroom teacher and the departmental or speech supervisor, others by the teacher or the supervisor without reference to other personnel). (pp. 224–225)

The results are based on conditions in the 21 programs that responded to the questionnaire. It is probable that conditions in other programs are not as good.

Nickerson (1975) conducted an extensive review of speech training and speech reception aids for the deaf, including sections about auditory aids, instantaneous visual displays, visual displays with time history, multifeature visual displays, and display systems and tactile displays. Nickerson concluded that communications science and engineering have done little to benefit those with disabling communications problems (p. 97). He stated (1975):

It is well known that the speech of the deaf tends not to be very intelligible, and it is possible to list a variety of things that are wrong with it, . . . but nobody can yet say very precisely how much each of these deficiencies contributes to its overall lack of intelligibility or its generally poor quality. (pp. 98–99)

Methods of Teaching Speech

Although at present few programs follow one identifiable method of teaching speech, it is helpful to be aware of how some of the more widely used techniques and systems developed and to perceive them within a broader perspective. In terms of labeling methods, we might use categories such as *analytic* (or *elemental*) versus *whole word*, *formal* versus *informal* (or *natural*), or *unisensory* versus *multisensory*.

Perhaps one of the most effective treatments of teaching speech to the deaf may be found in Bonet's work, the first book every published on education of the deaf (Bonet, 1620; Peet, 1850). Among other things, it deals with the relationships of speech, language, and reading, and it contains specific techniques for their development. On a more general level, Dalgarno's (1680) theoretical treatise may be considered of importance because of its influence on Alexander Graham Bell, who exerted such great influence on education of the deaf in the United States. However, despite such historical precedents as the work of Bonet and Dalgarno, and even the awareness of the existence of residual hearing in most deaf people as long ago as ancient Rome, the foundations for the teaching of speech to the deaf were established principally in the nineteenth century. To a large degree, they did not involve incorporation of techniques developed in Germany by "German" or "oral method" teachers, but rather they represented relatively independent systems. Short treatments are presented about the following: Visible Speech and the element method, the babbling method, the acoustic method, the concentric method, and the TVA method.

Visible Speech and the element method   Visible Speech, a system designed to represent any sound the human mouth can utter, was developed by Alexander Melville Bell and grew out of his work as a phonetician. Bell started work on the system in the 1840s and developed it over a period of years, with many of the publications printed in several editions (A. M. Bell, 1898, 1904, 1932). The system was based not upon sounds but upon the actions of the vocal organs in producing them. Visible Speech was first used with the deaf by his son, Alexander Graham Bell, in London in 1869. The younger Bell claimed that his four students, ages 7 to 12, learned nearly all the elementary sounds of English in a few days (A. G. Bell, 1872, p. 5). He taught the system to teachers in Boston in 1871 and stated at the same time that adult deaf mutes had acquired all the sounds of English in 10 lessons of Visible Speech (p. 6). It was Bell's contention that perfect articulation could be obtained through Visible Speech. He made no claims for its effect on rhythm and modulation, seeing these as separate branches of training (p. 19).

Alexander Graham Bell introduced his father's system at a time when a majority of educators of the deaf in America were committing themselves for the first time to the teaching of speech. His ideas were enthusiastically accepted because they were advanced as being applicable both to oral-only and oral-manual programs. A. G. Bell stated (1872):

The system takes *no part* in the contest between articulation, on the one hand, and signs and manual alphabets on the other. In presenting his system for adoption all the

Table 11.5   Northampton chart: Consonant sounds

Consonant sounds				
h__				
wh	w__			
p	b	m		
t	d	n	l	r—
k	g (1)	ng		
c		n(k)		
ck				
f	v			
(1) ph / th	(2) th			
(1) s	z			
c(e)	(2) s			
c(i)				
c(y)				
sh	zh	y x = ks		
	(3) s			
	(2) z	qu = kwh		
	j			
ch				
tch	(2) g—			
	—ge			
	dge			

SOURCE: Reproduced with permission of the Clarke School for the Deaf, Northampton, Mass.

inventor means to say is this: "Here is a means by which you can obtain perfect articulation from deaf mutes; *make what use of it you choose.*" (p. 9)

As noted in Chapter 3, Bell himself used the system with a form of manual communication — Dalgarno's two-handed alphabet — in his early efforts, especially with his prize pupil, George Sanders. Although the system was used by Bell within an analytic, or elemental, framework, he later changed his position to favor a whole-word method (A. G. Bell, 1906); but he continued to have reservations about the possible dangers of such an approach.

The principles on which Visible Speech were developed have had a general effect on the teaching of speech to the present day. Alexander Melville Bell's books on the subject all enjoyed multiple editions, a few over periods of 50 years or more. The influence of Visible Speech is such that more than 100 years after its conception by Bell senior, it could be claimed: "The system of

Table 11.6   Northampton chart: Vowel sounds

Vowel sounds					
1 oo	2 oo	o—e	aw	—o—	
(r)u—e		oa	au		
(r)ew		—o	o(r)		
		2 ow			
ee	—i—	a—e	—e—	—a—	
—e	—y	ai	2 ea		
1 ea		ay			
e—e					
	a(r)	—u—	ur		
		—a	er		
		—ar	ir		
		—er			
		—ir			
		—or			
		—ur			
		—re			
a—e	i—e	o—e	ou	oi	u—e
ai	igh	oa	1 ow	oy	ew
ay	—y	—o			
		2 ow			

SOURCE: Reproduced with permission of the Clarke School for the Deaf, Northampton, Mass.

Visible Speech . . . is even today the basis for the method used in teaching the deaf to talk" (Streng et al., 1955, p. 5).

To a large extent the same situation holds true today. This does not mean that Visible Speech is employed in the classroom — it is not. Rather, the work of the Bells had a great influence on the development of methods of teaching speech to the deaf at the Clarke School for the Deaf. In turn, the methods developed at Clarke have been adopted, or adapted, by many programs in America. The single most influential work was Yale's *Formation and development of elementary English sounds* (1939). Yale was principle of the Clarke school for years, and she incorporated the genius of the Bells's system into her work. Although other educators perhaps have developed more complete sets of exercises (e.g., Joiner, 1936) utilizing the element method, the foundation was set by Yale. The *Northampton charts* of vowel and consonant sounds (Tables 11.5 and 11.6) — also known as *Yale charts* — still are used commonly by teachers of the deaf.

The babbling method The babbling method was developed by Avondino (1918, 1919, 1924) on the basis of what she believed to be the natural order of speech acquisition for children with normal hearing. It is essentially a system of syllable drills and stresses voice rhythm and breath control as opposed to drill on isolated elements.

The system relies on constant repetition until fluency is obtained. There are three stages. In the first, there is drill on single syllables in groups of three, spoken with rapidity. At the second stage, words of two syllables are combined, with the accent on the second syllable. By the third stage, two syllables, each beginning with a consonant, are combined. The accent may fall on either syllable.

Words are introduced by syllable drills as follows (Streng et. al., 1955):

fah	fah	fah
faw	faw	faw
fee	fee	fee
foo	foo	foo
faht	faht	faht
fawt	fawt	fawt
feet	feet	feet
foot	foot	foot (p. 316)

Although the method is advanced as following "natural" patterns of development, there is little evidence that hearing children develop speech by constant repetition of meaningless syllables. As with other methods of teaching speech, its effectiveness must remain a matter of conjecture because of a lack of empirical evidence.

The acoustic method The acoustic method was introduced by Goldstein in the United States at the St. Joseph School for the Deaf in St. Louis. It was incorporated in the Central Institute for the Deaf from its founding in 1914 and has been the basis, at least in part, for most of the acoustic methods used in the United States.

Within his definition of the acoustic method Goldstein (1939) included voice and musical sounds; sound vibration as sensed by tactile impression to interpret pitch, rhythm, accent, volume, and inflection; analysis of speech sounds by tactile differentiation; synthesis and speech construction by tactile impression; sound waves and their significance as appreciated by visual perception.

The method concentrates on developing the auditory sense within the context of the speech program. Training is conducted on a daily basis and includes instrumental as well as vocal stimulation. The program may be perceived in two parts: passive education and active education. *Passive education* does not involve conscious effort on the part of students. Musical instruments and sustained amplified tone frequencies are utilized. *Active education* involves "analytic" exercises (which concentrate on interpretation of vowels, consonants, and syllables independent of ideas or words) and "synthetic" exercises (which are concerned with actual speech or language).

The concentric method   The concentric method, developed by Rau (Moores, 1972a), is the official method of teaching speech in the Soviet Union. Unlike the dominant American methods, it incorporates the use of fingerspelling in the teaching of speech. The central principle is to start the speech development of children by beginning with a limited number of phonemes. The method is based on the premise that normally hearing children use an abbreviated phoneme system; that is, they may use a limited number of sounds to express the phonemes of their language.

At the beginning of instruction, children are expected to master only 17 of the 42 Russian phonemes. These consist of 12 voiceless consonants and 5 vowels, the 17 phonemes of the inner circle of Figure 11.2. At this stage, difficulty in understanding, because of poor speechreading — or in expression, because of poor speech — is eliminated by the simultaneous use of fingerspelling. Thus, children might have difficulty articulating the initial distinctions between *pat, bat,* and *mat* (to use an English analogue) and yet be understood by means of fingerspelling.

At first, an approximated pronunciation of sounds is allowed, and then the related sounds are introduced. The teaching of pronunciation has three phases:

1. A preparatory period involving development of imitative processes, breathing habits, phonation and articulation.

2. A second stage involving systematic work in sound production.

3. A final stage involving perfection of pronunciation skills and correction of deficiencies.

By age 9, children are expected to have mastered all 42 phonemes and to use them appropriately. Description and rationale for the concentric method may be found in Karsunshaya (1969) and Rau (1960).

The TVA method   The TVA (tactile, visual, auditory) method is a multisensory, "natural" approach to the development of speech. In the United States it is closely associated with the speech program of the Lexington School for the Deaf. It more accurately might be called a philosophy than a strict method. Children are encouraged to use speech spontaneously at all times, and a whole-word approach is utilized. The approach is both synthetic and analytic, but the analytic aspects are not primary. For example, articulation is seen as an outgrowth of the speech process, not a foundation for it. The emphasis is on a meaningful, interesting, and relevant communication as opposed

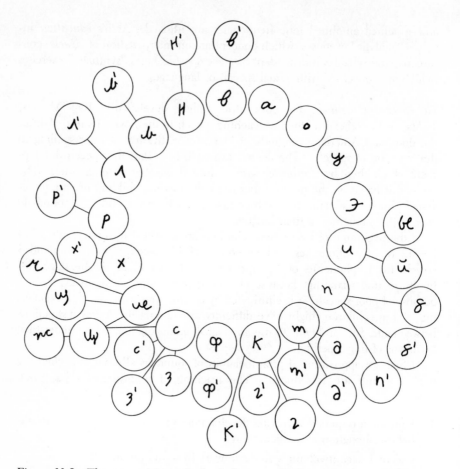

Figure 11.2 The concentric method of phoneme development (Rau). (From D. Moores, "Neo-Oralism and Education of the Deaf in the Soviet Union," *Exceptional Children*, 38 [1972], 377–384. Used by permission.)

to meaningless drill in elements or syllables. Rhythm and voice qualities receive relatively great attention.

The speech program obviously is well coordinated with the natural language program at Lexington. Children are bombarded by natural, informal spoken language and are expected to develop it in a manner approximating that of normally hearing children.

Present Status

Over a period of generations there apparently have been no improvements in techniques of teaching speech to the deaf. Ironically, improvements in methods of teaching speech seemed to come to an end at the same time that the oral-only philosophy became dominant. Some breakthroughs obviously are needed, especially involving the use of techniques appropriate to combined oral-manual techniques. At present only the program in development by Maestas y Moores (1974), which involves the use of fingerspelling to improve articulation and rhythm, shows promise of meeting current needs.

Viewed within a larger context, the lack of progress in teaching speech is not surprising. Since the 1950s major breakthroughs have been made in the areas of psycholinguistics and developmental psycholinguistics. There has been at least the beginning of a symbiotic relationship between theory and practice. As a result, educators of the deaf have been stimulated to develop and assess alternate approaches to the development of language in deaf children. There is even evidence for existence, if only in embryonic form, of universal theories of language development.

Unfortunately there have been no major theoretical advances in the field of speech corresponding to the development of generative-transformational grammar. No universal theory of speech development has been advanced and embraced. No real insights have even been announced. Finally, the relation between theory and practice is tenuous at best.

In short, the field of speech, as well as its subfield of teaching speech to the deaf, is in sad disarray. At this time it is incumbant upon educators of the deaf to rededicate themselves to helping deaf children develop their speech skills to the highest possible degree. With theoretical and practical advances in the broad field of speech, our task will be facilitated. But with or without these advances, the job must be done.

The Utilization of Residual Hearing

Acoupedics

One approach, which has been limited to very young children, perhaps deserves special mention at this point. The techniques or series of procedures — variously termed the *aural method, acoustic method, unisensory method, auditory method,* and *acoupedics* — received wide attention during the 1960s. Some of its advocates (Griffiths, 1967a, 1967b; Pollack, 1964, 1967, 1970; Stewart, Pollack, & Downs, 1964) viewed it as the final breakthrough in education of the deaf. In fact, Griffiths (1967a, pp. 42–50) has claimed that her procedures may cure deafness if instituted before 8 months of age.

It must be emphasized that the proponents of acoupedics, the term coined by Huizing in Holland (Pollack, 1971), view it as a radical departure from techniques commonly employed in the past. It has been acknowledged as early as Roman times that many individuals classified as deaf possess at least some amounts of residual hearing. Systematic procedures for the training of hearing abilities have been in existence for over 200 years (Buchner, 1770). In 1868,

E. Gallaudet reported on training a "deaf" college student to rely on hearing. And in 1884 Gillespie, working at the Nebraska School for the Deaf, developed and implemented an aural system for students with residual hearing.

Acoupedics represents a departure in that it emphasizes the primacy of audition over vision. The major base for this in the United States may be traced to the work of Goldstein (1939) and his acoustic method. Goldstein argued that children should focus attention on sound without division from watching the face or hands. For even the most profoundly deaf child the role of vision is deemphasized on the basis that the child, if allowed, will become too dependent on vision and will not develop auditory-vocal proficiency. Advocates of acoupedics, then, are critical not only of combined oral-aural-manual methods but also of the most common oral-aural approaches, which employ multisensory (auditory-visual-tactile) techniques. For example, emphasis on lipreading with young children is considered a hindrance to the development of hearing. According to Pollack (1971), children taught in this way will continue to rely on visual skills and may ignore sound. Acoupedics, then, does not represent merely an improvement in techniques of auditory training. According to its purest advocates, it cannot be incorporated into an oral-aural or oral-aural-manual program. It is unisensory and must stand alone.

The major impetus for this development grew out of work in Europe during and shortly after World War II. A program was initiated in Holland in 1943 to provide hearing aids to rural deaf children under 3 years of age in order to prepare them for subsequent entrance into residential schools. It was discovered that with early fitting and guidance, many children did not have to enter the residential programs. Some could be integrated into regular classes, and others could attend classes for the hard of hearing (Huizing, 1959). Shortly after this, reports of work in Sweden by Wedenberg (1951, 1954) and in England (Fry & Whetnall, 1954; Whetnall & Fry, 1964) indicated great benefits from the utilization of residual hearing with young children. Related work in the United States has been reported on by Griffiths (1967a, 1967b), McCroskey (1968), Pollack (1964, 1967, 1970), Simmons (1967), and Stewart, Pollack, and Downs (1974).

Viewed from the perspective of a quarter-century or more, it is difficult to appreciate the impact of these findings. The widespread use of powerful hearing aids was only beginning, and with few exceptions the methods employed — oral, manual, or combined — did not assign much importance to hearing. With the evidence that reliance on vision alone was not satisfactory for all children, it was only a matter of time for the pendulum to swing to the other extreme and for some educators to advocate the use of audition alone for all children.

The term *acoupedics* is not restricted only to early auditory training. It is a "comprehensive habilitation program for the hearing impaired infant and his family which includes an emphasis upon auditory training without lipreading instruction" (Pollack, 1970, p. 13). It is based upon the development of an auditory function and is made possible by: (1) early detection; (2) fitting of power-ful hearing aids; (3) intensive and systematic training; (4) heavy involvement, especially by mothers; and (5) deemphasis of nonauditory cues.

The importance of early identification and fitting is related to the idea of a critical period for the development of the use of hearing. Griffiths reports on a child who received aids at 21 days of age (1975). Downs suggests that a decision be made at a very early age, stating (1967):

> If by the time a child is a year and a half old, we have determined that no auditory per-ceptions can be developed, the visual orientation program is clearly laid out for us — whether by lip reading and oral approaches, fingerspelling and manual techniques or a combination of both of these. (p. 749)

Children are expected to wear their hearing aids at least during all waking hours. Most programs utilize binaural, as opposed to bilateral, aids; that is, the child is fitted with two microphones, two power controls, and two receivers.

The demands upon the mother are great. In the foreword to Pollack's book on acoupedics (1970), Wedenberg stated: "My wife gave up her profession* and devoted all of her time to our son. I have found it is the mother's efforts which will determine if the work will succeed or not." Pollack also places the major responsibility on the role of the mother with very little concern for the father and his obligations. She claims that the clinician working with the pro-gram should be a mother herself and that all children under age 3 are more naturally drawn to a woman than to a man.

Although the individuals who have developed acoupedic programs con-tinually stress its unisensory nature, examination of their procedures clearly il-lustrates that they actually also rely heavily on visual and tactual modalities. In reality, the human being, including the very young human being, functions as an integrated organism. The young child relies on sensorimotor experience. Hearing, vision, and touch constantly interact with and complement each other. As such it is almost impossible to place all emphasis first on audition. Examination of descriptions of techniques employed in acoupedic programs seem to support this, as illustrated by the following examples:

> Receptive ability at first is measured by the child's ability to "track" *with eyes or hand*. (Griffiths, 1975, p. 38; emphasis added)

> Once an infant can sit up and *watch* people, it is very important to *show* him that you can hear too. (Pollack, 1967, p. 245; emphasis added)

> For the baby who is from one month to five or six months of age when he starts auditory training, the techniques have to lie *within the range of watching and listening*. (Grif-fiths, 1967b, p. 764; emphasis added)

---

* Both Mr. and Mrs. Wedenberg were dentists.

The mother *places her hands over her ears* with a pleasant surprised expression and says, "I hear that. Listen! What's that?" Then she *shows* the baby what she hears. (Pollack 1971, p. 329; emphasis added)

Toys are selected . . . that have a *manipulative* aspect. (Griffiths, 1967a, p. 34; emphasis added)

In reading the above it is difficult to understand how the authors seriously believe that they are using a unisensory method. From the beginning, visual cues, manipulation of objects, gestures, bodily posture, facial expressions, and kinesthetic feedback, as well as hearing, are all integral parts of the training program. A program that prohibits formal signs and deemphasizes lipreading does not automatically become unisensory. Children usually have both their eyes and ears open. The statements of the authors themselves clearly illustrate the multisensory nature of their training, despite their strongest efforts to maintain otherwise.

Objective research on the effectiveness of such programs reveals more modest results when compared with other types of programs. As previously noted, McCroskey (1968) found few differences between children trained in an auditory-based preschool and children with no preschool training, and the differences that existed tended to favor no preschool training. As reported by Moores, Weiss, and Goodwin (1974) two auditory-based programs were involved in a longitudinal evaluation of eight early intervention programs for the deaf. One of the two auditory-based programs withdrew from the study after the results of the first year's data gathering were published. The remaining program, along with a program that employed manual communication, was one of the top two in use of residual hearing. However, when the mouth was uncovered, scores of these children improved less and fell below the average of children in the other six programs. Overall, children from this program scored sixth (out of seven) in receptive communication; fifth in expressive communication; and seventh in reading, arithmetic achievement, amount of classroom interaction, quality of classroom interaction, and academic achievement.

In recent years enthusiasm for the unattainable — and probably undesirable — goal of a unisensory method has waned. Despite the position of its strongest advocates, many of the techniques have been incorporated into admittedly multisensory programs (e.g., Hartbauer, 1975; Sanders, 1971). Educators of the deaf do owe a debt to the work of these workers in at least two major areas. First has been the emphasis placed on early detection and intervention, and on the role of the parent, or at least the mother. Second has been the demonstration that even severe hearing losses do not preclude the utilization of residual hearing as part of everyday functioning.

Table 11.7   Essential characteristics of the auditory global method

---

1. Maximum emphasis on use of hearing
   a. Early use of amplification
   b. Periodic reexamination of hearing
   c. Selection of optimum amplification systems
   d. Periodic examination of hearing aid
   e. Constant usage
2. Comprehensive intervention
3. Emphasis on corrected speech

SOURCE: Adapted from D. Calvert & R. Silverman, *Speech and Deafness.* Washington, D.C.: A. G. Bell Association, 1975, pp. 148–156.

The Auditory Global Method

Calvert and Silverman (1975) developed the label *auditory global method* to characterize the techniques incorporated under the terms *acoupedic, unisensory, auditory, aural,* and so on. The essential characteristics of the method are presented in Table 11.7. Calvert and Silverman state that the primary, though not always exclusive, channel for speech development is auditory and that the input should consist of fluent connected speech (p. 148).

Calvert and Silverman recommend the auditory global method as the initial method for all children (pp. 156, 168) but acknowledge that it will not be satisfactory for all children. They recommend specific procedures for assessing children's progress in order to make decisions about alternate approaches.

Speechreading

Speechreading — traditionally known as *lipreading* — involves visual interpretation of communication of a speaker. It is a highly complex process by which a speechreader must utilize situational and motivational variables as well as a mastery of the grammar of a language while decoding messages containing elements that are not visible or of lower visibility (e.g., sounds made in the back of the throat, such as the italic sections of the following words: *k*ey, sti*ng,* *g*un) as well as elements that may sound different but appear similar on the lips. A classic example of the difficulty of dealing with these homophones may be provided by the fact that the usual sounds for the phonemes /p/, /b/, and /m/ are *homophonous;* that is, they are articulated in a similar way and look similar on the lips. The same is true for the sounds /t/, /d/, and /n/. Therefore, in isolation the following nine words would look similar to a speechreader:

BAT   MAT   PAT
BAD   MAD   PAD
BAN   MAN   PAN

Bruhn (1949) noted that about 50% of the words in the English language have some other word or words homophonous to them. She listed the following homophonous sounds:

1. f — v — ph — (gh as in cough or laugh)
2. m — b — p — mb — mp
3. w — wh — (qu)
4. s — z — soft c
5. sh — ch — j — soft g
6. d — t — n — nt — nd
7. k — hard c — hard g — ng — nk
8. (l has no sound homophonous to it) (p. 13)

Although technically *l* has no homophones, it should be pointed out that articulation is similar to that of the homophones in item 6 in the list. For example, articulation of *l*ook, *t*ook, and *n*ook are similar. Bruhn (1949) points out that, although theoretically there are no homophonous sounds among vowels, some vowels are difficult to distinguish during rapid speech.

The above examples should illustrate how difficult the process of speechreading can become. In fact, some writers have argued that the term *speechreading* is unsatisfactory to express the complexity of the function. Mason (1943) suggested that the term *visual hearing* be used. O'Neill and Oyer (1961) have proposed that *visual listening* be considered as a more appropriate term. Although both terms may be more accurate, they have not replaced *speechreading* as the term most commonly used by professionals.

In a review of the literature on speechreading, Farwell (1976) pointed out that no commonly accepted definition of the term existed. Some argued that it was entirely dependent on vision, while others saw it as complementing audition, at least to some extent. The most serious disagreement has been over the role of speechreading in the development of language. Much of the confusion may be traced to the current status of speechreading in education of the deaf.

Although, as noted in Chapters 2 and 3, speechreading was incorporated into programs developed to educate deaf children as early as the seventeenth century, the methods used in the twentieth century reflected different goals and techniques. Of the various approaches to speechreading perhaps four different methods deserve mention: the Jena, the Mueller-Walle, the Nitchie, and the Kinzie.

The Jena Method

Developed in Jena, Germany, by Brauckmann (DeLand, 1931), the Jena method incorporates basic principles of kinesthesis, imitation, and rhythm.

Although Brauckmann directed a school for deaf children, the method originally was developed for hard-of-hearing and deafened adults. Procedures attempted the integration of speech, speechreading, reading, and writing, and they involved memorization and practice in analytic drills initially of a syllabic nature. The Jena method was introduced into the United States in the 1870s, and the most complete English treatment of the method is provided by Bunger (1961).

The Mueller-Walle Method

Mueller-Walle, like Brauckmann, had been a teacher of the deaf. When he began teaching speechreading to hard-of-hearing adults, he found the need for different instructional techniques and developed a six-week course relying on rapid syllable drill and rhythmic speech (Bruhn, 1949; DeLand, 1931). At first, the most visible sounds are introduced, and then less visible elements are added gradually. The system was introduced to the United States in 1902 by Bruhn, a teacher of French and German in Massachusetts who had lost her hearing and went to Germany to be trained by Mueller-Walle. Bruhn translated Mueller-Walle's work and adapted it to English. By 1949 her book in the Mueller-Walle method was in its seventh edition (Bruhn, 1949).

The Nitchie Method

Although he lost his hearing at 14 years of age and had no training in speechreading, Edward Nitchie was able to attend Amherst College and graduate Phi Beta Kappa. After graduation he was trained by Lillie Warren, an early teacher of lipreading who had developed a method of "expression reading" (DeLand, 1931). Building on Warren's work Nitchie developed an analytic system utilizing a set of symbols by which speechreading ability could be developed through mirror practice. Nitchie gradually moved from an analytic to a synthetic approach to speechreading and came to emphasize training the individual to grasp thoughts as wholes (Nitchie, 1912). It was Nitchie who consciously was the first to utilize psychological principles in a method of speechreading.

The Kinzie Method

This method was developed by Cora Kinzie, who lost her hearing when training to become a medical missionary, and her sister Rose, who joined her to develop a school of speechreading. After losing her hearing, Cora Kinzie was trained by Bruhn; she then established her own Mueller-Walle school of lipreading. While running her school, she studied under Nitchie. Kinzie and Kinzie (1931) utilized Nitchie's psychological principles and the Mueller-

Waller classification of introductory sounds to develop a graded series of speechreading exercises.

A number of factors should be considered in discussing the most popular approaches to speechreading in the United States. Most of the methods were developed for hard-of-hearing or deafened adults who already had acquired a mastery over spoken language and could use it to acquire skills in speechreading. Even many of the American leaders in the field — including Nitchie, Kinzie, and Bruhn — were individuals who lost their hearing after acquiring speech and language. Although intensive efforts were devoted to applying the techniques to deaf children, the bases of the methods had been grounded in work with hard-of-hearing adults. The speechreading task for deaf children, who have no foundation of oral language to draw from, is far different than for adult native users of a language.

An additional consideration is the fact that there are no objective data to choose between the various approaches. Miller, Ransey, and Goetzinger (1958) and Farwell (1976) have remarked on the lack of experimental evidence in the area of speechreading.

In addition, methods employed in the education of deaf children — especially those of preschool age — in recent times in the United States have tended to minimize the importance of speechreading. Advocates of the acoupedic (auditory global) approach tend to deemphasize the visual channel and discourage formal training in speechreading. Although the concept of total communication encompasses speechreading, the author has observed that for some reason speechreading tends to receive less emphasis than other components, such as signs, speech, auditory training, fingerspelling, and writing.

The review of research by Farwell (1976) presents some discouraging results. It has been well established that most deaf individuals are not good speechreaders. However, there is no evidence to suggest that deaf individuals cannot become good speechreaders. The lack of innovation in teaching speechreading is as poor as the previously mentioned lack in teaching speech. Aside from the utilization of film in teaching speechreading (Morkovin, 1960), no new methods have been developed since 1930 (O'Neill & Oyer, 1961). Apparently, new techniques in reality involve combinations of old methods.

What is needed is the development of a series of activities designed for use with young deaf children from time of identification of the hearing loss. The activities should be based on principles of child development, visual and auditory perception, linguistics, and learning. They should be designed specifically for young children with a severe hearing loss, not adapted from a series of drills for hard-of-hearing adults.

Speechreading ability is an invaluable tool for any deaf individual. Why processes of developing speechreading — and speech — have received so little genuine attention in the past 50 years from both oralists and combined oral-manual proponents must remain a mystery.

Summary

Methods that are utilized in helping deaf children acquire language proficiency and expressive and receptive communication skills typically were developed generations ago. With the exception of technical improvements, such as those in hearing aids, progress has been minimal. Particularly disheartening is the fact that, despite the ascendancy of the oral method for most of the twentieth century, there have been few advances in methods of developing speech, speechreading, and listening skills. Educators of the deaf continue to draw on the legacy of work done 30 or more years ago. The field cries out for theoretical and applied investigations into the acquisition of speech, language, speechreading, and listening skills of deaf children as developmental processes. The efforts of innovative and creative minds must be brought to bear on these processes if we are to take advantage of advances in linguistics and in speech and hearing science.

12

Elementary and
Secondary Education

Educational Placement and Programming

As data presented in Chapter 1 indicate, a large majority of deaf students currently are educated in day class programs and residential schools for the deaf. Enrollment in separate day schools, as opposed to day classes located within schools for children with normal hearing, is decreasing. A substantial number of day class students are integrated part time into classes for the normally hearing, and a relatively small, but growing, population of children are integrated into neighborhood schools and receive supportive services from itinerant teachers and speech therapists.

Educators of the deaf historically have been subject to two conflicting forces concerned with educational placement. First has been the desirability of having children educated near their homes, in the neighborhood school, if possible. Opposed to this was the fact that, because deafness is a low-incidence condition, a large population base is considered necessary for establishment of a comprehensive program.

The rapid urbanization and suburbanization of the United States in the twentieth century, coupled with the increased willingness of public schools to attempt to meet the needs of all children, has contributed to the spread of day class programs.

The growth of day class programs, however, has not been an unmitigated blessing. Great concern has been expressed, especially over the proliferation of very small programs — even as small as one class of children — in school districts that did not have the resources to provide complete services. The problem was considered to be of such import that in 1967 a National Research Conference on Day Programs for Hearing Impaired Children, funded by the U.S. Office of Education, was held (Mulholland & Fellendorf, 1968). Some of the problems discussed were the lack of trained teachers in the smaller programs, the scarcity of supervising teachers, the excessive travel time involved in busing some students long distances, and the inability of smaller districts to obtain the frequently expensive special equipment needed to educate deaf children. Very few state plans had been developed, and the development of pro-

244

grams seemed to be haphazard at best. In a summary report of the conference Kopp (1968a, p. 29) concluded that the liabilities of small day class programs outweighed their assets and advocated consolidation of such programs wherever possible. The day school region could range from a single urban area to an interstate facility. The region should be established on the basis of transportation feasibility and density of the hearing-impaired population, rather than along political boundaries.

The development of state plans in several states, most notably the more populous ones, helped to alleviate the situation. However, in 1973, the Conference of Executives of American Schools for the Deaf established an ad hoc committee to develop recommendations for the establishment of educational programs. The outcome was a series of recommended organizational policies for programs for the deaf (Brill, Merrill, & Frisina, 1973). In the report a number of pressures for local programs were identified, the major one being the logical and natural desire of parents to keep their children at home. Some other factors, less compelling educationally, were nevertheless real. In the report the opinion was expressed that professional educators of hearing children generally were not aware of the specialized services needed by deaf children. It was stated further that many parents felt their children's needs could be met simply through provision of speech and speechreading therapy and fitting of a hearing aid. Finally, it was noted that local programs might appeal to cost-conscious legislators because they appeared to be less costly. In this context, Brill, Merrill, and Frisina (1973) state:

Unfortunately they [legislators] are not aware that in the long run inadequate educational programs are most costly, both to the inadequately educated individual and to society. It is in reality a return to the "little red schoolhouse" which may be nostalgic, but hardly comparable to today's unified, comprehensive schools. (p. 10)

Brill, Merrill, and Frisina identified the following as requirements that should be met by educational programs for the deaf:

1. Sufficiently large in size to ensure homogeneous grouping
2. Qualified teachers
3. Supervision by qualified individuals who are highly knowledgeable about the education of the deaf
4. Provision of an appropriate curriculum for deaf children
5. The availability of supplementary services such as audiological and psychological by personnel who are knowledgeable about deaf children and their educational problems
6. The opportunities for extracurricular activities that will round out the deaf child's educational program, one in which he is able to participate
7. Provision of vocational training and counseling
8. Provision of appropriate equipment such as amplification equipment, captioned films and other educational media. (pp. 19–20)

Investigations of Achievement in Standard English

Written Language

Because of the difficulty inherent in comprehension of the speech of most deaf children, most studies concerned with assessing their expressive language proficiency have been limited to written compositions. Such studies have indicated that on Standard English usage deaf children significantly lag behind children with normal hearing.

Heider and Heider (1940a) analyzed compositions describing a short motion-picture written by deaf students from 11 to 17 years of age and hearing students from 8 to 14 years of age. Results indicated relatively rigid, immature, and simple written patterns by the deaf students. The investigators stated that the differences between the deaf and hearing children were of such a nature as to prevent their description in completely quantitative terms. The differences were seen as resulting not merely from different skills in the use of language but also from dissimilar thought processes. This may be contrasted to the results obtained by the same authors on the basis of four experiments on color sorting with young deaf and hearing children (Heider & Heider, 1940b), indicating that the performance of the deaf was similar to that of younger hearing children, which suggests a quantitative, rather than a qualitative, difference in intellectual functioning. From this Heider and Heider concluded that the thought of deaf children, in regard to color sorting, is essentially similar to that of hearing children and is not distorted by inadequate or imperfect concepts.

Walter (1955) studied the written sentence construction of 102 children from the ages of 6 years, 0 months to 12 years, 11 months at a school for the deaf in Australia and noted a lack of flexibility and an absence of sentence complexity. Walter (1959), in a later study of three Australian and four English schools for the deaf, analyzed written work of a total of 58 children from 9 years, 11 months to 12 years, 11 months. She noted similar patterns of language development and usage, although the level of sentence complexity and forms of sentence structure were somewhat more complex than in the original study.

Thompson (1936) investigated the written language of 800 students and reported an average of 104 mistakes per 1,000 words. The classification of mistakes, based on standard methods of analysis for that period, is presented in Table 12.1. Thompson concluded that — because mistakes in the *words* category accounted for almost 50% of the errors in the written composition of deaf children, while the *syntax and case* category accounted for a relatively small 20% of the errors — the language instruction program for deaf children should shift in emphasis from grammatical structure to the proper use of words. Thompson's conclusions may have been influenced by the categories under which the errors were classified. It may be argued that the use of excess words or the omission of words, for example — which together account for more than 25% of all errors — should be classified as *syntax* errors. Furthermore, because the categories were not defined operationally, the basis for assigning an error to a specific area is not clear. Thus, no explanation is given for placing the omission of an article or its incorrect use under *syntax* while assigning omissions and wrong use of all other parts of speech to mistakes in the *words* category. In a later study employing similar techniques, Birch and Stuckless (1963) reported a total of 5,044 grammatical errors from a corpus of 50,050 words, or slightly more than 100 errors per 1,000 words. The results were similar to those reported by Thompson almost 30 years previously.

Myklebust (1964) developed a *syntax score* to measure written language. Using the syntax score, he compared deaf and hearing children from the ages of 7 to 15 and reported statistically significant differences at every level in favor of the hearing. In fact, the mean score for 7-year-old hearing children (86.8) was similar to that of 15-year-old deaf children (86.2). Myklebust noted that in the hearing children significant differences appeared between the age groups of 7 and 9 and between 9 and 11, but differences did not occur after age 11. From this he concluded that the structure of written language conforms closely to the spoken form and that maturity in the syntax of written English is based upon previously developed maturity in spoken language. It would be interesting to investigate whether the reported maturity of hearing children in written language syntax would be evident at an even younger age than 11 if errors of punctuation were not included in the syntax score.

Wells (1942) attempted to identify differences in growth of what he identified as abstract and concrete forms between deaf and normal children. He concluded that deaf children were equal to hearing children in the use and understanding of concrete words but were four to five years retarded in their understanding of abstract terms. However, the terms *abstract* and *concrete* were not well defined by Wells. Without behavioral definitions, such terms tell us little concerning processes of understanding. See Chapter 7 for a discussion of the use and misuse of the terms *abstract* and *concrete*.

Table 12.1   Average number of errors made by deaf subjects per 1,000 words

Syntax and case	
Wrong number of noun	3
Wrong tense of verb	4
Omission of article	3
Wrong form of verb	3
Wrong article	1
Wrong number of pronoun	1
Miscellaneous	6
Total	21
Clauses	
Incoherent sentence	5
Improper word order	2
Incomplete sentence	1
Run-on sentence	1
Choppy sentence	1
Miscellaneous	4
Total	14
Words	
Excess	13
Wrong	13
Omitted	16
Poor choice	2
Word order	2
Miscellaneous	4
Total	50
Punctuation	
Lack of comma	8
Lack of period or question mark	4
Capitalization	3
Miscellaneous	4
Total	19

SOURCE: W. Thompson, "An Analysis of Errors in Written Composition by Deaf Children." *American Annals of the Deaf*, 1936, *81*, 99.

Simmons (1959) investigated word usage of 54 students at the Central Institute for the Deaf and 112 hearing students attending public schools by means of a *type-token ratio* (*TTR*), a measure of vocabulary diversity. Analyzing five written compositions and one spoken composition from each subject, she reported that the deaf children tended to use more stereotyped, rigid, and redundant structures and vocabularies. Even grammatically correct and understandable sentences were marked by a lack of richness and spontaneity, as illustrated by the following example:

A girl threw a ball to a boy. The boy bat a ball. The boy bat the ball to the window and the window was broken. The mother heard the boy broke the window. The mother saw a broke the window. She went to see the ball game. (p. 35)

Where hearing children would vary their reference to a boy in a picture with such terms as *kid, boy, urchin, friend, him, Tom,* and so on, deaf children repeatedly would use the noun *boy.* Four verbs tended to be used by the deaf children: *have, be, go,* and *feel.* Also, compared with the hearing, deaf children tended to underuse possessives and definite articles such as *these, that,* and *those.*

Reading Achievement

Investigations of performance of deaf students on standardized tests of reading comprehension suggest that deaf students encounter great difficulty in processing Standard English. In an investigation of performance by more than 5,000 deaf students in the United States and Canada on the Elementary Level Battery Reading subtest of the Metropolitan Achievement Test, Wrightstone, Aranow, and Moskowitz (1963) reported that less than 10% of the children over 10 years of age read at the fourth-grade level. In commenting on these findings, Furth (1966b) emphasized that the average reading score of the deaf students increased only from grade 2.6 to grade 3.4 between ages 11 and 16, less than one year of growth over a period of five years of age.

Myklebust (1964) compared the reading vocabularies of deaf and hearing students at 9, 11, 13, and 15 years of age and reported higher average scores for 9-year-old hearing subjects (21.37) than for 15-year-old deaf subjects (11.32) on the Columbia Vocabulary Test. Scores for the deaf subjects tended to plateau around age 13, thus allowing the hearing students to increase their relative advantage in adolescence.

Pugh (1946) tested children on the Iowa Silent Reading Test at 54 day and residential schools for the deaf. No group scored above the sixth-grade level on any subtest. She reported very little improvement in reading achievement scores from the seventh to thirteenth year of schooling.

Goetzinger and Rousey (1959) obtained similar results from a study of achievement of 101 students at a residential school for the deaf. They reported that scores in Vocabulary and Paragraph Meaning subtests of the Standard Achievement Test tend to level off between the ages of 14 and 21.

Results of investigations by Pugh, by Goetzinger and Rousey, and by Wrightstone, Aranow, and Moskowitz all highlight an apparent leveling off of achievement by adolescent deaf children, at least as measured by standardized reading achievement tests.

One must be careful to emphasize that written achievement scores are not a measure of linguistic achievement for deaf students, or for any other students. Reading tests measure skills commonly acquired during the educational process. Children — or adults — may possess quite competent language skills but still be unable to read, as Cooper and Rosenstein (1966) have pointed out.

For children with normal hearing and with proficiency in Standard English, interpretation of reading scores may be relatively straightforward. For children whose primary language is different from that of the classroom, say Spanish-speaking children tested in English, interpretation is much less easy. For deaf children the difficulty is even greater. The tests assume the presence of a common English usage and have been standardized for children who fit such an assumption. By an early age children with normal hearing have mastered the basic principles of their language and can handle the most common structures automatically. Linguistic proficiency is established before reading instruction. Deaf children, however, have not internalized the structure of English. Poor reading scores for such children could be attributed either to inadequate proficiency in Standard English or to inadequately developed skills specific to the reading process. Mastery of English cannot be assumed.

It is possible that standardized tests have been administered to deaf students under the assumption that they possess English skills which in reality are lacking. Since most standardized reading tests give students a choice of responses usually restricted to one grammatical category, they might artificially raise estimates of reading ability in that all answers would be at least grammatically correct.* Fusfeld (1955), for example, reported that the written compositions of deaf students in the preparatory class of Gallaudet College were far below what would be expected on the basis of their achievement in Vocabulary and Paragraph Meaning subtests of the Stanford Achievement Test. He reported that the written compositions represented a "tangled verb type of expression in which words occur in profusion but do not align themselves in orderly array" (p. 69).

"Linguistic" Analyses

Moores (1970) investigated the use of the cloze procedures to differentiate between 37 deaf students with an average age of 16 years, 9 months matched to

---

* An example might be:

A whale is a(n): (a) amphibian, (b) reptile, (c) mammal

All three answers are grammatically correct.

37 hearing students with an average age of 9 years, 10 months. The mean grade reading achievement of the deaf group on the Metropolitan Achievement Test was 4.77, compared with 4.84 for the hearing group. The performance of the hearing students in the cloze task (filling in words deleted from passages) was superior on passages at three different levels of difficulty. Analysis suggested that the lower performance of the deaf students resulted both from poorly developed English grammatical skills and from limited vocabulary. The results support the hypothesis that standardized reading tests overestimate English skills of deaf students.

In a partial replication of the Moores study, Marshall (1970) used cloze procedures to compare 24 deaf students whose mean grade reading level was 4.5 with 24 hearing students whose mean reading level was grade 4.4. Marshall reported that the hearing students were superior on verbatim, form-class, and verbatim-given-form-class scores. The differences were statistically significant, with a probability of less than .01 for the first two measures, but they did not reach significance for the verbatim-given-form-class scores.

Schmitt (1968) used a transformational-generative model of language to explore the abilities of 8-, 11-, 14-, and 17-year-old deaf children to comprehend and produce sentences varying on the dimensions of transformations (kernal, negative, passive, passive-negative) and tense (past, present progressive, future) and to contrast them with 8- and 11-year-old hearing students. Both groups of hearing children were superior to the deaf subjects of all ages. Qualitative analysis of the data led Schmitt to postulate that the deaf children were using incorrect underlying rules to process English sentences and that three rules could account for most errors. He designated these: (1) the NP_2-NP_1 *rule,* which permits reversal of noun phrase 1 and noun phrase 2 in transitive-verb reversible sentences; (2) the *passive-active rule,* which specifies the ignoring of passive sentence markers and treating sentences as actives; and (3) the *no negative rule,* which specifies the ignoring of negative markers and permits the processing of negative sentences as positives. Tervoort (1970) investigated the ability of deaf children from ages 10 to 18 in the Netherlands to understand passive sentences. On a task in which two hearing 6-year-olds and two hearing 12-year-olds obtained perfect scores, deaf children under age 13 scored 27.5% correct (chance was 20%), and those over 13 scored 74% correct — the higher scores for the older children reflected more effective processing of nonreversible than reversible passives.* Consistent with Schmitt's results, Tervoort reported that if the grammatical subject at the beginning of a sentence was the acted-upon object, the sentences were refused or acted upon randomly. He concluded that deaf students first master the simple active and that they use it almost exclusively thereafter.

Quigley and associates (Montanelli & Quigley, 1974; Power, 1971; Quigley,

---

* An example of a reversible passive is: "The boy was pushed by the girl." Compare this with the nonreversible passive: "The house was painted by the girl." The understanding of the first sentence obviously requires more grammatical knowledge than that required for the second.

Smith, & Wilbur, 1973; Quigley, Wilbur, & Montanelli, 1974; Wilbur & Quigley, 1972) have developed an experimental Test of Syntactic Ability (TSA) that was designed to study deaf individuals' comprehension of specific syntactic structures occurring in English. The experimental TSA consists of 22 subtests measuring the following structures: relativization, question formation, the verb system, complementation, conjunction, pronominalization, reflexivization, and negation. The investigation is aimed at describing the acquisition and development of syntactic structures in written language of deaf students and operates under the assumption that the written language of deaf persons, like all natural languages, is generated by a grammar of rules which can be examined and described by techniques of generative-transformational grammar.

The sample for the major longitudinal investigation consisted of a stratified random sample of 450 subjects from 16 programs for the deaf across the United States ranging from 10 years to 18 years, 11 months in age. There were 50 subjects — 25 females and 25 males — at each of the 9 age levels (10+, 11+, 12+, etc.). Although some of the reports from the project utilize different or smaller samples (e.g., Power, 1971), the age range under consideration was always from approximately 10 to 18 years.

Results of analysis to date are similar to those of previous studies and suggest that deaf students tend to interpret and produce English sentences in terms of a subject-verb-object surface order of constituents. The results have been clear in the understanding and use of passive voice (Power, 1971); for example, "The girl was pushed by the boy" is read as "The girl pushed the boy." It was also quite evident in the processing of relative clauses. For example, 80% of the subjects, when responding to the sentence "The girl who hit the boy went home," interpreted the sentence to mean the boy went home (rather than the girl went home), suggesting that they were reading the surface order of the sentence (Wilbur & Quigley, 1972).

The deaf subjects were generally able to recognize correct sentences involving negation, but their production may not be the same as Standard English in that the negative marker may occur at the "wrong" point of a sentence, or *no* and *not* may be substituted for each other (Montanelli & Quigley, 1974).

In the area of question formation, deaf subjects' scores increased from 58% at age 10 to 94% at age 18 for yes-no questions, from 44 to 71% for tag questions,[*] and from 45 to 80% for Wh-questions.[†] Hearing control subjects aged 10 scored 100% for the yes-no and tag questions and 99% for Wh-questions (Quigley, Wilbur, & Montinelli, 1974).

The results of all the studies of the understanding of various written English (and in one case, Dutch) syntactic structures for deaf students of elementary and secondary school age are consistent with those reported for younger children, including both written and person-to-person communication by Moores and associates (Moores, 1975; Moores, Weiss, & Goodwin, 1974). The re-

---

[*] An example of a tag question is: "John went to town, didn't he?"
[†] Wh-questions begin *who, what, when, where.*

sults, as discussed in Chapter 10, also suggest that deaf students tend first to learn a simple subject-verb-object order and then to process sentences within that framework.

Academic Achievement

Given the traditional emphasis on English in programs for the deaf, it should come as no surprise that investigations into achievement in other academic areas such as social studies, science, and mathematics have been relatively limited in number and usually have involved limited samples of students. However, one excellent source has gathered and disseminated data on thousands of hearing-impaired students from preschool through college age: the Office of Demographic Studies located at Gallaudet College, which in 1968 established the Annual Survey of Hearing Impaired Children and Youth. The survey was designed to collect, process, and disseminate information of concern to educators, psychologists, legislators, and audiologists.

In 1972 the Office of Demographic Studies published achievement data based on scores of 16,908 deaf students who had taken one of five batteries of the Stanford Achievement Test, or SAT (Gentile, 1972). It is pointed out that scores on achievement tests standardized on students with normal hearing should be interpreted with great caution. Indeed, the staff of the center has devoted considerable attention to item analyses of the responses of deaf students on the Stanford Achievement Test. It is also obvious that for the most part deaf students frequently are administered test batteries designed for younger children. For example, a total of 6,986 deaf children, ranging in age from under 6 to over 21, were administered the SAT Primary I Battery (Gentile, 1972, p. 4), which is designed for children up to the middle of second grade, or an approximate chronological age (CA) of 7.5. An additional 5,933 students received the Primary II Battery, designed to test children up to the end of third grade, or an approximate CA of 9. Thus 11,919 of 16,908 deaf students, or more than 70%, were tested on batteries designed for children 9 years of age or younger, although more than 85% of the deaf students (14,414 of 16,908) were age 10 or older (Gentile, 1972, p. 4).

The achievement results, however, provide great insights into academic achievement of deaf students, as measured by a standardized test. For the purposes of the present chapter they are important in that they reveal deaf students' patterns of difficulty in different academic areas. Table 12.2 presents grade equivalents earned by deaf students on five batteries of the SAT. Scores are presented by subtest in rank order, from highest to lowest, for each battery.

Although the subtests are not identical for all batteries, some definite patterns appear. First, scores in Spelling and Arithmetic Computation are consistently high, compared to other subtests. This is also true, to a somewhat lesser extent, for scores in Language. At the other end may be found consistently lower

Table 12.2 Grade equivalent scores of 16,908 deaf students tested on five batteries of the Stanford Achievement Test, Form N, 1964 Edition

Subtest by rank order	Primary I[a] (N = 5,986)		Primary II[b] (N = 5,933)		Intermediate I[c] (N = 2,821)		Intermediate II[d] (N = 1,441)		Advanced[e] (N = 727)	
	Subtest	Grade equivalent	Subtest	Grade equivalent	Subtest	Grade equivalent	Subtest	Grade equivalent	Subtest	Grade equivalent
1	Spelling	2.04	Arithmetic Computation	4.22	Arithmetic Computation	5.92	Spelling	7.71	Spelling	9.24
2	Word Reading	2.00	Spelling	3.62	Spelling	5.84	Arithmetic Computation	7.12	Arithmetic Computation	8.68
3	Paragraph Meaning	1.80	Language	3.44	Social Studies	4.92	Arithmetic Applications	6.26	Arithmetic Concepts	8.41
4	Arithmetic	1.77	Arithmetic Concepts	3.02	Arithmetic Concepts	4.81	Arithmetic Concepts	6.05	Arithmetic Applications	7.84
5	Word Study Skills	1.75	Paragraph Meaning	2.78	Arithmetic Applications	4.64	Social Studies	5.85	Language	7.67
6	Vocabulary	1.38	Word Meaning	2.50	Science	4.25	Language	5.77	Social Studies	7.50
7			Science & Social Studies	2.33	Language	4.15	Paragraph Meaning	5.29	Science	7.48
8			Word Study Skills	2.15	Word Meaning	3.87	Science	5.09		
9					Paragraph Meaning	3.83	Word Meaning	4.83	Paragraph Meaning	7.33
10					Word Study Skills	3.23				

[a] P. 11. [b] P. 17. [c] P. 22. [d] P. 28. [e] P. 34.

SOURCE: A. Gentile, Academic Achievement Test Results of a National Testing Program for Hearing Impaired Students, United States: Spring 1971. Washington, D.C.: Annual Survey of Hearing Impaired Children and Youth, Office of Demographic Studies, Gallaudet College, Ser. D, No. 9, 1972.

achievement in Word Meaning, Paragraph Meaning, Social Studies, Science, and Word Study Skills.

Quite obviously achievement is highest in those areas which require "mechanical" skills and place little reliance on proficiency in Standard English. It should be pointed out that the term *Language* is a misnomer. To a large extent scores on this subtest are dependent on knowledge of English punctuation; it is not essentially a test of what is commonly considered language.

Grade equivalent scores on the lower end — for example, Word Meaning, Paragraph Meaning, and Science — are dependent on proficiency in Standard English and illustrate difficulties most deaf students face in this sphere. Such an interpretation of the results is supported by scores achieved on various arithmetic subtests. Without exception, higher grade equivalent scores are earned for Arithmetic Computation, which requires computational skill but little knowledge of Standard English, than for Arithmetic Applications or Arithmetic Concepts, subtests that place more emphasis on reading.

For two of the subtests, Paragraph Meaning and Arithmetic Computation, scores were averaged at each age to obtain weighted average grade equivalent scores. For example, all scores of 10-year-olds were averaged for each of the two subtests, regardless of which battery was administered. The results (pp. 39 and 40) show an increase in Paragraph Meaning from an average grade equivalent of 1.61 at age 6 to 4.36 at age 19. Scores for students over 19 were slightly lower. It was postulated that students 20 or more years old still in school are usually lower achievers. In Arithmetic Computation, the average grade equivalent increased from 1.46 at age 6 to 6.73 at age 19.

In a later analysis of the data (Gentile, 1973b) mean grade equivalent scores on Paragraph Meaning were compared at four age levels (8, 11, 14, 17) by sex. The results (Figure 12.1) indicate essentially no differences between deaf males and females on either subtest at any age. Deaf females score somewhat higher at each level on Paragraph Meaning. Deaf males score lower at ages 8, 11, and 14 on Arithmetic Computation, but higher at age 17. Since in no case does the difference exceed two-tenths of a grade, the functioning of deaf males and females on the two subtests may be considered essentially identical. Scores certainly are much closer than those obtained for hearing students on the SAT, in which males consistently achieve at higher levels in Arithmetic Computation, and females do so in Paragraph Meaning (Kelley, Madden, Gardner, & Rudman, 1966).

Figure 12.1 does clearly illustrate, however, the differential rates of growth in achievement on the two subtests. At age 8 the mean grade equivalent scores are similar in Paragraph Meaning (1.90) and Arithmetic Computation (1.85), with both slightly under grade 2. By age 11, Arithmetic Computation scores are approximately .5 grades higher, with the difference increasing to 1.5 grades by age 14. For the average 17-year-old deaf student, Arithmetic Achievement is approximately two years in advance of Paragraph Meaning, grade 6.03 to grade 4.02.

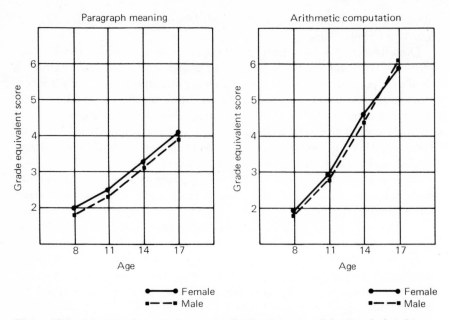

Figure 12.1 Mean grade equivalent scores for five batteries of the Stanford Achievement Test and selected ages by sex from the Annual Survey's 1971 Achievement Testing Program. (From A. Gentile, *Further Studies in Achievement Testing, Hearing Impaired Students, United States: Spring 1971*, Series D, Number 13, Annual Survey of Hearing Impaired Children and Youth, Washington, D.C., Gallaudet College, Office of Demographic Studies, 1973, p. 5.)

Both scores are a shameful indictment of our educational programs. By definition, a 17-year-old student should achieve at the twelfth-grade level. Thus deaf students at age 17 achieve six years below their potential on a standardized test of Arithmetic Computation, one of their highest areas of achievement, and eight years below on a test of Paragraph Meaning.

From another perspective, in examining rates of growth in achievement from ages 8 to 17, it is obvious that achievement in Arithmetic Computation is much greater. In nine years achievement improved from grade 1.85 to 6.03, or somewhat in excess of 4 grades, for an average yearly increase of almost .5 grades. Average yearly increments for Paragraph Meaning were only half as great, or less than .25 grades per year over nine years, or a total improvement of only 2.12 grades (1.90 to 4.02) over nine years of instruction.

However the figures are viewed and interpreted, they should give no educator of the deaf reason for complacency.

Special Curricular Methods

Although the education of the deaf is viewed by much of the lay public and, unfortunately, by many of its practitioners as an esoteric, somewhat mystical process, very little has been done in the way of development of special curricula outside of language and speech teaching and auditory training. In other areas, especially those involving traditional academic subjects, the tendency is to rely on texts, courses of study, syllabi, and curricula designed for students with normal hearing. Sometimes the material is adapted without change, and sometimes it is modified — which typically involves a simplification of vocabulary used.

The most comprehensive compilation of information on curriculum materials for the deaf is the monograph *Curriculum: Cognition and Content*, edited by Kopp (1968b). It is divided into eight sections: Natural Sciences, Social Science, Mathematics, Learning Theory, Resources, Art, Language, and Social and Physical Development. Although the publication contains a wealth of information, a reading of the various sections highlights the lack of development or modification of curricula specifically suited for deaf students. For example, in the area of social studies, Behrens and Meisegeier (1968) note:

A review of the literature on curricula for social studies for deaf children published in the two American periodicals on education of deaf children can be quite a shock. From the paucity of articles on this subject, one might conclude that social studies is not considered important for our children. If the number of publications listed under each category in the Bibliography on Deafness * were rank ordered, papers on general educational issues would seem to be most important, followed by articles on language, speech, speechreading and psychology. These categories have received six to nine times as much written attention as social studies. The other content areas of arithmetic and science would appear to have been considered as low, or perhaps even lower, in their importance to the field of education of deaf children. (p. 46)

The comments of Behrens and Meisegeier reflect a number of factors that exist in education of the deaf. Because speech and language have been seen as the major need for deaf children, content areas such as mathematics, science, and social studies have received insufficient attention. Traditionally, because teachers of the deaf have been expected to be teachers of language and speech, even class time designed for academic subjects often has been devoted entirely to speech and language remediation. Since most teachers of the deaf have not been trained in specific academic areas, the tendency to sacrifice content is intensified. This neglect of the intellect has been the basis for much of Furth's criticism of education of the deaf, and the basis for his plea for more cognitively based learning experiences in education (Furth, 1966, 1973).

* Fellendorf, 1966.

On the other hand, it should be noted that, aside from language arts, perhaps there is little need for elaborate curriculum development in the major academic areas. It can be argued that — although methods of teaching reading, speech, and Standard English to the deaf may be quite unique and specific — the content of a social studies, mathematics, or science unit need not be different from that for hearing students. Given the increased numbers of deaf children in public school programs, many of whom are integrated on a part-time basis, there is an added impetus to make the subject matter conform closely to that which is used by normally hearing students.

Although several schools for the deaf, and a few of the larger metropolitan programs, have developed curricula in various subject areas, most efforts along this line have been neither consistent nor comprehensive. One exception to this should be noted. Over a period of years Ball State University conducted a series of summer workshops in which experienced educators of the deaf developed curricula, or curriculum guides, in several content areas. Unfortunately the material is out of print and no longer available.

Summary

At the present time more than one-half of deaf children are educated in public schools, with school placement ranging from self-contained classes to complete integration in regular classrooms with support services by a teacher of the deaf. Substantial numbers of children still are educated in residential schools, but the proportion of deaf children in residential settings has been declining steadily.

Investigations of expressive and receptive use of English consistently report that deaf children generally fall behind hearing norms in written language and reading. The tendency is to produce subject-verb-object orders and to interpret sentences in the same manner.

Academic achievement is lowest in areas that rely on knowledge of English. Deaf students have difficulty with subjects such as reading and science, and they experience most success with subjects such as spelling and arithmetic computation. Aside from special methods for teaching speech and English, little attention has been devoted to the development of curricula specifically designed for deaf children.

13

Postsecondary Education and the Economic Status of Deaf Americans

Introduction

At the time of their establishment early in the nineteenth century the first schools for the deaf in America were designed to provide students with all the skills necessary for success in the world of work. No thought was given to the establishment of college or advanced technical training programs. Schools for the deaf in the United States were among the leaders in the provision of vocational training. For example, the American School for the Deaf introduced industrial training in 1822, five years after its founding (Jones, 1918). Historically, schools for the deaf organized their programs to provide technical-vocational skills to the majority of students. Usually an increasing proportion of the students' day was spent on vocational training as they progressed through school, until, in their last few years, a relatively small percentage of time was devoted to academic subjects. Given that the majority of students entering these schools were adolescents or young adults and that the total number of years of schooling they received was small, the situation functioned relatively effectively.

Such a condition was not suprising in the nineteenth century, and even in the early twentieth century, when only a small proportion of the general population of the United States consisted of high school graduates. But as the country evolved from a rural, agrarian society to one that was increasingly urban, suburban, and industrial, the type of training provided by the schools for the deaf could no longer meet the increasingly technical demands of the working world. What once had been adequate vocational preparation now could be considered only prevocational in nature.

In the case of individuals with normal hearing, the years following World War I produced a great increase in the proportion of the population receiving secondary and postsecondary education. An even greater increase occurred after World War II, when postsecondary opportunities were expanded, especially for males, with the aid of the GI Bill. By the 1960s a majority of students graduating from American high schools could look forward to some type of postsecondary training.

Educational opportunities for deaf individuals did not keep pace. Except for Gallaudet College, specifically established for the deaf in 1864, no postsecondary programs were available for the deaf before World War II. In essence, because Gallaudet was a liberal arts college, no postsecondary vocational or technical training opportunities existed for deaf students. Partly because of the lack of adequate programs of training to meet the increasing demands of industry, deaf individuals saw their position deteriorate from general economic parity with the hearing population in the nineteenth century to that of economic inferiority by the middle of this century (Moores, Fisher, & Harlow, 1974).

The deaf population did not share in the expansion of educational opportunities that occurred after World War II. The situation remained unchanged until the mid-1960s, with a few notable exceptions, such as the Riverside (California) program, which was established through the cooperation of the Riverside School for the Deaf and Riverside Community College.

One thus must come to the incredible conclusion that postsecondary opportunities for deaf students in general remained static from 1864 to 1964. Deaf students either could attend a liberal arts college for the deaf (Gallaudet) or could attempt to succeed in a regular college, university, or technical school with no supportive services. Because Gallaudet was not accredited until 1958, students attending before that date faced additional obstacles in that they had difficulty transferring credits to other institutions of higher learning and frequently were unable to gain admittance to graduate schools on the basis of undergraduate study at Gallaudet College.

Early Efforts toward Postsecondary Education

The fact that Gallaudet College was established as long ago as 1864 and as recently as 1964 remained the only postsecondary program in the world specifically developed for the deaf attests to its special and unique character. Even today it remains the only liberal arts college for the deaf in the world. Its special nature can be illustrated by the facts that (1) no liberal arts college for the deaf has ever been established in any other country and (2) no comparable postsecondary agricultural, vocational, or technical schools for the deaf have ever been established.

The establishment of the college, then, must be attributed to a fortuitous set of circumstances that, unfortunately, was never duplicated. The two protagonists were Edward Minor Gallaudet and Amos Kendall (M. Boatner, 1959). Gallaudet had been hired in 1857 at age 19 by Kendall to head the Columbia Institution for the Deaf (now the Kendall School for the Deaf) in Washington, D.C., and he wished to develop advanced programs for qualified deaf students. Kendall supported Gallaudet's plans, and the two brought to bear an impressive array of talents in their efforts. Gallaudet was young, brilliant, persuasive, and aggressive. Kendall was older, highly successful, philanthropic, well connected, and equally aggressive. Still, it is unlikely that they would have succeeded in a location other than Washington, D.C., or at a time other than the decade of the 1860s. The United States was engaged in the bloody Civil War, and the nation was divided. The establishment of a national college in the federal capital during the Civil War was one of many ways the federal government emphasized its concern with national interests while in the midst of a war that threatened to split the nation in two permanently. It was not without accident, then, that the school first was established as the National Deaf-Mute College. The name was changed later, in honor of Thomas Hopkins Gallaudet, the father of Edward Minor Gallaudet. For a full treatment of the establishment of the college, see M. Boatner's definitive biography (1959) of E. M. Gallaudet.

Gallaudet College was, and to a large degree remains, the primary source of deaf leadership in the United States. Its graduates not only have provided deaf teachers of the deaf to residential schools but also have gone on to success in a wide variety of professions. If Gallaudet (both the individual and the college) had not existed, postsecondary training for deaf individuals also would not have existed.

As an aside it should be stated that the normal (teacher training) program established by the college in 1892 to train individuals with normal hearing as teachers of the deaf also has had a profound impact on education of the deaf in the United States. A large number of leading educators of the deaf in the past have been products of the Gallaudet training program. Even today a large proportion of school administrators, teacher training personnel in colleges and universities, and researchers received their first training in the area of deafness at Gallaudet College.

Other than the opportunities presented by Gallaudet College, the postsecondary situation for deaf students was bleak. Contemporary concerns involving technical-vocational education of the deaf were anticipated by the expressed dissatisfaction of nineteenth-century educators. Speaking at a meeting of the Eleventh Convention of American Instructors of the Deaf in 1886, F. D. Clarke declared: "The high honor of establishing the first schools in the country where any persistent attempt was made to teach trades belongs to the institution of the deaf. But, though we began first, I hardly think we are keeping abreast of those who started later in the race."

A review of topics in the *American Annals of the Deaf* over its more than 120 years of existence provides ample evidence of the importance with which educators of the deaf have considered vocational, technical, and agricultural — as well as academic — education. Wilkinson (1885) recommended the establishment of mechanics arts schools to train deaf students from ages 12 to 19. Even the idea of postsecondary technical training for the deaf first was expressed in the nineteenth century. Arguing that deaf students require more special preparation than the hearing, Rogers (1888) recommended that a national polytechnic institute for the deaf be established to provide the vocational preparation which could not be supplied by individual schools for the deaf.

Several educators also supported the expansion of Gallaudet College to provide technical and agricultural education as well as liberal arts. The college actually did establish an agricultural department in the early 1900s (Jones, 1918, p. 23), but it was short-lived. Representing a committee on technical education, Fay (1893) recommended that a technical department, equivalent to liberal arts, be established at Gallaudet College. Fay's recommendations later were echoed by Morrison (1920), who advocated the addition of industrial training to the basically liberal arts program at Gallaudet. Morrison urged:

Add to the National College for the Deaf more industrial teaching, with the idea of giving more technical training than is possible in the state and other schools. Let it in great measure set the standard for attainment for the deaf along industrial as well as academic and scientific lines. (p. 223)

For secondary programs Morrison recommended: (1) drop training in obsolete fields, (2) emphasize machine skills, (3) intensify efforts in a few trades, (4) anticipate trades with growing demands, (5) foster close cooperation between shop and classroom, and (6) provide more attention to placement. Before the United States entered World War II, Barnes (1940a, 1940b) proposed the separation of academic and vocational education of deaf students through the creation of job training centers in urban areas and the establishment of a nonprofessional National School of Trades, Agriculture and Vocational Training for the Deaf for students 18 years of age and older.

Investigations of the Vocational Status of the Deaf

The first comprehensive study of the vocational status of the deaf concerned the employment of 422 employed graduates of the American School for the Deaf. In the school's seventieth annual report, Superintendent J. Williams stated (1886) that more than 50% of the employed men were clustered in seven occupations: 70 farmers, 27 shoe-factory operators, 21 mill operators, 20 shoemakers, 20 mechanics, 17 carpenters, and 15 teachers. Of the 54 employed women, 27 were mill operators. One male graduate had established his own insurance company; it had flourished, and he continued as the major shareholder. He was listed as a capitalist. The graduates also included 3 ordained clergymen, 1 successful patent lawyer, and 1 artist. Although some of the success might be attributed to the higher proportion of adventitiously deafened individuals at that time, it is of particular interest to note Williams's statement that the wages of the 422 employed men and women were equivalent to general wages in New England. Wages appeared to be consistently high, and there was no indication that the economic status of the school's graduates was below that of the hearing. It seems, then, that in the late nineteenth century, despite previously noted concerns, schools for the deaf could prepare their students to compete effectively in the economic marketplace.

Robinson, Park, and Axling (1904) reported responses of 14 employers of 64 deaf workers to questionnaires on the industrial status of the deaf. The deaf individuals were considered good workers. Difficulties of communication presented the major problem. Consistent with Williams's report, it was found that deaf workers invariably received the same wages as the hearing for the same class of work.

Fusfeld (1926) investigated the occupations of graduates of 29 schools for the deaf in relation to the vocational training they had received. Evidence from the schools' reports suggested that approximately 50% of the graduates entered occupations for which they were trained. Printing, carpentry, farming, shoe repair, and dressmaking were the most commonly reported occupations. Only one school reported cooperation with local and state rehabilitation agencies, and only two employed placement workers.

Lunde and Bigman (1959) in a questionnaire sample of more than 10,000 deaf men and women reported that among the men approximately 10% reported no training; 40% reported training in the printing trades; 20% in carpentry; 15% in shoemaking; 10% in woodworking, cabinet making, and baking; and 5% in other areas. For the women, 15% had been taught clerical skills, while others had sewing, cooking, and domestic science. Major areas of employment were printing, tailoring, and shoemaking. Lunde and Bigman reported a median income of $3,465, well above the national reported income of $2,818 at that time. The discrepancy in favor of the deaf was attributed to the nonrepresentativeness of the samples. Minorities, women, the very young, and the very old — groups that traditionally have faced economic discrimination — were all underrepresented.

Rosenstein and Lerman (1963) investigated the vocational status of 121 women graduates of the Lexington School for the Deaf. In relation to their positions at the time of the investigation, 25% responded that no specific skills were required, 12% indicated that necessary training had been received at the Lexington school, 15% had received training in other schools, 10% had received on-the-job training, and 36% had acquired their skills in similar previous jobs. (Percentages do not add up to 100 because of rounding.)

Impetus for establishment of postsecondary programs for the hearing impaired was provided with the publication of a study by Boatner, Stuckless, and Moores (1964) and Moores (1969d) on the occupational status of young deaf adults in New England. The results were interpreted as demonstrating the need for regional, postsecondary, technical-vocational training centers. Among its major findings were:

1. Young deaf adults were underemployed; the majority were engaged in semi-skilled or unskilled positions (cf. Williams, 1886).

2. The wages of young deaf adults were 22% below those of their hearing siblings (cf. Williams, 1886).

3. Training provided by the programs for the deaf in New England was, in reality, prevocational training and did not provide the students with necessary competitive skills.

4. The unemployment rate of 20% was approximately four times that of the New England region.

5. Of 840 specific occupations rated as to necessary aptitude levels, 753 were seen as suitable for one or more students. Among the general fields were:

library science	artistic arranging
managerial, industrial	quantity cooking
routine recording	bench work
mechanical repair	electrical repair
complex machine operation	structural crafts
typing, stenographic	graphic arts
food serving	inspecting and testing

6. Deafness itself precluded relatively few skilled occupations. However, most of the positions were not available to deaf students because they lacked appropriate training.

7. Deaf students and young deaf adults received insufficient vocational counseling and placement services (cf. Morrison, 1920). Friends and relatives helped in obtaining jobs in 59% of the cases.

8. Immediate supervisors of 95% of the employed adults rated them average or better in job performance.

9. The greatest problem noted by supervisors related to difficulties of communication (cf. Robinson, Park, & Axling, 1904).

10. More than 90 percent of the parents of current and former students of schools for the deaf and 73% of the young deaf adults approved of the concept of regional technical-vocational centers at the post-secondary level. (pp. 101–102)

These results, the authors concluded, supported the position that vocational education for the deaf could best be conducted for most deaf students on a regional basis, under a faculty of vocational educators specially prepared to provide instruction and ancillary services to the deaf.

The study was replicated in seven southern and southwestern states by Kronenberg and Blake (1966). The purpose was the same as that of the New England study, to assess the occupational status and opportunities for young deaf adults. The results, essentially similar, also supported the concept of preparation programs for postschool employment. The authors reported:

1. The rates of unemployment, occupation level, wage, and opportunities for advancement for the deaf — when compared with the same age group of the general United States adult population — are inferior.

2. Employed young deaf adults performed well in their jobs, as evidenced by the favorable reports of most supervisors regarding job performance, willingness to have one or more deaf subordinates, and willingness to advance them if further training were received.

3. The vocational preparation resources for the deaf are limited.

4. The opportunities for young deaf adults to advance under their present employment situations were limited. In spite of their employer's ratings of "average" or "above average" in the performance of their jobs, only a few of the

employed young deaf adults could advance beyond their present occupational levels without retraining and/or relocation.

5. The need for updating and upgrading vocational training and ancillary services for young deaf adults appeared long overdue.

6. A majority of current students, former students, and parents perceived a need for postsecondary training and indicated support for such programs if the opportunity were available. A majority of parents preferred that postschool training for young deaf adults be provided in a facility for hearing students where modifications, including additional staff, would be introduced to serve deaf trainees. Approximately 40% of the young deaf adults had a preference to be trained with deaf peers.

Deaf Students in Hearing Colleges

In every generation there have always been some deaf people who have managed to attend and graduate from institutions of higher learning. For example, Ferreri (1908) mentioned that he met with and interviewed four deaf students at Harvard in 1901 who appeared to be adjusting and achieving quite satisfactorily. However, except for anecdotal reports, there was little information about those deaf individuals who were able to negotiate successfully the demands of hearing colleges and universities. Although one may assume that these individuals would tend to have adventitious hearing losses and more residual hearing than the general deaf population, these assumptions can be neither verified nor disproved when considering past generations.

Except for studies by Bigman (1961) and Breunig (1965), most information about students attending hearing colleges before 1965 came from efforts of some of the private schools for the deaf to follow up their graduates and from the Alexander Graham Bell Association for the Deaf's annual surveys of deaf graduates of schools and colleges for the hearing. The results were published each year from 1930 to 1952, with the exception of 1942 and 1948 (Davidson, 1930, 1931, 1932, 1933, 1934, 1935, 1936, 1937, 1938, 1939, 1940, 1941, 1943, 1944, 1945, 1946, 1947, 1949, 1950, 1951, 1952). There was then a 10-year hiatus, because of a lack of funds (Quigley, Jenne, & Phillips, 1968), until 1962, when the listing was reinstituted (Davidson, 1962).

For all its benefits, the annual listings provided little more than an enumeration of individuals. In addition, most of the listings were composed of individuals who attended high schools, not colleges, large numbers of whom actually were in day programs for the deaf and receiving supportive services.

Quigley, Jenne, and Phillips (1968), with the cooperation of several groups and associations, attempted a comprehensive survey of deaf individuals who had attended colleges for the hearing. The Alexander Graham Bell Association was the major initial source of information, and funds were provided to the association to fill in the gaps for the 10 years in which the surveys were not conducted (p. 14). Also involved in the project were the National Association of the Deaf, Gallaudet College, and various state vocational rehabilitation agencies.

Results of the survey were based on questionnaire responses of 653 individuals who had attended an institution of higher learning between 1910 and 1965. The responses indicated a far more complex situation than had been anticipated in terms of extent of hearing loss, age of onset of loss, and type of education received. A pattern emerged in which five distinct groups were identified (Quigley, Jenne, & Phillips, 1968):

1. *Group A.* Deaf or hard of hearing individuals with at least a four year undergraduate degree from a regular institution of higher education. $n = 224$
2. *Group B.* Deaf or hard of hearing individuals who attended a regular institution of higher education but did not graduate. $n = 131$
3. *Group C.* Deaf or hard of hearing individuals enrolled in a regular institution and working toward an undergraduate degree at the time of the investigation. $n = 161$
4. *Group D.* Deaf or hard of hearing individuals who transferred to Gallaudet College from other institutions of higher learning, most of whom were in attendance in the first semester of the 1964–65 academic year. $n = 39$
5. *Group E.* Deaf or hard of hearing individuals who had graduated from Gallaudet College and later attended graduate school in other colleges and universities. $n = 98$ (p. 24)

The study contains a great amount of fascinating data, and readers are referred to the original source for complete details. A number of characteristics of the different groups, and of the sample itself, must be mentioned. Quigley, Jenne, and Phillips (p. 28) identified 457 respondents as deaf and 196 as hard of hearing. The *hard of hearing* category included all unaided hearing losses up to 64 dB, and the *deaf* category encompassed losses of 65 dB and greater. In most cases the losses were estimated on the basis of questionnaire responses. Respondents were classified further by age of onset of hearing loss into *prelingual* (birth to age 3) and *postlingual* (age 4 and older) categories (p. 33). Using criteria of a 65-dB loss or greater incurred before age 4 to indicate prelingual deafness, examination of the data reveals that only 281 of 653, or 43%, of the respondents may be classified as prelingually deaf individuals. Examination of Table 13.1 indicates that only 113 prelingually deaf graduates of regular colleges and universities were identified from 1910 to 1965! One must agree with the investigators' conclusions that their results are underestimates (p. 159), but still it is disquieting to note that the combined efforts of the Alexander Graham Bell Association, the National Association of the Deaf, the United States Vocational Rehabilitation Administration, state vocational rehabilitation agencies, and the University of Illinois Institute for Research on Exceptional Children were involved. It is doubtful that any other set of organizations could have produced a more complete listing of individuals.

Examination of data might suggest that graduation from Gallaudet College is

Table 13.1   Percentage of hearing-impaired students identified as attending regular colleges and universities classified as prelingually deaf

| Group | Respondent data | | |
	Total responding	Number prelingually deaf	Percentage prelingually deaf
A. College graduates of regular colleges and universities	224	113	50.4
B. Attended but did not graduate	131	63	48.1
C. In attendance at time of survey	161	63	39.1
D. Transferred to Gallaudet	39	13	33.1
E. Gallaudet graduates who later attended graduate school	98	29	29.4
Totals	653	281	40.0

SOURCE: Adapted from S. Quigley, W. Jenne, & S. Phillips, *Deaf Students in Colleges and Universities.* Washington, D.C.: A. G. Bell Association, 1968, p. 33. Used with permission.

better preparation for graduate school than graduation from an undergraduate school for students with normal hearing — an amazing conclusion, since most of the individuals identified in group E graduated before Gallaudet's accreditation. Information presented in Table 13.1 suggests that the Gallaudet graduates who went on to graduate school before 1965 represent an atypical sample. Only 29 of 98, or 29.4%, may be considered prelingually deaf, the smallest percentage of any of the five groups involved. As such, more than two-thirds of this group consists of postlingually deaf or hard-of-hearing individuals. The extent to which one can generalize from this group to the present-day Gallaudet student population is limited.

Given the degrees of hearing loss and ages of onset of loss reported, it is not surprising to find that only 8 of the 457 deaf respondents relied on manual communication alone, 299 used both manual communication and speech, and 150 used speech alone. The respondents appeared to exhibit a great deal of flexibility concerning mode of communication, regardless of whether they previously were taught in oral-only or combined oral-manual settings. For four of the five groups, both oral and manual communication was used by a majority of respondents. For the fifth group, those attending hearing colleges and institutions, 34% used manual communication and speech — a figure Quigley, Jenne, and Phillips considered "surprising" (p. 50), since these students for the most part were educated in programs that did not allow manual communication. The survey did not differentiate between methods of communication used by the prelingually and postlingually deaf groups. One may speculate that an even higher percentage of the prelingually deaf group utilized both manual and oral communication. Either way, it is obvious that deaf individuals exhibit great flexibility in the methods of communication they employ.

Quigley, Jenne, and Phillips concluded that the provision of special services to deaf students would make it possible for many more deaf individuals to attend college successfully. Trends since publication of their study have supported such a conclusion.

Crammatte (1968) interviewed 87 individuals identified as leading deaf professionals and reported that their backgrounds essentially were similar to those of hearing professionals. They tended to come from upper-middle- and upper-class families with highly educated parents. Of the 87 interviewees, 82 had attended college, and 70 had graduated. In terms of graduate study, 17 had a master's degree, and 5 had doctorates.

Approximately two-thirds, 56 of 87, had been educated primarily in programs for the deaf: 30 in public residential schools, 15 in day programs, 10 in private residential schools, and 1 who spent equal time in a private residential and a day school for the deaf (p. 36). Those who attended schools for the hearing represent predominantly a postlingually deaf population. Only 7 of 31 lost their hearing before age 6, and less than one-half, 15 of 31, were identified as losing their hearing before age 12 (p. 36). For the entire group, 43 lost their hearing before age 3, and 44 lost it after age 3.

Consistent with the Quigley, Jenne, and Phillips findings, Crammatte's interviewee's showed great flexibility concerning methods of communication. Over 90% relied on oral communication to some extent at work, where their colleagues had normal hearing, and more than 80% of them used manual communication with their deaf friends (p. 28). High skill in speech generally was acquired without training; that is, two-thirds of those with the best speech had lost their hearing after age 6.

Development of Programs for the Deaf at Postsecondary Institutions for Students with Normal Hearing

Based on the studies of Quigley, Jenne, and Phillips (1968) and Crammatte (1968), it may be concluded that few prelingually deaf people are able to matriculate at colleges designed for students with normal hearing and graduate without some type of supportive services. The majority of individuals identified as graduates of such programs in reality are hard of hearing or adventitiously deaf. Although no comparable studies were conducted on attendance of deaf students at vocational and technical schools for students with normal hearing, the results of studies of the vocational status of young deaf adults in

New England and the southwest (Boatner, Stuckless, & Moores, 1964; Kronenberg & Blake, 1966) suggested that the majority of young deaf adults were unable to obtain adequate postsecondary vocational-technical training.

Quigley mentioned the possibility of providing services to deaf clients within existing rehabilitation centers that are concerned with many types of disabilities (Quigley, Jenne, & Phillips, 1968, p. 2). Although this has occurred in regard to individuals classified as multiply handicapped, the major development in postsecondary education of the deaf has been the establishment of programs within existing facilities for students with normal hearing. The major impetus for such a development has come from three different types of federal legislation, and funding, that have affected national, regional, and state programming.

At the national level, Congress, in 1965, authorized the establishment at the National Technical Institute for the Deaf (NTID). Following submission of proposals by several leading technical schools, the Rochester Institute of Technology (RIT) was chosen as the host facility. The first NTID class opened in 1968, and by 1972 enrollment had grown to 389 full-time deaf students out of a total RIT enrollment of 5,942 (Stuckless & Delgado, 1973). A majority of beginning students enter a vestibule (preparatory) program that offers career sampling, technical mathematics, science, English, and personal social and cultural development programs. Training may lead to a certificate program or to an associate or a baccalaureate degree. Support services include manual interpreting and notetaking; tutoring; vocational, personal, and social counseling; training in speech, hearing, and manual communication; supervised housing; and vocational placement. The NTID program is viewed as the technical counterpart of Gallaudet College, that is, as a national program serving highly qualified deaf students.

The second thrust came with the establishment of three regional, federally funded model vocational-technical programs for the deaf, which again were established within existing facilities for students with normal hearing. The programs were located at Delgado Vocational Technical Junior College in New Orleans (Louisiana), at Seattle (Washington) Community College, and at St. Paul (Minnesota) Technical Vocational Institute. The Delgado program was begun in 1968, and the Seattle and St. Paul programs were started the following year.

Each of the three programs offers preparatory training, including instruction in mathematics and English, job sampling, and orientation. Similar to NTID, the programs offer a number of supportive services, including manual interpreting and notetaking; vocational, personal, and social counseling; manual communication training; and vocational placement. The duration of a training program varies according to individual needs but tends to be somewhat shorter than that offered at NTID.

Another cluster of programs developed out of federal legislation which specified that states were obligated to spend significant portions of federal money in support of vocational education to provide training for handicapped students.

As might be expected, several states elected to invest funds in the vocational education of deaf students at the postsecondary level. A large number of new programs came into existence between 1969 and 1975. The growth of programs was so rapid that 27 postsecondary programs for the deaf were identified by 1972 (Stuckless & Delgado, 1973), and this expanded to more than 40 programs by 1975 (Rawlings, Trybus, Delgado, & Stuckless, 1975).

Although the majority of programs have been in the vocational-technical area, there have been some exceptions. The most notable one was at California State University at Northridge (CSUN), which in 1964 first accepted deaf graduate students into its National Leadership Training Program in the Area of the Deaf. Before then, all students in the program had possessed normal hearing. With the provision of notetaking and manual interpretation services, the students successfully completed requirements for MA degrees, and since that time the program has accepted deaf students on a regular basis (R. Jones, 1972).

In 1969, CSUN initiated a graduate program to train teachers of the deaf and encouraged applications from deaf individuals. Educational and support services for deaf students were broadened to include all graduate programs in the university. As of summer 1975, CSUN had a total of 153 deaf graduates who had earned a master's degree.* This is an amazing figure when compared with the totals found by Quigley, Jenne, and Phillips for the entire United States from 1910 to 1965, and it illustrates how a modest investment in support services such as notetaking and interpreting can increase greatly the numbers of deaf individuals who can take advantage of college and university programs designed for students with normal hearing.

The proliferation of postsecondary programs for the deaf proceeded in an unsystematic way. Given the absence of standards, guidelines, and established procedures, the extent and quality of services provided varied widely. Because postsecondary programs for the deaf — with the exception of Gallaudet College — are a recent phenomenom, research literature concerning the students and quality of such programs has been sparse. Craig, Newman, and Burrows (1972) discussed the characteristics of the deaf students in the three model postsecondary programs (Delgado, Seattle, TVI) in order to draw a composite profile. They reported:

1. The students tend to come from states closest to the regional program; to come from a variety of high school backgrounds, though most frequently from residential schools; and to have brought with them the handicaps imposed by being deaf throughout most of their lives.

2. The students enroll in a wide range of courses, though more than half of them follow career lines in office practices, graphic arts, and data processing.

---

* Personal communication with Dr. Ray Jones, Director of CSUN Programs in Deafness, October 1975.

However, the selection of vocational areas appeared to the authors to be restricted unnecessarily.

3. Two-thirds of the students who left before graduation left by individual choice. Through counseling and career guidance, an increased number of those cases might be reduced. Test scores taken from the evaluation reports would suggest strongly that deaf students should succeed in schools that provide special tutoring and supportive services.

Examination of the information provided for 27 postsecondary programs in existence in 1972 (Stuckless & Delgado, 1973), and of the 43 programs in 1975 (Rawlings, Trybus, Delgado, & Stuckless, 1975), gives insights into their nature and functions. The 27 programs enrolled a total of 2,271 deaf undergraduates, with the two largest programs (Gallaudet, 926; NTID, 389) accounting for 58% of all students enrolled. The 14 programs identified as being established between 1969 and 1972 (excluding the 3 model programs) enrolled a total of 287 students. Only 1 program, La Puente (California) Valley Vocational Adult School, with 90 students, had more than 25 deaf students, and 4 programs had 10 students or fewer. Geographic distribution was uneven. In the south the only program east of Louisiana was St. Petersburg (Florida) Junior College, with 21 students. In the entire northeast, the only program was the Community College of Philadelphia, with 5 deaf students.

By 1975 the number of programs had grown to 43, with a student population of 2,903. The two largest programs continued to account for more than 50% of all students enrolled. Although Gallaudet's enrollment dropped slightly to 894, NTID reached its projected full enrollment and had 630 students. Other programs appeared more stable than in 1972, and the mean enrollment was 34 students, with no programs enrolling fewer than 10 students. Geographic distribution, however, continued to be uneven, with relatively few programs in the south and northeast.

Perhaps because of the pragmatic nature of postsecondary education, the burning issues that are debated with such intensity at the early intervention, elementary, and secondary years have been resolved with a refreshing lack of emotion and recrimination. This is especially evident in the lack of controversy concerning manual communication and mainstreaming. In 1972 all 27 programs reported using manual communication, and 26 of the programs have been established within facilities for students with normal hearing. In 1975 all but 1 program used manual communication, and all but 1 were within facilities for students with normal hearing. The moves have been accepted as practical, and little dissension has resulted.

There has been concern, however, over the rapid increase of small programs unable to offer effectively the range of necessary services to deaf postsecondary vocational-technical students. In cooperation with the three model demonstration programs in New Orleans, St. Paul, and Seattle, the University of

Minnesota Research, Development and Demonstration Center in Education of Handicapped Children conducted a comprehensive study (Moores, Fisher, & Harlow, 1974) with the following objectives:

1. To provide post secondary programs with guidelines for developing programs for the deaf.
2. To determine as precisely as possible the nature of the three demonstration programs in relation to:
   a. Population served
   b. Courses of study offered
   c. Supportive services provided
   d. Cost of services
3. To determine the effectiveness of the type of post secondary programming offered by the three demonstration programs in:
   a. Course success
   b. Employment success
   c. Attrition
   d. Comparison of student and non-student success
4. To consider student characteristics in an attempt to derive implications for specific vocational instructional procedures. (p. 3)

The objectives encompassed two components. The first dealt with the three federally funded demonstration programs for which formative evaluation was conducted as a means of improving their effectiveness. The results were reported in a series of research monographs (Fisher, Harlow, & Moores, 1974; Fisher, Moores, & Harlow, 1974; Harlow, Fisher, & Moores, 1974; Harlow, Moores, & Fisher, 1974; Moores, Harlow, & Fisher, 1974). The final outcome of the investigation, based on the summative evaluation of the demonstration programs, concerned the summary of findings and establishment of guidelines for new programs (Moores, Fisher, & Harlow, 1974). Readers are referred to the original sources for complete details. Some of the major findings and implications of the study were as follows:

1. A majority of former students (73%) approved of the idea of technical-vocational programs for the deaf, were positive toward their programs, and most were appreciative of the training and supportive services afforded them.
2. Compared to investigations of the occupational status of young deaf adults ten years previously (Boatner, Stuckless & Moores, 1964; Kroneberg & Blake, 1966) the occupational status of former students of the three post secondary programs under study provided evidence that the programs facilitated an upward movement in the job market for their students.
3. The upward movement, however, showed no major shifts in or breakthroughs to new types of occupations, but rather a general upward trend within the framework of positions traditionally held by deaf people. There was a tendency to cluster in certain occupations, such as general office practice for females and printing for males.

4. Training, placement opportunities, salaries and chances for advancement for deaf females were much more restrictive than for deaf males.

5. Former students report more job satisfaction than had been found in previous studies.

6. Comparative figures suggest that the young deaf adults interviewed earn higher salaries than hearing adults of equivalent ages. There is a tendency for this advantage to disappear with older interviewees.

7. Consistent with previous studies, the deaf worker identified communication difficulties as the major on the job problem. It is a factor in limiting advancement of deaf individuals.

8. In spite of the counseling and placement services provided by the programs, a substantial proportion of jobs were located through the aid of parents, friends and relatives.

9. Immediate supervisors regarded deaf workers as desirable employees with high job performance and were willing to hire more deaf workers.

10. However supervisors regarded opportunities for advancement for their deaf workers as limited, even with further training.

11. The majority of parents favored post secondary programs for the deaf within ongoing programs for students with normal hearing.

12. Most parents expressed satisfaction with their children's vocational-technical training.

13. The majority of vocational rehabilitation counselors felt that the training received by their deaf clients in post secondary programs was adequate.

14. Vocational Rehabilitation Counselors tended to be more critical of the education their clients had received prior to their vocational technical training.

15. Nearly 90% of the current students interviewed were satisfied with the training they were receiving. Most approved of the idea of vocational-technical programs for the hearing impaired and most preferred to attend school with both hearing and hearing-impaired peers.

16. Occupational choices tended to fall along traditional and sex lines. Nearly 40% of males chose graphic arts/printing or cabinet making/carpentry as their future occupations. Sixty percent of the females' choices came under the category of general office practice.

17. The educational preparation of the preparatory program teachers was not geared to the post secondary level.

18. Courses offered in the preparatory programs were heavily remedial in nature, stressing math and English.

19. Preparatory program teachers felt that deaf students had not been provided basic academic skills by the time of secondary school graduation.

20. Regular classroom teachers were nearly unanimous in expressing support for interpreters and obviously regarded them as the catalyst permitting deaf students to receive technical-vocational training with hearing students.

21. Regular classroom teachers were supportive of and enthusiastic about the programs for the deaf. Many expressed a need for more background information concerning deafness.

22. Analysis of scores of deaf subjects on the Stanford Achievement Test, the General Aptitude Test Battery and the Weschsler Adult Intelligence Scale, indicates they are the intellectual equals of hearing adults and may be superior in areas demanding spatial and

perceptual skills. Therefore deaf individuals should have no more difficulty in meeting the cognitive demands of any job than anyone else. The high ratings which supervisors and regular classroom teachers give deaf workers and students tend to support such a position.

23. Because deaf people are underemployed, a deaf person is more often than not the intellectual superior of hearing people employed in the same type of work.

24. Problems arise not because of the cognitive demands of a job but because of difficulties in communication, especially insufficient command of the English language.

25. The effectiveness of well-run secondary vocational-technical programs for the deaf has been documented. However, they are hampered by the poor education students received prior to the post secondary level. (pp. 16–29)

Summary

With the exception of Gallaudet College — the world's only college for the deaf, which was established in 1864 — postsecondary education was available only to those individuals who were able to enroll in colleges and universities for students with normal hearing. Evidence suggests that few deaf individuals have graduated from such institutions over the years and that the majority of those who have were in reality hard of hearing or postlingually deaf.

The economic status of deaf workers in the nineteenth and early twentieth centuries in America was comparable to that of hearing workers, but it deteriorated as industry demanded more and more specialized workers, and training opportunities for the deaf did not keep pace with those for the hearing. By 1965 it was evident that the deaf were a depressed group economically, with high rates of unemployment, low wages, and little chance for advancement.

The establishment of the National Technical Institute for the Deaf on the campus of the Rochester (New York) Institute of Technology and the establishment of three regional model vocational-technical programs in New Orleans, St. Paul, and Seattle in 1968 and 1969 provided the major thrust for the growth of postsecondary programs for the deaf. All were affiliated with existing host facilities serving students with normal hearing.

Evidence suggests that deaf students are as capable as hearing students intellectually and can handle cognitive demands of a work situation with relative ease. Over several generations of research, deaf individuals have been rated as good, even superior, workers. Over the same generations, their major obstacle on the job has been related to difficulty of communication, which has restricted job mobility and advancement.

Evaluation of the model programs in New Orleans, St. Paul, and Seattle indicated that the programs have aided their students in terms of upward job mobility, although no major breakthroughs have been made, and that choice of training and occupation for deaf students, especially female deaf students, remains limited.

It is doubtful that any postsecondary program, no matter how exemplary, can overcome the inadequate education most deaf individuals receive in the early intervention, elementary, and secondary years. Until education of the deaf, in general, begins to provide students with basic skills and helps them to develop to the limits of their potential, the economic position of deaf adults will continue to be below that which they are capable of obtaining.

14
Multihandicapped Deaf Individuals

Introduction

Although it commonly is acknowledged that a large proportion of deaf individuals suffer from additional handicaps, the nature and extent of the problem has never been subjected to systematic investigation. A primary obstacle is the lack of agreement over what indeed constitutes a handicap. Almost all human beings have problems of one kind or another — for example, color blindness, overbite, curvature of the spine, deviated septum, astigmatism, depression, and so on — that may be bothersome but may not necessarily affect everyday functioning adversely. The major emphasis of the present chapter will be on disabilities that may have handicapping implications for educational and psychological functioning. Within this context, the terms *disability* and *handicap* are consistent with their usage as described in Chapter 1. Terms such as *deafness, blindness,* and *mental retardation* are restricted to disabilities caused by various impairments. Disabilities may be expressed in terms of such variables as speech reception threshold, visual acuity, and IQ test scores. A handicap represents the extent to which a person's overall functioning is limited by a particular disability or set of disabilities.

Although numerous studies have reported incidence figures on various types of disabilities related to deafness, present data must be treated as imprecise estimates. For the most part, the figures represent children enrolled in programs and identified by one means or another as multihandicapped. There is no way of knowing how many additional such children exist who may not be enrolled in any programs. Therefore, it is not wise to generalize to the total population on the basis of present incidence figures. Second, categories and definitions tend to be imprecise. Procedures for classifying deaf children as retarded, aphasic, learning disabled, and so on have been inconsistent and frequently result in inappropriate, harmful labeling.

With only a few notable exceptions, it may be said that studies of the existence of other handicaps in deaf populations have provided either incidence data with no definitions or definitions with no incidence data.

Table 14.1 Multihandicapped deaf children enrolled in programs, October 1974

Category	Number
Deaf blind	965
Deaf mentally retarded	3,165
Deaf aphasic	983
Deaf and all other handicaps	5,863
Total deaf multihandicapped	10,976

SOURCE: W. Craig & H. Craig (Eds.), Directory of Services for the Deaf. *American Annals of the Deaf*, May
1977, *120*, p. 175.

Incidence of Multiple Handicaps

General incidence figures suggest that the numbers of multihandicapped deaf
students are increasing rapidly. For example, Weir (1963) reported that there
were 1,069 multihandicapped deaf students in 1954 and 3,050 in 1960. Using
data from the 1968 Annual Survey of Hearing Impaired Children and Youth,
Rawlings and Gentile (1970) reported that over 7,000 of a total of 21,000 deaf
students were identified by their programs as having at least one additional
handicap. This represents one-third of the sample. If generalized to the total
enrollment of deaf students in the United States, it would mean that currently
16,000 to 20,000 multihandicapped deaf children are enrolled.

Ries (1973b) conducted an analysis of data from the 1971 Survey of Hearing
Impaired Children and Youth. He reported (p. 50) that for a total of 41,109
deaf students, 23,874 had no additional handicaps, and information was not
available for 6,255 individuals. The remaining 10,980 had a total of 13,662
other handicaps. If one computed the number of multihandicapped deaf students (10,980) in relation to the total in the survey (41,109), it could be concluded that approximately one-fourth of deaf students might be included in this
category. If the 6,255 students for whom information was not available are
excluded, then the incidence figure rises to approximately one-third, or 10,980
out of 34,954.

The incidence figures from the annual surveys are higher than those supplied by the Directory of Services of the American Annals of the Deaf (Craig &
Craig, 1975), which reported that 10,976, or 21% of 53,009 deaf students
enrolled in programs in 1974, were categorized as multihandicapped. Table
14.1 presents a breakdown of figures by major categories.

It must be empahsized, however, that for the large-scale surveys (Craig &
Craig, 1975; Rawlings & Gentile, 1970; Reis, 1973b) the various programs re-

Table 14.2 Power and Quigley: Proposed classification system for categorizing multihandicapped deaf students

Remedial conditions		Adjustable conditions
Medically treatable	Educationally treatable	
Epilepsy	Educable mental retardation	Gross visual defect
Cleft palate	Learning disorder	Trainable mental retardation
Most visual defects	Behavior disorder	Crippling conditions

SOURCE: Derived from D. Power & S. Quigley, *Problems and Programs in the Education of Multiply-disabled Deaf Children.* Urbana: University of Illinois, 1971, pp. 7–12.

ported their figures by categories without reference to clear definitions. One can assume only that the assignment of children to respective categories varied greatly from program to program. In a review of the literature Power and Quigley (1971) estimated that approximately 25% of all deaf children in the United States have another disability. The authors, however, emphasized the dangers in generalizing from existing incidence figures and recommended first that a report on definitions of multiple disabling conditions be commissioned. Following the development of clear definitions, an adequately sampled survey then could be conducted to ascertain the overall incidence of multiple disabilities among deaf children (Power & Quigley, 1971, p. 2).

It cannot be emphasized too strongly that an unknown number of multihandicapped children may be receiving no education or services. Burns and Stenquist (1960) pointed out that multihandicapped children often remain at home or are placed in institutions. Calvert (1970) stated that there might be more multihandicapped deaf children outside of school than in it.

Power and Quigley (1971) advanced a tentative classification system that is presented in condensed form in Table 14.2. They suggested a basic distinction be made between *remediable* conditions, which can be alleviated to a large extent by appropriate medical or educational treatment, and *adjustable* conditions, which at present cannot be removed. In the latter case, the emphasis would be on adapting as much as possible to a disability. Remediable conditions are subcategorized into *medically treatable* and *educationally treatable* components. The medically treatable problems do not require special educational treatment, and the educationally treatable areas are conditions that, at present, are not medically treatable.

The three major adjustable conditions, as presented by Power and Quigley, represent in general more severe handicapping conditions. For example, at present most visual defects are considered medically treatable (by glasses, minor surgery, etc.), but gross visible defects are not. Similarly children classified as educable mentally retarded are considered educationally treatable by Power and Quigley, but those classified as trainable mentally retarded are not. Obviously, when dealing with disabilities ranging over continua from mild to severe, the establishment of criteria by which "remediable" and "adjustable" conditions are differentiated are crucial. The problem is probably most acute when dealing with educational implications of children in the *educable mental retardation, learning disorder,* and *behavior disorder* categories.

Unfortunately, there has been no response to the request for the establishment of precise definitions for identification of multihandicapped deaf children. Lacking such definitions, all reported incidence figures must be taken with a grain of salt.

Educationally Caused Handicaps

It may be argued — indeed it has been argued — that the major cause of multihandicapped conditions among the deaf may be attributed to the inadequate education deaf children receive. Along these lines Vernon (1971) stated:

Ironically, it is not deafness or the secondary physical problems associated with it which are the primary causes of severe handicaps among deaf adults. Instead the primary causes are the counselling and programming provided by professionals in speech pathology, education, audiology, medicine, psychology, and other specialties in the field of deafness.

Thus, we have in the majority of deaf clients individuals whose primary disability is not their deafness. It is the gross educational, psychological, and social deprivation forced upon them by anachronistic parent counseling followed by an educational system equally inappropriate, both of which are promulgated by professionals insensitive to and unaware of the needs of deaf people and oblivious to existing research data in deafness. (p. 10)

Stewart (1974) argued in a similar vein and noted the distinction between a handicap and a disability; that is, a person may have a physical disability and still not be handicapped educationally. Stewart developed the position that the great majority of deaf people may be considered multihandicapped in that their academic achievement is far below their intellectual potential and in that their communicative ability is impaired. He concluded (1974, pp. 21, 22) that neglect of the educational, social, and psychological needs of the child is the major cause of multiple handicaps in the deaf.

The position of Stewart and Vernon suggests that a major new category be identified — that related to handicaps caused by inappropriate educating and counseling. The situation is similar to that of iatrogenic conditions, that is, disabilities whose causes may be medical in nature. The best-known examples are probably (1) the effects of the drug thalidomide on the development of the fetus and (2) the effects of the exposure of premature babies to excessive amounts of oxygen. The first situation is well known to the general public and needs no detailed discussion. The second situation relates to the precaution of placing premature babies in an incubator after birth. In many cases the babies received too much oxygen, causing the development of fibrous growths in the eye (retrolental fibrophasia). The result was a tremendous increase in the incidence of blindness over a period of several years, before the relationship between exposure to excessive levels of oxygen and blindness was established (Kirk, 1972). Following the discovery, the incidence of iatrogenic catagenetic blindness was reduced appreciably through a more careful monitoring of oxygen during incubation.

To the best of the author's knowledge, relatively few cases of deafness are iatrogenic in nature, and there is little reason to believe that it is a significant factor in causing multiple handicaps in the deaf population. The major cause of multihandicapping conditions in deaf individuals may be said to be educational in nature; that is, they are caused by inappropriate educational diagnosis, prescription, and treatment.

Current Major Identified Educational Handicaps Related to Deafness

In a discussion of other handicapping conditions related to deafness, it is necessary to devote some attention separately to the interaction of deafness with a number of other disabilities. Two populations that have received a great deal of attention — and some educational service — are the deaf blind and the deaf retarded. Two other groups recently have received considerable attention but little in the way of services: These are the deaf individuals also classified as having emotional and/or behavioral problems.

Mental Retardation

Studies of the incidence of deafness combined with mental retardation generally come from two sources: (1) children enrolled in schools and classes for the deaf and (2) individuals, including children and adults, in schools and institutions for the retarded. Power and Quigley (1971) suggest that children in schools and classes for the deaf primarily represent an *educable mentally retarded* (EMR) category, and those in institutions for the retarded tend to fall within the *trainable mentally retarded* (TMR) grouping. The extent to which this generalization has applied since 1971 is questionable. The trend in most states has been to reduce their institutional populations of severely retarded individuals while developing programs at local or regional levels. Many state residential schools for the deaf and some large metropolitan school systems have expanded the scope of their services for deaf children to include those with severe mental retardation.

The percentage of children identified as mentally retarded in programs for the deaf — the majority of whom presumably would be within the EMR category — has remained fairly stable over a period of years, until the late 1960s. Frisina (1955) reported an incidence of 11 to 12% in residential schools for the deaf. Weir (1963) reported an incidence of up to 11% in day and residential programs for the deaf. In a study of educational services available to retarded students in six schools for the deaf, Anderson and Stevens (1969a) reported that 304 students (19% of the total population of the schools) had measured IQs to below 83; of these children, 132 (8% of the total) were classified by their school as retarded. Calvert (1970) reported that 10 to 12% of deaf students were either EMR or TMR. Rawlings and Gentile (1970) found that 8.05% of students were reported as retarded in programs for the deaf participating in the 1968 Annual Survey of Hearing Impaired Children and Youth. In the 1971 survey (Ries, 1973c, p. 50) 2,400 of 41,109 students, or approximately 5.9%, were reported as retarded. Excluding the students for whom information was not available, the incidence of reported mental retardation in programs for the deaf rises to approximately 7%. Craig and Craig (1975) reported a total of 3,165 deaf/retarded children out of an enrollment of 53,009 in the United States in 1974. This represents 6% of the enrollees, a figure consistent with the 1968 and 1971 surveys.

The data above suggest some trends which seem to contradict the unquestioned assumption that the absolute numbers *and* relative incidence of multiple handicaps in deaf children have increased tremendously in recent years (Power & Quigley, 1971) and that there is no evidence of any decline in the near future (Vernon, 1969). Such does not seem to be the case in the relative incidence of children in programs for the deaf who are classified as deaf and retarded. There has been a definite decline in the percentage of deaf children placed in this category since the late 1960s.

Reasons for the decline, which is counter to the trend for other multihandicapping conditions, are subject to speculation, but a number of factors should be taken into consideration. First, the traditional estimates that 10 to 12% of deaf students in residential schools also were retarded were probably gross overestimates and included many children who were in fact intellectually normal. Too often deaf children have been classified as retarded by professionals who had no knowledge of the communication problems faced by deaf individuals and who operated under the mistaken assumption that language and speech problems are symptoms of mental retardation. Although such inappropriate diagnoses are still made, the abuse is not as widespread as in the past.

A second factor has been the growing reluctance of educators in general to label a child as retarded. In some cases the child merely has been assigned a new label, for example *learning disabled*. In other cases teachers may work with the child and avoid the use of any label at all, causing a decline in the reported incidence figures. Still, it also must be acknowledged that 6 to 8% of students in programs for the deaf continue to be classified as retarded. This represents a far greater percentage than the incidence rate of retardation for the general population, which is estimated at 3 percent (Kirk, 1972). The author speculates that some reasons for the relatively high rate might be: (1) several of the major etiologies of deafness are also factors in mental retardation (see Chapter 4); (2) intelligence testing of deaf children often is conducted by professionals who cannot communicate with their subjects, and the results frequently underestimate the intellectual ability of the children (see Chapter 8); and (3) intellectually normal deaf children frequently are labeled retarded inappropriately on the basis of low academic achievement.

The incidence of hearing loss for individuals in programs and institutions for the retarded is a matter of even greater uncertainty. For example, Nober (1968) referred to 49 studies published between 1951 and 1968 in which the reported incidence of hearing loss for the retarded ranged from 6 to 65%! The wide range in reported incidence probably is explained by differing interpretations of the term *hearing loss*. The majority of major studies tend to place estimates of hearing loss in institutionalized populations at 25% or below. Rigrodsky, Prouty, and Glovsky (1961) reported 25% of the population of the Vineland Training School had "educationally significant" hearing losses. Studies by Johnson and Farrell (1956) and MacPherson (1952) produced an incidence figure of 24%. Lloyd and Reed (1967) reported hearing impairment of 15% in an institutionalized mentally retarded population. They also found an increased incidence of hearing loss as they moved down the scale of intelligence. This implies that the more severely retarded an individual is judged, the more likely he or she is to have other handicaps. Lloyd and Moore (1972) concluded that 15% of children in schools for the retarded have educationally significant hearing losses. Leenhouts (1960) reported that 15% of the population in the California State Hospital programs for the retarded had hearing losses.

Again, the definition of what is entailed by an "educationally significant" hearing loss for a retarded individual is unclear, and criteria vary from one study to another. Still, it is obvious that the incidence of hearing impairment is greater in institutions for the retarded than in the general population. Although estimates vary, there are large numbers of deaf individuals in institutions for the retarded. For example, in a survey of nine New York State schools for the retarded, Colpoys (1972) found a reported incidence of deafness (as opposed to hearing loss) ranging from 1.1 to 11.1%. Even though responses from each school surveyed came from the head of that school's speech and hearing department, the definition of deafness varied from school to school, ranging from "lack of hearing for speech when presented at a level of

75 dB" to "eliciting no response at any frequency at the maximum output of the audiometer" (Colpoys, 1972, p. 18). It is therefore safe to assume that the incidence figures vary to a large extent as a function of the definitions employed. Given such large divergence in a relatively sophisticated system of state programs for the retarded — all of which had professionally staffed speech and hearing departments — one must conclude that generalizations from studies of incidence of hearing loss in programs for the retarded can be made only with the utmost caution. Although the statement by Sonies and Healey (1974) that the majority of deaf retarded individuals are in institutions for the retarded is probably true, any accurate estimate of absolute numbers at present is impossible.

Even though the scope of the problem is unclear, a number of factors must be considered. It is reasonable to assume that many people in institutions for the retarded are inappropriately classified as deaf retarded on the basis of poorly developed communication skills. On the other hand, there are probably large numbers of individuals classified as retarded who, in reality, suffer from deafness as their primary disability. It also may be assumed that there is a large but unknown number of deaf/retarded individuals receiving no service at all, either from programs for the retarded or from those for the deaf. The situation is horrendous and will not be alleviated until precise definitions are developed, incidence figures are obtained, and programs are initiated. Educators of the deaf should be aware of the trend in many states to reduce institutionalized populations. In the years to come, it is probable that residential schools and local programs for the deaf will have to assume major responsibility for the education of even the most severely retarded deaf individuals.

Educational provisions   Investigations of educational provisions for deaf retarded students have been conducted both for schools for the deaf (Anderson, Stevens, & Stuckless, 1966) and for schools for the retarded (Mitra, 1970). As might be expected, the extent and quality of programs are uneven, and criteria for inclusion are inconsistent. For the most part, educational programs for deaf retarded individuals are low on the list of priorities, are poorly staffed, and receive limited administrative support. The poor state of affairs is highlighted by a study of Anderson and Stevens (1969b) of the qualifications of teachers of mentally retarded deaf pupils in residential schools for the deaf. On the basis of responses by 150 teachers, Anderson and Stevens (1969b) reported:

1. Deaf teachers accounted for 43% of the respondents, representing a far higher percentage than those employed to teach deaf children with no other handicap.

2. Less than one-fourth of the respondents were teaching deaf retarded children by choice. The remainder (78%) were placed by administrative assignment.

3. Approximately two-thirds of the teachers of retarded children stated that they preferred to teach deaf children with *no* other handicap. Of the remainder, 5% had no preference, and 28% preferred to teach deaf retarded children.

4. A need for additional training was expressed by 86% of the teachers.

In sum, a majority of teachers of deaf retarded students in residential schools for the deaf are not trained to teach mentally retarded deaf children, did not choose to teach such children, and would prefer *not* to teach such children. One may conclude that the effectiveness of such teachers is less than ideal.

The paucity of training programs specifically designed to develop teachers of mentally retarded deaf children has been a major hindrance to the development of effective programs. Apparently it is not sufficient to take course work in deafness and in mental retardation. The deaf mentally retarded child presents qualitatively different problems than either a deaf child or a retarded child. Anderson and Stevens (1969b) quote from a teacher with 14 years of experience with retarded deaf children:

If I felt courses for helping the deaf mentally retarded were available, I certainly would take them. In my mind I cannot accept courses for the teaching of the mentally retarded child as being of value for the teaching of mentally retarded deaf children. . . . In other words I see a completely new field in special education, the education of the deaf mentally retarded child. This child requires special techniques, materials, and curriculum to do him justice. . . . The help I need will not come from taking courses on mental retardation or courses on deafness. It will come from courses in the mentally retarded deaf. (p. 31)

The teacher's comments point up an important fact that cannot be ignored in dealing with deaf individuals who have additional handicaps. The problems of an individual who is both deaf and retarded are not additive. They cannot be understood as representing the sum of the problems of deafness plus retardation. Instead, the deafness and retardation interact in a multiplicative way, presenting unique, qualitatively different patterns. Just as the problems faced by a deaf retarded individual differ from those of a deaf person or a retarded person, the training and qualifications of professionals working with the deaf retarded must be qualitatively different from those working with the deaf or with the retarded. Naturally, the same holds true for those working with deaf and blind or other multihandicapped individuals.

Blindness

Before the 1963–1965 rubella epidemic, with only a few notable exceptions such as the program at the Perkins Institute for the Blind, very little effort had been made to identify and educate deaf blind children. Both deafness and blindness are low-incidence conditions, and the combination of the two is relatively rare. Therefore, there was little motivation for the development of comprehensive programs. The impetus for movement grew out of the aftermath of the 1963–1965 rubella epidemic and the uncertainty over what its impact would be. There was uncertainty over the number of children who might have been affected. A sharp rise in the number of multihandicapped children was predicted, but there was considerable confusion over just how great the increase might be. The United States Senate exhibited considerable foresight by anticipating needs and authorizing in January 1968 the development of comprehensive regional centers for deaf blind children (Centers and Services for Deaf-Blind Children, 1969). By 1970, 10 regional centers serving all 50 states were established and funded through the Bureau of Education for the Handicapped. The immediate tasks of the centers included the following charges (Dantona, 1970):

1. Identification of deaf-blind populations
2. Identification of resources available
3. Identification of children served
4. Identification of population not served
5. Determination of economic cost factors
6. Development and expansion of the number of facilities, programs and services
7. Development of meaningful inservice training programs
8. Coordination of all community resources
9. Stimulation of the development of teacher-training programs
10. Coordination of all existing federal resources to supplement the program needs of the centers (pp. 4–6)

As might be expected, when the programs began their activities, far more deaf blind children were identified than had been anticipated. According to data supplied by the Bureau of Education for the Handicapped (Dantona, 1970), in the 1967–1968 academic year — before the establishment of regional centers for the deaf blind — a total of 256 children were receiving what might be considered adequate educational services. Of these, 100 children were enrolled in six different residential programs for the deaf blind, and the remaining 156 were in various public and private school programs for the deaf or the blind. By 1970 a total of 2,461 deaf blind children had been located by the surveys. Of this number, 802 were enrolled in educational programs — more than a 300% increase in the 1967–1968 enrollment over a two-year period. This represents tremendous movement in a short period of time. Still, it must be remembered that in 1970 less than one-third (802 of 2,461) of the children were in an adequate educational program. An additional 347 children, approximately 14%, were in institutions for the retarded. The remaining 1,349 children, accounting for more than half of those identified, were at home.

The majority of children identified by 1970 were under 9 years of age, reflecting the impact of the 1963–1965 rubella epidemic. However, more than 1,100 of the children were 9 years of age or older, a large proportion of whom had received no educational services at all.

In the intervening years, the regional centers for deaf blind children have been working effectively toward providing educational services to deaf blind children, even though the numbers to be served have exceeded original estimation. For example, the 10 regional centers reported 4,200 deaf blind children in 1972 and 5,300 in 1973 (Stewart, 1974). As a whole, the efforts of the regional centers stand as an endorsement of the systematic development of regional programs — utilizing local, state, regional, and federal resources — to meet the needs of individuals suffering from severe handicaps that are of low incidence.

Special Learning and Behavioral Problems

If the problems of diagnosing and educating deaf individuals who also are classified as mentally retarded or blind are great, they still do not match the confusion related to deaf individuals who have been identified as having behavioral and/or learning problems. No field of education has been so abused by specialists, and it will probably be generations until the effects of their well-intentioned but nevertheless harmful policies have been neutralized. Writing about the term *minimal brain dysfunction*, Anderson (1971) describes the situation as follows:

Minimal brain dysfunction is one of fifty or more terms which describes the same set of symptoms. Experts in the field, representing various professional disciplines, have introduced terminology derived from their own professional orientations; as a result, much confusion has been created. In effect the same behavioral phenomena have been observed from different frames of reference. Terms such as perceptual cripple, interjacent child, developmental dyslexia, hyperkinetic child syndrome, and minimal brain damage have been used. . . .

As communication has increased among the disciplines, there has been an increasing tendency to utilize the term learning disability rather than minimal brain dysfunction or minimal brain damage to describe the syndrome. (pp. 31–32)

Not only are different labels used for the same types of conditions, but also the same label frequently has been used for different types of conditions. For example, children have been labeled *brain damaged* on the basis of lack of educational progress, and not because of any medical evidence of neurological impairment.

If the situation is confused for children with normal hearing, it is logical to assume that it is worse for deaf children. In discussing the concept of learning disorders related to deafness, Power and Quigley (1971) referred to the descriptions of other authors in the field and somewhat bitingly concluded: "So many different concepts are linked together by these writers so as to make their concept of learning disorder meaningless. Many of the behaviors could well be subsumed under emotional disturbance and motor disfunction" (p. 9).

In the author's opinion, terms such as *emotional disorder, behavioral disorder*, and *learning disorder* have not been differentiated sufficiently to warrant separate treatment in this chapter. Given the major current etiologies related to deafness, it might be predicted that a somewhat higher proportion of deaf children than hearing children suffer from additional learning and behavioral problems. Inappropriate educational and counseling procedures would be expected to add to the numbers. At present it is unclear just what percentage of deaf children also might have educationally significant learning and behavioral problems. It is probable that the numbers could be reduced through appropriate counseling of parents, mental health programs designed to facilitate optimal development in deaf individuals, and more effective educational programs.

Many of the issues involved in the development of mental health programs to foster positive growth and to prevent the development of severe psychological difficulties have been discussed in Chapter 8. It cannot be emphasized too strongly that many serious disturbances can be treated relatively simply when diagnosis is made and treatment is begun at early stages. For example, Stewart (1974) has noted that, as a whole, mentally ill deaf people struggle along without help until the strains become so pronounced that they are institutionalized.

In terms of incidence figures, out of reports for 41,109 students Ries (1973c) counted 3,338 children labeled as having emotional and behavioral problems; 1,885 as having perceptual motor disorders; 910 as having learning disabilities; and 168 as being brain damaged. Again, since the students were identified by their own educational programs, it is assumed that definitions varied and that there was great overlap among categories.

Jensema and Trybus (1975) reported an overall incidence of 7.9% of deaf children identified as having "educationally significant emotional/behavioral problems." Differences among the definitions of the terms was highlighted by the fact that the proportion of students reported by their programs as having emotional/behavioral problems varied from 1.6 to 28% in schools of comparable size (p. 11). Despite the wide variation, some noteworthy trends appeared. First, the rate was much higher for males (9.8%) than for females (5.6%). Even the apparently straightforward relationship between sex and *reported* disturbance is highly complex, however. For example, for students born before 1954 there was essentially no difference: 5.8% for males and 5.6% for females. However, for those born in years 1958–1959 and 1964–1965, the reported incidence of reported emotional/behavioral problems for males was 11.7% and 12% respectively. For females it was 6% and 6.4% (p. 5). There appears, then, to be much more variability among males as a function of the year of birth, although the same periods (1958–1959 and 1964–1965) represent the highest figures for both groups. Since both periods represent aftermaths of rubella epidemics, it is not surprising to find that maternal rubella is the etiology most frequently associated with reported emotional/behavioral problems, particularly among males, with a reported incidence of 13.9% (p. 9).

The problems of deaf children with severe learning and emotional problems are unknown for the most part, and little has been done to serve them outside of a few model programs. Calvert (1970) reported that of 984 deaf children in California under age 15 who were identified as multihandicapped, one-half were classified as emotionally disturbed. Consistent with the plight of so many

Table 14.3   Distribution of students with and without additional handicapping conditions by ethnic origin: United States, 1971–1972

Ethnic origin	Students with no additional handicaps		Students with additional handicaps		Total number and % of students for whom information on additional handicaps was available	
	Number	Percent	Number	Percent	Number	Percent
White	15,667	67.6	6,520	32.3	23,187	100
Black	2,567	63.3	1,490	36.7	4,057	100
Spanish-American	1,426	69.2	634	30.8	2,060	100
Other specified [a]	331	67.8	157	32.2	488	100
Information on ethnic origin not available	2,820	72.0	1,099	28.0	3,919	100
Total	22,811	67.7	9,900	32.3	33,711	100

[a]*American Indian, Oriental, mixed parentage*, and *other*.

SOURCE: Adapted from A. Gentile & B. McCarthy, *Additional Handicapping Conditions among Hearing Impaired Students, United States: 1971–72*. Annual Survey of Hearing Impaired Children and Youth. Washington, D.C.: Gallaudet College, Office of Demographic Studies, Ser. D, No. 14, 1973, pp. 9 and 27.

multihandicapped deaf children, large numbers were at home receiving no services.

Power and Quigley (1971, p. 4) have recommended that a number of regional centers for deaf children who are severely emotionally disturbed be established, based on the model of the regional centers for deaf blind children. Their proposal has not met with any action.

Ethnic Origins of Multihandicapped Deaf Students

One area of interest is the delineation of the incidence of additional handicapping conditions in deaf individuals of various ethnic origins. Gentile and McCarthy (1973) reported that 9,900 or 32.3%, of a group of 33,711 deaf students had been identified as having at least one handicap in addition to deafness. Numbers and percent distribution by ethnic origin are presented in Table 14.3. There appeared to be only minor variation in the incidence of additional handicaps in the four major categories (*white, black, Spanish-American,* and *other specified*), although a somewhat higher percentage of deaf

Table 14.4   Percent distribution of deaf children with additional handicaps and total number of deaf students by ethnic origin: United States, 1971–1972

Ethnic origin	Total population for whom information on additional handicaps was available (percentage)	Population identified as having one or more additional handicaps (percentage)
White	68.8	69.3
Black	12.0	13.5
Spanish-American	6.1	5.6
Other specified[a]	1.4	1.5
Not available	11.6	10.2
Total[b]	99.9	100.1

[a]Includes *American Indian, Oriental, mixed parentage,* and *other.*

[b]Percentages do not add to 100 because of rounding.

SOURCE: Adapted from A. Gentile & B. McCarthy, *Additional Handicapping Conditions among Hearing Impaired Students, United States: 1971–72.* Annual Survey of Hearing Impaired Children and Youth. Washington, D.C.: Gallaudet College, Office of Demographic Studies, Ser. D, No. 14, 1973, p. 28.

blacks (36.7%) and a somewhat lower percentage of deaf Spanish-Americans (30.8) were reported to have additional handicaps (see Figure 14.1). In other words, as illustrated in Table 14.4, black children make up 12% of the total deaf student population in the survey and 13.5% of the total deaf multihandicapped population. Spanish-American children make up 6.1% of the total deaf student population and 5.6% of the total deaf multihandicapped population.

The differences in overall incidence figures appear to be slight across the various ethnic categories. However, analysis of the data by specific handicapping conditions, as shown in Table 14.5, reveals some interesting differences. One noteworthy item is the relatively high incidence of cerebral palsy in whites. Since the Rh factor is less common in American blacks than in American whites, and since deafness and cerebral palsy frequently are related to Rh-factor blood incompatibility (see Chapter 4), one would expect the incidence of cerebral palsy to be lower in deaf black students. Why it is also lower in the *Spanish-American* category, which is predominantly a white/Indian mixture, is not so apparent. Deaf blacks and deaf Spanish-Americans exhibit a higher incidence of heart disorders — 14.6% and 10% of that category, respectively.

The one category that shows gross distortion, however, is that of *mental retardation.* Table 14.5 indicates that black students account for 12% of the total deaf population but 22% of the category *mental retardation.* That is, 656 students — or 16.2% of the total deaf black sample of 4,057 — were classified

Table 14.5 Percentage distribution of additional handicapping conditions by type of condition and ethnic origin: United States, 1971–72

Ethnic origin	Total number students	Type of additional handicapping condition										
		Brain damage	Cerebral palsy	Epilepsy	Heart disorders	Mental retardation	Orthopedic disorders	Perceptual motor disorders	Emotional or behavioral problems	Visual defects	Other	Total
White	68.8	72.3	79.2	72.8	65.4	59.4	72.5	68.5	72.3	69.5	73.1	69.3
Black	12.0	12.2	7.7	11.2	14.6	22.0	11.3	10.7	11.8	12.2	11.4	13.5
Spanish-American	6.1	5.4	3.5	5.9	10.0	4.6	5.6	8.1	5.0	5.3	5.4	5.6
Other specified[a]	1.4	1.8	1.4	2.0	1.8	1.1	0.5	1.2	1.4	1.5	2.8	1.5
Not available	11.6	8.3	8.1	8.1	8.1	12.8	10.2	11.6	9.5	11.5	7.2	0.2
Total[b]	99.9	100.0	99.9	100.0	99.9	99.9	100.1	100.1	100.0	100.0	99.9	100.1

[a] American Indian, Oriental, mixed parentage, and other.

[b] Totals may not add to 100 because of rounding.

SOURCE: Adapted from A. Gentile & B. McCarthy, Additional Handicapping Conditions among Hearing Impaired Students, United States: 1971–72. Annual Survey of Hearing Impaired Children and Youth. Washington, D.C.: Gallaudet College, Office of Demographic Studies, Ser. D, No. 14, 1973, p. 28.

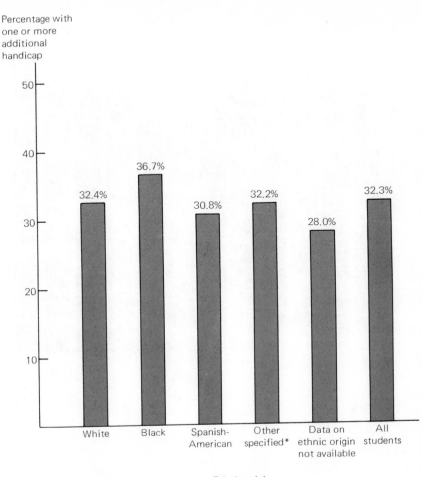

Percentage with
one or more
additional
handicap

*American Indian, Oriental, mixed parentage, and "Other"

Figure **14.1**   Percentage of students by ethnic origin for whom one or more additional handicapping conditions were reported: United States, 1971–1972. (Adapted from A. Gentile and B. McCarthy, *Additional Handicapping Conditions among Hearing Impaired Students, United States: 1971–72,* Annual Survey of Hearing Impaired Children and Youth, Series D, Number 14, Washington, D.C., Gallaudet College, Office of Demographic Studies, 1973, p. 8.)

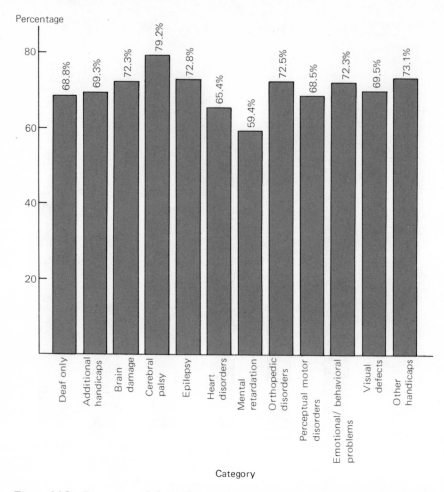

Figure **14.2** Percentage of deaf white students by type of handicapping condition. (Adapted from A. Gentile and B. McCarthy, *Additional Handicapping Conditions among Hearing Impaired Students, United States: 1971–72*, Annual Survey of Hearing Impaired Children and Youth, Series D, Number 14, Washington, D.C., Gallaudet College, Office of Demographic Studies, 1973, p. 8.)

as retarded. For the other groupings, 7.6% of *white,* 7% of *other specified,* and 6.7% of *Spanish-American* children were labeled retarded (p. 29). Figures 14.2 through 14.4 illustrate the differences in incidence for the *white, black,* and *Spanish-American* groups. Data from the *other specified* group were not graphed because of the relatively small numbers of children in them, which was especially apparent in the breakdown by categories.

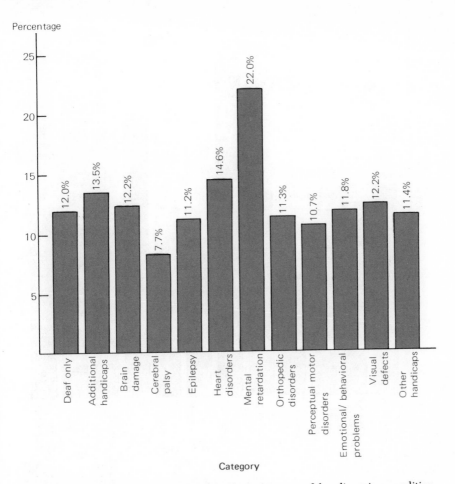

Figure 14.3 Percentage of deaf black students by type of handicapping condition. (Adapted from A. Gentile and B. McCarthy, *Additional Handicapping Conditions among Hearing Impaired Students, United States: 1971–72*, Annual Survey of Hearing Impaired Children and Youth, Series D, Number 14, Washington, D.C., Gallaudet College, Office of Demographic Studies, 1973, p. 8.)

There is no reason why there should be such a disproportionate number of deaf black students who also are classified as retarded. Many factors may contribute to this. At least part of the problem may be laid to inappropriate diagnostic and assessment procedures and to an insensitivity to cultural differences. This area lacks objective evidence by which firm conclusions can be made.

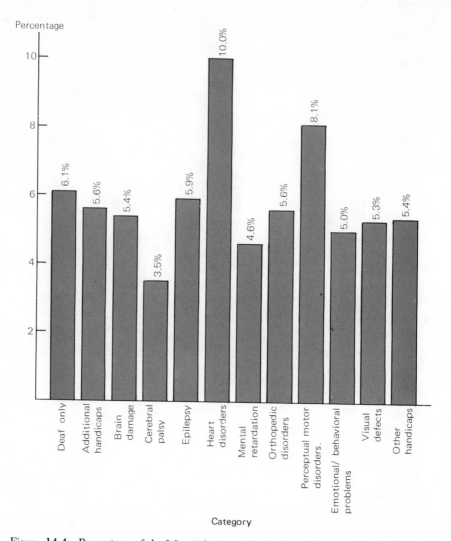

Figure 14.4   Percentage of deaf Spanish-American students by type of handicapping condition. (Adapted from A. Gentile and B. McCarthy, *Additional Handicapping Conditions among Hearing Impaired Students, United States: 1971–72,* Annual Survey of Hearing Impaired Children and Youth, Series D, Number 14, Washington, D.C., Gallaudet College, Office of Demographic Studies, 1973, p. 8.)

Mild Impairments

One repeated theme throughout this book has been an emphasis on the fact that many deaf children, for a number of reasons, suffer from impairments and disabilities in addition to deafness. The scant evidence available suggests (1) that deaf children may have more additional impairments than hearing children and (2) that deaf children less frequently receive appropriate treatment, even when their difficulties may be removed or ameliorated.

Evidence from investigations of the incidence of vision defects provides a clear example of the potential for damage to deaf children when "mild" impairments are not diagnosed and remediated. The same presumably would be true for areas other than vision, but unfortunately there is a dearth of information to test this presumption.

Given the importance of vision to a deaf child, diagnosis of any type of visual impairment is of extreme importance. The evidence suggests that there is a relatively high incidence of visual impairment in the deaf population. Braly (1938), Stockwell (1952), and Lawson and Myklebust (1970) have reported up to twice the incidence of eye defects among deaf children than among children with normal hearing. Frey and Krause (1971) reported that color blindness was more than twice as prevalent among deaf children than hearing children.

A greater prevalence of color blindness or higher incidence of visual defects does not necessarily constitute cause for alarm. Millions of people with normal hearing are color blind to varying degrees, but they are not hampered greatly in their everyday functioning. Even more millions have a wide range of visual defects, the majority of which are correctable to some extent.

Because the cochlea and retina are formed at the same developmental stage from the same embryonic level, it is not surprising that both hearing and vision frequently show impairment. What is shocking is the evidence that many deaf children with correctable vision defects have never been diagnosed. The chances of misdiagnosing a deaf child with a correctable visual defect as being hearing disabled, mentally retarded, distractable, minimally brain damaged, and so on obviously are great and even may constitute a self-fulfilling prophecy. Such a misdiagnosis can destroy a life.

Suchman (1968) tested 103 deaf children aged 4 years to 12 years, 9 months at a program for the deaf. Of this group, 43 had normal vision, and 60 had some visual abnormality. Results are consistent with findings of other studies that reported relatively high incidence. The disturbing finding relates to diagnosis and treatment. The 60 children identified as having visual impairments constituted 58% of the total sample. Of these 60 children, 54, or 90%, had visual impairments that could have been corrected by medical treatment. To the best of the examiner's knowledge only 7 had received visual correction; the remaining 47 with treatable visual defects had never been diagnosed. The most shocking finding dealt with those 25 children who simply had less than normal visual acuity, ranging from 20-30 to 20-70, with no other visual problems. Only 1 of these children had glasses. The visual acuity defects of the other 24 apparently had never been observed!

Obviously, it should be mandatory that complete physical examinations be made regularly of deaf children, especially in the area of vision. Many professionals may be reluctant to work with deaf children. For example, Suchman reported that the ophthalmologists who participated in her study admitted to misconceptions regarding the feasibility of testing deaf children. After their experiences, they admitted to both surprise and pleasure at the ease of testing. In many cases educators will have to convince other professionals that deaf children can be tested efficiently in all areas. It can be — and must be — done.

Training for Academically Low-achieving Adults

Mention should be made of the development of services for deaf adults with inadequately developed communication skills and low academic achievement. Although the term *multihandicapped* has been used in this context, it should be interpreted in most cases as referring to a handicap exacerbated by inappropriate educational procedures.

Rice (1973a, 1973b) reported that one-third of deaf youth who leave school each year do not possess the qualifications to continue their education or become employed. The characteristics of such young adults, categorized as multihandicapped or low-achieving, were presented as follows (Rice, 1973a):

1. Severely limited communication skills
2. Low academic achievement levels
3. Emotional immaturity
4. Secondary disabilities
5. Poor vocational preparation (p. 2)

It is obvious from the listing that the "multihandicaps" frequently are related to inadequate educational training. Secondary disabilities (e.g., retardation, visual defects, etc.) rank fourth on the list. It is apparent that better education and counseling at younger ages would significantly reduce the numbers of deaf adults in this category. Stewart (1971a) has emphasized that the cause of many of the problems faced by multihandicapped deaf adults goes back to unmet preschool needs. He notes that there is abundant information on physical bases of multihandicapping conditions but that little attention has been paid to sociocultural and family-interaction variables.

A number of demonstration projects have been conducted to investigate the feasibility of serving low-achieving school leavers in existing rehabilitation facilities. Lawrence and Vescovi (1967) reported on a program that served 126 deaf clients at the Boston Morgan Memorial over a two-year period. Communication difficulties were the biggest problem for clients, and it was concluded that a knowledge of manual communication was imperative for staff members, an interesting conclusion given the fact that at that time not one school program for the deaf in Massachusetts allowed manual communication. Of the clients, 40% achieved full-time employment, and an additional 20% enrolled in advanced training courses.

In a five-year project conducted by the St. Louis Jewish Vocational Service (Hurwitz, 1971), a total of 265 deaf clients received training in prevocational adjustment and vocational skills. Before training, 85% of the clients were financially dependent. A follow-up indicated that this figure dropped to 24% after training and revealed that 64% of a random sample were employed, with the largest number being in semiskilled and unskilled occupations and a relatively small percentage in sheltered workshops.

The Chicago Jewish Vocational Service developed a program of counseling, training, and referral services that served 710 deaf clients over a five-year period (CJVS Project, 1972). Follow-up revealed that one-half the clients who received substantial services (approximately 500 clients) were employed, and an additional 15% were in advanced training.

Blake (1970) reported on a project conducted by the Hot Springs (Arkansas) Rehabilitation Center from 1966 to 1968, which provided services to 131 deaf clients. Despite a dropout rate of 38%, follow-up revealed that 41% of all clients were employed full time. Of the graduates of the training programs, 61% were employed full time. It was estimated that 85% of all clients received some observable benefit from their training.

The results of the four projects summarized above suggest that at least one-half of low-achieving deaf adults can be habilitated with a core program of vocational and social services, but that a substantial number require more extensive services (Rice, 1973a, p. 8).

A five-year project extending from 1968 to 1973, growing out of the pilot project summarized by Blake (1970), was conducted at the Hot Springs Rehabilitation Center to provide comprehensive medical, social, psychological, and vocational services to low-achieving deaf adults (Rice, 1973a). The center provided extensive services to 212 deaf individuals from 29 states, the District of Columbia, and the Virgin Islands. Most clients were within the normal range of intelligence. The most commonly noted problem was impoverished communication (Stewart, 1971b). Motivation tended to be low, and clients frequently exhibited inappropriate, inadequate, and impulsive behavior. Stewart noted that such behavior apparently was accepted in the school programs from which the students came and recommended a restructuring of such programs.

In spite of a past history of academic failure, poor communication, and low motivation, 55% of the clients provided services by the center completed training. The most common areas of training were in printing and laundry work (see Table 14.6).

Rice (1973a) reported that over 60% of the clients were gainfully employed as a result of the training they received. He also stated that, even though the center served clients from more than half the states, the majority were from Arkansas and adjacent states. He concluded that in order to serve low achieving adult deaf clients effectively, comprehensive rehabilitation services for the deaf should be provided on a regional basis.

Table 14.6 Most common areas of training for
deaf clients at the Hot Springs Rehabilitation
Center, 1968–1973

Training area	Percentage of deaf clients enrolled
Printing	19.4
Laundry	17.1
Body and fender	7.0
Furniture repair	7.0
Furniture upholstery	7.0
Key punch	7.0

SOURCE: B. Rice, A Comprehensive Facility Program for
Multiply-handicapped Deaf Adults: Final Report. Fayette-
ville: Arkansas Rehabilitation Research and Training
Center, 1973, pp. 18–19.

Conclusions

Examination of conditions concerning deaf individuals who may have additional handicaps leads to some grim conclusions. First, there are large
numbers of deaf individuals who, incorrectly, are also classified as being retarded, learning disabled, brain damaged, and so forth. Frequently the classification is based upon such factors as poor communication skills and low academic achievement, conditions that more appropriately should be attributed to
poor training and inadequate education. There is also evidence that many deaf
individuals suffer from minor, easily correctable, visual defects. Poor or nonexistent diagnostic procedures place additional burdens on deaf individuals.

The presence of a handicap in addition to deafness does not merely add to an
individual's problems; it compounds them in a multiplicative way. Experience
and training in work with the deaf and with the blind, for example, does not
prepare one to deal with deaf blind individuals. Their special needs are qualitatively different and demand skills that training in the separate areas of
deafness and blindness do not provide.

With the exception of multihandicaps such as deafness and blindness, current incidence figures can be considered only rough estimates. Accurate incidence figures will be impossible to obtain until specific definitions are developed and accepted, and until comprehensive surveys are conducted.

Teacher training programs, with only a few exceptions, do not train people
to work with multihandicapped deaf individuals. There is evidence that the
majority of teachers of deaf retarded children not only are trained inadequately
but would prefer not to teach multihandicapped deaf children.

There is also a need for curriculum methods and materials specifically designed for multihandicapped deaf children. More adequate counseling techniques must be developed to help parents of multihandicapped deaf children and to facilitate the optimal development of deaf children.

Prevention programs could and should be developed to reduce the incidence of multihandicapped deaf individuals. These would include activities in such diverse areas as basic research on medical and psychological causes, development and initiation of mental health curricula for deaf students, genetic counseling, widespread vaccination programs, and parent counseling. Last, but far from least, educational programs for deaf children, from preschool to postsecondary levels, must be improved and humanized. This last step alone probably would cut in half the incidence of multihandicaps among deaf individuals.

Appendix A Periodicals in the United States
Concerned Primarily with Deafness

American Annals of the Deaf
5034 Wisconsin Avenue, N.W.
Washington, D.C. 20016

The *American Annals of the Deaf* is the official organ of the Convention of American Instructors of the Deaf and of the Conference of the Executives of American Schools for the Deaf. It was first published in 1848.

Published six times per year.

Deaf American
5125 Radnor Road
Indianapolis, Ind. 46226

The *Deaf American* is the official journal of the National Association of the Deaf. It was originally published as the *Silent Worker* in 1892.

Published four times per year.

Journal of Rehabilitation of the Deaf
7427 Leahy Road
New Carrollton, Md. 20786

The *Journal of Rehabilitation of the Deaf* is the official organ of the Professional Rehabilitation Workers with the Adult Deaf. It has been published since 1967.

Published four times per year.

Volta Review
1537 35th Street, N.W.
Washington, D.C. 20007

The *Volta Review* is published by the Alexander Graham Bell Association for the Deaf. It was first published in 1899 as the *Association Review*.

Published nine times per year.

Appendix B Major Organizations Serving the Deaf in the United States

Alexander Graham Bell Association for the Deaf, Inc.
3417 Volta Place, N.W.
Washington, D.C. 20007

Conference of Executives of American Schools for the Deaf
5034 Wisconsin Avenue, N.W.
Washington, D.C. 20016

Convention of American Instructors of the Deaf
5034 Wisconsin Avenue, N.W.
Washington, D.C. 20016

Council of Organizations Serving the Deaf
4201 Connecticut Avenue, N.W.
Suite 210
Washington, D.C. 20008

International Parents Organization
Alexander Graham Bell Association for the Deaf
3417 Volta Place, N.W.
Washington, D.C. 20007

National Association of the Deaf
814 Thayer Avenue
Silver Spring, Md. 20910

National Association of Parents of the Deaf
814 Thayer Avenue
Silver Spring, Md. 20910

National Fraternal Society of the Deaf
6701 West North Avenue
Oak Park, Ill. 60302

Professional Rehabilitation Workers with the Adult Deaf
Department of Special Education
University of Tennessee
Knoxville, Tenn. 37901

Appendix C   Recommended Books on Language
Acquisition and Function

Anderson, J. *The grammar of case.* New York: Cambridge University Press, 1971, 244 pp.

Balinger, D. *Aspects of language.* New York: Harcourt, Brace, Jovanovich, 1968, 326 pp. Paperback.

Bar Adon, A., & Leopold, W. (Eds.) *Child language,* Englewood Cliffs, N.J.: Prentice-Hall, 1971, 477 pages.

Bernstein, L. *Linguistic aspects of science.* Chicago: University of Chicago Press, 1939, 59 pp. Paperback.

Bowerman, M. *Early syntactic development: A cross linguistic study with specific reference to Finnish.* New York: Cambridge University Press, 1973, 302 pp.

Brown, R. *Words and things.* New York: Free Press, 1958, 398 pp.

Brown, R. *A first language: The early stages.* Cambridge, Mass.: Harvard University Press, 1973, 437 pp.

Carroll, J., & Freedle, R. (Eds.). *Language comprehension and the acquisition of knowledge.* New York: Wiley, 1972, 380 pp.

Cazden, C. *Child language and education.* New York: Holt, 1972, 314 pp.

Cazden, C., John, V., & Hymes, D. *Functions of language in the classroom.* New York: Teachers College Press, 1972, 394 pp. Paperback.

Chafe, W. *Meaning and the structure of language.* Chicago: University of Chicago Press, 1970, 360 pp.

Chomsky, N. *Syntactic structures.* The Hague: Mouton & Company, 1957, 118 pp. Paperback.

Chomsky, N. *Aspects of the theory of syntax.* Cambridge, Mass.: M.I.T. Press, 1965, 251 pp.

Chomsky, N. *Language and mind.* New York: Harcourt, Brace, Jovanovich, 1968, 88 pp. Paperback.

Cook, W. *On tagmemes and transforms.* Washington, D.C.: Georgetown University Press, 1964, 68 pp. Paperback.

D'Arcais, G., & Levelt, W. (Eds.). *Advances in psycholinguistics.* New York: American Elsevier, 1970, 454 pp. Paperback.

De Cecco, J. (Ed.). *Psychology of language, thought and instruction.* New York: Holt, 1967, 446 pp.

Deese, J. *Psycholinguistics.* Boston: Allyn & Bacon, 1970, 149 pp. Paperback.

Dixon, T., & Horton, D. (Eds.). *Verbal behavior and general behavior theory.* Englewood Cliffs, N.J.: Prentice-Hall, 1968, 596 pp.

Fillmore, C., & Langendoen, D. (Eds.). *Studies in linguistic semantics.* New York: Holt, 1971, 299 pp.

Fodor, J., Bever, T., & Garrett, M. *The psychology of language.* New York: McGraw-Hill, 1975, 537 pp.

Fodor, J., & Katz, J. (Eds.). *The structure of language: Readings in the philosophy of language.* Englewood Cliffs, N.J.: Prentice-Hall, 1964, 612 pp.

Gleason, H. *An introduction to descriptive linguistics.* New York: Holt, 1955, 503 pp.

Hayes, J. (Ed.). *Cognition and the development of language.* New York: Wiley, 1970; 370 pp.

Hook, S. (Ed.). *Language and philosophy.* New York: N.Y.U. Press, 1969, 301 pp.

Hughes, J. *Linguistics and language teaching.* New York: Random House, 1968, 143 pp. Paperback.

Irwin, J., & Marge, M. (Eds.). *Principles of childhood language disabilities.* New York: Appleton Century Crofts, 1972, 406 pp.

Jacobs, R., & Rosenbaum, P. *Readings in English transformational grammar.* Waltham, Mass.: Ginn, 1970, 277 pp.

Jakobovits, L., & Miron, M. (Eds.). *Readings in the psychology of language.* Englewood Cliffs, N.J.: Prentice-Hall, 1967, 636 pp.

Kavanagh, J., & Mattingly, I. (Eds.). *Language by ear and eye: The relationships between speech and reading.* Cambridge, Mass.: M.I.T. Press, 1972, 398 pp.

Koutsoudas, A. *Writing transformational grammars.* New York: McGraw-Hill, 1966, 368 pp.

Koutsoudas, A. *Workbook in syntax.* New York: McGraw-Hill, 1969, 218 pp. Paperback.

Lavatelli, C. *Language training in early childhood education.* Urbana: University of Illinois Press, 1971, 185 pp. Paperback.

Lenneberg, E. *Biological foundations of language.* New York: Wiley, 1967, 489 pp.

Lenneberg, E. *New directions in the study of language.* Cambridge, Mass.: M.I.T. Press, 1966, 194 pp. Paperback.

Lyons, J. *Noam Chomsky.* New York: Viking, 1970, 143 pp. Paperback.

Menyuk, P. *Sentences children use.* Cambridge, Mass.: M.I.T. Press, 1969, 165 pp.

Osgood, C. & Sebeok, T. (Eds.). *Psycholinguistics.* Bloomington: Indiana University Press, 1965, 307 pp. Paperback.

Piaget, J. *The language and thought of the child.* New York: Harcourt, Brace, Jovanovich, 1926, 238 pp.

Schiefelbusch, R., & Lloyd, L. *Language perspectives: Acquisition, retardation and intervention.* Baltimore: University Park Press, 1974, 697 pp.

Skinner, B. *Verbal behavior.* New York: Appleton Century Crofts, 1947, 478 pp.

Slobin, D. *Psycholinguistics.* Glenview, Ill.: Scott, Foresman, 1971, 148 pp. Paperback.

Slobin, D. *The ontogenesis of grammar.* New York: Academic, 1971, 247 pp.

Sokolov, A. *Inner speech and thought.* New York: Plenum, 1975, 283 pp. Paperback.

Steinberg, D., & Jakobovitz, L. *Semantics.* New York: Cambridge University Press, 1974, 599 pp. Paperback.

Vygotsky, L. *Thought and language.* Cambridge, Mass.: M.I.T. Press, 1962, 168 pp. Also available in paperback.

Wyatt, G. *Language learning and communication disorders in children.* New York: Free Press, 1969, 372 pp.

Zale, E. *Language and language behavior.* New York: Appleton Century Crofts, 1968, 342 pp.

General List of References

Abernathy, E. An historical sketch of the manual alphabets. *American Annals of the Deaf*, 1959, *104*, 232–240.

Abeson, A. Movement and momentum: Government and the education of handicapped children. *Exceptional Children*, 1972, *39*, 63–66.

Abeson, A. Movement and momentum: Government and the education of handicapped children — II. *Exceptional Children*, 1974, *41*, 109–115.

Adams, M. A preschool experiment. *American Annals of the Deaf*, 1928, *73*, 169–171.

Alcocer, A. (Ed.). *Proceedings of the Working Conference on Minority Deaf.* Northridge: California State University at Northridge, 1974.

Aldous, J. Occupational characteristics and males' role performance in the family. *Journal of Marriage and the Family*, 1969, *31*, 707–712.

Alford, H. *The proud people.* New York: Mentor, 1972.

Altshuler, K. Psychiatric considerations in the adult deaf. *American Annals of the Deaf*, 1962, *107*, 560–561.

Altshuler, K. Sexual patterns and family relationships. In J. Rainer, K. Altshuler, & F. Kallman (Eds.), *Family and mental health problems in a deaf population.* New York: New York State Psychiatric Institute, 1963, pp. 187–204.

Altshuler, K. Theoretical considerations in development and psychopathology of the deaf. In J. Rainer & K. Altshuler (Eds.), *Psychiatry and the deaf.* Washington, D.C.: U.S. Department of Health, Education, and Welfare, Social and Rehabilitation Service, 1967, pp. 65–84.

Altshuler, K., & Rainer, J. (Eds.). *Mental health and the deaf: Approaches and prospects.* Washington, D.C.: U.S. Department of Health, Education, and Welfare, Social and Rehabilitation Service, 1968.

Amman, J. *The speaking deaf.* London: Howkins, 1694. (Originally published in Latin in 1692)

Amman, J. *A dissertation on speech.* London: Low, Marston, Low & Searle, 1873. (Originally published in Latin in 1700)

307

Anderson, G., & Bowe, F. Racism within the deaf community. *American Annals of the Deaf*, 1972, *117*, 617–619.

Anderson, R. Minimal brain dysfunction and the rehabilitation process. In L. Stewart (Ed.), *Toward more effective rehabilitation services for the severely handicapped deaf client.* Hot Springs: Arkansas Rehabilitation Research and Training Center, 1971, pp. 31–49.

Anderson, R., & Stevens, G. Practices and problems in educating deaf retarded children in residential schools. *Exceptional Children*, 1969, *38*, 687–697. (a)

Anderson, R., & Stevens, G. Qualifications of teachers of mentally retarded deaf pupils in residential schools for the deaf. *Special Education in Canada*, 1969, *43*, 23–32. (b)

Anderson, R., Stevens, G., & Stuckless, E. *Provisions for the education of mentally retarded deaf students in residential schools for the deaf.* Pittsburgh: University of Pittsburgh, 1966.

Antinucci, F., & Parisi, D. Early language acquisition: A model and some data. In C. Ferguson & D. Slobin (Eds.), *Studies of child language development.* New York: Holt, 1971, pp. 607–618.

Arnold, T. *Aures surdis: The education of the deaf and dumb.* London: Elliot Stock, 1879.

Arrowsmith, J. *The art of instructing the infant deaf and dumb.* London: Taylor & Hessey, 1819.

Avondino, J. The babbling method. *Volta Review*, 1918, *20*, 667–671.

Avondino, J. The babbling method. *Volta Review*, 1919, *21*, 273–282.

Avondino, J. *The babbling method: A system of syllabic drills for natural development of speech.* Washington, D.C.: Volta Bureau, 1924.

Ayers, J. Home education for the deaf and dumb. *American Annals of the Deaf*, 1849, *2*, 177–187.

Babbidge, H. Education of the deaf in the United States., *Report of the Advisory Committee on Education of the Deaf.* Washington, D.C.: U.S. Government Printing Office, 1965.

Ballard, M. Reflections of a deaf-mute before instruction. *American Annals of the Deaf*, 1881, *26*, 34–41.

Baratz, J. Language and cognitive assessment of Negro children. *ASHA*, 1969, *11*, 87–91.

Baratz, J., & Shuey, R. Teaching black children to read. Washington, D.C.: Center for Applied Linguistics, 1969.

Barnard, F. *Analytical grammar with symbolic illustrations.* New York: E. French Company, 1836.

Barnes, H. A cooperative job training center for the deaf — if. *American Annals of the Deaf*, 1940, *85*, 347–350. (a)

Barnes, H. The need for separating advanced vocational training from the elementary school atmosphere. *American Annals of the Deaf*, 1940, *85*, 449–451. (b)

Baroff, G. A psychomotor, psychometric and projective study of mentally defective twins. Unpublished doctoral dissertation, New York University, 1955.

Barry, K. *The five slate system: A system of objective language teaching.* Philadelphia: Sherman & Company, 1899.

Bartlett, D. Family education for young deaf-mute children. *American Annals of the Deaf,* 1852, *5,* 32–35.

Behrens, T., & Meisegeier, R. Social studies in the education of deaf children. In H. Kopp (Ed.), *Curriculum: Cognition and content.* Washington, D.C.: A. G. Bell Association, 1968, pp. 44–48.

Bell, A. G. Visible speech as a means of communicating articulation to deaf mutes. *American Annals of the Deaf,* 1872, *17,* 1–21.

Bell, A. G. *Memoir upon the formation of a deaf variety of the human race.* Washington, D.C.: National Academy of Science, 1883. (a)

Bell, A. G. Upon a method of teaching language to a very young congenitally deaf child. *American Annals of the Deaf,* 1883, *28,* 124–139. (b)

Bell, A. G. Fallacies concerning the deaf. *American Annals of the Deaf,* 1884, *29,* 32–60.

Bell, A. G. *The mechanism of speech.* New York: Funk & Wagnalls, 1906.

Bell, A. M. *The faults of speech: A self-corrector.* Washington, D.C.: Volta Bureau, 1898.

Bell, A. M. *Popular manual of vocal physiology and visible speech* (3rd ed.). Washington, D.C.: Gibson Brothers, 1904.

Bell, A. M. *English visible speech in twelve lessons* (6th ed., revised by Yale). Washington, D.C.: Volta Bureau, 1932.

Bellugi, U. Studies in sign language. In T. O'Rourke (Ed.), *Psycholinguistics and total communication.* Silver Spring, Md.: American Annals of the Deaf, 1972, pp. 68–84.

Bemiss, S. *Report on the influence of marriages of consanguinity.* Philadelphia: Collins, 1858.

Bender, R. *The conquest of deafness.* Cleveland: Case Western Reserve, 1970.

Bereiter, C., & Englemann, S. *Teaching disadvantaged children in the preschool.* Englewood Cliffs, N.J.: Prentice-Hall, 1966.

Berger, K. *The hearing aid: Its operation and development.* Detroit, Mich.: National Hearing Aid Society, 1970.

Berko, J. The child's learning of English morphology. *Word,* 1958, *14,* 150–177.

Bernstein, B. Language and social class. *British Journal of Sociology,* 1960, *11,* 271–276.

Bernstein, B. Aspects of language and learning in the genesis of the social process. In D. Hymes (Ed.), *Language in culture and society.* New York: Harper & Row, 1964, pp. 251–263.

Bernstein, B. A critique of the concept of compensatory education. In C. Cazden, V. John, & D. Hymes, *Functions of language in the classroom.* New York: Teachers College Press, 1972, pp. 135–154.

Best, H. *Deafness and the deaf in the United States.* New York: Macmillan, 1943.

Bigman, S. The deaf in American institutions of higher learning. *Personnel & Guidance Journal*, 1961, *39*, 743–749.

Biklen, D. Deaf children vs. the board of education. *American Annals of the Deaf*, 1975, *120*, 382–386.

Binet, A., & Simon, T. An investigation concerning the value of the oral method. *American Annals of the Deaf*, 1910, *55*, 4–33.

Birch, J. *Mainstreaming: Educable mentally retarded children in regular classes.* Reston, Va.: Council for Exceptional Children, 1974.

Birch, J. *Hearing impaired pupils in the mainstream of education.* Reston, Va.: Council for Exceptional Children, 1975.

Birch, J., & Stuckless, E. *Programmed instruction as a device for the correction of written language in deaf adolescents.* Pittsburgh: University of Pittsburgh, 1963.

Birmingham, S. *The Grandees.* New York: Harper & Row, 1971.

Blake, G. *An experiment in serving deaf adults in a comprehensive rehabilitation center.* Little Rock: Arkansas State Board for Vocational Rehabilitation, 1970.

Bloom, L. *Language development: Form and function in emerging grammars.* Cambridge, Mass.: M.I.T. Press, 1970.

Bloomfield, L. *Language.* New York: Holt, 1933.

Boatner, E. Articulation at the American School. *New Era*, 1937, *23*, 50–51.

Boatner, E. Edward Miner Gallaudet. *New Era*, 1938, *24*, 49–50.

Boatner, E., Stuckless, E., & Moores, D. *Occupational status of the young deaf adults of New England and the need and demand for a regional technical vocational training center.* West Hartford, Conn.: American School for the Deaf, 1964.

Boatner, M. The educational psychology of Edward Miner Gallaudet. Unpublished doctoral dissertation, Yale University, 1952.

Boatner, M. *Edward Miner Gallaudet: The voice of the deaf.* Washington, D.C.: Public Affairs Press, 1959. (a)

Boatner, M. The Gallaudet papers. *Library of Congress Quarterly Journal of Current Acquisitions*, 1959, *17*, 1–12. (b)

Bonet, J. *Reducion de las letras y arte para ensenar a hablar los mudos.* Madrid: Par Francisco Arbaco de Angelo, 1620.

Bonvillian, J., Charrow, V., & Nelson, K. *Psycholinguistic and educational implications of deafness.* Stanford University Institute for Studies in the Social Sciences, Technical Report No. 188, 1972.

Booth, E. Thinking in words and gestures. *American Annals of the Deaf*, 1878, *23*, 223–225.

Bordley, J., Brookhauser, P., Hardy, J., & Hardy, W. Observations of the effect of prenatal rubella on hearing. In F. McConnell & P. Ward (Eds.), *Deafness in childhood.* Nashville: Vanderbilt University Press, 1967, pp. 123–141.

Bowe, F. Non-white deaf persons: Educational, psychological and occupational considerations. *American Annals of the Deaf*, 1971, *116*, 357–361. (a)

Bowe, F. Dr. Luther Robinson and mental health care for deaf persons. *Deaf American*, 1971, *23*, 3–6. (b)

Bowerman, M. *Early syntactic development: A cross-linguistic study with specific reference to Finnish.* New York: Cambridge University Press, 1973.

Braine, M. The ontogeny of English phrase structure: The first phase. *Language*, 1963, 39, 1–14.

Braly, K. A study of defective vision among deaf children. *American Annals of the Deaf*, 1938, 83, 192–193.

Brasel, K., & Quigley, S. *The influence of early language and communication environments in the development of language in deaf children.* University of Illinois Institute for Research on Exceptional Children, 1975.

Brasel, K., & Quigley, S. The influence of certain language and communication environments in early childhood on the development of language in deaf individuals. *Journal of Speech and Hearing Research*, in press.

Breunig, L. An analysis of a group of deaf students in colleges with the hearing. *Volta Review*, 1965, 67, 17–27, 94.

Brill, R. Mainstreaming: Format or quality? *American Annals of the Deaf*, 1975, 120, 377–381.

Brill, R., Merrill, E., & Frisina, D. *Recommended organizational policies in the education of the deaf.* Washington, D.C.: Conference of Executives of American Schools for the Deaf, 1973.

Brown, K. The genetics of childhood deafness. In F. McConnell and P. Ward (Eds.), *Deafness in childhood.* Nashville: Vanderbilt University Press, 1967, pp. 177–203.

Brown, K., Hopkins, L., & Hudgins, M. Causes of childhood deafness. *Proceedings of International Conference on Oral Education of the Deaf.* Washington, D.C.: A. G. Bell Association, 1967, pp. 77–107.

Brown, R. *Words and things.* New York: Free Press, 1958.

Brown, R. *A first language: The early stages.* Cambridge, Mass.: Harvard University Press, 1973.

Brown, R., & Bellugi, U. Three processes in the acquisition of syntax. *Harvard Educational Review*, 1964, 34, 133–151.

Brown, R., & Fraser, C. The acquisition of syntax. In C. Cofer and B. Musgrave (Eds.), *Verbal behavior and learning.* New York: McGraw-Hill, 1963, pp. 158–196.

Bruce, R. *Bell: Alexander Graham Bell and the conquest of silence.* New York: Little, Brown, 1973.

Bruce, R. *Alexander Graham Bell: Teacher of the deaf.* Northampton, Mass.: Clarke School for the Deaf, 1974.

Bruce, W. Assignment of the seventies. *Volta Review*, 1970, 72, 78–80.

Bruhn, M. *The Mueller-Walle method of lipreading for the hard of hearing.* Washington, D.C.: Volta Bureau, 1949.

Buchner, A. *An easy and very practical method to enable deaf persons to hear.* London: Howes, Clark & Collins, 1770. (Translated from German)

Buell, E. *A comparison of the Barry five slate system and the Fitzgerald key.* Washington, D.C.: Volta Bureau, 1931.

Bulwer, J. *Philocophus; or, The deafe and dumbe man's friend.* London: Humphrey Moseley, 1648.

Bunger, A. *Speechreading, Jena method* (4th ed.). Danville, Ill.: Interstate Press, 1961.

Burlingham, R. *Out of silence into sound: The life of Alexander Graham Bell.* New York: Macmillan, 1964.

Burns, D., & Stenquist, G. The deaf-blind in the United States: Their care, education and guidance. *Rehabilitation Literature,* 1960, *21,* 334–344.

Buxton, D. *An inquiry into the causes of deaf-dumbness, congenital and acquired.* Liverpool: Brakell, 1858.

Calvert, D. Multi-handicapped deaf children: Problem and response. *Proceedings 1969 Conference of American Instructors of the Deaf.* Washington, D.C.: U.S. Government Printing Office, 1970, pp. 58–66.

Calvert, D., & Silverman, R. *Speech and deafness.* Washington, D.C.: A. G. Bell Association, 1975.

Carhart, R. *Human communication and its disorders.* Bethesda, Md.: National Institutes of Health, Public Health Service, 1969.

Carton, L'Abbe. *L'Education des sourds-muets (In Miscellaea).* Paris: A. Dubrand & M. Dupont, 1883.

Case, etc., et al. v. *Department of Education, et al.* Superior Court of the State of California for the County of Riverside, No. 101679, Findings of Fact and Conclusions of Law, 1973.

Cazden, C. Environmental assistance to the child's acquisition of grammar. Unpublished doctoral dissertation, Harvard University, 1965.

Centers and Services for Deaf Blind Children: Policies and Procedures. Washington, D.C.: Bureau of Education for the Handicapped, 1969.

Charlesworth, W. *Contributions of ethology to education.* University of Minnesota, Research, Development and Demonstration Center in Education of Handicapped Children, Occasional Paper No. 24, 1973.

Charlesworth, W. Human intelligence as adaptation: An ethological approach. Paper presented at University of Pittsburgh Conference on the Nature of Intelligence, 1974.

Charrow, V. *Deaf English.* Stanford University Institute for Studies in the Social Sciences, Technical Report, 1974.

Chenoweth, A. Planning for a mass attack on Rubella. *Children,* 1969, *16,* 94–95.

Chicago Jewish Vocational Service (CJVS) Project for the Deaf. Chicago: Chicago Jewish Vocational Service, 1972.

Chomsky, N. Review of Skinner's *Verbal behavior. Language,* 1959, *35,* 26–58.

Chomsky, N. *Aspects of the theory of syntax.* Cambridge, Mass.: M.I.T. Press, 1965.

Chomsky, N. The formal nature of language. In E. Lenneberg, *Biological foundations of language.* New York: Wiley, 1967, pp. 397–442.

Chomsky, N. *Language and mind.* New York: Harcourt, Brace, Jovanovich, 1968.

Chung, C., & Brown, K. Family studies of early childhood deafness ascertained through the Clarke School for the Deaf. *American Journal of Human Genetics,* 1970, *22,* 630–644.

Cicourel, A., & Boese, R. Sign language and the teaching of deaf children. In C. Cazden, V. John, & D. Hymes (Eds.), *Functions of Language in the Classroom.* New York: Teachers College Press, 1972, pp. 32–62.

Clark, C., & Greco, J. *MELDS glossary of rebuses and signs.* University of Minnesota Research, Development and Demonstration Center in Education of Handicapped Children, Occasional Paper No. 18, 1973.

Clark, C., & Moores, D. Minnesota early language development sequence (MELDS). *Proceedings of the 1973 Meeting of the Convention of American Instructors of the Deaf.* Washington, D.C.: U.S. Government Printing Office, 1973, pp. 676–678.

Clark, E. How children describe time and order. In C. Ferguson & D. Slobin (Eds.), *Studies in child language development.* New York: Holt, 1973, pp. 585–606.

Clarke, F. Paper presented at the Eleventh Convention of Instructors of the Deaf. Hartford, Conn.: 1886. (Untitled)

Clerc, L. Some hints to teachers of the deaf. *Proceedings of Second Convention of American Instructors of the Deaf and Dumb.* Hartford, Conn.: Case, Tiffany & Company, 1851, pp. 64–75.

Collins, J. Communication between deaf children of preschool age and their mothers. Unpublished doctoral dissertation, University of Pittsburgh, 1969.

Colpoys, B. The mentally retarded deaf in New York. In L. Stewart (Ed.), *Deafness and mental retardation.* New York University Deafness Research and Training Center, 1972, pp. 17–21.

Connor, L. *Speech for the deaf child: Knowledge and use.* Washington, D.C.: A. G. Bell Association, 1971.

Cooper, R., & Rosenstein, J. Language acquisition of deaf children. *Volta Review,* 1966, 68, 58–67.

Cornett, O. Cued speech. *American Annals of the Deaf,* 1967, 112, 3–13.

Cornett, O. In answer to Dr. Moores. *American Annals of the Deaf,* 1969, 114, 27–29.

Costello, M. A study of speech reading as a developing language process in deaf and in hard of hearing children. Unpublished doctoral dissertation, Northwestern University, 1957.

Craig, W. Effects of preschool training on the development of reading and lipreading skills of deaf children. *American Annals of the Deaf,* 1964, 109, 280–296.

Craig, W., & Craig, H. (Eds.). Directory of services for the deaf. *American Annals of the Deaf,* April 1975, 120.

Craig, W., Newman, J., & Burrows, N. An experiment in post-secondary education for deaf people. *American Annals of the Deaf,* 1972, 117, pp. 606–611.

Crammatte, A. Deaf persons in professional employment. Springfield, Ill.: Charles C Thomas, 1968.

Cronbach, L. The two disciplines of scientific psychology. *American Psychologist,* 1957, 12, 671–684.

Crouter, A. Preliminary home training. *American Annals of the Deaf,* 1885, 30, 226–228.

Dalgarno, G. *Didascopholus; or, the deaf and dumb man's tutor.* Oxford: Timothy Halton, 1680. (Reprinted in *American Annals of the Deaf,* 1857, 9, 14–64)

Dantona, R. *Centers for the deaf blind.* Washington, D.C.: Bureau of Education for the Handicapped, 1970.

Davidson, S. Deaf graduates of schools and colleges for hearing students. *Volta Review,* 1930, 32, 73–75; 1931, 33, 71–73; 1932, 34, 631–633; 1933, 35, 499–501; 1934, 36, 715–720; 1935, 37, 725–729; 1936, 38, 703–705; 1937, 39, 687–689; 1938, 40, 773–775; 1939, 41, 690–691; 1940, 42, 515–518; 1941, 43, 716–720; 1943, 45, 686–691; 1944, 46, 691–694; 1945, 47, 693–694; 1946, 48, 770–773; 1947, 49, 552–555; 1949, 51, 10–16; 1950, 52, 7–11; 1951, 53, 58–61; 1952, 54, 113–118; 1962, 64, 229–313.

Davis, H. Abnormal hearing and deafness. In H. Davis & R. Silverman (Eds.), *Hearing and deafness.* New York: Holt, 1970, pp. 83–139.

Day, H., Fusfeld, I., & Pintner, P. *A survey of American schools for the deaf, 1924–1925.* Washington, D.C.: National Research Council, 1928.

Degerando, J. De l'education des sourds-muets de naissance. Paris: Cher Mequignon L'Aine Pere, (Ed.), 1827.

De Ladsbut, L. *A collection of the most remarkable definitions and answers of Massieu and Clerc, deaf and dumb, to the various questions put to them of public lectures of the Abbé Sicard in London.* London: Cox and Baylis, 1815.

Deland, F. An ever-continuing memorial. *Volta Review,* 1923, 25, 34–39.

Deland, F. *The story of lipreading.* Washington, D.C.: Volta Bureau, 1931.

Denmark, J., & Eldridge, R. Psychiatric services for the deaf. *Journal of Rehabilitation of the Deaf,* 1971, 5, 1–20.

Di Lorenzo, L. *Prekindergarten programs for the disadvantaged.* Albany: New York State Education Department, Office of Research and Education, 1969.

Doctor, P. (Ed.). Directory of services for the deaf. *American Annals of the Deaf,* 1962, 107.

Donoghue, R. The deaf personality: A study in contrasts. *Journal of Rehabilitation of the Deaf,* 1968, 2, 35–51.

Downs, M. Early identification and principles of management. *Proceedings of International Conference on Oral Education of the Deaf.* Washington, D.C.: A. G. Bell Association, 1967, pp. 746–757.

Doyle, J. *Histories of the American schools for the deaf and dumb,* Hartford, Conn.: American School for the Deaf, 1893.

Dunn, L. Special education for the mildly retarded: Is much of it justified? *Exceptional Children,* 1968, 35, 13–20.

Duvall, E. *Family development* (4th ed.). Philadelphia: Lippincott, 1970.

Early home training of deaf-mute children. *American Annals of the Deaf,* 1879, 24, 9–26. (Translated from 1869 Report of the Royal Wurtemberg Institution for the Deaf)

Education of deaf children: The possible place of fingerspelling and signing. London: Department of Education and Science, Her Majesty's Stationery Office, 1967.

Erikson, E. *Childhood and society.* New York: Norton, 1963.

Erikson, E. *Insight and responsibility.* New York: Norton, 1964.

Erikson, E. *Identity, youth and crisis.* New York: Norton, 1968.

Erikson, E. *Identity and the life cycle.* New York: International Universities Press, 1969.

Falberg, R. National Association of the Deaf Communicative Skills Program Advisory Board Meeting. Tucson, Ariz.: February 1971.

Fant, L. *Ameslan.* Silver Spring, Md.: National Association of the Deaf, 1972.

Farber, B. An index of marital integration. *Sociometry,* 1957, *20,* 117–134.

Farber, B. *Effects of a severely retarded child on family integration.* Society for Research on Child Development Monograph, Vol. 24, No. 2, 1959.

Farber, B. *Family organization and crisis.* Society for Research on Child Development Monograph, Vol. 25, No. 1, 1960.

Farber, B. *Mental retardation: Its social context and social consequences.* Boston: Houghton Mifflin, 1968.

Farrar, D. *Arnold on the education of the deaf.* London: Francis Carter, 1923.

Farwell, R. Speechreading: A research review. *American Annals of the Deaf,* 1976, *121,* 19–30.

Fay, E. Report of the Committee on a Technical School. *American Annals of the Deaf,* 1893, *38,* 279–280.

Fay, E. *Marriages of the deaf in America.* Washington, D.C.: Volta Bureau, Gibson Brothers, 1898.

Fay, E. What did Lucretius say? *American Annals of the Deaf,* 1912, *57,* 213.

Fellendorf, G. *Bibliography on deafness.* Washington, D.C.: A. G. Bell Association, 1966.

Ferreri, G. *The American institutions for education of the deaf,* Philadelphia: Pennsylvania Institute for the Deaf, 1908.

Fisch, L. (Ed.). *Research in deafness in children.* London: Billing & Sons, 1964.

Fisher, S., Harlow, M., & Moores, D. *Post secondary programs for the deaf: Monograph II: External views.* University of Minnesota Research, Development and Demonstration Center in Education of Handicapped Children, Research Report No. 61, 1974.

Fisher, S., Moores, D., & Harlow, M. *Post secondary programs for the deaf: Monograph III: Internal views.* University of Minnesota Research, Development and Demonstration Center in Education of Handicapped Children, Research Report No. 67, 1974.

Fitzgerald, E. *Straight language for the deaf.* Staunton, Va.: McClure Company, 1929.

Frey, R., & Krause, I. The incidence of color blindness among deaf children. *Exceptional Children,* 1971, *38,* 393–394.

Frisina, R. A psychological study of the mentally retarded deaf child. Unpublished doctoral dissertation, Northwestern University, 1955.

Frisina, R. (Chairman). *Report of the Committee to Redefine Deaf and Hard of Hearing for Educational Purposes,* 1974. (Mimeo)

Fry, D., & Whetnall, E. The auditory approach in the training of deaf children. *Lancet*, 1954, 266, 584–587.

Furfey, P., & Harte, T. *Interaction of deaf and hearing in Frederick County, Maryland*. Washington, D.C.: Catholic University, 1964.

Furfey, P., & Harte, T. *Interaction of deaf and hearing in Baltimore City, Maryland*. Washington, D.C.: Catholic University, 1968.

Furth, H. Research with the deaf: Implications for language and cognition. *Psychological Bulletin*, 1964, 62, 145–162.

Furth, H. *Thinking without language*. New York: Free Press, 1966. (a)

Furth, H. A comparison of reading test norms for deaf and hearing children. *American Annals of the Deaf*, 1966, 111, 461–462. (b)

Furth, H. *A thinking laboratory for deaf children*. Washington, D.C.: Catholic University, 1969.

Furth, H. Education for thinking. *Journal of Rehabilitation of the Deaf*, 1971, 5, 7–71.

Furth, H. *Deafness and learning: A psychological approach*. Belmont, Calif.: Wadsworth, 1973.

Furth, H. The role of language in the child's development. *Proceedings of the 1973 Convention of American Instructors of the Deaf*. Washington, D.C.: U.S. Government Printing Office, 1974, pp. 258–261.

Fusfeld, I. National Research Counsel's Committee on the Survey of Schools for the Deaf. *American Annals of the Deaf*, 1926, 71, 97–135.

Fusfeld, I. The academic program of schools for the deaf. *Volta Review*, 1955, 57, 63–70.

Gallagher, J., & Martin, E. *Windows on Russia*. Reston, Va.: Council for Exceptional Children, 1974.

Gallaudet, E. (Chairman, panel discussion on articulation). *Procedures of the National Conference of Principals of Institutions for the Deaf and Dumb*. Washington, D.C.: Gallaudet College, 1868, pp. 60–90.

Gallaudet, E. Is the sign language used to excess in teaching deaf mutes? *American Annals of the Deaf*, 1871, 16, 26–33.

Gallaudet, E. History of the education of the deaf in the United States. *American Annals of the Deaf*, 1886, 31, 130–147.

Gallaudet, E. The value of sign language to the deaf. *American Annals of the Deaf*, 1887, 32, 141–147.

Gallaudet, E. *The life of Thomas Hopkins Gallaudet*. New York: Holt, 1888.

Gallaudet, E. Must the sign language go? *American Annals of the Deaf*, 1899, 44, 221–229.

Gallaudet, E. The present state of deaf mute education in America. *Report of the International Conference on Education of the Deaf*. Edinburgh: Darwin Press, 1907, pp. 18–24.

Gallaudet, T. *An elementary book for the use of the deaf and dumb*. Hartford, Conn.: American Asylum for the Deaf and Dumb, 1817.

Gardner, B., & Gardner, R. Two way communication with an infant chimpanzee. In A. Schrier & F. Stollvitz (Eds.), *Behavior of nonhuman primates*, vol. IV. New York: Academic, 1971, pp. 117–184.

Gardner, R., & Gardner, B. Teaching sign language to a chimpanzee. *Science*, 1969, 165, 664–672.

Garnett, C. *The exchange of letters between Samuel Heinicke and Abbe' Charles Michel de l'Epée*. New York: Vantage, 1968.

Garrison, M., & Hamil, D. Who are the retarded? *Exceptional Children*, 1971, 38, 13–20.

Gentile, A. *Summary of selected characteristics of hearing impaired students: 1969–1970*. Annual Survey of Hearing Impaired Children and Youth. Gallaudet College Office of Demographic Studies, Ser. D, No. 5, 1971.

Gentile, A. *Academic achievement test results of a national testing program for hearing impaired students: 1971*. Annual Survey of Hearing Impaired Children and Youth. Gallaudet College Office of Demographic Studies, Ser. D, No. 9, 1972.

Gentile, A. *Further studies in achievement testing, hearing impaired students: 1971*. Annual Survey of Hearing Impaired Children and Youth. Gallaudet College Office of Demographic Studies, Ser. D, No. 13, 1973.

Gentile, A., & McCarthy, B. *Additional handicapping conditions among hearing impaired students, United States, 1971–1972*. Washington, D.C.: Gallaudet College Office of Demographic Studies, Ser. D, No. 14, 1973.

Gerankina, A. *Practical work in sign language*. Moscow: Institute of Defectology, 1972.

Gillespie, J. The aural system for the semi-deaf. *Proceedings of the Convention of Articulation on Teachers of the Deaf*. Albany, N.Y.: Voice Press, 1884, pp. 46–59.

Gleason, J. Do children imitate? *Proceedings of International Conference on Oral Education of the Deaf*. Washington, D.C.: Alexander Graham Bell Association, 1967, pp. 1441–1448.

Goetzinger, C., & Rousey, E. Educational achievement of deaf children. *American Annals of the Deaf*, 1959, 105, 221–224.

Goldstein, M. *The acoustic method for the training of the deaf and hard of hearing*. St. Louis: Laryngoscope Press, 1939.

Goodhill, V. Nuclear deafness and the nerve-deaf child: The importance of the Rh factor. *Transactions of the American Academy of Ophthalmology and Otolaryngology*, 1950, 54, 671–687.

Goodhill, V. Rh child: Deaf or "aphasic"? I. Clinical pathological aspects of kernicteric nuclear deafness. *Journal of Speech and Hearing Disorders*, 1956, 21, 407–410.

Goodhill, V. Auditory pathway lesions resulting from Rh incompatibility. In F. McConnell & P. Ward (Eds.), *Deafness in childhood*. Nashville: Vanderbilt University Press, 1967, pp. 215–228.

Goodhill, V. Deafness research. *Volta Review*, 1968, 70, 620–629.

Gordon, J. Deaf-mutes and the public schools from 1815 to the present day. *American Annals of the Deaf*, 1885, 30, 121–143. (a)

Gordon, J. Hints to parents. *American Annals of the Deaf*, 1885, 30, 241–250. (b)

Goss, R. Language used by mothers of deaf children and mothers of hearing children. *American Annals of the Deaf,* 1970, *115,* 93–96.

Grant, J. *Proceedings of a Workshop on the Preparation of Personnel in Education of Bilingual Hearing Impaired Children; Ages 0–4.* San Antonio, Texas: Trinity University, 1973.

Green, F. *Vox oculis subjecta: A dissertation on the most curious and important art of imparting speech and the knowledge of language to the naturally deaf and (consequently) dumb.* London: White, 1783.

Greenberg, J. *Universals of language.* Cambridge, Mass.: M.I.T. Press, 1963.

Greenberger, D. The natural method. *American Annals of the Deaf,* 1879, 24, 33–38.

Griffiths, C. *Conquering childhood deafness.* New York: Exposition Press, 1967. (a)

Griffiths, C. Auditory training in the first year of life. *Proceedings of International Conference on Oral Education of the Deaf.* Washington, D.C.: A. G. Bell Association, 1967, pp. 758–772. (b)

Griffiths, C. The auditory approach: Its rationale, techniques and results. *Audiology and Hearing Education,* 1975, *1,* 35–39.

Grinker, R. Conference summary. In J. Rainer & K. Altshuler (Eds.), *Psychiatry and the deaf.* Washington, D.C.: U.S. Department of Health, Education, and Welfare, Social and Rehabilitation Service, 1967, pp. 147–154.

Groht, M. Language as taught at the Lexington Avenue School. *American Annals of the Deaf,* 1933, 78, 280–281.

Groht, M. *Natural language for deaf children.* Washington, D.C.: A. G. Bell Association, 1958.

Grossman, H. *Manual on terminology and classification of mental retardation.* American Association on Mental Deficiency, Special Publication No. 2, 1973.

Gustason, G., Pfetzinger, D., & Azwolkow, E. *Signing exact English.* Rossmoor, Calif.: Modern Signs Press, 1972.

Hardy, W. Trends. In L. Connor (Ed.), *Speech for the deaf child: Knowledge and use.* Washington, D.C.: A. G. Bell Association, 1971, pp. 335–344.

Harlow, M., Fisher, S., & Moores, D. *Post secondary programs for the deaf: Monograph V, Follow-up data.* University of Minnesota Research, Development and Demonstration Center in Education of Handicapped Children, Research Report #79, 1974.

Harlow, M., Moores, D., & Fisher, S. *Post secondary programs for the deaf: Monograph IV: Empirical data analysis.* University of Minnesota Research, Development and Demonstration Center in Education of Handicapped Children, Research Report No. 75, 1974.

Hartbauer, R. *Aural habilitation.* Springfield, Ill.: Charles C Thomas, 1975.

Heider, H., & Heider, G. A comparison of sentence structure of deaf and hearing children. *Psychological Monographs,* 1940, 52 (1, Whole No. 232), 42–103. (a)

Heider, H., & Heider, G. A comparison of color sorting behavior of deaf and hearing children. *Psychological Monographs,* 1940, 52 (1, Whole No. 232), 6–22. (b)

Heider, F., & Heider, G. *Studies in the psychology of the deaf. Psychological Monographs,* Vol. VIII. Evanston, Ill.: American Psychological Association, 1941.

Hersch, L., & Solomon, M. A comprehensive approach to understanding deafness. *American Annals of the Deaf*, 1973, *118*, 34–36.

Hester, M. Manual communication. *Proceedings of International Congress on Education of the Deaf*. Washington, D.C.: U.S. Government Printing Office, 1963, pp. 211–222.

Hill, M. *Die Geistlichen und Schullehrer im Dionste der Taubstummen* (Pastors and teachers in the service of deaf mutes). Weimar: H. Bohlan, 1868.

Hill, R., Foote, N., Aldous, J., Carlson, R., & MacDonald, R. *Family development in three generations*. Cambridge, Mass.: Shenkman Publishing Company, 1970.

Hinde, R. *Animal behavior*. New York: McGraw-Hill, 1966.

Hirsch, D. Advice to parents. *American Annals of the Deaf*, 1877, *22*, 93–103.

Hodgson, K. *The deaf and their problems*. New York: Philosophical Library, 1954.

Hoffmeister, R., Moores, D., & Ellenberger, R. Some procedural guidelines for the study of the acquisition of sign language. *Sign Language Studies*, Silver Spring, Md.: 1975, *7*, 121–137.

Hofsteator, H. *An experiment in preschool education: An autobiographical case study*. Washington, D.C.: Gallaudet College, 1959.

Holcomb, R. The total approach. *Proceedings of International Congress on Education of the Deaf*. Stockholm: 1970, pp. 104–107.

Hubbard, G. *The First Annual Report of the Clark Institution for Deaf Mutes*. Boston: Wright & Potter, 1868.

Hubbard, G. Response to Gallaudet. *American Annals of the Deaf*, 1884, *29*, 64–67.

Hudgins, C., & Number, M. An investigation of intelligibility of speech of the deaf. *Genetic Psychology Monographs*, 1942, *25*, 289–392.

Hudgins, R. Causes of deafness among students of the Clarke School for the Deaf. *Clarke School for the Deaf, 106th Annual Report*. Northampton, Mass.: 1973, pp. 59–60.

Huervas y Panduro, L. *Escuela Espanola de sordo-mudos o'Arte para ensenarles a escribir hablar el idioma Espanol*. Madrid: En La Imprenta Real, 1795.

Huizing, H. Deaf-mutism: Modern trends, treatment and prevention. *Advances in Otolaryngology*, 1959, *5*, 74–106.

Hurwitz, S. *Habilitation of deaf adults: Final report*. St. Louis: Jewish Employment and Vocational Service, 1971.

Jacobs, J. A synopsis and exposition of primary lessons for the deaf and dumb. *Proceedings of Fifth Convention of American Instructors of the Deaf*. Afton, Ill.: Currier Steam Book & Job Printing House, 1859, pp. 219–232.

James, W. Thought before language: A deaf-mute's recollections. *American Annals of the Deaf*, 1890, *35*, 135–145.

Jenne, W., & Farber, B. *Interaction between severely retarded children and their normal siblings*. Paper read at Institute for Research on Exceptional Children Conference, Allerton Park, Ill., May 1957.

Jensema, C., & Trybus, R. *Reported emotional/behavioral problems among hearing impaired students in special educational programs*. Washington, D.C.: Gallaudet College Office of Demographic Studies, Ser. R, No. 1, 1975.

Johnson, P., & Farrell, M. Auditory impairments among residential school children at the Walter E. Fernald State School. *American Journal of Mental Deficiency*, 1956, 58, 640–644.

Joiner, E. *Graded lessons in speech.* Morganton: North Carolina School for the Deaf, 1936.

Jones, J. One hundred years of history in the education of the deaf in America and its present status. *American Annals of the Deaf*, 1918, 63, 1–47.

Jones, R. The Northridge plan. *American Annals of the Deaf*, 1972, 117, 612–616.

Joos, M. Language and the school child. *Harvard Educational Review*, 1964, 34, 203–210.

Karlin, S. Et tu oralist? *Volta Review*, 1969, 71, 478e–478g.

Karnes, M., Hagens, A., & Teska, J. An evaluation of two preschool programs for disadvantaged children. *Exceptional Children*, 1968, 34, 667–676.

Kelley, T., Madden, R., Gardner, E., & Rudman, H. *Stanford Achievement Test.* New York: Harcourt, Brace, Jovanovich, 1966.

Kindergarten method. *American Annals of the Deaf*, 1875, 20, 120–124.

Kinzie, C., & Kinzie, R. *Lipreading for the deafened adult.* Chicago: Winston, 1931.

Kirk, S. *Educating Exceptional Children.* Boston: Houghton Mifflin, 1972.

Kirk, S. Labeling, categorizing and mainstreaming. Paper presented at International Conference of Special Education. Kent, England: 1975.

Klima, E. Language in a different mode. Talk presented for the Human Learning Center, University of Minnesota, January 1975.

Klima, E., & Bellugi, U. Teaching apes to communicate. In G. Miller (Ed.), *Communication, language and meaning.* New York: Basic Books, 1973, pp. 95–106.

Knapp, P. Emotional aspects of hearing loss. *Psychosomatic Medicine*, 1968, 10, 203–210.

Knox, L., & McConnell, F. Helping parents to help deaf infants. *Children*, 1968, 15, 183–187.

Kohl, H. *Language and education of the deaf.* New York: Center for Urban Studies, 1966.

Konigsmark, B. Hereditary deafness in man, Pt. 1. *The New England Journal of Medicine*, 1969, 281, 713–720. (a)

Konigsmark, B. Hereditary deafness in man, Pt. 2. *The New England Journal of Medicine*, 1969, 281, 774–778. (b)

Konigsmark, B. Hereditary deafness in man. Pt. 3. *The New England Journal of Medicine*, 1969, 281, 827–832. (c)

Konigsmark, B. *Genetic hearing loss with no associated abnormalities: A review.* Maico Audiological Library Series, 1972, Vol. XI, Report 6. (a)

Konigsmark, B. *Genetic hearing loss with no associated abnormalities: A review.* Maico Audiological Library Series, 1972, Vol. XI, Report 7. (b)

Konigsmark, B., & McKusick, U. Hereditary deafness. *Volta Review*, 1966, 68, 336–341, 380.

Kopp, H. Summary report. In P. Mulholland & G. Fellendorf (Eds.), *National Research Conference on Day Programs for Hearing Impaired Children.* Washington, D.C.: A. G. Bell Association, 1968, pp. 27–34. (a)

Kopp, H. (Ed.). *Curriculum: Cognition and content.* Washington, D.C.: A. G. Bell Association, 1968. (b)

Korsunskaya, E. A *method of teaching speech to preschool deaf children.* Moscow: Institute of Defectology, 1969.

Kronenberg, H., & Blake, G. *Young deaf adults: An occupational survey.* Hot Springs: Arkansas Rehabilitation Service, 1966.

Kumata, H., & Schram, W. A pilot study of cross-cultural methodology. *Public Opinion Quarterly,* 1956, 23, 63–66.

Kuriloff, P., True, R., Kirp, D., & Buss, W. Legal reform and educational change. *Exceptional Children,* 1974, 41, 35–42.

Labov, W. *The social stratification of English in New York City.* New York: Center for Applied Linguistics, 1966.

Ladefoged, D. *Elements of acoustic phonetics.* Chicago: University of Chicago Press, 1962.

Lamson, M. *Life and education of Laura Dewey Bridgeman, the deaf, dumb and blind girl.* Boston: New England Publishing Company, 1878.

Lancaster, J. Primate communication systems and the emergence of human language. In P. Jay (Ed.), *Primates: Studies in adaptation and variability.* New York: Holt, 1968, pp. 234–247.

Lappe, M. Genetic knowledge and the concept of health. *Hastings Center Reports,* 1973, 3, 1–3.

Lawrence, C., & Vescovi, G. *Deaf adults in New England. An exploratory service program.* Boston: Morgan Memorial, 1967.

Lawson, L., & Myklebust, H. Ophthalmological deficiencies in deaf children. *Exceptional Children,* 1970, 37, 17–20.

Leenhouts, M. The mentally retarded deaf child. *Proceedings of the 1960 Convention of American Instructors of the Deaf.* Washington, D.C.: U.S. Government Printing Office, 1960, pp. 55–64.

Lenneberg, E. The capacity for language acquisition. In J. Fodor and J. Katz (Eds.), *The structure of language.* Englewood Cliffs, N.J.: Prentice-Hall, 1964, pp. 579–603.

Lenneberg, E. Prerequisites for language acquisition. *Proceedings of International Conference on Oral Education of the Deaf.* Washington, D.C.: A. G. Bell Association, 1967, pp. 1302–1362. (a)

Lenneberg, E. *Biological foundations of language.* New York: Wiley, 1967. (b)

Lenneberg, E. Biological approach to language. *American Annals of the Deaf,* 1970, 115, 67–72.

Lenneberg, E. Biological aspects of language. In G. Miller (Ed.), *Communication, language and meaning.* New York: Basic Books, 1973, pp. 49–60.

Levi-Strauss, E. *The savage mind.* Chicago: University of Chicago Press, 1966.

Levine, E. An investigation into the personality of normal deaf adolescent girls. Unpublished doctoral dissertation, New York University, 1948.

Levine, E. *Youth in a soundless world.* New York: New York University Press, 1956.

Levine, E. *The psychology of deafness.* New York: Columbia University Press, 1960.

Levinson, R. (Ed.). *A Plato reader.* Boston: Houghton Mifflin, 1967.

Lindsey, J. Congenital deafness of inflammatory origin. In F. McConnell & P. Ward (Eds.), *Deafness in childhood.* Nashville: Vanderbilt University Press, 1967, pp. 142–155.

Ling, D. An auditory approach to the education of deaf children. *Audecibel,* 1964, 4, 96–101.

Lloyd, L., & Moore, E. Audiology. In J. Wortis (Ed.), *Mental retardation, Vol. IV.* New York: Grune & Stratton, 1972, 374–398.

Lloyd, L., & Reed, M. The incidence of hearing impairment in an institutionalized mentally retarded population. *American Journal of Mental Deficiency,* 1967, 72, 746–763.

Long, D. Teaching language to the deaf. Unpublished master's thesis, Gallaudet College, 1918.

Lowell, E. Research in speech reading: Some relationships to language development and implications for the classroom teacher. *Proceedings of the 34th Convention of American Instructors of the Deaf,* 1959, 68–73.

Lunde, A., & Bigman, S. *Occupational conditions among the deaf.* Washington, D.C.: Gallaudet College, 1959.

Luria, A. Speech development and the function of mental processes. In M. Cole & I. Maltzman (Eds.), *A handbook of contemporary Soviet psychology.* New York: Basic Books, 1969, pp. 121–162.

Mackay, H., & Ware, E. Cross-cultural use of the semantic differential. *Behavioral Science,* 1961, 6, 185–190.

MacKenzie, C. *Alexander Graham Bell: The man who contracted silence.* Boston: Houghton Mifflin, 1929.

MacNamara, J. Cognitive basis of language learning in infants. *Psychological Review,* 1972, 79, 1–14.

MacPherson, M. The status of the deaf and/or hard of hearing mentally deficient in the United States. *American Annals of the Deaf,* 1952, 97, 375–386, 448–469.

Maestas y Moores, J. The use of fingerspelling in teaching speech to the deaf. Paper presented at Minnesota Speech and Hearing Association Annual Convention, Alexandria, Minn., 1974.

Magner, M. Techniques of teaching. In L. Connor (Ed.), *Speech for the deaf child: Knowledge and use.* Washington, D.C.: A. G. Bell Association, 1971, pp. 245–264.

Mangan, K. The deaf. In S. Kirk & B. Weiner (Eds.), *Behavioral research on exceptional children.* Washington, D.C.: Council for Exceptional Children, 1963, pp. 183–225.

Mangan, T. Integration of the hearing impaired into community programs. In J. Maestas y Moores (Ed.), *Education of the deaf: Some practical considerations.* Minneapolis: University of Minnesota, 1975, pp. 111–116.

Marshall, W. Quantitative and qualitative analysis of the written language of deaf children. Unpublished doctoral dissertation, University of Illinois, 1970.

Martinovskaya, E. The influence of fingerspelling on the reproduction of the sound-syllabic structure of a word. *Spetsial Shkala*, 1961, *102*, 22–28.

Masland, R. Rubella can rob children of their hearing. *Volta Review*, 1968, 70, 304–307.

Maslow, A. *Motivation and personality.* New York; Harper & Row, 1954.

Mason, M. A cinematographic technique for testing visual speech comprehension. *Journal of Speech Disorders*, 1943, 8, 271–278.

Mayne, R. The Bell family and English speech. *Volta Review*, 1929, *31*, 453–456.

McCabe, B. The etiology of deafness. *Volta Review*, 1963, 65, 471–477.

McCahill, P. A case of disinterest: The deaf in Puerto Rico. *American Annals of the Deaf*, 1971, *116*, 413–415.

McClure, G. The history of LPF. *Proceedings of the 1961 Convention of American Instructors of the Deaf.* Washington, D.C.: U.S. Government Printing Office, 1961, pp. 103–108.

McClure, W. Historical perspectives in the education of the deaf. In J. Griffith (Ed.), *Persons with hearing loss.* Springfield, Ill.: Charles C Thomas, 1969, pp. 3–30.

McCroskey, R. Early education of infants with severe auditory impairments. *Proceedings of International Conference on Oral Education of the Deaf.* Washington, D.C.: A. G. Bell Association, 1967, pp. 1891–1905.

McCroskey, R. Final progress report of four year home training program. Paper read at A. G. Bell National Convention, San Francisco, June 1968.

McNeill, D. Developmental Psycholinguistics. In F. Smith & G. Miller (Eds.), *The genesis of language.* Cambridge, Mass.: M.I.T. Press, 1966, pp. 65–84.

McWilliams, C. *North from Mexico.* New York: Greenwood Press, 1968.

Mead, G. *Mind, self and society.* Chicago: University of Chicago Press, 1934.

Meadow, K. The effect of early manual communication and family climate on the deaf child's development. Unpublished doctoral dissertation, University of California, Berkeley, 1966.

Meadow, K. Early manual communication in relation to the deaf child's intellectual, social and communicative functioning. *American Annals of the Deaf*, 1968, *113*, 29–41. (a)

Meadow, K. Parental responses to the medical ambiguities of deafness. *Journal of Health and Social Behavior*, 1968, 9, 299–309. (b)

Meadow, K. Self image, family climate and deafness. *Social Forces*, 1969, 47, 428–438.

Meier, M. Role of non verbal signals in education of the deaf. *Proceedings of 1961 convention of American Instructors of the Deaf.* Washington, D.C.: U.S. Government Printing Office, 1961, p. 148.

Mercer, J. *Labelling the mentally retarded.* Riverside: University of California Press, 1973.

Miller, J. Oralism. *Volta Review*, 1970, 72, 211–217.

Miller, J., Ransey, C., & Goetzinger, C. An exploratory investigation of a method of improving speechreading. *American Annals of the Deaf*, 1958, *103*, 473–478.

Mills v. Board of Education of the District of Columbia, 348, F. Supp. 866, 868, 875, D.D.C., 1972.

Mindel, E., & Vernon, M. *They grow in silence.* Silver Spring, Md.: National Association of the Deaf, 1972.

Minnesota course of study: A brief exposition of the Wing's symbols. Faribault: Minnesota School for the Deaf, 1918.

Mitra, S. Educational provisions for mentally retarded deaf students in residential institutions for the retarded. *Volta Review*, 1970, *72*, 225–236.

Montague, H. Mr. Bell's private school. *Volta Review*, 1940, *42*, 325–326, 395.

Montanelli, D., & Quigley, S. *Deaf children's acquisition of negation.* Institute for Research on Exceptional Children, University of Illinois, 1974.

Montgomery, G. The relationship of oral skills to manual communication in profoundly deaf adolescents. *American Annals of the Deaf*, 1966, *111*, 557–565.

Moores, D. Cued speech: Some practical and theoretical considerations. *American Annals of the Deaf*, 1969, *114*, 23–27. (a)

Moores, D. A question of accuracy and sufficiency. *American Annals of the Deaf*, 1969, *114*, 29–32. (b)

Moores, D. The vocational status of young deaf adults in New England. *Journal of Rehabilitation of the Deaf*, 1969, *2*, 29–41. (c)

Moores, D. *Education of the deaf in the United States.* University of Minnesota Research, Development and Demonstration Center in Education of Handicapped Children, Occasional Paper No. 2, 1970. (a)

Moores, D. Psycholinguistics and deafness. *American Annals of the Deaf*, 1970, *115*, 37–48. (b)

Moores, D. Evaluation of preschool programs: An interaction analysis model. *Proceedings of International Congress on Education of the Deaf.* Stockholm: 1970, pp. 1964–1968. (c)

Moores, D. Review of B. Tervoort & A. Verbeck, Analysis of communicative structure patterns in deaf children. *American Annals of the Deaf*, 1970, *115*, 12–17. (d)

Moores, D. An investigation of the psycholinguistic functioning of deaf adolescents. *Exceptional Children*, 1970, *36*, 645–654. (e)

Moores, D. *Recent research in manual communication.* University of Minnesota Research, Development and Demonstration Center in Education of Handicapped Children, Occasional Paper No. 7, 1971.

Moores, D. Neo-oralism and education of the deaf in the Soviet Union. *Exceptional Children*, 1972, *38*, 377–384. (a)

Moores, D. Mental health and the hearing impaired. *Deaf American*, 1972, *23*, 7–12. (b)

Moores, D. Communication: Some unanswered questions and some unquestioned answers. In T. O'Rourke (Ed.), *Psycholinguistics and total communication.* Silver Spring, Md.: American Annals of the Deaf, 1972, pp. 1–10. (c)

Moores, D.   Families and deafness.   In A. Norris (Ed.), *Deafness annual*, Silver Spring, Md.: Professional Rehabilitation Workers with the Adult Deaf, 1973, pp. 115–130.

Moores, D.   Non vocal systems of verbal behavior.   In R. Schiefelbusch & L. Lloyd (Eds.), *Language perspectives: Acquisition, retardation, and intervention*.   Baltimore: University Park Press, 1974, pp. 377–417.

Moores, D.   A review of education of the deaf.   In L. Mann and D. Sabatino (Eds.), *Third review of special education*.   New York: Grune & Stratton, 1976, pp. 19–52. (a)

Moores, D.   Early childhood special education for the hearing impaired.   In H. Spicker & N. Anastasiow (Eds.), *Early childhood special education*.   Minneapolis: University of Minnesota Press, 1976, pp. 91–110. (b)

Moores, D., Fisher, S., & Harlow, M.   *Post secondary programs for the deaf: Monograph VI: Summary and guidelines*.   University of Minnesota Research, Development and Demonstration Center in Education of Handicapped Children, Research Report No. 80, 1974.

Moores, D., Harlow, M., & Fisher, S.   *Post secondary programs for the deaf: Monograph I: Introduction and overview*.   University of Minnesota Research, Development and Demonstration Center in Education of Handicapped Children, Research Report No. 60, 1974.

Moores, D., & McIntyre, C.   *Evaluation of programs for hearing impaired children, Report of 1970–1971*.   University of Minnesota Research, Development and Demonstration Center in Education of Handicapped Children, Research Report No. 27, 1971.

Moores, D., McIntyre, C., & Weiss, K.   *Evaluation of programs for hearing impaired children: Report of 1971–1972*.   University of Minnesota Research, Development and Demonstration Center in Education of Handicapped Children, Research Report No. 39, 1972. (a)

Moores, D., McIntyre, C., & Weiss, K.   An analysis of signs, language and speech in the communication of young deaf children, *Sign Language Studies*, 1972, 9–28. (b)

Moores, D., & Quigley, S.   Cloze procedures in assessment of language skills of deaf persons.   *Proceedings of the International Conference on Oral Education of the Deaf*. Washington, D.C.: A. G. Bell Association, 1967, pp. 1363–1395.

Moores, D., Weiss, K., & Goodwin, M.   *Evaluation of programs for hearing impaired children: Report of 1972–1973*.   University of Minnesota Research, Development and Demonstration Center in Education of Handicapped Children, Research Report No. 57, 1973. (a)

Moores, D., Weiss, K., & Goodwin, M.   Receptive abilities of deaf children across five modes of communication. *Exceptional Children*, 1973, 39, 22–28.

Moores, D., Weiss, K., & Goodwin, M.   *Evaluation of programs for hearing impaired children: Report of 1973–1974*.   University of Minnesota Research, Development and Demonstration Center in Education of Handicapped Children, Research Report No. 81, 1974.

Moreva, N.   Learning dactyl reading by various age groups.   Unpublished doctoral dissertation.   Moscow: Institute of Defectology, 1964.

Morkovin, B.   Rehabilitation of the aurally handicapped through the study of speechreading in life situations. *Journal of Speech and Hearing Disorders*, 1947, *12*, 363–368.

Morkovin, B.   Experiment in teaching deaf preschool children in the Soviet Union. *Volta Review*, 1960, *62*, 260–268. (a)

Morkovin, B.   Through the barriers of deafness and isolation.   New York: Macmillan, 1960. (b)

Morozova, N.   *Development of the theory of preschool education of the deaf and dumb.* Moscow: Institute of Defectology, 1954.

Morris, O.   Consanguineous marriages, and their results in respect to deaf-dumbness. *American Annals of the Deaf*, 1861, *13*, 29–34.

Morrison, J.   Industrial training: What shall we subtract and what should we add in the new century of education of the deaf? *American Annals of the Deaf*, 1920, *65*, 213–224.

Mulholland, A., & Fellendorf, G. (Eds.).   *National Research Conference on Day Programs for Hearing Impaired Children.*   Washington, D.C.: A. G. Bell Association, 1968.

Myklebust, H.   Towards a new understanding of the deaf child.   *American Annals of the Deaf*, 1953, *98*, 345–357.

Myklebust, H.   *The psychology of deafness.*   New York: Grune & Stratton, 1964.

Myklebust, H., & Brutten, M.   A study of visual perception of deaf children.   *Acta Otolaryngologica*, Supplementum, *105*, 1953.

Nelson, M.   The evolutionary process of teaching language to the deaf.   *American Annals of the Deaf*, 1949, *95*, 230–294, 354–396, 491–511.

Newman, L.   As a deaf teacher sees it.   *Deaf American*, 1971, *23*, 11–12.

Nickerson, R.   *Speech training and speech reception aids for the deaf.*   Cambridge, Mass.: Bolt, Branek, & Newman, Report No. 2980, 1975.

Nitchie, E.   *Lipreading: Principles and practice.*   New York: Stokes, 1912.

Nober, E.   *The audiometric assessment of mentally retarded patients.*   Syracuse: Syracuse University, 1968.

Norden, K.   The structure of abilities in a group of deaf adolescents.   *Proceedings of International Congress on Education of the Deaf.*   Stockholm: 1970, pp. 238–251.

O'Neill, J., & Oyer, H.   *Visual communication for the hard of hearing.*   Englewood Cliffs, N.J.: Prentice-Hall, 1961.

Osgood, C.   On understanding and creating sentences.   *American Psychologist.* 1963, *18*, 735–751.

Osgood, C.   Meaning cannot be an r_m?   *Journal of Verbal Learning and Verbal Behavior*, 1966, *5*, 402–407.

Osgood, C.   Toward a wedding of insufficiencies.   In F. Dixon & D. Horton (Eds.), *Verbal behavior and general behavior theory.*   Englewood Cliffs, N.J.: Prentice-Hall, 1968, pp. 495–519.

Osgood, C., Suci, G., & Tannenbaum, P.   *The measurement of meaning.*   Urbana: University of Illinois Press, 1957.

Peet, D. The remote and proximate causes of deafness. *American Annals of the Deaf*, 1856, 8, 129–158.

Peet, H. Analysis of Bonet's treatise on the art of teaching the dumb to speak. *American Annals of the Deaf*, 1850, 3, 200–211.

Peet, H. Memoir on origin and early history of the art of instructing the deaf and dumb. *American Annals of the Deaf*, 1851, 3, 129–161.

Peet, H. *Statistics of the deaf and dumb*. New York: Egbert, 1852.

Peet, H. *Thirty-fifth Annual Report of the New York Institution for the Instruction of the Deaf and Dumb*. New York, 1854.

Peet, H. Notions of the deaf and dumb before instruction, especially in regard to religious subjects. *American Annals of the Deaf*, 1855, 8, 1–44.

Peet, H. Memoirs on the history of the art of instructing the deaf and dumb. *Proceedings of the Fifth Convention of American Instructors of the Deaf*. Alton, Ill.: Currier Steam Book and Job Printing House, 1859, pp. 286–344.

Peet, H. The order of the first lessons in language for a class of deaf mutes. *Proceedings of the Sixth Convention of American Instructors of the Deaf*. Washington, D.C.: U.S. Government Printing Office, 1868, pp. 19–26.

Peet, H. Family instruction. *American Annals of the Deaf*, 1886, 31, 260–271.

Pennsylvania Association for Retarded Citizens (PARC) v. *Commonwealth of Pennsylvania*, 343 F. Supp. 279, E.D. Pa., 1972.

Pettengill, B. Home education for deaf mutes. *American Annals of the Deaf*, 1874, 19, 1–10.

Pettengill, B. The natural method of teaching language. *American Annals of the Deaf*, 1876, 21, 1–10.

Pettengill, B. Methods of teaching language. *American Annals of the Deaf*, 1882, 27, 203–208.

Phillips, W. Influence of preschool training on language arts, arithmetic concepts and socialization of young deaf children. Unpublished doctoral dissertation, Columbia University, 1963.

Piaget, J. *The language and thought of the child*. New York: World, 1962.

Piaget, J. Language and intellectual operations. In H. Furth, *Piaget and knowledge*. Englewood Cliffs, N.J.: Prentice-Hall, 1969, pp. 121–130.

Pintner, R., Eisenson, J., & Stanton, M. *The psychology of the physically handicapped*. New York: Crofts and Company, 1941.

Pintner, R., Fusfeld, I., & Brunswig, L. Personality tests of deaf adults. *Journal of Genetic Psychology*, 1937, 51, 305–317.

Pollack, D. Acoupedics: A uni-sensory approach to auditory training. *Volta Review*, 1964, 66, 400–409.

Pollack, D. *Educational audiology for the limited hearing child*. Springfield, Ill.: Charles C Thomas, 1970.

Pollack, D. The development of an auditory function. *Otolaryngology Clinics of North America*, 1971, 4, 319–335.

Pollack, D. The crucial year: A time to listen. *International Audiology*, 1976, 243–247.

Pope, A. History of the five slate system. *Proceedings of the Twenty-eighth Convention of American Instructors of the Deaf.* Washington, D.C.: U.S. Government Printing Office, 1935, pp. 18–23.

Porter, S. Professor Porter's paper on grammar. *Proceedings of the Sixth Convention of American Instructors of the Deaf.* Washington, D.C.: U.S. Government Printing Office, 1868, pp. 144–145.

Porter, S. The instruction of the deaf and dumb in grammar. *Proceedings of the National Conference of Principals of Institutions for the Deaf and Dumb.* Alton, Ill.: Currier Steam Book and Job Printing Company, 1869, pp. 136–158.

Power, D. Deaf children's acquisition of the passive voice. Unpublished doctoral dissertation, University of Illinois, 1971.

Power, D., & Quigley, S. *Problems and programs in education of multiply disabled deaf children.* Urbana: University of Illinois Institute for Research on Exceptional Children, 1971.

Premack, D. Language in chimpanzee? *Science*, 1971, *172*, 808–822.

Premack, D. Cognitive principles. In J. McGuigan and Lunsalen (Eds.), *Contemporary approaches to conditioning and learning.* Washington, D.C.: Winston & Sons, 1973, pp. 287–308.

Premack, D., & Premack, A. Teaching visual language to apes and language deficient persons. In R. Schiefelbusch & L. Lloyd (Eds.), *Language perspectives: Acquisition, retardation and intervention.* Baltimore: University Park Press, 1974, pp. 347–376.

Pronovost, W. The Horace Mann planning project. *Proceedings of International Conference on Oral Education of the Deaf.* Washington, D.C.: A. G. Bell Association, 1967, pp. 372–386.

Pugh, G. Summaries from the appraisal of silent reading abilities of acoustically handicapped children. *American Annals of the Deaf*, 1946, *91*, 331–349.

Quigley, S. *The influence of fingerspelling on the development of language, communication and educational achievement of deaf children.* Urbana: University of Illinois, 1969.

Quigley, S., & Frisina, D. *Institutionalization and psycho-educational development of deaf children.* Washington, D.C.: Council for Exceptional Children, 1961.

Quigley, S., Jenne, W., & Phillips, S. *Deaf students in colleges and universities.* Washington, D.C.: A. G. Bell Association, 1968.

Quigley, S., Smith, N., & Wilbur, R. *Comprehension of relativized sentences by deaf children.* University of Illinois Institute for Research on Exceptional Children, 1973.

Quigley, S., Wilbur, R., & Montanelli, D. *Development of question formation in the written language of deaf students.* University of Illinois Institute for Research on Exceptional Children, 1974.

Rainer, J., & Altshuler, K. (Eds.). *Comprehensive mental health services for the deaf.* New York: New York State Psychiatric Institute, Columbia University Press, 1966.

Rainer, J., & Altshuler, K. (Eds.). *Psychiatry and the deaf.* Washington, D.C.: U.S. Department of Health, Education, and Welfare, Social and Rehabilitation Service, 1967.

Rainer, J., & Altshuler, K. (Eds.). *Expanded mental health for the deaf.* Washington, D.C.: U.S. Department of Health, Education, and Welfare, Social and Rehabilitation Service, 1970.

Rainer, J., Altshuler, K., & Kallman, F. (Eds.). *Family and mental health problems in a deaf population.* New York: New York State Psychiatric Institute, Columbia University Press, 1963.

Rau, F. *Teaching pronunciation to the deaf.* Moscow: Institute of Defectology, 1960.

Rawlings, B., & Gentile, A. *Additional handicapping conditions, age of onset of hearing loss, and other characteristics of hearing impaired students, United States, 1968–1969.* Annual Survey of Hearing Impaired Children and Youth. Gallaudet College Office of Demographic Studies, Ser. D, No. 3, 1970.

Rawlings, B., Trybus, R., Delgado, G., & Stuckless, E. (Eds.). *A guide to college/career programs for deaf students: Revised 1975 edition.* Washington, D.C.: Gallaudet College; and Rochester, N.Y.: National Technical Institute for the Deaf, 1975.

Ray, L. Thoughts of the deaf and dumb before instruction. *American Annals of the Deaf,* 1848, *1,* 149–157.

Ray, L. Family education for young deaf mute children. *American Annals of the Deaf,* 1852, *5,* 32–35.

Reed, M. Preprimary education. *Proceedings of the 1963 Convention of American Instructors of the Deaf.* Washington, D.C.: U.S. Government Printing Office, 1963, pp. 543–550.

Renden, A. *Chicano manifesto.* New York: Collier, 1971.

Report of the Joint Special Committee of the Massachusetts Legislature of 1867 on the Education of Deaf-Mutes. Boston: Wright & Potter, 1867.

Rice, B. *A comprehensive facility program for multiply handicapped deaf adults.* Fayetteville: Arkansas Rehabilitation Research and Training Center, 1973. (a)

Rice, B., & Milligan, T. A structuring approach to independent living training for young multiply handicapped deaf adults. *Journal of Rehabilitation of the Deaf,* 1973, *6,* 38–43. (b)

Ries, P. *Reported causes of hearing loss for hearing impaired students: 1970–1971.* Annual Survey of Hearing Impaired Children and Youth. Gallaudet College Office of Demographic Studies, Ser. D, No. 11, 1973. (a)

Ries, P. *Further studies in achievement testing, hearing impaired students, spring, 1971.* Annual Survey of Hearing Impaired Children and Youth. Gallaudet College Office of Demographic Studies, Ser. D, No. 13, 1973. (b)

Ries, P. *Additional handicapping conditions among hearing impaired students; United States: 1971.* Annual Survey of Hearing Impaired Children and Youth. Washington, D.C.: Gallaudet College Office of Demographic Studies, Ser. D, No. 14, 1973. (c)

Rigrodsky, S., Prouty, F., & Glovsky, L. A study of the incidence, types and associated etiologies of hearing loss in an institutionalized mentally retarded population. *Training School Bulletin,* 1961, *58,* 30–44.

Robinson, W., Park, A., & Axling, P. The industrial status of the deaf. *American Annals of the Deaf*, 1906, 49, 460–464.

Rogers, D. A plea for a polytechnic institute for deaf mutes. *American Annals of the Deaf*, 1888, 33, 184–185.

Rosen, E. A cross-cultural study of semantic profiles and attitude differences. *Journal of Social Psychology*, 1959, 49, 137–144.

Rosenstein, J. Perception, cognition and language in deaf children. *Exceptional Children*, 1961, 27, 276–284.

Rosenstein, J., & Lerman, A. *Vocational status and adjustment of deaf women.* New York: Lexington School for the Deaf Research Series, 1963.

Ross, A. *The exceptional child in the family.* New York: Grune & Stratton, 1964.

Sanders, D. *Aural rehabilitation.* Englewood Cliffs, N.J.: Prentice-Hall, 1971.

Sank, D., & Kallman, F. The role of heredity in early total deafness. *Volta Review*, 1963, 65, 461–476.

Schein, J., & Delk, M. *The deaf population of the United States.* Silver Spring, Md.: National Association of the Deaf, 1974.

Schlesinger, H. A child first. *Volta Review*, 1969, 71, 461–467.

Schlesinger, H., & Meadow, K. *Deafness and mental health: A developmental approach.* San Francisco: Langley Porter Neuropsychiatric Institute, 1971.

Schlesinger, H., & Meadow, K. *Sound and sign: Childhood deafness and mental health.* Berkeley: University of California Press, 1972. (a)

Schlesinger, H., & Meadow, K. Development of maturity in deaf children. *Exceptional Children*, 1972, 39, 461–467. (b)

Schlesinger, I. The grammar of sign language and the problem of language universals. In J. Morton (Ed.), *Biological and social factors in psycholinguistics.* Cambridge, Mass.: Logos Press, 1971.

Schmitt, P. Language instruction for the deaf. *Volta Review*, 1966, 68, 85–105.

Schmitt, P. Deaf children's comprehension and production of sentence transformations and verb tenses. Unpublished doctoral dissertation, University of Illinois, 1968.

Schneider, M. The thought and language of the deaf mute. *American Annals of the Deaf*, 1908, 53, 483–492; 1909, 54, 173–190, 254–263, 327–339, 402–412; 1910, 55, 164–171, 254–268, 474–485; 1911, 56, 1–17.

Scouten, E. *A revaluation of the Rochester method.* Rochester, N.Y.: Rochester School for the Deaf, 1942.

Shif, Zh. *Language learning and deaf children's thought development.* Moscow: Institute of Defectology, 1969.

Simmons, A. A comparison of the written and spoken language from deaf and hearing children at five age levels. Unpublished doctoral dissertation, Washington University, 1959.

Simmons, A. A comparison of the type-token ratio of spoken and written language of deaf and hearing children. *Volta Review*, 1962, 64, 417–421.

Simmons, A.   Home demonstration teaching for parents and infants in Central Institute for the Deaf. *Proceedings of International Conference on Oral Education of the Deaf.* Washington, D.C.: A. G. Bell Association, 1967, pp. 1862–1873.

Simmons, A.   Language and hearing.   In L. Connor, (Ed.), *Speech for the deaf child: Language and use.*   Washington, D.C.: A. G. Bell Association, 1971, pp. 280–291.

Sinclair-de-Zwart, H.   Developmental psycholinguistics.   In D. Elkind & J. Flavell (Eds.), *Studies in cognitive development: Essays in honor of Jean Piaget.*   New York: Oxford University Press, 1969, pp. 315–336.

Skinner, B.   *Verbal behavior.*   New York: Appleton-Century-Crofts, 1957.

Slobin, D.   Cognitive prerequisites for the development of grammar.   In C. Ferguson & D. Slobin (Eds.), *Studies of child language development.*   New York: Holt, 1973, pp. 175–208.

Soloman, J.   Psychiatric implications of deafness.   *Mental Hygiene,* 1943, *17,* 37–52.

Sonies, B., & Healy, W.   *The deaf mentally retarded.*   Washington, D.C.: American Speech and Hearing Association, 1974.

Spicker, H.   Intellectual development through early childhood education.   *Exceptional Children,* 1971, *37,* 629–641.

Springer, N., & Roslaw, R.   A further study of the psychoneurotic responses of the deaf and hearing child.   *Journal of Educational Psychology,* 1938, *29,* 590–615.

Stafford, C.   Fingerspelling in the oral classroom.   *American Annals of the Deaf,* 1967, *110,* 483–485.

Stein, L., Merrill, N., & Dahlberg, P.   Counseling parents of hearing impaired children: A psychotherapeutic model.   Paper presented at American Speech and Hearing Association National Convention, Las Vegas, Nev., November 1974.

Stevenson, E.   A study of the educational achievement of deaf children of deaf parents.   *California News,* 1964, *80,* 143.

Stewart, J., Pollack, D., & Downs, M.   A unisensory approach for the limited hearing child.   *ASHA,* 1964, *6,* 151–154.

Stewart, L.   Problems of severely handicapped deaf.   Implications for educational programs.   *American Annals of the Deaf,* 1971, *116,* pp. 362–368. (a)

Stewart, L. (Ed.).   *Toward more effective rehabilitation services for the severely handicapped client.*   Fayetteville: Arkansas Rehabilitation Research and Training Center, 1971. (b)

Stewart, L.   *Multiply handicapped deaf people.*   Keynote address, Conference on Multiply Handicapped Deaf People.   Brainerd, Minn.: October 1974.

Stinson, M.   A comparison of the acquisition of the achievement motive in hearing and hearing impaired children.   Unpublished doctoral dissertation, University of Michigan, 1972.

Stockwell, E.   Visual defects in children.   *Archives of Ophthalmology,* 1952, *48,* 428.

Stokoe, W.   *Sign language structure.*   University of Buffalo, Studies in Linguistics, Occasional Paper No. 8, 1958.

Stokoe, W.   *Semiotics and Human Sign Languages.*   The Hague: Mouton, 1972. (a)

Stokoe, W. *The study of sign language.* Silver Spring, Md.: National Association of the Deaf, 1972. (b)

Stokoe, W. The use of sign language in teaching English. In J. Maestas y Moores (Ed.), *Proceedings of the Minnesota Special Study Institute in Education of the Deaf.* Minneapolis: University of Minnesota, 1975, pp. 62–85.

Stokoe, W., Croneberg, C., & Casterline, D. A *dictionary of American Sign Language.* Washington, D.C.: Gallaudet College, 1965.

Storrs, R. Methods of deaf-mute teaching. *American Annals of the Deaf,* 1880, 24, 233–250.

Streng, A., Fitch, W., Hedgecock, L., Phillips, J, & Carroll, J. *Hearing therapy for children.* New York: Grune & Stratton, 1955.

Streng, R. *Syntax, speech and hearing.* New York: Grune & Stratton, 1972.

Stuckless, E., & Birch, J. The influence of early manual communication on the linguistic development of deaf children. *American Annals of the Deaf,* 1966, 111, 452–460, 499–504.

Stuckless, E., & Delgado, G. A *guide to college/career programs for deaf students.* Rochester, N.Y.: National Technical Institute for the Deaf; and Washington, D.C.: Gallaudet College, 1973.

Suchman, R. Visual impairment among deaf children: Frequency and educational consequences. *Volta Review,* 1968, 70, 31–37.

Suci, G. A comparison of semantic structure in American southwest cultural groups. *Journal of Abnormal and Social Psychology,* 1960, 61, 25–50.

Suppes, P. A *survey of cognition in handicapped children.* Stanford University Institute for Mathematical Studies in the Social Sciences, Technical Report No. 197, 1972.

Survey of children born in 1947 who were in schools for the deaf in 1962–63. Report of the Chief Medical Officer of the Department of Education and Science. London: H.M. Stationery Office, 1964.

Tervoort, B. Esoteric symbolism in the communicative behavior of young deaf children. *American Annals of the Deaf,* 1961, 106, 436–480.

Tervoort, B. The understanding of passive sentences by deaf children. In G. Flores D'Arcais & W. Levelt (Eds.), *Advances in psycholinguistics.* New York: American Elsevier, 1970, pp. 166–173.

Tervoort, B. *Developmental features of visual communication.* Amsterdam: North Holland Publishing Company, 1975.

Tervoort, B. and Verbeck, A. *Analysis of communicative structure patterns in deaf children.* Groningen, The Netherlands: Z.W.O. Onderzoek, N.R.: 583–15, 1967.

Thielman, V. John Tracy Clinic Correspondence Course for Parents of Preschool Deaf Children. *Proceedings of the International Congress on Education of the Deaf.* Stockholm: 1970, pp. 156–158.

Thompson, W. Analysis of errors in written composition by deaf children. *American Annals of the Deaf,* 1936, 81, 95–99.

Thorndike, E., & Lorge, J. *The teacher's word book of 30,000 words.* New York: Teachers College Press, 1944.

Titova, M. Peculiarities in mastering pronunciation amongst deaf children who are beginning to learn speech through dactylic language. *Spetsial Shkala*, 1960, 97, 20–28.

Tomas, T. *Juan Pablo Bonet*. Barcelona: Imprenta de la Casa de Curitat, 1920.

Turnbull, H. Accountability: An overview of the impact of litigation on professionals. *Exceptional Children*, 1975, 42, 427–433.

Turner, W. Causes of deafness. *American Annals of the Deaf*, 1848, 1, 25–32.

Turner, W. Hereditary deafness. *Proceedings of the National Conference of Principals of Institutions for the Deaf and Dumb*. Washington, D.C.: 1868, pp. 91–96.

Van Uden, A. Some problems in the education of deaf children aged 0:0–6:11 years. *Proceedings of International Congress on Education of the Deaf*. Stockholm: 1970, pp. 272–286.

Vernon, M. Rh factor and deafness: The problem, its psychological, physical and educational manifestations. *Exceptional Children*, 1967, 34, 5–12. (a)

Vernon, M. Meningitis and deafness. *Laryngoscope*, 1967, 10, 1856–1874. (b)

Vernon, M. Prematurity and deafness: The magnitude and nature of the problem among deaf children. *Exceptional Children*, 1967, 34, 289–298. (c)

Vernon, M. Relationship of language to the thinking process. *Archives of Genetic Psychiatry*, 1967, 16, 325–333. (d)

Vernon, M. Current etiological factors in deafness. *American Annals of the Deaf*, 1968, 113, 106–115.

Vernon, M. *Multiply handicapped deaf children: Medical, educational and psychological considerations*. Washington, D.C.: Council for Exceptional Children Research Monograph, 1969.

Vernon, M. Psychological evaluation of the severely handicapped deaf client. In L. Stewart (Ed.), *Toward more effective rehabilitation services for the severely handicapped deaf adult*. Hot Springs: Arkansas Rehabilitation Research and Training Center, 1971, pp. 6–30.

Vernon, M., & Brown, D. A guide to psychological tests and testing procedures in the evaluation of deaf and hard of hearing children. *Journal of Speech and Hearing Disorders*, 1964, 29, 414–423.

Vernon, M., & Koh, S. Effects of manual communication on deaf children's educational achievement, linguistic competence, oral skills, and psychological development. *American Annals of the Deaf*, 1970, 115, 527–536.

Vernon, M., & Koh, S. Effects of oral preschool compared to manual communication on education and communication in deaf children. In E. Mindel & M. Vernon, *They grow in silence*. Silver Spring, Md.: National Association of the Deaf, 1972.

Vernon, M., & Prickett, H. Mainstreaming, past and present: Some issues and a model plan. *Audiology and Hearing Education*, 1976 (in press).

Vorce, E. Speech curriculum. In L. Connor (Ed.), *Speech for the deaf child: Language and use*. Washington, D.C.: A. G. Bell Association, 1971, pp. 221–244.

Vorce, E. *Teaching speech to deaf children*. Washington, D.C.: A. G. Bell Association, 1974.

Vygotsky, L. *Thought and language.* Cambridge, Mass.: M.I.T. Press, 1962.

Waldo, M. Early home instruction. *American Annals of the Deaf,* 1859, *11,* 170–192.

Walter, J. A study of the written sentence construction of a group of profoundly deaf children. *American Annals of the Deaf,* 1955, *100,* pp. 235–252.

Walter, J. Some further observations on the written sentence construction of profoundly deaf children. *American Annals of the Deaf,* 1959, *104,* 282–285.

Warfield, G. *Mainstream concepts. Reprints from Exceptional Children, 1968–1974.* Reston, Va.: Council for Exceptional Children, 1974.

Washburn, A. *Seeing Essential English.* Denver: Community College of Denver, 1971.

Waterman, J. *Perspectives in linguistics.* Chicago: University of Chicago Press, 1970.

Watson, J. *Instruction of the deaf and dumb.* London: Darton & Harvey, 1809.

Watson, J. *Behaviorism.* Chicago: University of Chicago Press, 1924.

Wedenberg, E. Auditory training of deaf and severely hard of hearing children. *Acta Oto-Laryngologica,* Supplementum, 94, 1951, pp. 1–130.

Wedenberg, E. Auditory training for severely hard of hearing preschool children. *Acta Oto-Laryngologica,* Supplementum *110,* 1954, pp. 1–82.

Weikert, D. Comparative study of three preschool curricula. Paper presented at meeting on the Society for Research on Child Development, Santa Monica, Calif., March 1968.

Weir, R. Impact of the multiple handicapped deaf in special education. *Volta Review,* 1963, *66,* 287–289, 325.

Weiss, K., Goodwin, M., & Moores, D. *Evaluation of programs for hearing impaired children: 1969–1974.* University of Minnesota Research, Development and Demonstration Center in Education of Handicapped Children, Research Report No. 91, 1975.

Weld, L. *Twenty-eighth Annual Report of the American Asylum at Hartford for Education of the Deaf and Dumb.* Hartford, Conn., 1844.

Weld, L. *Twenty-ninth Annual Report of the American Asylum at Hartford for the Education of the Deaf and Dumb.* Hartford, Conn., 1845.

Wells, C. *The development of abstract language concepts in normal and deaf children.* Chicago: University of Chicago Press, 1942.

Westerveldt, Z., & Peet, H. The natural method as applied to the instruction of young children. *American Annals of the Deaf,* 1880, *25,* 212–216.

Wever, E. *Theory of hearing.* New York: Dover Publications, 1949.

Whetnall, E., & Fry, D. *The deaf child.* Springfield, Ill.: Charles C Thomas, 1964.

Whorf, B. *Language, thought and reality.* Cambridge, Mass.: M.I.T. Press, 1956.

Wilbur, R., & Quigley, S. Deviant processing of relative clauses by deaf children. Paper presented at National Convention of the American Speech and Hearing Association, San Francisco, 1972.

Wilkinson, W. Mechanics arts schools. *American Annals of the Deaf,* 1885, *30,* 177–187.

Williams, J. *Seventieth Annual Report: American Asylum for the Deaf.* Hartford, Conn., 1886.

Wing, G. The theory and practice of grammatical methods. *American Annals of the Deaf*, 1887, 32, 84–89.

Wolff, S., & Wolff, C. *Games without words.* Springfield, Ill.: Charles C Thomas, 1973.

Woodruff, L. Primary instruction of the deaf and dumb. *American Annals of the Deaf*, 1848, 1, 46–55.

Wright, J. Familiarity with language the prime factor. *Volta Review*, 1917, 19, 222–223.

Wrightstone, J., Aranow, M., & Moskowitz, S. Developing reading test norms for deaf children. *American Annals of the Deaf*, 1963, 108, 311–316.

Yale, C. *Formation and development of elementary English sounds.* Northampton, Mass.: Clarke School for the Deaf, 1939.

Zeckel, A. Psyche and deafness. *American Journal of Psychotherapy*, 1953, 321, 7–15.

Zemlin, W. *Speech and Hearing Science Anatomy and Physiology.* Englewood Cliffs, N.J.: Prentice-Hall, 1968.

Zukov, S. *Textbook for deaf children.* Moscow: Institute of Defectology, 1962.

Author Index

Subject Index